APPROACHES TO POST-SCHOOL MANAGEMENT

APPROACHES TO POST-SCHOOL MANAGEMENT

A Reader

edited by
Oliver Boyd-Barrett, Tony Bush,
Jane Goodey, Ian McNay and
Margaret Preedy

at the Open University

Harper & Row, Publishers
in association with
The Open University

Harper & Row, Publishers
London

Cambridge San Francisco
Mexico City São Paulo
New York Singapore
Philadelphia Sydney

Reprinted 1987

Harper & Row Ltd
28 Tavistock Street
London WC2E 7PN

British Library Cataloguing in Publication Data

Approaches to post-school management
    1. Adult education—Great Britain—Administration
    2. Education Higher—Great Britain—Administration
    I. Boyd-Barrett, Oliver
    374'.068   LC5256.G7

    ISBN 0–06–318263–7

Typeset 10 on 12pt. VIP Plantin
by Inforum Ltd, Portsmouth
Printed and bound by Butler & Tanner Ltd, Frome and London.

CONTENTS

Section 4: INSTITUTIONAL POLICY-MAKING AND
LEADERSHIP

Section 5: CURRICULUM POLICY AND CONTROL

PREFACE

This reader comprises a collection of papers published in connection with the Open University course E324, entitled 'Management in Post-Compulsory Education'. As only one part of a total learning package it does not claim to offer a completely comprehensive picture of the issues with which it deals. Nevertheless, the editors have aimed to provide a balanced representation of the major themes, with a view to developing the critical understanding of students and other readers. Opinions expressed in the volume are not necessarily those of the course team nor of the university. The reader has been designed mainly to deal with post-school education but it also covers aspects of 16–19 provision in school contexts.

It is not necessary to become an undergraduate of the Open University in order to take the course associated with this reader. Further information about the course may be obtained by writing to: The Admissions Office, The Open University, P.O. Box 48, Walton Hall, Milton Keynes, MK7 6AB.

INTRODUCTION

The present decade has a better claim than most to designation as one of 'crisis' for post-compulsory education. Many articles in this reader represent attempts to understand the nature and implications of this crisis and to suggest appropriate response strategies, while others propose various conceptual frameworks and analytical models likely to be of value in the management of change. The crisis has many interrelated facets, the most important of these being concerned with resources, demographic change, public confidence and esteem, curriculum control and relevance, sectoral and institutional reorganization, staff management and development. Major problems in all these areas have highlighted the great need for better management and improved management education for those involved with the post-compulsory sector of education.

What kind of management education is this likely to be? The present volume, together with the Open University course of which it is a part, provides a number of clues. Together, they suggest it should be:

1　Firmly rooted in the educational context;

2　Resourceful in its application of theory and analysis from outside the educational context and across national frontiers;

3　Comprehensive in its coverage of different kinds of educational institution, levels of provision and categories of staff, student and client in the post-compulsory sector;

4　Pluralist in its generation and adoption of conceptual models and theoretical approaches;

5　Of direct help to educationalists in the management of change, whether responding to external pressures or in the autonomous generation of change.

This volume is companion to an earlier reader entitled *Approaches to School Management* (Harper & Row, 1980) which was, in turn, related to an Open University course, 'Management and the School' (E323). Two of the editors of that companion volume are editors of the present one and all the present editors have contributed to both the associated Open University courses. It is the editors' judgement that at the time of preparing this volume, the literature on educational management in the post-school sector had not yet reached a level of development comparable to the literature covering schools. The editors' task, therefore, has been more difficult in some respects, if no less rewarding in the end. The difficulty also reflected the very great heterogeneity of provision in the post-compulsory sector, which includes universities, polytechnics, colleges of further education, institutes of higher education, central institutions, monotechnics, tertiary and sixth-form colleges and school sixth forms. All of this, therefore, underlines the importance of the editors' foremost objective in putting together such a volume at the present time: to improve the quality of management understanding appropriate to the post-compulsory sector.

The reader has been organized into sections which reflect different aspects of post-school management. The most important criteria for inclusion have been quality and relevance. Another important criterion has been that most of the articles should be set reading for the course associated with this reader. The editors have been concerned to maintain a balance between different areas of the subject, and between different kinds of institutional context within the post-compulsory sector. The main emphasis has been upon British material, though several articles draw on international comparisons. Very many of the contributions are addressed to the management of educational change in a period of crisis, and this theme may be considered as the implicit subtitle of the volume.

The introduction to the companion volume outlined the importance of developing an analysis of educational management that was specifically related to the educational context. It indicated a number of ways in which educational institutions differed sharply from industrial plants: objectives are less easy to define; the 'raw material' is human; managers and staff share a common professional background; and the output of educational institutions is less amenable to measurement or evaluation. These differences largely hold true for the post-school sector as well, although the professional background of staff is much more heterogeneous. There are, of course, a number of important differences between the school and post-school sectors. One of these is that client participation is largely compulsory in the former and voluntary in the latter. This difference has important implications for the way in which educationalists in the post-school sector relate to their various 'markets'.

In recognizing the differences between school and post-school sectors, the editors have also been concerned to represent their interdependence and interpenetration. The widespread development of concern for the 16–19 age-range in recent years has helped bring about important initiatives in course provision, examining structures and institutional form that cut across the traditional boundaries. The character of provision in further and higher education greatly influences, and is greatly influenced by, the character of school provision. This volume therefore includes material which is relevant to the final years of schooling and to 'school' education provided in college contexts, such as sixth-form colleges.

The first section of the reader provides two different but complementary conceptual frameworks for an analysis of post-school education, in articles by Weaver and by Becher and Kogan. Although they are written mainly in relation to higher education, they clearly have broader relevance.

The theme of Section 2 – Student Pathways – is the process of transition from school to college, workplace or unemployment and between institutions in the post-compulsory sector. The range and quality of student experience during processes of transition are seen as an essential concern for effective management. Gordon examines the range of social, economic and school-related factors that influence the educational choice of young people between the ages of 15 and 18. The extract from the Macfarlane Report that follows provides a useful categorization in terms of 'client groups' of different routes available to young people at age 16. The FEU report on vocational preparation focuses on a particular range of these routes in relation to educational and training provision for 16–19-year-olds.

The interrelationships between ideology, strategy and the institutional environment provide the central theme of Section 3. Collier provides a useful summary of major ideologies which compete for influence in the educational system. The element of ideological conflict is present in a number of subsequent readings. Weir considers the various ways in which education can seek to provide relevant services to the traditional 'non-participant'. In the European context, Neave looks at the relationship between demographic and expenditure decline and the shifts in power between 'education' and 'training' authorities. Also in a European context, Fulton et al. examine the impact of manpower-based plans for higher education and their associated guidance, counselling and job-placement implications. It is weaknesses of planning that provide the focus for Fowler, whose contribution includes a critical review of the impact of Robbins and of Crosland's binary policy. Silver's concern is that the diversity of provision which seems so healthy in a period of expansion can lead to policy chaos in a period of contraction. A study by Reid and Filby of the development of sixth-form colleges neatly explores the frailties of school-based and party political ideologies in relation to one important development in 16–19 education in the 1970s.

Section 4 goes inside the institutions to look at issues of policy-making and leadership. Davies and Morgan examine various aspects of institutional response to long-term contraction and uncertainty, and the consequences for leadership priorities and roles. Latcham and Cuthbert propose a systems approach to college management as an aid to analysis of the relationship between college objectives and college resources. The theoretical analysis which follows is taken from a classic work by Cohen and March and provides a useful conceptual framework for an understanding of decision-making and leadership in the further education context. Preedy investigates the tertiary colleges in an analysis which relates to many general issues of reorganization strategy, organizational structure, curriculum provision and pastoral guidance. Peeke investigates the phenomenon of role strain in the FE college. Very relevant to Peeke's analysis is the paper by Oxtoby which looks at the role of the head of department in a context of greatly increasing institutional complexity. Handy argues that society is developing a dominant model for institutional and human relations, one which he labels 'the organization of consent', and which he sees as characteristic of educational contexts. Hewton's contribution on organizational, subject and intra-subject 'cultures' and culture conflicts identifies one of the most essential as well as distinctive features of further and higher education; 'culture' is clearly a major factor which must be taken into account if management is to be effective.

The curriculum itself provides the focus for Section 5. Readings by Wheeler and Marsh critically adopt the terminology of 'quality control' for education. This theme is further developed by Adelman and Alexander, who review the principal modes, strengths and weaknesses of evaluation strategies for higher education. Readings by Russell, and by Mansell and Parkin, examine the significant role of major external agencies of curriculum control: the examination, validation and 'controlling bodies' whose influence has become more pervasive in recent years.

The first reading of Section 6 on staff management and development is Jackson's introduction to industrial relations, which stresses the importance of taking a wider view of the subject than that of overt conflict. An extract from the NATFHE handbook of college administration outlines the principal features of industrial relations in further education. Rutherford discusses different strategies of staff development in relation to educational innovation. The contribution by Riches looks at the critical role of the interview as an instrument for staff recruitment, appraisal and staff development. Papers by Bone, Portwood and Moodie are all in different ways concerned with problems associated with institutional contraction and staff redundancy, as well as of staff development. Finally, Knight addresses the question of how far existing conditions of service for academic staff must be changed if there is to be improvement in the quality, quantity and efficiency of educational provision.

The inclusion or exclusion of any article from a reader is always a matter of judgement and the editors take full responsibility for those chosen here. If this reader serves to disseminate knowledge and develop understanding about post-school management we shall consider our selection justified.

SECTION 1

CONCEPTUAL FRAMEWORKS

CHAPTER 1.1

POLICY OPTIONS FOR POST-TERTIARY EDUCATION*
SIR TOBY WEAVER

Education in general and higher education in particular are facing a crisis [. . .]. At best, people have lost confidence in us. The high, and perhaps extravagant, hopes that they had of us during roughly 30 years of expansion, have not been realized. This disappointment is reflected in the demoralization of teachers, the faltering take-up of higher education places by potential students, the unease of employers, and the apparent lack of concern for the importance and welfare of our enterprise that our local and central governors seem to display. Grave problems call for radical changes in attitude and behaviour [. . .].

The participants in the educational enterprise fall roughly into three categories – those who learn, those who teach and those who facilitate (or inhibit) the enterprise by the way they provide for and control it. It may be helpful to visualize this total activity as taking place in a five-storeyed mansion in which the residents on each floor, though partially autonomous, are at the same time dependent (often heavily) on those who work on the floors above and below them.

The final purpose of the enterprise, where the aims of education are fulfilled, is consummated on the fifth floor, in the personal transaction between teacher and learner. Thereby the learner is helped to develop his capacities for thinking, for feeling and for action. All our activities as educators – academic, pedagogic, pastoral, financial, administrative – have no other purpose than to make that encounter fruitful. The floor below is

---

* *Higher Education Review*, spring 1982, vol. 14, no. 2, pp. 9–18. © Tyrrell Burgess Associates Ltd. Sir Toby Weaver was for many years a top civil servant at the DES and was Professor of Educational Administration and Management at the Open University from 1976 to 1978.

the home of the discipline, expressed through course and class and seminar, from which the teaching/learning encounter on the fifth floor takes its nourishment. Here the transaction between teacher and learner is modified by the intrinsic demands of the discipline, the quality of staff and students, the opportunities for research, the limitations of the timetable, the pressure of examinations, the demands of professional bodies and so on. All these factors help to modify the autonomy of both teachers and learners. The next floor represents the higher education institution – university, polytechnic or college – with its own traditions and its own dynamic. These in turn modify the freedom of the curriculum-makers on the floor above, thanks to the exigencies of the complex forms of organization and internal control which in any higher education institution govern standards, fix priorities and share out resources in the process of trying to harmonize a huge diversity of aims and interests. But the institution is itself far from sovereign. It is embedded in a system, represented by the second floor, where the providers and controllers of the system of which the particular institution is a part – the UGC, for example, for the universities, the LEAs, the CNAA and the regional advisory councils for the so-called public sector, the DES for the direct-grant colleges and for much else – modify the autonomy of the individual institution by the policies they lay down, the resources they provide and the strings they attach to them. Finally the controllers of systems are themselves the creatures of the powers who live and work on the first or bottom floor – the Queen in Parliament, the Cabinet, the political parties and the Treasury. [. . .]

So much for the politics of education which lie behind all policy-making. In the course of this sketch I touch on what I believe to form the four main problems that confront every educator, whether his task is to teach, to programme or to provide. I have labelled the four [. . .] in order of educational importance: *curriculum, access, structure* and *resources*.
[. . .]

1   What are potential learners to be helped to learn? *Curriculum* subsumes questions of method and process as well as content, of standards and the criteria by which they are set and assessed. More widely it includes the hidden curriculum – the sum of the attitudes and values implicit in the community life of the institution. [. . .]

2   Who is to have the opportunity for systematic higher education? *Access* subsumes such issues as the desirable length, level and pattern of courses, the qualifications for admission to them, educational

guidance, the level of fees and awards, and practical aids to accessibility by means of residence, refectories, transport and welfare services. [. . .]

3 How is a desirable pattern of institutions to be determined, organized and governed? *Structure* involves key questions about the differential functions of institutions, the problems of their internal management, and the distribution of control over their lives between the institution itself and local, regional and central authorities. The determination of such structure policies has become a central topic of debate. Since institutions in their educative (as opposed to their knowledge-creating and other social) functions are primarily means to the realization of curriculum and access, policies for the solution of these latter problems must be settled first.

4 How are staff, buildings, materials and money to be provided, distributed and accounted for? The problem of *resources* includes such questions as the number of teachers needed and how they should be recruited, trained, rewarded, and, alas, made redundant; the level of capital expenditure; building standards; above all, the determination of priorities as between subject and subject, teaching and research, institution and institution, sector and sector. [. . .]

In distinguishing these four separate aspects of policy I recognize that they are of course so closely interdependent that it is impossible to effect a change in any one of them without repercussions on all the others. If you alter access you affect resources – [. . .]; if you alter structure you affect curriculum; if you modify curriculum you affect access, and vice versa.

Since curriculum is the prime means of realizing the educator's aims, I see no way of avoiding some attempt to define them. But how? Only, I believe, in terms of the development of human capacities. I recognize that higher education institutions may well have more or less explicit social purposes, and certainly social effects for good or ill, other than the development of well-educated persons, such as the creation of an intellectual or social elite, the promotion of social mobility and equal opportunity, the production of skilled manpower or the expansion of knowledge. But it leads only to confusion to formulate the aims of education (as opposed to the wider social functions of the institutions in which they are pursued) in terms of the alleged needs of society. [. . .] It offers no practical guide to devising a curriculum, because it turns out that education is *for* every possible human activity. The notion of personal development as the educator's aim must start and finish with some concept of what it means to be a person. I offer, for ease of discussion, a mnemonic inventory of the distinctively human capacities that I should like to see every person, *qua* learner, given the opportunity to develop, to whatever extent his abilities and aspirations (both limiting factors) will allow.

First and foremost, he has the ability to acquire knowledge and reflect on it. His central motive may be to pursue it for its own sake, because he is consumed with intellectual curiosity simply to discover by scholarship and research what is the case, and to find ways of representing reality. [. . .] For the educator, as opposed to the scholar, knowledge and inquiry are not ends in themselves but means – means to the development of the learner's understanding. My first aim, then – the development through research, scholarship and reflection of the capacity to understand – I label *comprehension*.

But thinking, reflection, cognition, the basis of all scientific and scholarly activity, are only one expression of human genius. *Homo sapiens* is also an artist in the widest sense. Feelings and emotions are the source of his power to value – to discriminate between right and wrong, worthwhile and trivial, beautiful and ugly. They are the source of his value judgements, and supply the motive power to act on them. And since one familiar means of helping people to develop their critical appreciation of value is to initiate them into what has been called 'a selection of our cultural heritage', I call the second aim, in its double sense of process and product, *cultivation*. This is the liberal humanist ideal, now sadly at a discount.

John Macmurray and William Temple have been lifelong guides in helping me to come to terms with the relation between theory and practice and between reflection and feeling on one hand and action on the other. Macmurray's thesis is that reflection and feeling find their completion only in action. As Temple (1949) put it, the most disastrous moment in the history of Europe was when Descartes, after sitting all day in a stove, delivered the aphorism *'Cogito, ergo sum'*. Macmurray (1957, 1961) contends that it is man's essential destiny to *act* – and that he can do so effectively only in fellowship with other human beings. Therefore, he substitutes *'ago, ergo sum'*, and summarizes his thesis when he says: 'All meaningful knowledge is for the sake of action, and all meaningful action for the sake of friendship'. This leads me to identify four further aims for the educator, all of which are aimed at helping learners not only to understand and feel aright, but to live rightly and effectively.

Most people are able to be good at something which requires specialized skill for its achievement. [. . .] Every learner should have the chance to develop any capacity he has for some such achievement both for the satisfaction and confidence it brings to the individual and the contribution it makes to the quality of life. My third aim is to develop what for want of a richer word I call *competence*. It may or may not have a vocational content.

Except when we withdraw from the world for reflection or contemplation we spend our lives doing things and organizing things. To live is to work in the fullest sense of that word and to make decisions, usually in conditions of uncertainty. We have a general capacity to manage our lives, a capacity engendered to a great extent *ambulando*, by experience. We live and learn. But in the course of his history *homo sapiens* has developed an armoury of principles and techniques to help him to amplify his capacity to act wisely and effectively, to solve his problems whether personal, practical, social or political, and generally to use the world's resources to cope successfully with his environment. The capacity to use these powerful aids to the art of living needs to be developed: I call my fourth aim the enhancement of *capability*.

Next comes [. . .] what Martin Buber (1947) called 'the originator instinct'. This power and desire to design, to invent, to construct, to compose, to create something that was not there before [. . .] needs to be fed and exercised. It is the source of man's 'creative ingenuity' (Nuttgens, 1978). My fifth aim, then, is to nourish and channel *creativity*.

But man is not an island. His very life depends in fact, though not always in intention, on communication, cooperation and fellowship. [. . .] And yet our educational system conspires to promote *individual* prowess, and competition. We need to develop man's capacity for compassion, mutual dependence and support, moral sensitivity in action [. . .]. From its political aspect you can call it citizenship. I prefer to think of it, with its religious dimension, as the capacity for *communion*.

I have avoided the unhelpful distinction between liberal and vocational education. Both terms have been devalued to the point that they call forth automatic approval or derision, without conveying any agreed meaning. No education is liberal or vocational but thinking makes it so. [. . .]

I turn from educational philosophy to canvass some options for curriculum and access policy, both to be tested, by the scope they provide for the development of my six aims of education, my six Cs: comprehension, cultivation, competence, capability, creativity and communion. In what directions can the higher education curriculum (irrespective for the moment of the kind of institution in which it may be offered) be modified or expanded to help learners at any age from 18 onwards to develop what I see as their sixfold potentialities? Many current attempts to find practical answers, whether by way of content or process, are worth exploiting further. Sandwich courses, 'walking the wards' – in architecture, accountancy or other professional fields besides medicine – and other forms of high-level apprenticeship bring the curriculum closer to the world of action. There is a growing emphasis on learning by doing, under the guidance of people of skill and experience, not necessarily teachers – 'action learning' (Revans, 1980). Study service is being encouraged at Imperial College and elsewhere to develop capability and communion. The Royal Society of Arts (1981) is sponsoring, through its Education for Capability Manifesto, a 'recognition scheme' to identify and publicize original schemes to develop a better balance between the six Cs. A dedicated group within the North East London Polytechnic (Burgess, 1977) some years ago initiated remarkable programmes of independent study by which, under the guidance of a personal tutor, and with the resources of the whole polytechnic to call on, each student negotiates a personal DipHE or degree course tailored to the measure of his own motives and abilities.

These and similar experiments and achievements have a significant bearing on my second policy topic – access. [. . .] The Robbins axiom has to be liberalized. The ability to profit from higher education cannot be validly measured alone by the prior possession of two A-Levels or their equivalent; the success of the Open University and the NELP programme have proved it conclusively. The proper test of a person's access to post-tertiary education is whether he is qualified to profit from further personal development, and who potentially is not? The student's motives and maturity are half the battle. Moreover, none of the curriculum developments I have sketched poses a threat to standards, because only one, and that not the most important aspect of human excellence, can be measured by academic yardsticks. I look forward to the day when it will be as common to award degrees in capability, creativity and communion as it is now to accredit comprehension, cultivation and (selected forms of) professional competence.

Many other proposals for modifying the somewhat rigid rules for access have been canvassed which are less dependent on changes in curriculum. For example, modified patterns of courses, with a two-year stint as their staple, have been advocated. The protagonists of recurrent education emphasize man's constant need for renewal [. . .] as knowledge and technology expand, occupations change, leisure increases and aspirations alter. Their proposals also imply the need to liberalize conditions of entry. Others put their faith in home-based study combined with distance learning, or in further developing more conventional aids to access like part-time or short courses, grants and loans, or educational guidance. [. . .] There is no shortage of access options for the policy-makers on all floors to work on.

Now I turn to structure policies. On the second floor what I called the system-makers try to devise coordinating strategies for higher education. If any evidence was needed that ministers are not omnipotent, their hitherto abortive attempts to change the structure policy that has conditioned the so-called public sector since it was established should be conclusive. [. . .] I refer of course to the binary policy introduced to deal with the simple fact that not all higher education institutions are yet, or ever likely to become, universities.

Many proposals have been canvassed to devise the more coherent system of higher education for which the Robbins Committee called. Some people want to revert to the policy of continuous creation of universities out of public-sector institutions, of which the promotion of the colleges of advanced technology was the last example. Some put their faith in direct rule by the DES on the strength of their past experience of its liberal administration of the late voluntary colleges of education. Others advocate the creation of some central body, whether executive or consultative is not always clear [. . .]. Others place their hopes in shadowy regional bodies that lack political credibility, while select committees tend to support the creation of a megalithic council of over-arching potency.

[. . .] I am constrained by 'Weaver's Law', to question the ability of any large central body to make or operate a comprehensive plan to cover the public sector, let alone the whole, of higher education. What is at issue is the destiny of some hundreds of highly diverse institutions and of those who work in them. Consider the dimensions of the planners' task. It will require a closely integrated, not to say bureaucratic and politically adroit team, working full-time over a substantial period, to collect, digest and analyse the minimum data of facts and figures they need. They must find out about the strengths, weaknesses and aspirations of each institution before they can form a total picture out of which to devise even a provisional plan for the designation of its functions, the range of its courses, the number of its students, the distribution of resources to it and so on. I say a provisional plan, because it then has to run the gauntlet of an inevitably long process of consultation with dozens of interest groups. If and when a plan emerges from this ordeal it must, in the process of being translated into a viable policy, be negotiated at least in outline through the corridors of Whitehall before it can be presented to ministers to provide the resources. There it faces the competition for resources of other services and other parts of the education service. If you assume that the plan survives this trial of strength, and possibly the shoals of parliamentary debate intact enough to be translated into a policy document, it will then be ready to be promulgated through the labyrinthine channels of the higher education system. This must be done in terms sufficiently precise to enable each institution to act on it.

[. . .] Meanwhile the world will not have stood still. The march of events will have transformed the picture. While waiting for Godot a host of ad hoc decisions have had to be made to keep the show on the road, rendering the plan obsolete. Weaver's Law, then, may be formulated thus: the maximum speed with which it is possible to devise, negotiate and validate a central plan adequate to give each of some hundreds of institutions a practical guide to its tasks and a budget to support them, will always fall so far short of the speed of change in the situation with which it is designed to deal as to make the completed plan abortive. That, you may say, is a literally hopeless conclusion. Not at all. Not every large-scale human activity is susceptible to purely central determination. To few problems is there an ideal solution; often it is difficult to devise one that gets as far as what Herbert Simon (1957) called 'satisficing' – a compromise between satisfying and sufficing. If there is any such policy it will have two constituents: first, the maximum self-help by the individual institution in terms of exploiting its market; second, a broad set of rules for designation of institutional tasks and the raising and distribution of funds, to be negotiated in a revived partnership between the DES and the LEAs (despite all their warts) – and nobody else. That conclusion implies that I do not share the view that the precedent of the UGC (itself now being questioned) can be applied with modifications to the supervision of the public sector, let alone of all higher education institutions.

There are many other questions under the heading of structure in search of policy answers. To one such, 'Should different families of institutions be expected to accept some differentiation of their functions?', I have by implication answered 'yes'. Some external control of the market seems to me inevitable if the wasteful and frustrating results of a free-for-all are to be avoided. And here what I earlier called the institution's extrinsic social purposes and not just its person-educating functions come into question. Whatever external terms of reference, if any, this or that category of institution is given, each individual institution still has to come to terms with its own identity and functions. [. . .]

The universities have for the most part become, perhaps irreversibly, tight groupings of subject specialists properly intent on the possession, expansion and transmission of the knowledge they guard. This is an indispensable function needed by every civilized community. The problem is how to protect it compatibly with meeting the educational needs of the population. The organization that the maintenance of scholarship requires, based on the integrity of the discipline, lends itself, so far as the educative functions of the university are concerned, admirably to a training in limited forms of comprehension, a training, that is, in scholarship and professional expertise. But I can think of no specialized discipline which at the undergraduate stage, however liberally taught, is capable of offering a balanced opportunity to develop the sixfold capacities I posited as the proper aim of education. The choice for the universities may then be between limiting the vast majority of students who are not potential scholars or experts to a seriously attenuated educational experience and offering them a richer experience at the unacceptable expense of compromising their essential function. The trouble is not that more means worse; there are severe limits to the ability and willingness of students to embark on a life of scholarship but not to their educability as persons in directions I have suggested. The trouble is rather that no way has been found to staff or organize universities compatibly with the provision of what I called education for capability, creativity or communion. But the increasingly articulate demand of society, voiced by parents, employers, politicians and the students themselves is for just this wider service – wider in aims, wider in curriculum and wider in access.

I believe that the polytechnics and other public-service institutions should leave to the universities the essential functions of pursuing and transmitting specialist knowledge through research and scholarship, and that drawing on this knowledge should concentrate on the no less difficult and important task of meeting this wider demand from potential learners from the ages of 18 to 80. As I tried to indicate earlier, there is no shortage of access and curricular policies ready to be exploited. Teaching and learning methods, too, offer a rich field for research.

I recognize that for the universities the direction I am suggesting sounds conservative, indeed reactionary. I shall be told – irrelevantly, I believe, because being *sui generis* they will adapt to the future in their own inimitable way – that Oxford and Cambridge offer all that I am asking; that in all institutions teaching and research are indivisible; that there are thousands of scholar-educators in the universities (survivors from, I fear, a waning tradition); and that I am condemning the public sector to second-class status.

Unrepentant, I shall believe that in the long run this represents the logical development of both the Robbins principle and the binary policy. There is an unfulfilled need for people to be helped to learn how to use the world's store of knowledge for the solution of personal and social problems. That brings me, shortly, to my last policy issue – resources.

During the long and now nostalgic period of higher education expansion our central and local governments proceeded on the logical basis that they should decide their objectives and then supply the resources to achieve them. There is strong evidence that this process has been reversed. From now on governments will stand this policy on its head, dictate the resources to be available and leave their clients – with invocations to freedom – to make the best of it. Whatever governments are in store for us, cuts will continue.

This prompts us to ask whether those who carry the main burden of policy-making on the third floor of the higher education mansion can face the tough decisions over priorities involved in any policy changes radical enough to deal with the higher education predicament. Better, for example, to rethink what is essential to the doctrines of institutional autonomy, academic freedom, and lifelong tenure than for institutions to perish in too automatic a defence of them.

Challenging questions of priority creates acute tensions between the residents on the third floor of the higher education building and between them and the policy-makers on the first and second floors. There are signs, too, that the system controllers are floundering. But confrontation stiffens positions. There will need to be much more amicable inter-floor cooperation if answers to the questions I have raised are to be found in time to avert chaos or catastrophe. [. . .] Who will make the first move towards rapprochement?

References

This article is an edited text of a lecture given at the University College, Swansea on 29 October 1981.

Buber, M. (1947) *Between Man and Man*. London, Kegan Paul, p.85.
Burgess, T. (1977) *Education after School*. London, Gollancz, pp. 147–159.
Journal of the Royal Society of Arts, May 1981, pp. 324–331.

Macmurray, J. (1957, 1961) The Gifford Lectures 1953–54: (i) *The Self as Agent*, (ii) *Persons in Relation*. London, Faber and Faber.
Nuttgens, P. (1978) *Learning to Some Purpose*. Society of Industrial Artists and Designers.
Revans, R.W. (1980) *Action Learning*. London, Blond and Briggs.
Simon, H.A. (1957) *Administrative Behaviour*. New York, Collier MacMillan.
Temple, W. (1949) *Nature, Man and God*. London, Macmillan, p.57.

CHAPTER 1.2

A MODEL FOR HIGHER EDUCATION*
TONY BECHER AND MAURICE KOGAN

Introduction

It can sometimes be helpful, in explaining complex social and political phenomena, to refer to a deliberately simplified representation of those phenomena. There are no obvious rules for constructing such representations, and no standard means of checking their validity. Often one is left with nothing more satisfactory than a sense of good fit, or of logical consistency, a feeling of appropriateness, a shock of recognition. Representations of reality in the social sciences may have certain features in common with striking caricatures, telling metaphors or good interpretations of a play or a musical score. They highlight particular aspects of the whole, at the expense of others; but do so in such a way as to enhance understanding rather than to distort reality.

In this chapter we attempt to develop a portrayal of higher education which meets the requirement of simplifying and making more readily comprehensible while at the same time remaining true to reality. We have so far referred to representations and portrayals; but it is probably in the end easier to follow current usage and adopt the terminology of constructing or setting out a model.

The term 'model' has come to have a variety of different meanings. We

* *Process and Structure in Higher Education*. London, Heinemann, 1980, pp. 10–25. ©Tony Becher and Maurice Kogan.
Some of the material in this chapter was first published in 'Research in Higher Education' (1979) by the Swedish National Board of Universities and Colleges.
Tony Becher is Professor of Education at the University of Sussex. Maurice Kogan is Professor of Government and Social Administration at Brunel University. Before that he spent 14 years in the DES where he was private secretary to Sir Edward Boyle.

shall employ it here in a non-technical sense, as a straightforward, but necessarily and deliberately simplified, set of categories for thinking about British higher education and looking at the relationships between its components. These categories, components and relationships can be compactly summarized in tabular form and it is the resulting figure to which we will refer as our model. We ascribe no special powers or properties to the model itself, other than those of conveniently presenting abstract ideas in concrete visual terms. It must, to be of any use, stand up to the test of being recognizable; it must succeed in reflecting without distortion important discontinuities in value; and above all it must provide a coherent and conceptually sound analysis of the complex phenomena of higher education.

We do not suggest that the model has predictive power of the kind offered by theories in the natural sciences; nor that it adequately incorporates the time dimension in a way that would make it a useful tool for the social historian. Our analysis relates to one particular decentralized system of higher education. It could be extended without much difficulty to other decentralized systems, or even to somewhat more centralized public services within the British welfare state: but a significantly different kind of model, especially in terms of relationships between components, would need to be developed for strongly centralized countries. Finally, the model sets out to portray the characteristic features of institutions which are primarily concerned with teaching. The networks for predominantly research-based individuals and units would overlap with, but show structural properties which differ in various ways from, those we discuss below.

The structural levels in the system

We now turn to the business of assembling the model itself. In the discussions which follow we distinguish between four familiar elements in the structure of any higher education system. The first is the central level, involving the various national and local authorities who between them are charged with overall planning, resource allocation and the monitoring of standards. The second level is that of the individual institution, as defined in law (through its charters or instruments of governance) and by convention (through its various decision-making bodies).

We have called the third level the 'basic unit', because its precise nature varies between different institutions. In many traditional universities, it corresponds with subject-based departments; but in some newer ones the basic unit may be a more broadly constituted 'school of study'. In other institutions again, it may be defined by a course team – namely, an interdisciplinary group of teachers who collectively provide a major component of the undergraduate curriculum. The main characteristics of such basic units are that they have academic responsibility for an identifiable course or group of courses, that they have their own operating budgets (and some discretion in disposing of them) and that they exercise some element of choice in the recruitment of professional colleagues (and often also of students). They may in certain cases engage in collective research activities, but this is far from being a defining feature.

Finally, the system is composed of individuals: teaching staff, researchers, students, administrators and ancillary workers. We shall focus in our discussion mainly on the teachers, as in British higher education they normally play the main role in shaping academic, institutional and curricular policy, though we shall also give some attention to students.

In the first stage in the construction of the model, then, we have merely identified four elements representing the different structural levels within the system (*Table 1*).

Table 1   The structural components of the model

Individual	*Basic unit*	*Institutional*	*Central authority*

Two considerations need to be emphasized in the interpretation of this part of the model. The first is that the elements are meant to represent functions rather than entities (to illustrate this, the same people may operate at some times as individual academics and at others as representing basic units; particular institutions can, in certain aspects of what they do, depart from their institutional role to act as central authorities, or even as basic units). The second consideration is that the fourfold categorization deliberately simplifies reality: the more complex components – and especially the central authority and the institution – will subsequently be seen to function in a variety of different styles and to embody a diverse collection of entities.

Two modes, and the development of a matrix

The second stage in the process depends on a less familiar set of distinctions. It separates two components in the everyday life of the academic world which are not in practice sharply distinguished. The first of these relates to the monitoring and maintenance of values within the system as a whole. It might be designated, briefly, as the *normative mode*. The second, in contrast, refers to the business of carrying out practical tasks at different levels within the system. It could be labelled as the *operational mode*.

Although these two modes obviously interact – and we shall go on, towards the end of this section, to discuss the nature of their interaction – their characteristics can be readily marked off one from another. Their inseparability in practice and clear differentiation in theory recall the familiar contrast between mind and body. Looked at in this light, the normative/operational distinction can be considered as denoting two aspects of the same state of affairs. The contrast between the one and the other is related to the difference between what people actually do – or what they are institutionally required to do – and what they count as important. The distinction also has some kinship with the familiar differences between fact and value and between everyday practice as defined by law and ideal practice as defined by morality. However, the best way to draw out the differences between the two modes is perhaps within the context of discussing the model itself in more detail.

Allowing still for a certain sketchiness in the delineation of the normative and operational components, we now have the basis of an eight-cell matrix which marks off the two modes in relation to each of the four structural components (*Table* 2).

Table 2   The eight elements of the model

	Individual	Basic unit	Institution	Central authority
Normative	1	2	3	4
Operational	5	6	7	8

The cells of the matrix

The next step must be to fill out the eight elements or cells of this matrix in sufficient detail to make it possible to discuss the interconnections between them. This task can best be tackled by taking the eight numbered elements in turn and commenting on the nature and implications of each.

Normative mode

1 The main characteristics at the individual level in the normative mode are an emphasis on fulfilling personal wants and meeting personal expectations, linked with a general concern to maximize job satisfaction. These might be called intrinsic features of the element in question. However, there is also an extrinsic characteristic, in that most individuals derive some sense of support from the working group to which they belong, and reciprocate this by subscribing to the group's norms. (As we shall see, the combination of intrinsic and extrinsic features also occurs at the other levels of the system.)

2 The basic unit, viewed in its normative mode, is mainly taken up with maintaining the group norms and values which give it its sense of coherence. It operates the collective credit system through which members of the immediate professional group, and the wider network of comparable groups in other institutions, obtain rewards, advancement and recognition. Thus, for example, a history department in a particular university is concerned to endorse the canons of historical scholarship and codes of good professional practice in the subject. In doing so, its own departmental reputation will be preserved and enhanced, and in addition its individual members may the more easily gain promotion in other history departments in other universities, whether at home or abroad. But at the same time, in the interests of survival, any such basic unit will also need to fall in with the extrinsic demands of the parent institution, which will not necessarily coincide with its own particular sectional concerns.

3 Academic institutions are predominantly engaged, in their normative aspect, in setting and monitoring rules rather than in making substantive judgements of quality. In other words, their role emerges most clearly in the maintenance of 'due process', although they also have important developmental functions. They seek to ensure that the proper procedures are followed by basic units in relation to academic appointments, the use of funds, the selection of students, the protocols of assessment and the like. Institutions as a whole do not normally lay down collective criteria for excellence. Rather, their tendency is to monitor the normative ambitions of basic units and to ensure that these conform to the shared interests of the group. In many higher education systems, institutions also have an extrinsic concern with meeting the requirements of central authorities, and of ensuring that the range of courses they provide matches the demands of applicants and employers.

4 Just as academic institutions monitor their basic units, so too the central authorities have the normative task of monitoring the standards of their constituent institutions. They are also, however, expected to identify the extrinsic requirements on higher education of the economy and of society at large. Assuming that they succeed in this slippery task, they are then expected to perform the even more remarkable achievement of changing the system itself to match such requirements. Their possible means of doing so are reviewed in 8 below.

At this point, we might conveniently summarize the elements in the normative mode, as shown in *Table 3*.

Table 3   The elements in the normative mode

Individual	Basic unit	Institution	Central authority
Intrinsic: job satisfaction; personal wants and expectations	Intrinsic: maintaining peer-group norms and values	Intrinsic: maintaining due academic process; initiating developments	Intrinsic: maintaining institutional standards
Extrinsic: subscription to group norms	Extrinsic: conformity with institutional requirements	Extrinsic: conformity to central demands	Extrinsic: meeting social and economic desiderata
(1)	(2)	(3)	(4)

Operational mode

5 Turning now to the operational mode, it is easy to see that at the individual level the main requirements are those of occupational tasks. Such tasks are laid down mainly by the basic units, and comprise, for example, the teaching and/or research commitments of staff, and the learning demands and subsequent assessment exercises of students.

6 In operational terms, the key function of the basic unit is to define the actual nature and content of the unit's everyday practice. It is thus concerned mainly with issues of the curriculum, and in some cases also of research. It has to specify the working programme in sufficient detail to make it capable of implementation, and to translate the result in terms of individual tasks.

7 The institution has an important part to play in forward planning, and

in implementing national or local policy decisions in return for the resources required for development. It is also concerned with the maintenance of established activities. It carries out these tasks mainly by the differential allocation of money and manpower between basic units.

8 The central authorities are operationally responsible for negotiating the recurrent funds made available for higher education by the legislature, and for allocating them between their constituent institutions. They are also in many cases charged with authorizing proposals for new developments or laying down specifications for new courses. By such means they can to a greater or lesser extent carry out their normative functions, as outlined in 4 above.[1]

A further summary is presented in *Table* 4.

Table 4   The elements in the operational mode

Individual	Basic unit	Institution	Central authority
Work required: research/teaching, learning	Operating process: curriculum and/or research programme	Maintenance of institution; forward planning; implementing policy	Negotiation and allocation of central resources; sponsorship of new developments
(5)	(6)	(7)	(8)

Relationships between elements

Before this initial exploration of the model is completed, it remains to say something more about the relationships between adjacent elements in the matrix which we have just discussed. There are, of course, two sets of relationships: those which are horizontal (between elements 1 and 2, 2 and 3, and so on), and those which are vertical (between elements 1 and 5, 2 and 6, etc.). We shall look at them briefly in turn.

It has been implicit in our discussion of the normative mode that all the relevant relationships involve appraisal or judgement. Thus basic units relate normatively to individuals in terms of matching an individual's standards against the values of the group (elements 1 and 2). Institutions and basic units are linked in terms of procedural judgements in which the units must be seen to conform to institutional codes of practice (elements 2 and 3). National authorities carry out their monitoring function in relation to institutions by evaluating the general effectiveness of their basic units and by appraising their professional competence (elements 3 and 4).

In comparable ways, all the main relationships in the operational mode can be characterized in terms of the allocation of resources, responsibilities and tasks. The individual's activities are set out in terms of the operational requirements of the basic unit to which he or she belongs (elements 5 and 6). The basic unit is related operationally to the institution in terms of the specification of its budget and the institutional requirements on its curricular and/or research programmes (elements 6 and 7). Each institution in its turn is dependent on the acceptance by the central authorities of new types of course provision and, in the autonomous sector, on the allocation of funds from the total pool available for the system as a whole (elements 7 and 8). This is so even where the central authority relies on academic peer assessments to guide its decisions: the final decision nevertheless rests with the authority itself.

The vertical relationships are different in character. Where the horizontal links ensure normal day-to-day working, the vertical links involve possible departures from convention. As long as the normative and operational modes are in phase with one another, the system as a whole can be said to be in dynamic equilibrium – if not in harmony, then at least in a state of balanced tension. But when the two modes become significantly out of phase, some kind of adjustment is necessary to avoid breakdown and to restore the possibility of normal functioning. On the whole, one would expect the normative level to exercise dominance over the operational. This would constitute a particular application of the general rule that, when there is a clash between what people do and what their basic values are, then the values will affect the actions more strongly than the actions affect the values. However, numerous examples of the opposite effect can be put forward.

Looking at the different relationships briefly in turn, we have noted that they are all characterized by developmental change designed to restore a sense of equilibrium. As far as the individual level is concerned (elements 1 and 5), the emphasis is on developments in working practice – for example, changes in a student's learning habits induced by changes in his or her beliefs; or changes in a researcher's emphasis and approach brought about by some new apprehension of the subject; or changes in a teacher's techniques generated by a new pedagogic ideal. The interaction between the normative and operational modes at the level of the basic unit (elements 2 and 6) will perhaps most often be characterized by developments in curricula, as group values develop in such a way as to call into question current activities – a recent example would be the effect on undergraduate courses of the changing conceptions of geography as a discipline. At the institutional level (elements 3 and 7), the characteristic product of a tension between norms and operations is some change in academic or administrative organization, designed to bring more closely into line what is done with what is held desirable. The comparable task at the level of the central authorities (elements 4 and 8) – namely, matching the provision within the system as a whole to major changes in the demands of society and the economy – often has to be tackled by a major structural reform (as in Sweden) or by the establishment of a series of new institutions (as in Britain).

The completion of the model

The various considerations brought forward so far can be effectively summarized by presenting them as in *Fig*. 1. The model which we have now set out contains no features which have not already been discussed. However, the act of bringing them together in a relatively compact form will, we hope, make it easier to keep the system as a whole in view – and hence to grasp more clearly the nature of its components and the interrelationships between them.

Some justifications and qualifications

It is important at this stage in the argument to reiterate that we are not making any sweeping claims for the model. In particular, we have no intention of implying that it is the only conceivable, or indeed the only allowable, representation of the higher education system in Britain. There could well be a number of such portrayals, not necessarily in competition one with another; different models might be concerned to emphasize different features and to develop distinct but not necessarily incompatible interpretations of shared phenomena. What we have been putting forward so far can be seen, perhaps, as a system of notation within which to spell out ideas and findings, hunches and categorical assertions about the workings of the enterprise and of its component elements, about the interactions between the parts and about their respective relationships with the whole.

That the choice of a particular kind of notation is not a purely arbitrary matter can be brought out by contrasting the Roman with the Chinese system of representing speech, or the Arabic with the Roman system of representing number. It is none the less incumbent upon anyone putting

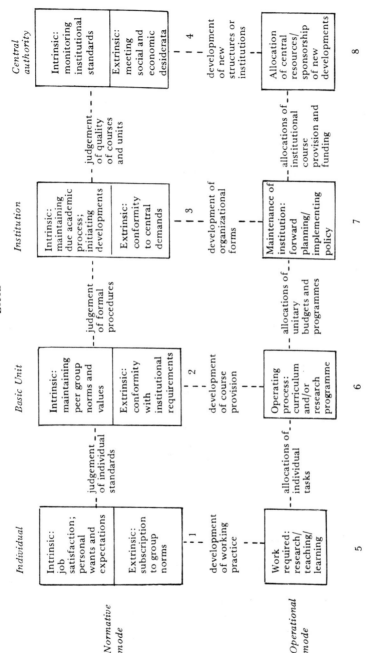

Figure 1 The completed model.

forward a schema such as ours to demonstrate that it makes reasonably good sense, and to acknowledge its limitations.

It may be asked, in the first place, whether the four levels defined in the model are generally useful. Outside the UK, admittedly, a number of systems (for example, those of Japan and the USA[2]) have nothing exactly corresponding to the level of 'central authority'. Even within the UK, its appropriateness could be questioned, since it might be argued that an additional tier is necessary in the maintained sector of polytechnics and colleges to accommodate the regional advisory councils (RACs). Similarly, in some small monotechnic institutions the level of 'basic unit' seems hardly to exist; in some very large institutions the position is complicated by the apparent existence of subinstitutions.

Earlier in this chapter we remarked that the levels should be seen as denoting different functions within the system, and not as categorizing particular entities: the same individual or corporate group might be identified at one time as performing a role at one level, and at another time, a different role at another level. However, it seems necessary – in addition to this particular means of giving flexibility to our descriptive vocabulary – to introduce a further ruling to take into account the type of objection just outlined. We shall therefore have recourse at this point to the mathematician's notion of a 'degenerate case' – although we shall use the term 'special case' to avoid possible connotations of debauchery or disintegration.

In so far as we might wish to extend our model to other decentralized systems, we could say that, just as a straight line is a special (degenerate) case of a circle – that is, a circle with infinite radius – so too a system without any single central authority is a special case of a system. It will usually have a series of governing authorities (trustees for private institutions, state administrations for public) rather than a single and unifying one. Nevertheless, these authorities severally will discharge the kinds of function attributed in our model to the unitary central agency. Similarly, the absence of basic units in small institutions can be seen as a special case of the model, in which the second and third levels – and the normative and operational functions of the institution and basic unit – are combined in one entity.

If the apparent absence of a particular level is usefully regarded as a special case of the model, the suggested addition of further levels raises different problems about the ways in which values, entering through the normative mode, are expressed in institutional form. Following the principle of Occam's razor, we should not elaborate levels beyond those necessary for explanation. In this spirit, the RACs need not be regarded as constituting a distinct level between the central authorities and the institutions because, ultimately, the RACs merely make recommendations upon which the central authorities then take decisions. Equally, the existence of federal institutions (the universities of London and Wales) does not call for an elaboration of the model, since the functions ascribed by the model to the institution are merely in these instances distributed to components of the aggregate.

To clarify this point, a distinction may be drawn between the constitutional framework of higher education – which can be depicted as a particular constellation of managerial elements arranged in formally designed organizational tiers – and the underlying structure of the system, which our model seeks to portray.

While the number of tiers is a matter of administrative definition, the number of levels can be marked off in terms of significant differences in value sets. The central authority has the responsibility for collating the demands of society on the higher education system, in terms of its consumers (the employers of graduates and the potential students) and of its sponsors (the tax-paying public and its elected representatives). It has the further responsibility of seeing that the system meets such demands to an acceptable degree. The institution has its own distinctive values. Its primary task is to maintain and develop a collective character, style and reputation, incorporating but reaching beyond those of its constituent basic units; and as part of this to respond to internal and external demands by the initiation of new units and new programmes. It also has an important secondary task, of acting in its fiduciary role of collating values and monitoring the procedures of constituent units. The basic unit has the very different responsibility of responding to and maintaining academic norms within its particular field of relevance. And the values of the individual are again separable from, though comprising part of, those of the basic unit.

The distinction which is embodied in the model between the two modes, normative and operational, can also be called into question. For example, the allocation of resources within an institution can properly be seen as a value-laden activity – in other words, one which reflects judgements of merit as well as answering functional needs. But even allowing for the close interrelationships between the normative and the operational modes, there is a familiar and recognizable difference between the rationale of a group or organization and what it does in practice, between its espoused causes and its functions, its values and its tasks. The distinction is useful precisely because it separates for the purposes of analysis two quite different perspectives from which the workings of the higher education system and its constituents can be viewed. The duality is in no sense meant to imply that we are dealing with two separate systems, or two systems which are interconnected in some mysterious way: it is, as we suggested earlier, the same system, analysed from two different perspectives.

The remaining constituent of the model, namely the set of relationships between the different levels and different modes, is similarly open to qualification. Our model clearly implies that the only connecting links are those between adjacent elements. In so far as there are links between components other than those directly shown (for example, between institution and individual, leapfrogging the basic unit, in the normative mode; or diagonally between central authority in the normative mode and institution in the operational mode), we prefer to redescribe them in terms of the existing model so as to preserve its simplicity, unless this does violence to the facts. (In the examples above, we would reinterpret the leapfrogging as two horizontal moves, from institution to basic unit and basic unit to individual, with the basic unit as a dormant partner; and would redescribe the diagonal link as one vertical and one horizontal move, with the institution in its normative mode as a dummy agent.)

A further point arises which is empirical rather than conceptual: namely, what is the actual frequency, within higher education, with which diagonal, leapfrogging or other types of links are made between non-adjacent elements in the system as portrayed in our model? We suggest that the proportion of such connections is relatively low. Even in the apparently most common case, where a central authority would appear at the normative level to be directly judging the academic quality of basic units, it is not misleading to say that the institution plays some shadowy role. At the very least, its permission is formally sought for any site visitation. For the most part, we have been unable to identify clear cases of diagonal moves: the link between normative and operational modes is easily enough made at the same level in the system, but normally occurs only indirectly, it would seem, between elements at different levels. So the notation we have adopted is not only convenient in presentational terms, but also gives a fair reflection of existing practice.

An implicit component

The initial presentation and subsequent examination of our model have omitted one important component whose influence on higher education we shall have frequent occasion to note. We refer to the social and economic climate within which any given higher education system exists. It impinges most obviously on the central authority but also has a direct bearing on the institution, the basic unit and the individual within the system.

A society which holds higher education in considerable esteem, as do those of the USA and The Netherlands, for example, will give rise to a very different morale within academia from that generated by a society which denies its academic institutions any significance in the scheme of things (as was until recently the case in mainland China). But more specifically, institutions whose graduates do well on the job market will tend to have more confidence than those whose record in this respect is poor; the fortunes of particular basic units will wax and wane with the extent to which their particular areas of coverage match, or fail to match, the prevailing social mood (consider, for instance, theology); and individual academics' self-esteem will to some extent be affected by the comparability of their salary scales with those of other professionals, including fellow-academics in other countries.

Such considerations, though extraneous to the values of higher education per se, undeniably influence those values, and the ways in which they are operationalized. But they are not part of the higher education system – unless one regards the whole of society as being, in a sense, the higher education system. The social and economic climate pervades higher education and acts, to change the metaphor, as a field of force affecting the development of the values which express themselves through the normative mode – and hence the operations of higher education. Thus any historical treatment of higher education would take the social and economic background as an essential context within which to explain the way in which the academic enterprise has developed.

We propose, having drawn attention to this missing component, to leave it out of the structure of our model. That is to say, we propose to confine our model to the domain of higher education, rather than extending it to embrace the wider polity. However, we do not in any way intend by this to neglect or disallow the importance, in understanding how the higher education system functions, of more general social and economic considerations.

Notes

1   In ascribing these functions to central authorities we are deliberately telescoping the roles of the Department of Education and Science with respect to universities, and the local

education authorities in England and Wales with respect to polytechnics and colleges (the position of the central institutions being different in Scotland). The local education authorities, in our use of the term, are 'central' in so far as they take on a number of the functions we attribute to the central level in our model. This ruling gives rise to questions about the responsibilities of local government in relation to institutions which are partly national and partly local in character. But in any event, it should be noted that in the maintained sector of higher education, the allocation of capital resources and the approval of new developments are primarily a matter for the DES, even if recurrent funds are at the disposition of city or county hall.

2   It is in one sense an oversimplification to describe higher education in the USA as lacking a central component. Although the federal government has only a marginal role, some of the larger state networks – such as those of California and New York – can be seen as complete systems in themselves, with the state legislature functioning as the central authority. Taking the nation as a whole, however, there is no unitary system. In particular, the numerous private universities and colleges are answerable only to their individual governing bodies.

SECTION 2

STUDENT PATHWAYS

CHAPTER 2.1

THE EDUCATIONAL CHOICES OF YOUNG PEOPLE*
ALAN GORDON

This chapter examines the range of factors influencing the educational choices of young people between the ages of 15 and 18. [. . .]

The main factors reviewed here have been grouped under three headings. First, the influence of such social factors as home background, sex, parental education and attitudes and so on; second, the influence of school-related factors; and third, the effects of such economic variables as the material circumstances of the home, educational maintenance allowances, and young people's perceptions of the benefits and cost associated with continued education.

Social factors

Since 1944 a large number of research reports, some government sponsored, have drawn attention to the under-representation of young people from working-class home backgrounds in post-compulsory education. Parental occupation, education and attitudes have all been shown to be closely associated with a young person's progress (or lack of progress) through to the highest levels of the education system. [. . .]

Parental occupation

[. . .] Research evidence over a period of some 30 years indicates the scale

* *Access To Higher Education*, edited by Oliver Fulton. SRHE at University of Guildford, Surrey, 1981. © SRHE. Alan Gordon is Research Fellow at the Institute of Manpower Studies, University of Sussex.

of class differences in post-compulsory education and the ways in which very little has changed by the 1980s (see, for example, CACE, 1954, 1959; HMSO, 1963; Douglas et al., 1968; Schools Council, 1968; Fulton and Gordon, 1979a; Halsey et al., 1980). There are numerous well-researched commentaries that document:

> (the) well-known fact that working-class children (and particularly the children of unskilled manual workers) are under-represented in selective secondary and higher education; and that even at the same levels of ability they are far more likely than middle-class children to deteriorate in performance and to leave school at the earliest permitted age. (Craft, 1970)

[. . .] Similar inequalities in participation in higher education are found in most other developed countries too (OECD, 1970; Bockstael and Feinstein, 1970; King et al., 1974; Neave, 1976).

One of the Robbins Committee's most important findings was that the proportion of children from non-manual home backgrounds who obtained places in higher education was some six times as great as the children of people in manual occupations (HMSO, 1963). Indeed, the difference between professionals and those from unskilled manual families was of the order of twenty to one. [. . .] These differentials have scarcely narrowed even though the absolute age participation rates for all social classes have risen. Indeed, the university differentials are almost unchanged from the levels prevailing some 50 years ago – and are somewhat wider than those of the early and mid-1970s. [. . .]

The failure of working-class young people to carry on their full-time education beyond the age of 16 and into higher education might well cause less concern if it could be shown that ability, however measured, varied greatly between different social class groups, so that the education system was meritocratically keeping the most able within its care and attention. Much research and argument has taken place over the past two decades on the question of the extent to which equal opportunities[1] in education have been achieved for young people of similar abilities and attributes (e.g. Westergaard and Little, 1964). Halsey et al. (1980) suggest that, in fact, the ability threshold for working-class young people to enter university is markedly higher than for other young people with fathers in either service or intermediate occupations. Their research showed that, on average in the years 1950–1970, a would-be student from a working-class background had to be some 6.6 IQ points brighter than a similar higher education aspirant from a service family background (*Table* 5).

Table 5 IQ thresholds for university entry

Social class of father	IQ
Service class	120.8
Intermediate class	125.6
Working class	127.4
Service class/working class IQ handicap	6.6

Source: Halsey et al. (1980), Table 10.7.

Halsey et al. (1980) are particularly concerned that 'past selection processes, especially to the highest education in the universities, cannot satisfy either meritocrats, or still less egalitarians'. [. . .] But if we ask whether selection for university is more or less meritocratic than earlier selection processes, even very recent figures produced for upper-secondary and further education (e.g. Dean et al., '1979) indicate that young people with fathers in higher occupations are similarly over-represented in full-time education after 16. It seems in fact that it is at the minimum school-leaving age that the greatest amount of differentiation between the social classes occurs (see, for example, Gordon and Williams, 1977; Fulton and Gordon, 1979a; Halsey et al., 1980). [. . .]

To focus on application and participation rates in higher education, then, might well lead to a failure to appreciate the important policy issues of demand for, and access to, full-time post-compulsory education. If working-class young people survive in the education system until the age of 18, their chances of going on to higher education are not so very different from their middle-class classmates. Halsey et al. (1980) found that while 70 percent of boys from service class backgrounds who continued their full-time studies until the age of 18 went on to university, the figure for boys from intermediate and working-class families who did so was only a little lower at 60 percent. The expansion in non-university higher education, which occurred too late for most of Halsey's sample, may have moved these figures even closer together.

While it is, of course, necessary to review the scale of the influence of social class on young people's progress in the education system, this does not tell the reasons for class inequalities. As Neave (1976) points out, social class may be a good predictor of academic survival, but it does not explain. For that we must go beyond the statistics of differential demand and participation.

The pool of ability

In the early 1960s there was a belief in some quarters that the number of young people with the capacity to benefit from higher education was rigidly limited, and that any expansion in the number of places provided by institutions of higher education could only be filled by dredging the depths of this fixed pool of ability. [. . .]

More recent research, too, has stressed that fears of a limited 'pool of ability' are unjustified (Halsey et al., 1980). Indeed, a more common anxiety is the converse – that there still exist high levels of untapped ability amongst young people from manual home backgrounds and among girls. It is still true that 'many manual working class pupils who have the ability to benefit from a sixth year at school or college are failing to do so' (Douglas et al., 1968). In theory at least, the wastage of talent would be substantially reduced if the advantages 'conveyed by the chance of birth, as a male, into a professional family' (Fulton and Gordon, 1979a) could be made available to all young people.

Parental attitudes

Roberts (1980) is one of many to comment on the reasons for class-related disadvantage in the education system. Reviewing research on the benefits of those born into middle-class homes, he suggests that one advantage is 'having articulate and confident parents who recognise the relevance of education for life chances . . .'.

Moreover, Roberts (1980) has few doubts about the strength of middle-class parental expectations for their children:

> Middle class parents do not treat success as a prize reserved for the intellectually brilliant, but act on the assumption that it lies within the grasp of any industrious child of their own. [. . .]

Neave (1974) observed that external examinations, particularly CSE and GCE O-Levels, perform very different functions for middle-class and working-class parents. For middle-class parents the success the their children in examinations serves to justify further support and encouragement, while failure leads not to acceptance but to calls for additional work and effort. They are in fact more likely to offer support and encouragement throughout their child's schooling. On the other hand working-class parents (and those who were early-leavers themselves) generally only seem to offer the same kind of encouragement once good examination results are available as evidence of their child's academic potential. Morris (1969) suggests that parental encouragement is important at two stages: first, in supporting children's provisional intentions; and second, in reinforcing a student's determination to carry on with a course of action already started.

Parental education

Parents' experiences of post-compulsory education certainly influence their attitudes towards whether their children should continue their studies after the age of 16 or 18 (e.g. CACE, 1959; HMSO, 1963). In sixth forms, further education and higher education, students whose parents had themselves continued in full-time education are over-represented (Williams and Gordon, 1975; Dean et al., 1980). A large number of studies (e.g. Thomas and Wetherell, 1974; Rauta and Hunt, 1975) have pointed out the high correlation between the age at which parents and their children left school. In addition, Neave (1975) found that the amount of influence parents have over their child's decision to stay on in or leave full-time education was strongly associated with the amount of education they themselves had received. Parents who had left school before their fifteenth birthday were much less influential. Both middle-class and more highly educated parents generally take more interest in their children's schooling[2] (see, for example, Douglas, 1964; Douglas et al., 1968).

Peers

A possible influence on leavers is '. . . anti-school peer groups and subcultures . . .' (Neave, 1976). It is evident that among some groups of working-class pupils there is a deep-rooted cultural hostility towards the main objectives of secondary and continued education (Willis, 1977). But it seems that, for the decision to go on to university at least, the importance of the influence of peers depends on children's social background. The peer group is more important the less support is received from home, and peers are least influential for those young people whose parents have some experience of post-compulsory education themselves. In addition, for those hoping and planning to go on to higher education, 'the peer group appears to be influential for precisely those who already derive their main support from the school' (Neave, 1975). [. . .]

As far as a counter-school culture is concerned, however, some working-class pupils in compulsory education do derive great support from their peers: it can hardly be said that the secondary school regime supports their lack of interest or their disruption, but it acts as a common focus for disenchantment (Willis, 1977).

Sex

One of the anxieties expressed by the Robbins Committee was over the wastage of female talent. On grounds of economic efficiency, rather than equity, they felt that much better use had to be made of academically able women who represented 'what must be the greatest source of unused talent'. [. . .] Women's participation in all types of full-time higher education now stands at 43 percent of students (provisional figures: DES, 1981). In addition, it does appear that girls' educational ambitions in recent years have converged with those of boys (Fulton and Gordon, 1979a). If these ambitions materialized this would represent a further improvement in relative chances. In spite of these trends it seems still to be the case that the general environmental and educational disadvantages of working-class young people are compounded in the case of girls. Many working-class parents still attach more importance to their son's education than to that of their daughter. 'The resources – cultural, economic, psychological – necessary for a working-class child to overcome the obstacles on the way to a university place are very rarely expended on behalf of a girl' (Westergaard and Little, 1964).

Similar criticism has also been levelled at schools' attitudes towards girls' education. Blackstone and Weinreich-Haste (1980) have recently commented on the ways in which girls have been 'taught' to underachieve. Sharpe (1976) blames this underachievement and the low career aspirations of many girls on teachers and careers counsellors. A combination then of home and school environment prevents many girls from fulfilling their educational potential. The most important issue now, however, is probably not the general aspirations of girls, but their often limited choice of subjects.

General

Throughout the 1960s and 1970s there was a general expectation among both educationalists and policy-makers that the expansion of British higher education, together with the reorganization of secondary education along comprehensive lines, would lead to an opening up of higher education to those of lower social origins. The evidence above is unequivocal on this point: in spite of these developments the proportion of students who come from working-class backgrounds is virtually the same as half a century ago.

This is the 'sad statistic' to which Jackson and Marsden (1966) drew our attention more than 15 years ago. It is clear that:

> the expansion of educational provision has not involved a major redistribution of opportunities between children of different classes . . . as in the past the growth of student places in higher education from the early 1960s met a demand which, in effect, came mainly from professional, managerial and other non-manual homes. The scales remain heavily weighted against young people of manual working-class origin, though probably not quite so much as before. (Westergaard and Resler, 1975)

In view of the persistence of the social class inequalities in access to upper-secondary and higher education reviewed above, one has to ask whether Bernstein (1970) might have been correct in his assessment that 'education cannot compensate for society'. Westergaard and Little (1964) took a similarly pessimistic view: 'The persistent class differentials in educational opportunity in the final analysis are anchored in the equally persistent divisions of the society at large.' Others, however, are more hopeful about the possibilities of specific educational change in improving young people's opportunities and life chances.

The influence of school

The Robbins Committee clearly recognized that both the quality of primary and secondary education and the organization of schooling would affect the proportion of young people with the abilities and attitudes appropriate to higher education (HMSO, 1963). What the committee did not foresee was the growth in the number of pupils attending non-selective schools over the past two decades. [. . .]

Official pronouncements have, at least until recently, claimed that comprehensive[3] reorganization has already enhanced young people's chances of continuing their studies in higher education. A DES discussion paper on future trends in higher education commented that:

> . . . in the education field itself, comprehensive reorganization is already transforming secondary schooling; when this process is complete no children will be educated in institutions which, by their status, nature and organization, are apt to cut off their pupils from higher education opportunities.

Moreover,

> . . . in the climate which re-organization will have created higher education may be made a more attractive prospect for young people from poorer home backgrounds. (DES, 1978)

The hope that equalizing opportunities in secondary education will have a spill-over effect on participation in higher education has, of course, been a major spur to comprehensive reform. Intuitively, at least, one might expect that the reorganization of secondary education will affect not only the number of young people staying on in sixth forms, colleges and institutions of higher education, but also the social class mix of those staying on. This is, however, an area that has remained relatively unresearched, and the research evidence that does exist is somewhat contradictory.

Many studies have shown that remaining in full-time education after the age of 16 is closely connected to the type of school attended (e.g. Rauta and Hunt, 1975). A Schools Council survey of sixth-form pupils (Schools Council, 1970) found clear differences between different types of school in the participation rates of manual workers' children. Just over half of the sixth-formers in comprehensive schools came from manual working-class home backgrounds, compared with a third of those attending maintained grammar schools and a fifth of those in independent and direct-grant school sixth forms. A study undertaken in 1975 revealed a broadly similar pattern (Gordon and Williams, 1977): among those students studying for GCE A-Levels, 36 percent of pupils in comprehensive-school sixth forms came from manual working-class backgrounds, compared with 22 percent of those attending other forms of upper-secondary education. More recently still, however, when an even higher proportion of pupils were studying in comprehensive schools, a survey of just under 4500 16–19-year-olds in sixth forms and colleges found that different institutional types contained an approximately equal proportion of students from any one social class group (Dean et al., 1979). As a result, students from manual home backgrounds were similarly under-represented in all forms of 16–19-year-old education, whether comprehensive schools, grammar schools, sixth-form colleges, tertiary colleges or further education institutions. This finding is rather different from earlier ones and appears to belie the claim by Benn and Simon (1972) that 'the higher proportion of working-class students in sixth forms [is] also reflected in university entrants from comprehensive schools'. [. . .]

In a study of students who had attended comprehensive schools Neave (1975) found that 38 percent of university entrants came from manual social class families, compared with 28 percent of university entrants nationally. He felt that the delayed selection implied by a comprehensive system would allow universities and other higher education institutions '. . . to draw upon a far wider social reservoir than has hitherto been the case'. Neave remained convinced that comprehensive reform would mean '. . . a change in university clientele' and that it would have '. . . profound repercussions . . . on the type of student entering university'. His conclusions (based on students who entered university as long ago as 1968) have been criticized on a number of counts. In particular, it has been argued that any adequate assessment of the impact of reorganization has to grapple with the question of what the outcome would have been had comprehensive reform not taken place. As Bellaby (1977) points out, this question cannot be answered by surveying only the comprehensive population.

In addition, as noted earlier on, the number of students from manual working-class backgrounds as a proportion of all students in universities has remained virtually unchanged for the past 50 years, in spite of a threefold expansion in the number of places since 1960 and the introduction of widespread maintenance grants. Comprehensivization, then, has not in the short run conspicuously improved the relative rates of participation in higher education by traditionally under-represented groups – unless, as Fulton and Gordon (1979b) point out, in a drawn battle with other factors that would otherwise be worsening the situation.

The influence of the school goes beyond that of structural change however. The pedagogic experiences of pupils must also be important; and Lawton (1977) has suggested that one reason for the education system's failure to achieve what he calls social justice is the lack of attention that has been paid to curriculum issues. It is certainly the case that questions on the effects of the content of education and of teaching methods have been relatively neglected. One exception, however, was the 1970s debate on examination reform for upper-secondary students and the possible replacement of GCE A-Levels by a two-level five-subject curriculum and examination structure. This debate focused on the curricular and examination needs of sixth-formers, aiming both to provide a suitably rigorous academic preparation for those going on to higher education, and to have some currency for those students planning to leave full-time education for work at the age of 18 (Schools Council, 1973). A two-level curriculum that involved the study of three subjects to N (normal) and two to F (further) level for those planning to go on to higher education attracted some support, with the possibility remaining for upper-secondary students to study all five subjects at N level. As with comprehensive restructuring, the aim was, by providing a curriculum open to a wider range of abilities and interests, to postpone selection and streaming. In spite of Schools Council support this particular proposal for reform foundered, partly because of doubts about the effects of widening the knowledge base of higher education entrants, and partly because of the possible resource implications.

More recently, a British research team argued, on the basis of somewhat limited evidence, that 'secondary schools do have an important influence on their pupils' behaviour and attainments' (Rutter et al., 1979), and that schools could be a force for the good, even in deprived areas. Their work was acclaimed as contradicting the arguments of Jencks and his associates (1972) in the United States that educational change on its own is ineffective when set against the influence of wider society. Rutter's argument was that the effects of apparently similar educational institutions on young people's ambitions, attitudes and achievements do in fact differ widely, and that weak and strong educational practices can be found in any type of structural arrangement. A series of factors that can be described as the 'ethos' of the school are, if so, much more influential than the formal criteria by which a school selects or receives pupils and organizes them for teaching purposes: what may first appear to be a uniformly structured secondary education system will, on closer inspection, turn out to be a quite heterogeneous system with a wide range of practices, attributes and institutional structures. For the future, then, the policy issue may be to identify and try to promote good practice, rather than indulge in further structural reform.

To some extent, therefore, the debate has shifted from organizational issues to concern about curricula, method, assessment and standards. This is perhaps not surprising since nearly nine out of ten lower-secondary pupils in the state sector now attend nominally comprehensive schools (DES, 1980a). However, the structural arrangements for post-compulsory education are still a contentious issue. This particular debate encompasses such issues as the size of school sixth forms (including concern about falling group sizes), and the advantages or disadvantages of tertiary colleges, sixth-form colleges, school sixth forms and institutions of further education as centres of learning for 16–19-year-olds (Dean et al., 1979; King et al., 1975).

Whatever the evidence that can be harnessed to show the impact of school type or of pupils' educational experiences on the demand for and access to higher education, it is clear that for many secondary-school pupils higher education is at best an irrelevance. A large number of young people effectively cut themselves off from opportunities in higher education by their decision to leave school at the age of 16. And for many it is their experience in compulsory education that has led them to quit as soon as it is legally possible. It has to be recognized that for many young people 'school . . . is merely a dull though prolonged preamble to a working life that is itself to prove desultory and unchallenging' (Carter, 1966). Young people who have enjoyed and had success in their primary and lower-secondary education are much more likely to want 'to continue on paths they have a liking for or excel in' (Barnard and McCreath, 1970). On the other hand, of course, for other pupils where '. . . school life produces not passing fits of revolt but a real and continuous sense of frustration, the right thing is to leave' (CACE, 1954).

A survey of fifth-formers undertaken in 1975 found disenchantment with school or with teachers to be a major reason given for the decision to leave at 16. Thirty-eight percent of the boy-leavers questioned and 45 percent of the girls said that they had decided to leave because they were 'fed up' with school (Gordon and Williams, 1977).

Economic factors

There is also a range of economic factors that may influence some fifth- and sixth-formers. Alienation from school and the desire for money of their own are frequently given by young people as the two most important reasons for their decision to leave school.

> These two factors can be viewed in push and pull terms. The alienation from school will tend to push fifth-formers out of secondary education as soon as they are legally able to do so; this disaffection with education compelling potential leavers to search for alternatives at the earliest possible opportunity. The attractions of work, or rather the attractions of the money that will be gained from working, will tend to pull the fifth-former out of full-time education and into employment. (Gordon, 1976)

However, while money may well be a powerful influence on young people's decisions, it is only one of many economic factors that need to be taken into account when presenting an overall picture of influences on the demand for upper-secondary and higher education.

There are in fact several ways in which economic considerations might affect demand. The material circumstances of the home is one. A second is the direct and indirect costs of staying on at school or college, the impact of which on any individual is obviously affected by his or her material circumstances. A third is the prospective student's perceptions of the personal economic benefits to be derived from continued education. In addition, there may be more general economic, social and cultural benefits, perhaps related to labour market opportunities.

The material circumstances of the home

The desire for money of their own is one of the most common reasons given by fifth-form leavers for their decision to leave. [. . .] Ryrie et al. (1979) also reported that the opportunity to earn money was the most frequently expressed reason for leaving school. Another study (Dean et al., 1979) also found a strong emphasis on concern over lack of income, with 38 percent of the young people surveyed saying they were 'very much' influenced to leave because if they had continued their studies they 'would not be earning any money'. Even those who did stay on described shortage of money as the main disadvantage of post-16 education.

Earning one's own money, though, is only part of the problem. For some fifth-formers the option of remaining in full-time education after the minimum school-leaving age has never been realistic because of financial constraints at home. In one study 40 percent of the fifth-formers questioned (both intending stayers and leavers) thought that they ought to leave school for work to start helping their families financially; but very few sixth-formers who had stayed on felt the same obligation (Gordon, 1976). [. . .]

Educational maintenance allowances

More than 20 years ago Floud (1961) made the point that in low-income households 'fees cannot be paid nor can adolescent earnings be foregone by the family'. She went on to recommend that educational maintenance allowances be introduced for full-time pupils staying on past the minimum leaving age, but expressed the anxiety that even this would fail to prevent all wastage of talent from the 'able children of impoverished families'. Such a call for financial support to 16–19-year olds is one that has been taken up again relatively recently.

> It is evident that it is at the end of compulsory education that the full effects of social class and the financial position of pupils' parents are felt. If we wish to remedy the waste of human resources of those who leave full-time education prematurely, then one way of doing so is to make grants for 16-year-olds widely available at a level that will both provide an incentive to stay on for the pupil, and relieve the financial burden from the shoulders of parents. (Gordon, 1976)

Given the apparent importance of monetary influences, it is likely that the widespread introduction of educational maintenance allowances would have a positive effect on staying-on rates at the age of 16, and would probably have a subsequent spill-over effect on the number of entrants to higher education. A survey of 3000 fifth-formers undertaken in 1977 suggested that a uniformly available grant of £8 a week would, in the year of the study, have increased the number of boys staying on after 16 by 4.8 percent, and the number of girls by 5.6 percent (Fulton and Gordon, 1979a). [. . .]

Since the mid-1970s an additional disincentive has been the different kinds of income support schemes for young people who leave school. These have been usefully surveyed by Maclure (1979). [. . .] The difficulties which school-leavers are experiencing in finding jobs seem to be acting as an additional incentive for them to leave school at the earliest opportunity. If they cannot find a job, then at least they have not lost their entitlement to supplementary benefit. [. . .]

Student grants

In attempting to explain shifts in the demand for higher education Williams (1974) adopted an economic framework that suggested that there are three types of reason why demand may change: 'first, the costs may change; second, the benefits may change; third, people's perception of evaluation of the costs and benefits may change'.

[. . .] The research of Pissarides suggests that earnings and employment prospects are more significant in affecting demand than is the cost of the student maintenance grant. However, one unexpected aspect of the student grant system is worth attention. A 1975 study found that while 84 percent of the undergraduate population surveyed had the maximum maintenance grant reduced by a 'parental contribution', nearly three-quarters of these students in fact received less than the assessed contribution from their parents. For 29 percent of these students the shortfall was over £100. In all, therefore, some two-thirds of all undergraduates are maintaining themselves on less than the amount thought to be necessary.

Policies designed to replace the existing student support scheme in Britain by a system of student loans had an airing in 1980 and early 1981. [. . .] It is argued by opponents of loan schemes that any such increase in the costs of becoming a graduate would have a detrimental effect on the demand for places in higher education, and that loans would act as a particular disincentive for students from working-class backgrounds who would be especially unwilling to take on a long-term debt. The Robbins Committee also claimed that loans would deter women from seeking places in higher education: '. . . British parents would be strengthened in their age-long disinclination to consider their daughters to be as deserving of higher education as their sons . . .' (HMSO, 1963).

The formal economic benefits of higher education

It has been suggested that one factor in accounting for the stagnation in staying-on rates 'could be the reduction in the leavers' perceived value of spending extra years obtaining qualifications, in terms either of getting a job or of current or long-term salary prospects' (DE, 1976). Although there are, of course, 'many intangible benefits of higher education not susceptible to sordid economic analysis' (Williams, 1974) such tangible benefits as jobs and salaries do lend themselves to an economic approach.

Williams (1974) found new graduates taking longer to find suitable employment than previously. In addition, increasing numbers were entering occupations of lower status (i.e. non-traditional graduate jobs): during the 1970s this appears to have been particularly the case for business studies and arts graduates (DE, 1981). The prospects for all new labour market entrants have deteriorated substantially since the mid-1970s. However, even in the absence of severe economic recession, the longer-term employment prospects of graduates in the 1980s appear generally less good than those of graduates who entered the labour force in the 1960s and early 1970s (DE, 1974, 1978), although prospects for different subjects vary (DE, 1981).

There is, too, evidence that over the last 12 years or so the earnings of non-graduates have risen somewhat faster than those of graduates (DE, 1981). [. . .] However, the average lifetime earnings of graduates are still higher than those of other workers. *Figure 2* shows the actual age-earnings profiles of men and women with degrees, GCE A-Levels and no qualifications in 1975–1976 (the actual profiles are marked A). This kind of information has been used in the past to compute private rates of return to staying on at school or going on to higher education, taking into account wherever possible the different abilities and social class backgrounds of the people concerned (Ziderman, 1973; Psacharopoulos and Layard, 1979; Wilson, 1980; DES, 1980b). The aim has been to provide some answers to Ziderman's question, 'Does it pay to take a degree?' It appears that over the 1970s there have been some fluctuations in the private rate of return to higher education, but on a generally downward trend (DE, 1981). Wilson found a significant decline of about one-third in the private rate of return to becoming a qualified engineer or scientist in the decade to 1976–77, although it

Figure 2 Actual* and expected relative age-earnings profiles (median).

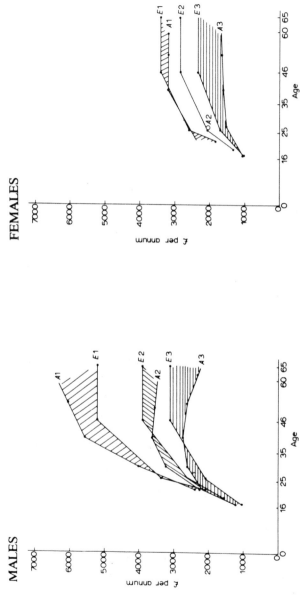

A – Actual, 1 – Degree, 2 – GCE A-Levels, 3 – No qualifications   E – Expected, 1 – Higher education, 2 – Upper-secondary, 3 – Work
* 'Actual' profiles for males derived from OPCS (1978) Table 7.9.
'Actual' profiles for females derived from SED 4A GHS 1975/76. Kindly made available by OPCS.
Only one observation of actual earnings, A2, is available for women with A-Levels.

Source: Williams and Gordon (1981).

appears that most of this drop occurred before 1973–74. He found private rates of return in 1976–77 varying from eight percent to ten percent depending on the discipline studied. But one of the most recently published calculations of marginal private rates of return to boys' education found a return of 19 percent for a first degree over A-Levels in 1978 (DES, 1980b).

Recently it has been demonstrated that it is possible not only to compare the actual private costs and benefits of post-compulsory education but also to find out what kind of return young people *think* there is from studying for GCE A-Levels or a degree. *Figure* 2 also shows the earnings expected by fifth-formers in 1977; they are grouped according to whether they planned to go on to higher education, to leave full-time education at 18, or to leave at 16 (see Williams and Gordon, 1981). This information has been used as a starting point to calculate ex ante (i.e. perceived) private rates of return to continued education. Taking into account the different family backgrounds, abilities and other relevant characteristics of those who do and do not plan to stay on after the minimum school-leaving age, the conclusion was reached,

> . . . that in 1977 16 year-old boys perceived the private rate of return from staying on to age 18 as 17 percent, with a further 10 percent from continuing further to take a degree. For girls the expected returns were lower: 9 percent for upper secondary and 8 percent for higher education. (Williams and Gordon, 1981)

It appears that at the end of compulsory schooling young people in general do have fairly accurate perceptions of the labour market opportunities with which they are confronted and the ways in which these opportunities are related to educational qualifications.

> The implications of these findings for an understanding of changes in the demand for higher education during the 1960s and 1970s are considerable. They lend support to claims that one of the prime motives for the rapid expansion of the 1960s and much slower growth of the 1970s was economic . . . . As far as policy is concerned, these results aid in the prediction of the demand for higher education in that they help to demonstrate that the demand is not autonomous but influenced by changes in the private economic costs and benefits of a degree level qualification. (Williams and Gordon, 1981)

The general economic benefits of higher education

Whenever potential or actual students in higher education have been questioned about their motives directly, the benefits in terms of job prospects, wider job choice, enhanced promotion prospects, higher salaries and so on have featured strongly in their answers.

Morris (1969) found that applicants to higher education saw it very much in terms of useful vocational preparation and as necessary for their future careers. According to Neave (1975), the most important reasons for going to university were to gain useful qualifications, and to study for a career that the student already had in mind. Another study, of second-year university undergraduates, found that 90 percent mentioned factors related in one way or another to their future occupations as one important consideration (Startup, 1972). In particular, they thought that a degree would give access to more interesting work (72 percent); a better-paid job (51 percent); a wider choice of occupations (47 percent); and more secure employment (24 percent). Two-thirds of the undergraduates questioned in another small study of second-year university students said that going to university would give them better career prospects (University of Reading, 1973). Other benefits included better chances of employment, the prospect of a more stable career, and higher earnings.

Cohen (1970), in a study of sixth-formers, found the vocational purposes of a university education strongly emphasized by his sample, and that 'Expectations were strong that learning at university and college should above all else be "applicable" '. The aim of gaining qualifications for a chosen career, or to enter higher education, or to improve career prospects generally all featured strongly in a survey of upper-secondary and further education students (Dean et al., 1979). Other such studies have come up with similar conclusions (e.g. Schools Council, 1970; King et al., 1974). In selecting specific courses in higher education too, the usefulness of the chosen course for a particular job has been found to be more important than any other factor (Gordon and Williams, 1977). In the United States, as well as in Britain, labour market opportunities have been found to be extremely influential (e.g. Dole, 1970).

It is clear from this brief review that while there is obviously a wide variety of reasons for staying on into the sixth form or going on to university, economic factors are extremely important.

> The motives that impel sixth formers to seek higher education are many, varied and seldom clear-cut. A minority wish to continue for its own sake the study in depth of a specialized subject to the top of their bent. . . . Some students have a specific career in mind. A larger number are anxious to develop over a wider field what the Robbins Committee called the general powers of the mind. . . . Some ask for no more than a stimulating opportunity to come to terms with themselves, and to discover where their real interests and abilities lie. Others have no better reason than involuntarily to fall in with

the advice of their teachers and the example of their contemporaries. But not far from the surface of most candidates' minds is the tacit belief that higher education will go far to guarantee them a better job. (HMSO, 1972)

A decade earlier the Robbins Committee was more forthright: 'We deceive ourselves if we claim that more than a small fraction of students in institutions of higher education would be where they are if there were no significance for their future careers in what they hear and read . . .' (HMSO, 1963).

Conclusions

[. . .] In spite of all changes in educational policy, the traditional under-representation of young people from working-class backgrounds persists in upper-secondary and higher education. It is clear from this research review that it is at the school-leaving age that most working-class dropout occurs. It is therefore in the period leading to and including the minimum school-leaving age that at least some public policies must be directed that are aimed at reducing social class inequalities. Educationalists and policy-makers cannot console themselves with the thought that participation in the higher levels of the education system is equally open to the equally talented: it would seem that notions of meritocracy have little to do with who does and who does not continue their education at key transition points.

[. . .] Education policies can be formulated that will whet the appetites of young people for continued study. Access can be improved; demand can be stimulated; and participation in upper-secondary and higher education by underrepresented groups can be increased. [. . .]

[. . .] But while specifically educational policies and practices may somewhat improve access to and participation in upper-secondary and higher education, they do have to be supported by other policies. Class inequalities are associated with, and perhaps exacerbated by, the inabilities of families to afford the cost of post-compulsory education. While financial support, albeit subject to parental means test, is widely available for the over-18s in higher education, there is little monetary help for young people (and their families) when they first choose to stay on beyond the minimum school-leaving age. Research evidence indicates that the introduction of educational maintenance allowances on a national basis would help to raise demand for post-compulsory education. Any government concerned with equalizing educational opportunities, and with the provision of highly skilled personnel for the future development of the economy, would do well to place the introduction of educational maintenance allowances very high indeed on an agenda of educational reforms.

Notes

1 Much depends, of course, on what is meant by equality of opportunity. A variety of interpretations are usefully discussed by Warnock (1975) and Bowman (1975).

2 Other analysts see class differences as primarily economic or political rather than educational or cultural in origin. There is in fact little research evidence that working-class parents have lower general educational ambitions for their children, except to the extent that they are unaware of opportunities available, or are unable to conceive that their own children are capable of competing on equal terms with other children. For both working-class parents and their children, the possibility of upward mobility through education 'seems so remote as to be meaningless' (Willis, 1977). It is certainly correct that working-class parents command fewer resources and have less power over educational institutions.

3 Comprehensive reorganization can take a number of different forms. There are still large numbers of secondary schools that carry the label 'comprehensive' but which are selective, or from which able pupils have been 'creamed off' (see Bellaby, 1977).

References

Barnard, G.A. and McCreath, M.D. (1970) Subject commitments and the demand for higher education. *Journal of the Royal Statistical Society Series A (General)*, vol. 132, no.3, pp. 358–408.

Bellaby, P. (1977) *The Sociology of Comprehensive Schooling*. London, Methuen.

Benn, C. and Simon, B. (1972) *Half Way There*. Harmondsworth, Penguin.

Bernstein, B. (1970) Education cannot compensate for society. *New Society*, no. 387, pp. 344–347.

Blackstone, T. and Weinreich-Haste, H. (1980) Why are there so few women scientists and engineers? *New Society*, no. 907.

Bockstael, E. and Feinstein, O. (1970) *Higher Education in the European Community*. New York, Heath Lexington.

Bowman, M.J. (1975) Education and opportunity: Some economic perspectives. *Oxford Review of Education*, vol. 1, no. 1, pp. 73–84.

Carter, M. (1966) *Into Work*. Harmondsworth, Penguin.

Central Advisory Council for Education (CACE) (1954) *Early Leaving*. London, HMSO.

Central Advisory Council for Education (CACE) (1959) *15 to 18* (Crowther Report). London, HMSO.

Cohen, L. (1970) Sixth form pupils and their views of higher education. *Journal of Curriculum Studies*, vol. 2, no. 1, pp. 67–72.

Craft, M. (ed.) (1970) *Family, Class and Education: A Reader*. London, Longman.

Dean, J., Bradley, K., Choppin, B. and Vincent, D. (1979) *The Sixth Form and its Alternatives*. Slough, NFER Publishing Company.

Department of Education and Science (DES) (1978) *Higher Education into the 1990s: A Discussion Document*. London, DES.

Department of Education and Science (DES) (1980a) Provisional statistics of schools – January 1980. *Statistical Bulletin 16/80*, December 1980. London, DES.

Department of Education and Science (DES) (1980b) *The Rate of Return to Post-Compulsory Education during the 1970s: An Empirical Study for Great Britain*. London, DES.

Department of Education and Science (DES) (1981) Higher education in Great Britain: early estimates for 1980–81. *Statistical Bulletin 6/81*, April 1981. London, DES.

Department of Employment (DE) (1974) *Employment Prospects for the Highly Qualified*. London, Department of Employment.

Department of Employment (DE) (1976) Young people leaving school. *Department of Employment Gazette*, vol. 84, no. 5, pp. 455–460.

Department of Employment (DE) (1978) *Employment Prospects for the Highly Qualified*. Manpower Paper No. 8. London, Department of Employment.

Department of Employment (DE) (1981) *Higher Education and the Employment of Graduates*. Research Paper No. 19. London, Department of Employment.

Dole. A.A. (1970) Stability of reasons for going to college. *Journal of Educational Research*, vol. 63, no. 8, pp. 373–378.

Douglas, J.W.B. (1964) *The Home and the School*. London, MacGibbon and Kee.

Douglas, J.W.B., Ross, J.M. and Simpson, W.R. (1968) *All Our Future*. London, Peter Davies.

Floud, J. (1961) Social class factors in educational achievement. In: Halsey, A.H. (ed.) *Ability and Educational Opportunity*. Paris, OECD.

Fulton, O. and Gordon, A. (1979a) The British pool of ability: how deep, and will cash reduce it? *Educational Studies*, vol. 5, no. 2, pp. 157–169.

Fulton, O. and Gordon, A. (1979b) *Admission Policies in Post-Secondary Education: The Impact of Structural Change on the Demand for Upper Secondary and Higher Education*, SME/ET/79.25. Paris, OECD.

Gordon, A. (1976) *Education for Employment? A Dilemma for Fifth Formers*. Paper presented to the Annual Meeting of the British Association for the Advancement of Science at the University of Lancaster.

Gordon, A. and Williams, G. (1977) *Attitudes of Fifth and Sixth Formers to School, Work and Higher Education*. University of Lancaster, IPCE (mimeo).

Halsey, A.H., Heath, A.F. and Ridge, J.M. (1980) *Origins and Destinations: Family, Class and Education in Modern Britain*. Oxford, Clarendon Press.

HMSO (1963) *Higher Education* (Robbins Report), Cmnd 2154. London, HMSO.

HMSO (1972) *Education: A Framework for Expansion*, Cmnd 5174. London, HMSO.

HMSO (1977) *Education in Schools: a Consultative Document*, Cmnd 6869. London, HMSO.

Hopkins, A. (1978) *The School Debate*. Harmondsworth, Penguin.

Jackson, B. and Marsden, D. (1966) *Education and the Working Class*. Harmondsworth, Pelican.

Jencks, C. (1972) *Inequality: A Reassessment of the Effect of Family and Schooling in America*. New York, Basic Books Inc.

King, E.J., Moor, C.H. and Mundy, J.A. (1974) *Post-Compulsory Education: A New Analysis in Western Europe*. London, Sage.

King, E.J., Moor, C.H. and Mundy, J.A. (1975) *Post-Compulsory Education 2: The Way Ahead*. London, Sage.

Lawton, D. (1977) *Education and Social Justice*. London, Sage.

Maclure, S. (1979) Financial support for the 16–18s. *Education Policy Bulletin*, vol. 7, no. 1, pp. 99–124.

Morris, R.N. (1969) *Sixth Form and College Entrance*. London, Routledge and Kegan Paul.

Neave, G. (1975) *How They Fared: The Impact of the Comprehensive School upon the University*. London, Routledge and Kegan Paul.

Neave, G. (1976) *Patterns of Equality*. Slough, NFER Publishing Company.

OECD (1970) *Group Disparities in Educational Participation and Achievement*. Paris, OECD.

Office of Population Censuses and Surveys (OPCS) (1978) *The General Household Survey 1976*. London, HMSO.

Psacharopoulos, G. (1973) *Returns to Education: An International Comparison*. Amsterdam, Elsevier.

Psacharopoulos, G. and Layard, R. (1979) Human capital and earnings: British evidence and a critique. *Review of Economic Studies*, vol. XLVI, pp. 485–503.

Rauta, I. and Hunt, A. (1975) *Fifth Form Girls: Their Hopes for the Future*. London, HMSO.

Roberts, K. (1980) Schools, parents and social class. In: Craft, M., Raynor, J. and Cohen, L. (eds) *Linking Home and School*, 3rd ed. London, Harper and Row.

Rutter, M., Maughan, B., Mortimore, P. and Ouston, J. (1979) *Fifteen Thousand Hours: Secondary Schools and Their Effects on Children*. London, Open Books.

Ryrie, A.C., Furst, A. and Lauder, M. (1979) *Choices and Chances*. London, Hodder and Stoughton.

Schools Council (1968) *Young School Leavers*. London, HMSO.

Schools Council (1970) *Sixth Form Pupils and Teachers*. London, Books for Schools.

Schools Council (1973) *Preparation for Degree Courses*. Schools Council Working Paper 47. London, Evans/Methuen Educational.

Sharpe, S. (1976) *Just Like a Girl: How Girls Learn to be Women*. Harmondsworth, Penguin.

Startup, R. (1972) Why go to the University? *Universities Quarterly*, vol. 26, no. 3, pp. 317–332

Thomas, R. and Wetherell, D. (1974) *Looking Forward to Work*. London, HMSO.

Turner, R.H. (1960) Modes of ascent through education: sponsored and contest mobility. In: Halsey, A.H., Floud, J. and Anderson, C. Arnold (eds) *Education, Economy and Society*. New York, Free Press.

Universities Central Council on Admissions (UCCA) (1980) *Statistical Supplement to the Seventeenth UCCA Report 1978–79*. Cheltenham, UCCA.

Universities Central Council on Admissions (UCCA) (1980a) *Seventeenth UCCA Report 1978–79*. Cheltenham, UCCA.

University of Reading (1973) *Student Motivation*. Reading, University of Reading (mimeo).

Warnock, M. (1975) The concept of equality in education. *Oxford Review of Education*, vol. 1, no. 1, pp. 3–8.

Westergaard, J.H. and Little, A.N. (1964) Educational opportunity and social selection in England and Wales: trends and policy implications. *British Journal of Sociology*, vol. 15, no. 4.

Westergaard, J.H. and Resler, H. (1975) *Class in a Capitalist Society*. London, Heinemann.

Williams, G.L. (1974) The events of 1973–74 in a long term planning perspective. *Higher Education Bulletin*, vol. 3, no. 1, pp. 17–44.

Williams, G.L. and Gordon, A.G. (1975) 16 and 18 year olds: attitudes to education. *Higher Education Bulletin*, vol. 4, no. 1, pp. 23–37.

Williams, G. and Gordon, A. (1981) Perceived earnings functions and ex ante rates of return to post compulsory education in England. *Higher Education*, vol. 10, no. 2, pp. 199–227.

Willis, P. (1977) *Learning to Labour*. Farnborough, Saxon House.

Wilson, R.A. (1980) The rate of return to becoming a qualified scientist and engineer in Great Britain, 1966–76. *Scottish Journal of Political Economy*, vol. 27, no. 1, pp. 41–62.

Woodhall, M. (1970) *Student Loans, A Review of Experience in Scandinavia and Elsewhere*. London, Harrap.

Ziderman, A. (1973) Does it pay to take a degree? The profitability of private investment in university education in Britain. *Oxford Economic Papers*, vol. XXV, pp. 262–274.

CHAPTER 2.2

A CLASSIFICATION OF 16–19s: CLIENT GROUPS*
DEPARTMENT OF EDUCATION AND SCIENCE/
COUNCIL OF LOCAL EDUCATION AUTHORITIES

1 . . . Local education authorities have a statutory duty, laid down in the Education Act 1944, to provide suitable educational opportunities for the 16–19 age range [. . .]. The Act does not specify in any precise way the range of opportunities which should be provided. Indeed, it is not easy to see how an Act could do that in a way which avoided meaningless generalities, recognized the essentially plural character of our education service and allowed for progressive development over the years. Although the ultimate test of whether an authority is properly fulfilling its statutory responsibilities under the Education Acts lies with the courts, individual authorities need in practice to consider for themselves how they should meet the duties laid upon them. We have therefore considered what might be viewed as a suitable range of opportunities for the age group, and what factors should be seen as conditioning decisions about its provision.

2 The primary purpose of the education service, for the 16–19 age range as for all other groups, must be to ensure that a range of opportunities is available of a quality that meets the realistic aspirations of young people, parents and society, and at a cost which the nation judges it right to pay. That is a commonplace which none would dispute, but it bears repetition, if only as a reminder that other considerations, however worthy or pressing, are essentially secondary. In this latter category one might include tradition, the aspirations of individual institutions and of teachers, the legal and administrative bases for school and college organization and governance,

* *Education for 16–19 Year Olds* (Macfarlane Report). London, HMSO, 1981, pp. 13–17.
Reproduced with the permission of the Controller, HMSO.

relationships between institutions and with maintaining local education authorities, salaries and conditions of service, political opinion, even the human considerations arising from change or the prospect of it. Such considerations may condition strongly the present system or the options for change – and in many cases rightly so – but they must not be allowed to become starting points for analysis. The only valid starting point, in our view, is an examination based on the needs and abilities of young people, conditioned by their aspirations and career prospects, and by the needs and expectations of the wider society.

3   The age group is far from homogeneous, and needs and aspirations are diverse and change with time. Nevertheless some classification must be attempted, if only to focus attention on the range of provision which needs to be made. The first main division is between those who leave full-time education at 16 and those who stay on in school or college. In the first category we find the following groups:

a those who enter employment and receive no structured part-time education or training;

b those who enter employment and who have the opportunity for systematic education and/or training leading normally to an educational, vocational or professional qualification;

c those without work or immediate prospects of work.

Among those who continue their full-time education we find:

d those staying on with a view to proceeding to higher education in due course;

e those seeking an essentially vocational qualification to fit them to enter employment at some stage up to 18 (but perhaps with the further prospect of proceeding to higher education later if they so decide);

f those who do not wish to be committed to a specific vocational objective, but who wish to continue their general education, personal development and pre-employment preparation. (Traditionally, this group includes many who seek to improve on previous O-Level or CSE performances, and some who take O-Level or CSE for the first time at about 17 because they need an extra year to reach the stage when they can do so successfully; it may also include some taking A-Levels but not intending to proceed to higher education);

g those who require remedial education to enhance their employment and life prospects.

4 [. . .] Such categorization over-simplifies, of course. Objectives may change during post-compulsory study. Some following A-Level courses may initially intend to enter higher education but later decide to proceed to non-advanced further education instead or to enter employment at age 17 or 18. Some may wish to re-enter full-time education after a period of work or unemployment, perhaps hoping to go on eventually to higher education. Others may wish to gain entry to higher education on the basis of essentially vocational studies. Local provision must be sufficiently flexible to allow such changes of objective and route. The composition of each category is also varied. Each will contain a spread of ability and motivation, and each will include some whose social, cultural, personal, medical or other circumstances militate against their achieving their full potential. Again, local provision has to be sufficiently flexible to provide properly for these minority groups too.

5 Despite the risks attendant on such over-simplification, we do see merit in rehearsing in this way the range of opportunities which needs to be available in the local area, and see it as a useful reminder of the differing needs of young people and as countering the superficial attractions of standardized 'solutions' to 16–19 provision. We comment in the following paragraphs on the main strands of provision which we see as essential to a balanced range of provision.

Group A

6 First, for those who enter employment of kinds which traditionally do not provide opportunities for part-time education and training, we see an urgent need for structured vocational programmes including such elements as the development of communication skills and numeracy, basic skills training, the sampling of various work-related activities, the enhancement of social and life skills, some understanding of social and economic organization and planned work experience. This is a large group, up to 300,000 strong in each year-group, and in the present financial climate we cannot hope for the massive new expenditure that universal provision for them would require. We welcome, nevertheless, the recently announced extension of schemes of Unified Vocational Preparation for young people in the relevant kinds of employment, and see it as an important step in developing the necessary wider provision. This will need also to build on pre-vocational work in schools and colleges, and in some cases resources released by falling rolls will enable them to offer additional provision at little or no extra cost.

Group B

7 For those who enter employment offering facilities for systematic education and/or training on a part-time basis, the education service has to provide a considerable variety of courses – for those employed as operatives, craftsmen and technicians in manufacturing and service industries, for clerical and secretarial employees, and for those working in other commercial and business fields, and for those in the social, welfare and caring professions. Most young people in this client group aim at vocational qualifications of national currency awarded by examining and validating bodies such as the Technician and Business Education Councils, the City and Guilds of London Institute and the Royal Society of Arts. Sometimes the courses in question are free-standing, not associated with matching on- or off-the-job training. Even so, across much of the craft and technician field there needs to be a close association of the education and training components, inside or outside formal apprenticeship structures. We therefore believe that there has to be close collaboration between authorities, colleges, employers and Industrial Training Boards. Many who received systematic part-time further education in the past now hold responsible positions in industry and commerce. We believe that the part-time route should be protected and promoted and look to employers to grant day-release more widely than at present, particularly to girls for whom the present rate of release is disappointingly low.

Group C

8 The third group who leave full-time education at 16 are those who find themselves without work or immediate prospect of work. Two main kinds of educational provision are needed for this client group. First, there has to be further education provision as part of many Youth Opportunities Programme (YOP) schemes devised and run by the Manpower Services Commission: we see that as an important area for development and are convinced of the benefits of blending education, training and work experience in that way for many of this client group. Secondly, there must be part-time pre-employment courses which will help the personal and educational development of young people and also increase their subsequent employability. Part-time provision in support of YOP activities and for the young unemployed must be designed so that young people can enter or leave at any time, since their continuing availability for study cannot be guaranteed; and

both kinds of provision must also often involve substantial remedial or 'second chance' education. We note also the contribution made by the Youth Service (both voluntary and LEA-provided) to opportunities for this group. The Youth Service provides valuable informal social education for many (as it may do for others in work or full-time education), either independently or in conjunction with YOP or more formal further education provision.

Group D

9 We turn now to consider the second main division of young people – those who stay on in full-time education beyond the period of compulsory schooling. A major group amongst them has always aimed at higher education, and will continue to do so. Most will travel the A-Level route. A-Level provision in schools and colleges will therefore be closely geared to higher education and its entry requirements. Alongside those will be a minority (from group F) taking A-Level courses, intending from the outset to enter employment on their completion; they may need different subject combinations from those taken in preparation for higher education. The range of A-Level subjects should be wide enough to cater for both groups and available on a basis which allows adequate variety in groupings of related subjects, as well as a reasonable range of choice corresponding to students' interests and personal strengths.

10 In considering how many A-Level subjects need to be on offer, a distinction must be drawn between the number provided at any one institution and the considerably greater number which needs to be accessible in the area. Thus, while 12–16 subjects is generally regarded as a reasonable range to be offered by a single institution, such a range would almost inevitably exclude many 'minority' subjects. Those at risk include all modern languages other than French and German, classical languages, ancient history, religious studies, geology, political science, law, music, home economics, needlework, craft and design, technical drawing, graphics and a whole range of potentially important but still not widely established subjects such as engineering sciences, computer science and electronics. Young people can very reasonably expect to be able to choose such subjects and, moreover, to opt for such combinations of subjects as may be best suited to their higher education plans. We also believe that it is important to develop newer A-Level subjects such as engineering science, and to allow combinations which span the traditional arts/science 'divide'

and are relevant to developing opportunities in higher education and employment. We therefore conclude that something like 24 A-Level subjects should be available in an area. We believe too that it is important that young people taking A-Level courses should be encouraged to broaden their programme beyond the scope of their A-Level subjects through the provision of supplementary non-A-Level studies. In practice timetabling and resource considerations must limit the range offered by individual institutions. For these reasons we think it is often over-narrow to see A-Level provision solely in terms of self-contained institutions. Where two or more in one locality each offer a limited number of subjects, the interests of pupils and students demand joint planning to ensure that local institutions together cover a wider range of options in satisfactory combinations than each could do separately. [. . .]

11 Alongside A-Level provision in schools and colleges, but on a much smaller scale, is the further education alternative of entry to higher education through Ordinary National Diplomas (now progressively being replaced by the corresponding Technician and Business Education Council qualifications). Such courses feed both degree and non-degree courses, and are a sensible choice of post-16 study for many. We believe that young people should have this option alongside the traditional A-Level opportunity.

Group E

12 Ordinary National Diplomas and their TEC and BEC replacements are particularly aimed at group E – those who seek a vocational qualification for direct entry to employment. These qualifications have substantial validity in the eyes of employers, and can be built on later by further study – in many cases to full professional qualifications. Those of lesser academic attainment at 16+ must also be provided for, and in each area there has to be a range of courses for industrial and commercial employment, for work in catering, hairdressing, community fields, etc. and for clerical and secretarial jobs. Many such courses are uncompromisingly vocational in character; few serve also as preparation for entry to higher education, though for many students the vocational content is a vehicle for wider general education.

Group F

13 This group consists of those who do not wish to be committed to a

specific vocational objective and who have no higher education aspirations, but who wish to continue their general education, personal development and pre-employment preparation. This group has been described for some years as the 'new sixth form' but it includes some fairly distinctive elements. Some young people take A-Levels with the directly vocational intention of finding employment in such areas as the civil service, local government and banking. Others take well-established vocational or semi-vocational courses in further education colleges. Efforts have been made in recent years to make appropriate provision in both schools and colleges of further education for those without clear aims. Linked courses and work experience can be particularly relevant to the whole group. Within the schools, valuable work has been done in developing the one-year Certificate of Extended Education (CEE). Whatever view one might take of the appropriateness of A-Level as a preparation for employment or of the merits of retaking O-Level or CSE to improve performances as compared (in both cases) with vocationally oriented alternatives, the fact remains that many major employers still base their recruitment practices on achievement in those traditional examinations. So long as that situation persists, young people will wish to follow post-16 courses with such examination targets. We believe, however, that for many continued study along these lines is not necessarily in their best interests: rather we look for the development of courses with a strong pre-employment character. We think it of the greatest importance that employers should come to value such a form of post-16 education as a preparation for employment, and be ready to accord it due recognition alongside the more traditional A-Level, O-Level and CSE courses. [. . .]

Group G

14 Our last group includes young people who have had difficulties in reaching reasonable standards of numeracy, communication and life skills, and who need time to catch up. Such young people cannot be expected to progress immediately to all the commoner forms of 16–19 study, whether full-time or part-time. The reasons for their lack of success in the past will be diverse and the rate at which they will develop variable and unpredictable. They need special attention, and the provision made for other groups may not always be adequate for their needs. Specific provision will be needed in schools and/or colleges for this group, so that as many as possible can pass on into satisfactory employment. There will remain those with grave mental or other handicaps for whom employment will be much more

Table 6 Client groups: estimates of size and of present provision for 16–19 year olds in a single year

	Client group	Potential numbers (000s)	Provision now made (000s)	Main types of provision
A.	Those who enter employment without any structured part-time education or training	200–300	5	UVP pilot schemes
B.	Those who enter employment and who have the opportunity for systematic education and/or training leading to an educational, vocational or professional qualification	500	280	Young operative courses; CGLI craft courses; TEC and BEC certificate courses; MSC/ITB courses; RSA courses; courses leading to professional qualifications or college awards
C.	Those without work or immediate prospects of work	200–300	190	YOP schemes (not all with educational component)
D.	Those staying on with a view to proceeding to higher education in due course	400	335	Full-time courses leading to A-level

E.	Those seeking an essentially vocational qualification to fit them for employment at some stage up to 18	200	140	CGLI craft courses, TEC and BEC diploma courses, OND courses; RSA courses; courses leading to professional qualifications or college awards
F.	Those who do not wish to be committed to a specific vocational objective, but who wish to continue their general education, personal development and pre-employment preparation	200	135	A-level, O-level and CSE courses; pre-employment and foundation courses; BEC General Certificate, TEC Level 1 units
G.	Those who require remedial education to enhance their employment and life prospects	50	5	Courses in literacy and numeracy; courses for physically and mentally handicapped; English language courses

The figures for potential numbers are estimates of the number of young people who might be provided for in a single year in the various ways shown. They are interdependent; the total size of groups A and C is put at some half million. The figures for provision now made show the number of young people actually receiving such education or training in a twelve-month period.

difficult to obtain and for some even an unrealistic goal. A number of authorities already do much for those with special educational needs. We welcome the Government's endorsement* of the emphasis put by the Warnock Committee on the importance of post-16 provision for those concerned and look to authorities generally to consider how existing arrangements can be improved.

15 The handicapped students in this group must be distinguished from those who will be found as members of groups A to F. The intellectual ability and attainments of the latter may be comparable with those of other members of these groups; their problems are normally those of access and communication. The system will need to adapt itself to provide for students for whom stairs are a problem and those with defective sight or hearing, if they are to enjoy equality of opportunity with their able-bodied contemporaries.

16 This brief rehearsal of the main client groups illustrates the range of provision which must be made. When one adds in the detail of the courses and options available, particularly in the further education sector, one arrives at a very diverse pattern indeed. We look to the period of compulsory education to provide the common educational basis for the later learning and believe it right that young people should branch out at the age of 16, each according to his or her abilities, aptitudes and career intentions. The present diversity of provision has developed over the years in response to the perceived needs of many, including industry and commerce; we find in its very existence a main part of its justification. Rather than a more closed and standardized system we believe that what is needed is a varied, open and progressive learning system which allows each young person to develop individually along a variety of routes each of which is thorough, purposeful and carries credibility as a base for work, further study or both. We say varied because the needs of the age group show great variety. We say open because many young people will want to change direction during the 16–19 years, either because they find themselves unsuited to their first path or because they have changed their minds about their ultimate destination. The system must allow for such changes and young people must not be locked into particular routes on the basis of decisions taken at the age of 16 or earlier. There have to be bridges across to other lines of development; ladders on to higher study for the able and determined; opportunities to retrieve past failure or to arrive at goals later than the average; and for those

---

* Special Needs in Education, Cmnd 7996.

who genuinely find themselves unable to cope with their studies as they first hoped, a fair chance to consolidate what they can achieve and to transfer to work or other education or training with full credit for that achievement. We say progressive because we believe there should be no educational cul-de-sac. It should be possible for each and every young person to aspire to continued study on successful completion of the current phase, whether that be general or vocational in character, full-time or part-time, undertaken end-on or in later life in a form variously described as post-experience, adult or continuing education.

CHAPTER 2.3

VOCATIONAL PREPARATION*
FURTHER EDUCATION CURRICULUM REVIEW AND DEVELOPMENT UNIT

The context of vocational preparation

1 The existing education and training provision for the 16–19 age group can be divided into three categories not necessarily related to conventional intelligence or capability.

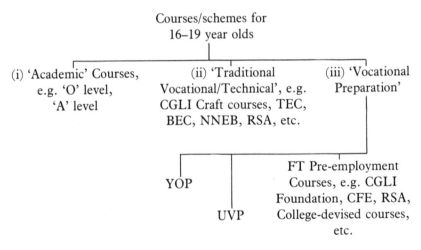

Figure 3   Education and training provision for 16–19-year-olds.

2 One major distinguishing feature, and justification for this categoriza-

---

* *Vocational Preparation*. London, Further Education Curriculum Review and Development Unit, 1981, sections II, III & IV, pp. 9–14.

tion, is the source of the curricula in each case (or the assumed destination of the participants).

i. The syllabus of an *academic subject* is usually supplied by an external examining board and determined to an important extent by the requirements of the next higher grade of academic course, for which it normally acts as an entry qualification. The syllabus aims emphasize cognitive development, although an individual's school sixth form or college programme may comprise a combination of academic syllabuses plus perhaps a number of non-examinable 'non-academic' activities.

ii. The crucial influence on the curricula of *traditional vocational/technical* provision, which are invariably provided by the vocational examining and validating bodies, is the claimed requirements of specific occupations, industries or professional associations, for which the young people concerned are being prepared or have already entered.

iii. For the *vocational preparation* schemes described above, neither of these sources is applicable. The participants are not necessarily intending to proceed to further academic study, nor are they necessarily motivated to study academic subjects for their own sake. At the same time, their curricula cannot necessarily be derived from the demands of a particular job, for reasons which include the following:

    a. the jobs to which they have been recruited make such limited demands in terms of specific job skills that these cannot provide an adequate 'source' for the curricula;

    b. there is an uncertainty about the kind of employment, if any, they will be able to get;

    c. the individuals concerned do not feel ready to make a firm commitment;

    d. there is a high probability that these young people will move, by choice or otherwise, in and out of a number of different jobs in the early part of their working life.

3 This does not mean to say that young people should not be encouraged to use an interest (perhaps ephemeral) in a particular job as a focus for their learning, but a main aim of *vocational preparation* must be the development of the capacities required to make a success of adult and working life in general. An example of such capacities is given by the common core suggested by FEU (June 1979, *A Basis for Choice*).

4 Often, only a matter of historical or geographical accident will determine which kind of *vocational preparation* a 16-year-old school-leaver receives. In some areas it will not be possible to get a *unified vocational preparation* traineeship because there are no available jobs. The school-leaver may therefore be offered one or other of the opportunities available under the *Youth Opportunities Programme*. It is also the case that some young people will have chosen to enrol in certain full-time college courses (not part of YOP) because of the scarcity of local jobs, or for a variety of other reasons. But even where individuals have stayed in full-time education voluntarily because of a desire to improve their basis for choice, they will still have many needs in common with those who have left school to find work. We refer to these three categories of provision as modes of *vocational preparation*.

5 In contrast to those following academic or traditional vocational/technical courses, these young people have not normally been selected on the grounds of level of previous attainment, or assumed destination, but they are generally those who remain after selection for the other two groups has taken place. It is about this group that this document has been primarily written and to whom we relate at this stage the term 'vocational preparation' in the classification shown in *Fig. 4*.

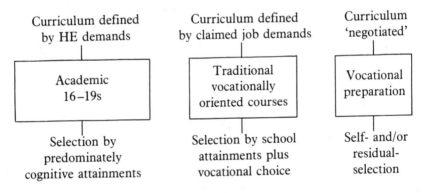

Curriculum defined by HE demands	Curriculum defined by claimed job demands	Curriculum 'negotiated'
Academic 16–19s	Traditional vocationally oriented courses	Vocational preparation
Selection by predominately cognitive attainments	Selection by school attainments plus vocational choice	Self- and/or residual-selection

Figure 4

6 Some young people will move from one mode of vocational preparation to another. For instance, someone on a work experience placement under YOP may be offered a permanent position by that or another employer – in which case he or she becomes (theoretically) eligible for the opportunities and support of a UVP scheme. Another common move can arise when an

individual on a full-time pre-employment course in a college is offered a job before the course has finished. In most cases, they will be encouraged by various advisers to take up the offer, rather than put themselves in a position of competing with a large number of other school- and college-leavers for a small number of jobs, by waiting until they have completed their course. The dilemma in which this places a student and the college would be much eased if it were possible and likely that the young person could complete this stage of their learning with the assistance of a UVP scheme which accompanied their first job.

7 If an individual fails to progress satisfactorily when following academic or traditional vocationally oriented provision, it may be perfectly permissible to say that he/she should never have been selected for the course in the first place; i.e. the course is right, but this particular student should not be on it. Such an approach cannot be adopted with regard to those who are receiving vocational preparation. It does not make sense, for instance, to say of someone who is failing to benefit from a YOP scheme that he should never have been unemployed in the first place.

8 The individual may prefer a different mode of vocational preparation, but in general terms it remains true that with regard to this form of provision the curriculum will have to be tailored to suit the needs of the learners, rather than the learners being selected to fit ready-made programmes. This means that diagnosis of learning needs and the identification of appropriate learning activities need to be discussed with the learners, as part of the curriculum process. A form of educational negotiation therefore becomes part of the role of all tutors responsible for vocational preparation.

9 That a young person may not have had a free choice of mode means that it is important to ensure that whichever he/she does follow offers the same range and quality of learning opportunities. That UVP, YOP and full-time pre-employment courses are each the responsibility of different agencies makes difficult the required coordination and equality of provision. At the moment.

- UVP is jointly administered by an inter-departmental group of the DES and DoE (MSC);
- YOP is the responsibility of the Special Programmes Division of MSC;
- Full-time pre-employment courses come under the combined influence of colleges, LEAs, and examining boards.[1]

This divided responsibility and, in particular, the fact that a variety of agencies – from the YMCA and ITBs to FE colleges – have been involved in implementation may not have been a bad thing, up to now. It has provided opportunities to call on a wide variety of expertise, to depart from inappropriate teaching and administrative practices and to experiment in new areas of curriculum development.

10 On the other hand, the disadvantage of continuing to view each mode in isolation is that there may be inequality between the learning opportunities in different modes; desirable transfer and cooperation between modes will be inhibited, and discontinuities in educational progression will continue to exist.

11 The FEU believes that the coordinated curriculum approach outlined later in the document is an essential development in the process of removing any inequality, discontinuity and inflexibility that exists in and between these modes.

12 In curriculum terms, it now makes more sense to talk of vocational preparation as work experience-based, employment-based and/or institution-based (i.e. college or school).

These curricular modes do not always simply correspond to the administrative modes referred to in paragraph 9 above. The relationship between the administrative and curricular modes is shown in *Table 7*. [. . .]

Table 7   Relationship between the administrative and curricular modes

Administrative mode	UVP	Full-time pre-employment	YOP
Curricular mode	Employment-based	Institution (usually college)-based	Mainly work-experience-based. Some college-based
Responsible bodies	DES + MSC(TSD) ↓ ↗ IDG + ITBS	Colleges/LEAs Examining bodies	MSC(SPD)

13 For instance, it is possible for a YOP trainee to be based on an employer's premises for a work experience placement (with possible day release to college), *or* for him or her to be based full-time in college (with the possibility of some work experience arranged by the college). Although most UVP schemes only involve day release to college, some have extensive

periods of block release. Some full-time LEA-funded courses have important work experience elements. Some college-based YOP schemes for low achievers and some training workshop schemes last for as long as the full-time courses investigated in *A Basis for Choice*. In spite of this complex network of provision we see no reason why similar curricula criteria should not apply to all such schemes.

14 Because of the developing situation and the uncoordinated provision, the FEU has itself published documents which treated UVP, YOP and full-time pre-employment courses in isolation. While these reports differ in the emphasis which they give to certain issues, it is now apparent that an approach or process developed and recommended in connection with one mode can be applied with advantage in the context of the other two. This and the arguments described earlier lead us to conclude that we must now give consideration to the features that all modes of vocational preparation should have in common.

The participants, the provision and the needs

15 We start from the point that in this document we are considering the developmental needs of adolescents in the 16–19 age range. The problems of adolescence, although often exaggerated, remain real and enduring, differing in the stage at which they are resolved for each young person. There is no lack of evidence to indicate that if a satisfactory transition to adulthood is to be made, some form of self-fulfilment has to be acquired by the adolescent. 'Without adequate feelings of self-value one has an inadequate sense of responsibility.'[3] For the low achiever, without the supportive framework of proven conventional academic success, and without a job or any foreseeable career development, the acquisition of self-achievement becomes a near impossible task. Any curriculum process which contributes positively to a young person's essential personal development can be defined therefore as an essential social process.

16 As well as identifying the common characteristics of vocational preparation schemes, it is important to develop an awareness of the distinctive differences which exist between vocational preparation and more conventional provision.

17 There is a substantial number of young people who do not form part of the target group for academic or traditional vocationally oriented courses. This is the group for whom vocational preparation is a prime necessity. We estimate that this is about half of the 16-year-old age-group. This total is

composed of some 90,000 of those who voluntarily stay on in full-time education in schools and colleges, over 200,000 who enter employment which offers no accompanying education or training, and an increasing number who leave school but fail to find a job.

18 A few young people who would benefit more from traditional vocational/technical courses may find their way into vocational preparation. Initial guidance, diagnosis and counselling may reveal that some should be reallocated to traditional courses of one kind or another. This may be because of earlier guidance failures, or because of late development of ability or motivation. There will also be some young people who are fully and realistically committed to certain trades and who, at other times, would have obtained an apprenticeship or some other formal training. Their personal and career development may be better promoted through college-based vocationally orientated education/training, rather than vocational preparation. Some of them could (and do) make a success of a full-time vocational/technical course but, without the supportive framework of an employers' training scheme, a complementary programme of vocational preparation is surely still necessary.

In addition, there will always be a case for some young people to follow a 'mixed economy' course. For instance, they may wish to gain an O-Level or two in subjects in which they have a particular interest, whilst still basically following a vocational preparation scheme. There has always been this kind of mixing of academic and traditional vocational/technical courses and qualifications, not only in order to satisfy the wishes of individual students, but also to ensure that the education they have received is recognized in as many quarters as possible.

19 There will be of course a small minority of young people with such severe learning difficulties that special provision may have to be continued for them after the age of 16. This may be because either they need more sheltered provision than vocational preparation would normally provide, or because they are not likely to achieve even the minimum standards of attainment in basic skills which we later argue should be specified. The 1980 Government White Paper[4] has proposed a framework for implementing some of the Warnock Committee proposals, although many curriculum problems remain.[5]

20 For all young people the transition from school or college to work or unemployment can be a traumatic experience. The ease of this transition has much to do with the stage of maturation of the young school-leaver and there is some evidence to indicate that the transition is a less acute problem

for the academic young person than the non-academic.[6] Traditionally the more academic pupil tends to 'buy time' by staying on in education. The apprentice, though perhaps less academic, tends to enter his world of work via protective agreements, invariably supported by release to college. The low achiever, who is probably the least able to come to terms with the outside world, is the least supported in this transition. When jobs are plentiful there is some evidence to indicate that they 'survive' this transition by frequently changing jobs in the initial stages. Increasing unemployment now precludes this strategy. It follows that for *all* young people some form of vocational preparation is a necessity and in the long term a more comprehensive provision of this element of education and training may well be seen as making a major contribution to the flexible workforce that our changing technologies appear to demand. For example, it is generally admitted that our present rather rigid apprenticeship system needs reappraising in the light of change. A first year of apprenticeship comprising broadly based vocational preparation would allow the design of a modular superstructure giving greater flexibility with respect to changing skill needs and entry to training, an opinion apparently shared by the MSC.[7]

In the short term, however, because of the particular problems facing the non-academic school-leaver, priority should be given to providing this group with vocational preparation.

21 This cohort does not form a simple target group with easily identifiable coherent and shared characteristics. It would be possible to identify subgroups within the cohort, but this would be a spurious solution. It is more constructive to explore for this group common curricular approaches which suit them rather than design a series of set courses into which learners are then fitted.

We regard this 'bespoke' principle as an essential feature of vocational preparation.

22 We would also argue that a coherent rationale for all modes of vocational preparation is needed, if only to provide a basis for quality control. There is a danger that vocational preparation will come to be regarded as the 'tertiary modern' sector of education/training – lacking in esteem, facilities and currency. (Our earlier division of 16–19 education into three categories, whilst serving a useful purpose, has ominous echoes of the division of secondary education into grammar, technical and modern.) Any remedy will lie not in insisting that a conventional approach be applied, but in promoting and demonstrating the quality of this alternative and appropriate provision, and in the development of levels of accreditation for more

vocationally committed education. Much work has been done, but more progress is necessary if the required changes in attitude are to be brought about.

Vocational preparation: its aims and components

23 In defining the process of vocational preparation we have been eclectic and have recognized the development of its definition over the last few years.[8] We would reiterate that such a process of preparation should be available to all school-leavers whether academic or non-academic, whether employed, unemployed or remaining in education.

The main aims of vocational preparation are:

a. to give to young people basic skills, experience and knowledge;

b. to help them assess their potential, to think realistically about jobs and employment prospects and to optimize their employability;

c. to develop their understanding of the working and social environment, both nationally and locally, so that they may understand the variety of roles possible for them to play as an adult member of society;

d. to encourage them to become progressively responsible for their own personal development.

24 Vocational preparation should be a combination of education and training designed both to assist the smooth transition from school to work, and to support a young person in the early stages of working life. The content and aims of vocational preparation are derived as much from the perceived needs of the young people themselves as from a predetermined range of disciplines; and the schemes accordingly demand an integrated approach to the planning of content. Its aims range more widely than those of many conventional courses; its content necessarily spans a wide range of disciplines, and a variety of strategies have been adopted to provide the type of learning which gives vocational preparation its distinctive characteristics.

25 Within these aims, there is an implied content of communication, numeracy, decision-making and problem-solving, physical and manipulative skills, interpersonal relationships, moral values, social, political and economic awareness, learning skills, self-confidence and adaptability. The background against which this learning takes place is the working and adult world, and the approach should be based on experience which is as direct as

possible. This may or may not include paid employment.

26 An analysis of the existing modes of vocational preparation leads us to conclude that they all do or should contain common basic components. [. . .] they are described briefly below. Many of the components of vocational preparation which follow are not unfamiliar to the sensitive and responsive teachers in mainstream further education. However, all are seen as necessary in vocational preparation to achieve, with young people whose needs do not form a conventional coherent pattern, the wide-ranging aims quoted above.

27 The curriculum for vocational preparation, like any other responsive programme of individual development, should be a matter for *negotiation* between the various participants including the young people themselves. Experience has shown that negotiation is likely to be made effective by the use of two mechanisms, each of which is becoming more widely used.

28 The first is the personal *programme* (or agenda), which results when a young person makes (with guidance) his/her own selection of the things he/she needs to learn, the way in which they will be learned and the vocational focus for this learning.

29 The second is the use of *contracts*; between the agencies which contribute to the different learning experiences within a scheme (e.g. employers, college, career and youth services); and between the young person (and his/her parents?) and the particular agency to whom he/she is responsible. Once the framework of desired learning experience has been constructed, it should be recognized that the implementation and administration of vocational preparation schemes require different agencies to contribute as negotiated to the learning contract. This component of *negotiation* is not a new feature in education, particularly in post-16 curricula. A-Level students in progressive institutions have long since arrived at their individual programmes of study at the end of discussions involving the young people themselves, tutors and parents. In further education, course tutors often carry out an intensive process of negotiation with the young person and his/her employer before placement is settled. (This particularly applies to modular curricula such as TEC.) For vocational preparation it appears necessary to define the process of negotiation explicitly because the overall situation is more complex, if not more critical. Motivation of the young person by giving him/her some real responsibility in the planning of his/her programme must be regarded as an essential element of his/her personal development.

30 Another essential component in the vocational preparation process is

that covering *counselling*, *guidance* and *assessment*. Counselling and guidance are necessary prerequisites to the fulfilment of that aim (see 23b above) concerned with helping the young person to assess realistically his/her potential and job prospects. Also an increased self-awareness by young people will help them to exploit their particular aptitudes and achievements in order to match labour markets, hence optimizing their employability. The complexity of the task of guiding young people within one scheme or through several schemes demands the establishment of a base for personal guidance. It may be possible to use existing systems of guidance and counselling, but these need to be equipped with a wider range of information and techniques than they have at present. For the immediate future, this function will have to be performed by those bodies responsible for the schemes but it should be possible to design an independent guidance base for counselling young people, orchestrating the contributions of local bodies to a given scheme, and the FEU has sponsored development work in this area.[9] The development and negotiation of individual programmes as described above clearly demand that tutors should develop counselling and guidance skills as a part of their teaching repertoire. There remains the problem of certification and recognition of vocational preparation. Rightly or wrongly, the importance attached to certification based on examinations appears to be a major feature of our society; it is the principal means by which educators, trainers and employers value young people. Attempts to achieve status without examinations have generally failed:[10] the pressures from parents, employers and young people alike are too great, and in the UK at least being 'non-examinable' is tantamount to a social stigma.

31 Individual student programmes based largely on developmental needs, demand the development of continuous and sensitive *assessment* procedures giving both formative (continuing) and summative (terminal) appraisals of progress. We would suggest that the student *profile* is an appropriate method of serving these needs, forming as it does a part of the guidance that should be available to all young people. This is particularly important when embarking on vocational preparation, or when transferring from one scheme to another. A profile record of attainment would facilitate progression from one scheme to another. It provides a common system of record-keeping and certification, making redundant the need for an overall pass/fail grade, allowing the recognition of important personal qualities which cannot be formally assessed. In short we are saying that the aims of vocational preparation make it necessary to regard counselling, guidance and assessment as a single component of closely inter-related elements.

Further, the profile method of recording assessments has been shown to be a progressive way of making possible this interrelationship. [. . .]

32 It will not be sufficient to simply equate any 'voc-prep' certificate with examinations currently existing. With few exceptions, these examinations are either dominated by the normal distribution of conventional (academic) ability or by levels of easily measured competence. Experiential learning and increased personal and social maturity are not amenable to simple, formalized measurement and grading and as such are neither recognized by the existing examination system nor by the public at large. By adopting the profile method of recording assessments we are suggesting that recognition should be given to those aspects alongside the more easily recorded and interpreted assessments of performance that will also exist.[11]

33 To support this process of revaluation of non-academic education, colleges need to encourage the holders of vocational preparation profiles to enrol in conventional courses; the national FE (and HE?) examining/validating bodies should make special reference to the profile when describing access to their schemes; and employers should consciously attempt to use *all* the information presented on the profile[12] in making their assessment of young people for employment.

34 A further major component of vocational preparation is the *acquisition of basic skills*. By this we mean a level of ability, achievement and understanding in essential areas of knowledge and skill which will increase a young person's chance of making a success of adult and working life. These skills should be broad-based and transferable, rather than specific and job restricted, and should include that range known as social and life skills. The study and mastery of specific craft tasks or topics may well be an essential element of this component, but primarily they should be taught as a means of obtaining this broad skill base. By defining a range of *basic* skills we imply that they must be generally regarded as essential. In this sense we have to ensure that all young people have the opportunity to acquire them. This calls for some form of generally acceptable *common core* which once constructed can be used as a checklist against which a young person's previous experience can be matched and in the light of which a possible programme and contracts can be negotiated. [. . .]

35 It is axiomatic that for most people learning is effective if it is seen to be relevant. This applies particularly to our target group and there is much evidence to indicate that for many young people *relevance* is related to *experience*. For young people this experience may be work or other real-life situations. A preferred vocational focus, even if ephemeral or vicarious,

Figure 5   A tentative model of curriculum development for vocational preparation.

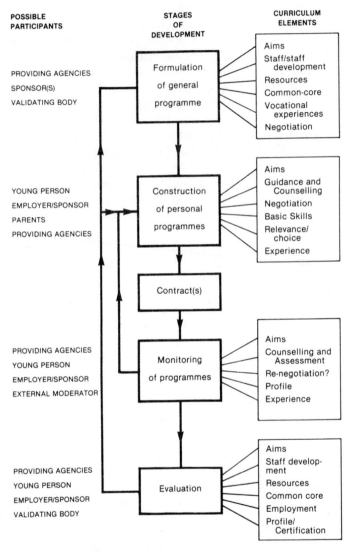

e.g. [. . .] For a college-based pre-employment course the *providing agency* would be the college; the *validating body* and *external moderator* may be an FE examining body. There may or may not be an *employer/sponsor* for individual students and the college may or may not require to negotiate with an outside body in the provision of an adequate range of experience.

often produces the necessary motivation for further learning and provides a base for development. All good teachers know the importance of starting any learning process by relating to the student's previous knowledge and experience and building on those. We contend that this group of young people often find it difficult to relate generalized deductive learning and teaching strategies immediately to their perceived needs. A more inductive approach based on their experiences, reinforced wherever possible with specific and concrete examples, has proved to be effective. This is a demanding task for any teacher and we discuss later the staff development implications of this approach. In the meantime we simply question whether the undoubted elegance of the deductive academic approach is always capable of producing the educational effects we require for these young people.

36 It follows from the above that we see some form of work-based, residential and/or simulated *experience* as essential to the process of vocational preparation. [. . .]

37 [. . . No] one mode of vocational preparation is uniquely suitable. All have advantages and defects: e.g. the range of experiences and the quality of basic skills acquisition in YOP schemes are difficult to control; the time allowed in many UVP schemes for the acquisition of basic skills is often insufficient; and college-based schemes cannot always provide the necessary work experience. What is required is more cooperation and coordination between the providing agencies. In identifying curriculum criteria common to all modes of vocational preparation, we hope that this document will make possible increased coordination, thus alleviating any disadvantages and discontinuities that exist.

Notes

1   See *Examinations 16–18*, a Government consultative paper, October 1980.
2   *Experience Reflection Learning* – suggestions for UVP organizers, April 1978; *Supporting YOP* – for colleges involved in YOP, July 1979; *A Basis for Choice* – study group on post-16 pre-employment course, June 1979.
3   Thomas (1980) gives a typical overview.
4   *Special Needs in Education*, Cmnd 7996, August 1980.
5   FEU response to Cmnd 7996 outlines some possible strategies, October 1980.
6   For a useful overview of research in this area see Clark (1980).
7   'The adoption of a modular approach to training in which basic foundation courses and specialist instruction could be combined should be considered.' MSC Chairman, BACIE Conference, November 1980.
8   *Vocational Preparation for Young People*, MSC (TSA) discussion paper, 1975; *A Better*

Start in Working Life; *16–18. Education and Training for 16–18 Year Olds*, Government consultative paper, February 1979; *A Basis for Choice*.

9   See FEU, *Project Information Bulletin* RP22. Personal Guidance Base.

10   The Beloe Report – *Secondary School Examinations other than the GCE* – (1960) is a typical example.

11   An analysis of the common core suggested in *A Basis for Choice* will show that the performance level required in the communication and numeracy areas correlates quite highly with that required in the first year of many vocational training schemes.

12   Employers contributed to the development of the profile used in the pilot studies for *A Basis for Choice*, and at the time of writing the FEU and CBI are discussing ways of promoting the use of this profile by employers.

References

Clark, Linda (1980) *The Transition from School to Work: A Critical Review of Research in the UK*. London, HMSO.

Thomas, J.B. (1980) *The Self in Education*. Slough, NFER.

SECTION 3

IDEOLOGY, STRATEGY AND THE INSTITUTIONAL ENVIRONMENT

CHAPTER 3.1

IDEOLOGICAL INFLUENCES IN HIGHER EDUCATION*
K.G. COLLIER

Plamenatz (1970) speaks of an ideology as 'a set of ideas or beliefs or attitudes characteristic of a group', which 'serves to hold a group together or to justify its activities and attitudes or to promote its interests'. Ideology is 'overtly descriptive and explanatory'; 'sets of beliefs or theories that are ideological purport to tell us how things are, and how they came to be so'; but many ideologies 'are also overtly prescriptive; they include injunctions and advice to men as to how they should behave. [. . .] Inherent in the common use of the word is that an ideology is not impartial, that its arguments cover a hidden self-interest; and that its adherents are blinkered, impervious to alternative views. The concept of ideology involves two components: a *perception* of the world to which the ideology is relevant; and a *set of values* relating to action in that world. These are distinguishable but not separable, they are fused into a picture of that world in which inheres a set of valuations, a sense of what ought to be. [. . .]

The idea of ideological influence is a commonplace in the discussion of school education, but figures less frequently in the debates on higher education. Marxists have led the way in these discussions (Dale et al., 1976; Finn et al., 1979). The opposition usually set up to a Marxist interpretation is one based on a 'liberal' ideology (Grace, 1978), or on a detailed dissection of the evidence (O'Keefe, 1979). The purpose of the present paper is to offer an alternative, more pragmatic, approach to the study of ideological influences. I wish to suggest that the development of

* *Studies in Higher Education*, 1982, vol. 7, no. 1, pp. 13–19.
K.G. Collier was Research Fellow at the University of East Anglia when this paper was written. Before that he was Principal of Bede College, University of Durham.

higher education in Britain has in the past half-century been especially influenced by four ideologies: the academic ideology; the ideology of economic renewal; the egalitarian ideology; and the ideology of consensus. [. . .]

The academic ideology

The adherent of the academic ideology sees the academic world as constituting a stronghold of certain values in an irrational and often barbaric society: a value for the basing of arguments and policies on evidence and logic, for the free flow of information both within and across national boundaries, and for the absence of discriminatory treatment on grounds of race, sex, religion or politics.

Secondly there is a deep involvement with the maintenance and development of the established academic disciplines. The teacher tends to identify himself with the development of an area of knowledge and investigation, and to see this as constituting a powerful bond of shared assumptions in a cosmopolitan brotherhood. The focus of his concern is on how to induct his students more fully and effectively into the recognition of the characteristic data of his discipline, the drawing of inferences and checking of evidence, the marshalling of relevant data from a variety of sources into a coherent conceptual structure, and the imaginative appreciation of the excitement of exploration in that area of study. He sees in his work the training ground – and sifting ground – for future researchers and for teachers in higher education. He sees the major criterion of competence for staff in higher education in the publication record, which is an indicator of the acceptance of the academic's work by his senior peers.

A third feature is the coincidence of a powerful emphasis on freedom for the individual academic with an essentially authoritarian system of training and testing. This involves the use of rigorous criticism in teaching and a machinery of examinations against whose verdict there is no appeal. Together these constitute an initiation process for admission to an academic elite. Once past the initiation the individual is accorded a high degree of independence to teach and research in his own way [. . .] so long as [he] stays within the boundaries set by that academic elite.

A further aspect is the emphasis on conceptual clarification and precision. In the context of the international peer-group of a particular discipline this emphasis tends in turn to generate an overemphasis on the print sources of academic debate, and thus thrusts students into a world of either intensely verbal or intensely mathematical abstractions. As a result the teaching often lumbers students with a mass of inert ideas remote from the observation of human realities.

Fifth, there is very little explicit discussion of value questions, that is, questions of the nature, validity and relative priorities of moral values in specific areas of (for example) literature or history. Such discussions entail an element of personal involvement in moral dispositions which goes beyond the cognitive. The advocate of Oxford 'Greats' in the nineteenth century had some ideal of the preparation of Platonic guardians or enlightened rulers, and value questions were at the heart of his teaching. The teacher who takes such matters seriously in his teaching now, like F.R. Leavis, is liable to become *persona non grata* to the academic establishment in his discipline. Even the values to which they are committed – of logic, precision and freedom of research – are not the subject of explicit discussion.

[. . .] The phenomenon of 'academic drift' or gradual intensification of aspirations towards higher academic status in institutions, must be an expression of the rise in status of the academic sphere in Western societies; but its connection with the academic ideology is not obvious. Nor can one see clearly the source of the defensiveness which seems to be the motive force behind the authoritarian tendencies.

The ideology of economic renewal

This involves the perception of Britain as an industrial society heavily dependent on its foreign trade and obliged therefore to be competitive in world markets for its manufactured goods; but lacking in certain of the prime conditions for successful competition, such as managerial skill, technical skill, aggressive marketing and technological innovativeness. It sees these as being mainly the concern of the further education side of the education system. This ideology tends to attach special value to occupations in industry and commerce as a counterweight to those in the older professions of medicine, law and so on; it tends to set a high value on those institutions and courses which devote their energies not to 'the origination of new knowledge' but to 'the development and application of what is known towards the fulfilment of the personal and professional concerns of their students and the solution of industrial and social problems' (DES, 1970). [. . .]

This ideology is found widely in government and other political circles in both major political parties and among industrial and trade union leaders. It was illustrated by the Chairman of ICI in 1964, who – as Eric Robinson (1968) reports – complained 'that the products of academic education were found wanting by industry and asked the universities to do something about it. He made reference to the inability of the academic to make decisions in real situations, and was particularly critical of postgraduate training'.

Here again there is sometimes a stridency of argument which seems to point to an element of defensiveness – perhaps against the apparently impregnable confidence of the university world in respect of intellectual training?

The egalitarian ideology

[. . .] The egalitarian ideology sees Britain as a society in which power and wealth are concentrated in a very small section of the population, and in which the criteria for admission to this elite are not simply ability and drive but a certain social style and membership of certain social layers. The values that characterize this ideology are for a less unequal distribution of wealth and power and a ready access of able children of manual workers to higher education and to top jobs.

Within this ideology we have 'soft' and 'hard' concepts of equality, the former being concerned primarily with equality of opportunity and of access to top positions, the latter more concerned with the distribution of wealth and power (Kogan, 1975; Finn et al., 1979).

After 1945 both major political parties in Britain accepted the soft concept of equality, and hence the meritocratic principle: to provide the maximum opportunity for the individual endowed with high intelligence and the enterprise to exploit his talents and thereby benefit society. Michael Young's (1958) formula 'Intelligence + Effort = Merit' encapsulates the view. Hence the reconstruction of the educational ladder in the immediate post-war years on the basis of open competition at each point.

But this machinery notoriously failed to work. [. . .] The expansion and diversification of institutions of higher education, intended to promote equality, have rather shown a tendency to reinforce the status differentiation and the links with social class differentiation.

Two types of response have emerged, representing what may be called 'moderately hard' and 'very hard' concepts of equality.

The moderately hard concept is represented by the abolition of the 11+ examination and the introduction of positive discrimination, compensatory education and the proposals for educational priority areas (EPAs) in the 1960s. It was summed up by Halsey (1972) in reviewing the EPA programme:

> Were we concerned simply to introduce a greater measure of justice into an educational system which traditionally selected the minority for higher education and upward social mobility out of the EPA district, leaving the majority to be taught, mainly by a huge hidden curriculum, a sense of their own relative incompetence and impotence – a modern, humane and even relatively enjoyed form of gentling the masses? Or could we assume a wide programme of social reform which would democratise local power structures and diversify local occupational opportunities so that society would look to its schools for a supply of young people educated for political and social responsibility and linked to their communities not by failure in the competition but by rich opportunities for work and life?

The 'very hard' concept is to a considerable extent a result of Marxist influence. But it has made relatively little headway in Britain, for reasons which are discussed in the next section.

The consensus ideology

Halsey emphasized the contrast between the traditions of political relations and industrial relations in this country:

> Political relations were able to rest more directly on social bonds outside the work place that were strongly antithetical to doctrines of class struggle. That is why it can be reasonably argued that the norms of political attitudes were ones of high trust by contrast with the established and enduring low-trust industrial relations. (Halsey, 1978)

He returns repeatedly to the continuing strength of the consensus tradition of politics, in spite of such traumatic events as the slump of the 1930s. When J.B. Priestley visited Jarrow in 1933, he

> marvelled that men in such economic conditions, not under the constraint of military force, but on the contrary politically enfranchised, should nevertheless have accepted their lot. That they did has to be explained largely by the strength of a consensual political culture. (Halsey, 1978)

[. . .] Adherents of the consensus ideology see society as naturally and inevitably prone to conflict, not as between the virtuous and the wicked but as between groups of different, and legitimate, persuasions or convictions. They attach a high value to the resolution of conflict by accommodation rather than by resort to force, threats or other forms of coercion; and they attach a consequential value to self-restraint in action and negotiation. Thus, as Embling (1974) has noted, much political negotiation and consultation are dominated by 'the search for the highest degree of common agreement among the large number of interests concerned and the minimum degree of public confrontation'. Underlying this outlook is a deep attachment to the freedom of action of the individual or the group: which is usually thought of as the heart of a 'liberal' ideology.

The maintenance of this tradition would appear to depend to a great extent on the style and manner of the exercise of authority by those in positions of power. [. . .]

Ideological influences on higher education

The academic ideology has, I believe, extended its influence very widely through the upper levels of the educational system in the period since 1945. It is not merely in the expansion of higher education but in the increased demands for formal academic qualifications, such as degrees or GCE A-Level passes, for entry to a variety of occupations – professional, semi-professional and technical – for which they were not formerly required. It is to be seen in the intensity of specialization in upper secondary schools and in the strength of resistance in the universities to proposals for a broadening of sixth-form courses. Various circles in government and industry regard it as a threat to the development of industry and commerce, since the orientation is not in general directed to the practical application of knowledge. It has stirred hostile reactions among adherents of the 'hard' concepts of equality, who see it as reinforcing an elitist social structure by adding academic attainment to the traditional ascriptive criteria for promotion.

The ideology of economic renewal has expressed itself in the creation of the binary system, which in some degree has served to protect the public sector of higher education from invasion by the academic ideology.

As regards the egalitarian ideology, the 'very hard' concept of equality appears to be rejected by a large part of British society. Halsey (1978) has remarked on the extreme combination of solidarity and hierarchy in British society. The ideology of consensus and the belief in individual freedom of action have a profound hold over a large part of the population in this country.

The influence of the ideology of consensus in higher education has been most clearly shown in two areas: the structure of control by central government over the universities via the UGC; and the evolution of staff–student relations in the stormy period of 1968–1970, illustrated by the concordat negotiated between the Committee of Vice-Chancellors and Principals and the National Union of Students (1968).

However, there does seem to have been a widespread sense of disenchantment over the slowness of movement towards a more egalitarian society in Britain. Perhaps this merely reflects an inflated expectation of what is possible in a decade or two in any society. But it is potentially explosive. The distribution of wealth and power has altered little in the post-1945 period and this seems certain to remain a source of disquiet and possibly of unrest. There seems to be a deadlock between those on the left who adhere to a hard concept of equality and those on the right who stubbornly resist it.

On the other hand it seems clear that the consensus and egalitarian ideologies do overlap at a crucial point, namely in a belief in shared decision-making. Over the last decade this convergence of values has resulted throughout higher education in a great extension of participation of junior academic staff, of non-academic staff and of students in decision-making and this has undoubtedly reduced the authoritarianism of the past, though sometimes at the expense of much precious time.

Conclusion

Above is a sketch of certain social forces which appear to have exerted a major influence on the development of higher education. This is not to say that there are no others: it would be possible to distinguish – for example – an anti-egalitarian, conservative ideology marked by an emphasis on hierarchy and conformity. It would be possible to point to the influence of certain traditions within the Christian churches on university or college life: traditions which have often expressed themselves in ideological form. The reality is of formidable complexity, of a 'matrix' of 'class, educational and political issues which impinge upon schooling' (Grace, 1978). Wherever we turn we uncover the 'hidden curriculum' of particular perceptions of social reality and particular value-orientations, sometimes explicit at a superficial level, but more usually unvoiced.

Is it possible to escape from the ideological trap, to break out of the blinkers imposed by ideological preconceptions? At all levels – whether of national or local government, institution, department or individual – we need to turn a searchlight on our own presuppositions, to identify our own unarticulated perceptions of society and unvoiced value-assumptions, which imprison us within ideological boundaries. At all levels also there is a need for bringing institutions' teaching, and students' learning, into more direct relationship with the human realities of the non-academic world, economic, political, personal and ethical, to give intellectual analysis and debate a firmer experiential basis. As Whitehead (1979) expressed it, 'First-hand knowledge is the ultimate basis of intellectual life. To a large extent book-learning conveys second-hand information . . . the learned world . . . is tame because it has never been scared by facts.'

References

Committee of Vice-Chancellors and Principals and National Union of Students (1968) *Joint Statement*. London, National Union of Students.

Dale, R., Esland, G. and MacDonald, M. (1976) *Schooling and Capitalism*. London, Routledge & Kegan Paul.

Department of Education and Science (DES) (1970) *The Polytechnics: Reports on Education 65*. London, HMSO.

Embling, J. (1974) *A Fresh Look at Higher Education*. Amsterdam, Elsevier.

Finn, D., Grant, N. and Johnson, R. (1979) *Social Democracy, Education and the Crisis*. University of Birmingham.

Grace, G. (1978) *Teachers, Ideology and Control*. London, Routledge & Kegan Paul.

Halsey, A.H. (1972) *Educational Priority: EPA Problems and Policies*, Vol. 1. London, HMSO.

Halsey, A.H. (1978) *Change in British Society*. Oxford, Oxford University Press.

Kogan, M. (1975) *Educational Policy-Making*. London, Allen & Unwin.

O'Keefe, D. (1979) Capitalism and correspondence: a critique of Marxist analyses of education. *Higher Education Review*, vol. 12, no. 1.

Plamenatz, J. (1970) *Ideology*. London, Macmillan.

Robinson, E. (1968) *The New Polytechnics*. Harmondsworth, Penguin.

Whitehead, A.N. (1979) *The Aims of Education*. London, Williams & Norgate.

Young, M. (1958) *The Rise of the Meritocracy*. London, Thames & Hudson.

CHAPTER 3.2

THE COST OF SURVIVAL: CHOICES FACING POST-COMPULSORY EDUCATION*
DOUGLAS WEIR

At 16 young people have the choice of whether to leave school or not. For many of them that time of life is also when they decide whether to stop their formal education or not. The consultative paper '*16–18s in Scotland*' (SED, 1979) has been interpreted as dealing with the question of whether school or college is the best institution for those continuing in education, the second problem, of those not continuing at all, is the more serious. No community can afford to allow half its members to discontinue their formal education at such an early age. The penalties in terms of a lowering of the quality of life, both economically and socially, are too severe.

The following discussion will therefore concentrate mainly on those who currently take no part in post-compulsory education. [. . .]

From time to time those in further education concerned to raise the proportion of any age-group attending their institutions have proposed compulsion – generally on the employer – to send his workers to day-release classes. For these educationists, compulsion is ideal because you can plan confidently. The courses are laid on by national examining bodies, the student numbers can be estimated in advance, there are sanctions which can be invoked against those who do not attend, and staff timetables are predictable. [. . .] Using compulsion in such a fashion provides the security which the secondary school has and to which many teachers in further education aspire. Indeed many of them left industry because education offered guaranteed wages, hours, tenure and even content.

---

* *Choice, Compulsion and Cost.* Scottish Education Department. Edinburgh, HMSO, 1980, pp. 56–61. © Crown Copyright 1980. Reproduced with the permission of the Controller, HMSO. Douglas Weir, Director of the Scottish Vocational Preparation Unit, at Jordanhill College of Education, was Director of the Education Resources Unit for the Youth Opportunities Programme.

However, [. . .] even with strong sanctions invoked by Industrial Training Boards, some employers ignore the pressure. Even where employers support day release, some young workers react against persuasion and pressure [. . .]. Some talk the employer round – not always the most difficult of tasks. Some attend irregularly or behave unacceptably, encouraging employer and college together to discontinue their attendance. Some attend in body only, the spirit remaining resistant to the attraction of the courses which the college offers.

[. . .] Their previous experience of formal education was not attractive. They did not like the demeaning way in which they were treated; they did not receive certificates or, more importantly, any feeling of their own worth; [. . .]. Being forced to attend college suggests more of the same to them and they therefore resist.

Even more important are the other young people in jobs and industries where continuing education is not normal. Many of them will have even less of a feeling for formal education and less of a respect for compulsory attendance. What purpose could be served by forcing them to attend college?

Colleges are not universally anxious to increase their student numbers especially in the areas where tailor-made courses do not exist. Over the country as a whole the numbers of students are growing without any strong promotional effort by colleges, and there are still the cushions provided by the Manpower Services Commission [. . .]. Only in those colleges struggling for numbers or imbued with genuine entrepreneurial ambition, are attempts being made to devise courses which will prove attractive on their own merits rather than because they are bolstered by compulsion, by certification or by economic necessity.

These arguments in favour of an expansionist further education sector are not adequate in themselves, emphasizing as they do college need rather than customer need. The 'customer need' issue also requires redefinition since, in further education, industry and commerce (i.e. the employers) are generally seen as the customers, while a new view of further education would see the student as the customer.

The consequences of moving away from the various elements of compulsion and the various aspects of service to employers are considerable and time consuming. The further education service is presently paid for on the understanding that it produces painters and nursery nurses and electricians and business machine operators rather than because it helps people to develop. Yet an examination of employer needs makes clear that they emphasize deficits in personal skills rather than in job skills when they criticize the calibre of young worker available to them. Furthermore an examination of many of this country's foreign competitors makes it clear that their success is associated with a solid base of general education where they have concentrated on first helping individuals with their personal development before turning to their vocational development.

[. . .] Further education should have the opportunity of redressing the balance. The messages which have to be conveyed to workers and young people alike are that no job is a job for life and that getting the most out of the type of complex society we live in depends as much on personal skills as on wage-earning capacity. Vocationally relevant courses are certainly necessary and offer a face validity to employers and young people, but the further education service's objectives in offering other courses are in the realm of personal growth and development.

A criticism of that argument might be that the educational input to the Youth Opportunities Programme (YOP) is supposed to have this objective and yet [. . .] only around one-quarter of the young people on YOP receive any education or training. If that very large-scale programme, full of carrots and sticks, has so little an impact in this respect and if UVP (Unified Vocational Preparation) with its £4 per day 'sweetener' for employers and colleges can only stimulate 30 schemes in Scotland, what chance is there for a wholesale change in emphasis in further education provision? Some colleges, disillusioned by their participation in YOP and UVP, wish to revert to their traditional markets.

Perhaps teachers, above all, need to learn that no job is a job for life: [. . .] our national economy is weak, the social costs of educational lassitude are high and the traditional college markets may soon disappear as ship-building, steel-making and car manufacturing cease to be British-based industries. Do we need to wait on large-scale redundancies among further education staff before attempts are made to generate new business?

Recent initiatives such as YOP and UVP have been discouraging. Much time and effort is required in contacting employers and sponsors (many of whom only employ one or two young people), in enthusing the young people, in course-building and staff development. At the end of all of this the young people may not attend and even if they do, the points for salary and staffing purposes which the college receives are so negligible as to make the exercise seem not worth tackling.

Each of these difficulties can be overcome and, indeed, has been overcome in some areas, particularly where the local authority has been prepared to make a redistribution or an extra investment of resources because of its belief in the importance of an educated population. The cost implications are not enormous, especially where the problem is largely one of attitudes. Where an employer says 'I can't afford to give this young worker a day off', or a young person says 'college is not for the likes of me' or where college staff say 'we don't have time to devise a new course', these problems generally need to be overcome only once. Having given day release once, the employer can more easily be persuaded to do it again; having come to college and lived to tell the tale, the young person spreads the word among his friends; having built the new course, the college staff find the exercise much less time-consuming second time round.

National and local government must therefore examine carefully the situations where judiciously applied pump-priming finance would have the best multiplier effect. A detached youth worker? An outreach careers officer? A curriculum development unit or resource centre? All of these are short-term investments with a long-term pay-off, and can be introduced quickly, if only the funding bodies see them as priorities when the falling rolls in primary and secondary school offer the opportunity for some shift in expenditure.

Arguments in favour of compulsion take an employer perspective, so arguments in favour of new provision take an institutional perspective, supporting the view that we have a further education system and we ought to make the best of that system. It is time to face squarely the choice and cost challenges of taking an individual perspective. The challenge is bluntly offered by the Advisory Council for Adult and Continuing Education (1979) when they say that 'we must look for the best educational potential for the needs of the student and provide it wherever he may be found, rather than expect him to fit into preconceived institutional structures'. [. . .]

It was indicated earlier that many young people have had enough of compulsion by the age of 16 and do not wish to return immediately to formal education. Another group, however, do not even have the confidence to return, however strong the motivation. The size and formalized structure of many educational institutions put them off. They were depersonalized before, at school, and do not want to risk that again.

Under those circumstances education must go to the people, indeed must become the service *of the people*. This demands practitioners who can do without the safety in numbers, the shelter of bricks and mortar, the security of a captive audience which are characteristic of much teaching. People meet in clubs, in pubs, in community associations, in trades unions, at work, in their homes. In these places a considerable amount of education already occurs – some by chance and some deliberately. Usually, however, it is unstructured or at least without a natural connection to the formal part of the education system.

Building these connections is a crucial task for the 1980s. The process can be imagined as developing in two major directions.

First, we need to know more about the circumstances which lead to people associating voluntarily for broadly educational purposes. Is it the company, the surroundings, the atmosphere, the topics – or some combination of all of these? How far can the formal education service imitate these attractions and encourage more people to take their interests further? What mechanism can be found for creating an acceptable network among the existing opportunities and between them and formal education?

This might be termed the 'responsive element' of the process, taking what exists a little further, and making it work a little better. Little capital expenditure would be required, few additional staff appointments, but considerable changes in attitudes within existing institutions so that when new clients progressed from the community learning situation to formal education they found similar characteristics, in the surroundings and the teachers, to those which they had previously experienced.

The second element of the process might be termed 'initiation'. Where people gather together spontaneously, what can education do to broaden their demands? Just as, to stave off death, professional theatre goes into village halls, pubs and clubs, so too education may have to follow. This means paying a great deal of attention to presentation of material, to a more professional understanding of 'what education is worthwhile', to being prepared to take up or drop lines of merchandise at a moment's notice.

Such an approach would be too insecure for many. Even in the community education service where entrepreneurship could be expected, some practitioners have yielded to the temptation to build community centres. This is exhibiting the same attitude as other parts of the education service do, namely 'here are the facilities, come and get them'. Perhaps more necessary from education today is the attitude of 'we have something important to tell you, can we come and talk to you about it?'

Of course the choices [. . .] are not as black and white as those presented above. The importance of these illustrations is to remind those of us in the education service that we have no divine right of survival. We are members of the community too, and have to respond to [. . .] educational need so as to benefit the whole community.

The formal education service [. . .], in order to survive, from time to time seeks an extension of compulsion in one form or another, without recognizing the alienating effects which compulsion can have.

[. . .] Constantly ignored, however, is the informal sector of education – the associations and groups which most people attend voluntarily and sporadically. In these lies the potential for a large expansion in educational provision if we see the need. That education would take on more of the characteristics of what people want rather than what educationists think they need although the long-term objective could appropriately be to reconcile needs and wants.

Under those circumstances the argument about provision in the post-compulsory years is not the simple 'school or college' choice. Certainly there is a continuing need for some institutional provision and for that provision to be more effectively utilized through generating more and new business. Equally, there is a need for a much larger 'informal' or 'community' sector, to meet the needs of those people who, at any time, have no need of formal education, and partly of those who are unable to re-enter the formal education they require until their confidence and competence have been increased. [. . .] Schools and colleges would then have the primary purpose of acting as a base for the mutual support of professional staff, leaving much of the contact amongst learners to take place elsewhere.

That scenario for the survival of the post-compulsory sector is a long way from the 'take it or leave it', 'come because you need the certificate' mentality which is still too prevalent. Genuine choice depends on having some education available where you want it and when you want it.

Costs need not be excessive. Some extra staffing will be needed to facilitate the development of those 'learning webs' which exist in all communities, but that staffing can be found from the resources released by the decline in primary and secondary rolls. Some teacher-training and curriculum development costs will arise but they too can be met from the funds released elsewhere.

Above all, if we get the take-up of education which can be envisaged there will be a saving in public expenditure. If education works it reduces such social costs as vandalism, ignorance and disadvantage. If education concentrates on attitude change then it affects both sides of industry by improving their understanding of the economic system. Then we could expect better labour relations, higher productivity and the creation of enough wealth to afford the educational system we aspire to.

If we wish to survive, have we a choice?

References

Advisory Council for Adult and Continuing Education (1979) *A Strategy for the Basic Education of Adults*. London, ACACE.

Scottish Education Department (SED) (1979) *16–18s in Scotland*. Edinburgh, HMSO.

CHAPTER 3.3

16–19 IN EUROPE:
DEMOGRAPHIC CHANGE AND PERSPECTIVES ON THE LINKS BETWEEN SCHOOL AND WORK*
GUY NEAVE

[. . .In] this brief *tour d'horizon*, I want to look at interrelated developments in Europe – the well-exercised topic of school populations and, second, developments in the 16–19 age-range, in particular the changing relationship between school-based and what, for lack of a better term, one might call experience-based education. Deliberately, I have avoided using the well-worn concept of general versus vocational education since to couch the issue in these terms is in effect to use a vocabulary that is not merely increasingly denuded of sense, but also poses a conceptual differentiation which, in the eyes of many planning authorities in Europe, is becoming increasingly redundant. For better or for worse, we are in a situation in which the classical definitions of what is 'academic' or 'general' and what is vocational is less a correspondence to the real world and rather a carry-over of ancient practice.

[. . . Let] us look at some of the demographic patterns that appear to be emerging in certain European countries with respect to the 15–19 age-range. I will take as the datum line the size of the age-cohort as it was in 1975 and compare it with the forecasted size over the next 10–15 years. At the present time, most European countries are still in a position where the mid-1960s mini baby boom is still working its way through upper-secondary and into post-secondary education (Hufner, 1982). In Belgium and Luxemburg the demographic decline will be apparent by 1985 in this age-group. Compared with 1975, it will be some 5.3 percent smaller in the

---

* *16–19 in Europe: Demographic Change and Perspectives on the Links Between School and Work.* Open University European Educational Policy Study Group, Occasional Paper No. 1, April 1982, pp. 1–12. Guy Neave is Senior Research Fellow, European Institute of Education and Social Policy, Paris.

former country and some 6.7 percent in the case of the latter (Eurydice, 1981).

By 1990, all member states of the EEC, with the exception of Ireland and Italy (+8.1 percent and 5.6 percent respectively) will see the size of the 15–19 age-cohort decline. All indications are that this will continue and reach its nadir around 1995.

The actual dimensions of this decline will be particularly dramatic in Germany, where the numbers of 15–19-year-olds will fall by some 34.8 percent compared to the 1975 level. And in Belgium, The Netherlands and Luxemburg, the reduction will be in the order of one in four. In Britain, the size of this group will fall by around one in five (19.3 percent) and in France and Denmark by around 12 percent.

Projections suggest that by the year 2000 there will be an upturn. It will be particularly marked in the case of the UK, France and The Netherlands, though in no instance will the upswing reach those levels of the 1975 cohort, with the possible exception of France and Greece. In the case of Belgium, Germany and Denmark, it will amount less to a revival than to a bottoming-out at the levels reached in 1995.

[. . . Before] reviewing some of the latest developments in the 16–19 age-range it is worth while setting the achievements of the 1970s in their perspective. If to many this decade was one when early euphoria gave way by 1974–1975 to deepening gloom, this, I would suggest, is somewhat of a rhetorical point. To be sure, the numbers of people who suddenly saw the advantage of de-institutionalizing education, of creating 'new alternatives' and new facilities, were considerable. But this is apt to disguise the very real quantitative expansion that continued despite 'the encircling gloom'. One indicator, though it gives no pointer towards 'qualitative improvements', is the staying-on rate. In 1970, this was some 46.5 percent for all 16–17-year-olds in the 10 EEC countries. By 1978, it had increased to 61.3 percent. [. . .] The probability of 16–17-year-olds remaining in full-time education improved during those eight years by one-third, for 17–18-year-olds by one-quarter and for the 18–19-year-olds by just under one-fifth.

If, at the start of the previous decade, post-compulsory education still remained a minority experience, by the end of the 1970s it had become the norm and in certain countries – for instance, France (with 75 percent of 16–17-year-olds), Belgium (77 percent) and The Netherlands (87.6 percent) – upper-secondary education has assumed all the characteristics of moving from a mass to a universal model.

Thus the full-time, school-based education system, despite doubts among many pundits, absorbed an unprecedented expansion during the 1970s. The prospect of demographic decline has led several governments to suggest that the time is now ripe to consolidate the quantitative expansion by more emphasis of what has been ambiguously called 'the qualitative aspect'. In some countries, such as Belgium, France and The Netherlands, this means, in effect, a lowering of the staff–student ratio.

In parallel with these developments in the 'traditional' sector of education, recent years have seen a remarkable shift in the balance of power between the authorities responsible for education that is school based and those newly established 'para-educational bodies', set up to deal with the problems of youth unemployment. The combination of sustained demographic decline which will directly affect the school system and the likelihood that the economic crisis will be with us at least for the next four years, suggests a further shift.

This shift in power between the traditional administration with responsibility for education and the penetration into what may be seen as a de facto area of education by the various Ministries of Labour, Employment, Labour Market Boards in Sweden, or the establishment of a Ministry for Vocational Training in France, is a development of the highest importance for several reasons. The first and most obvious of these is the direct financial power that these new agencies bring with them. It is a curious paradox that, while in most countries education budgets are being pegged to inflation, the growth of financial inputs from non-traditional sources in fact means that education budgets are continuing to grow. The difference is that most countries do not count such Youth Opportunities Programmes or the French equivalent, the *Plan Avenir Jeunes*, as part of the national education budget [, even] though, as the economic crisis continues, these programmes increasingly take on a long-term educational content and aspect. The second reason stems from the fact that even if not normally recognized as being within the administrative competence of national Ministries of Education, they do in effect amount to the development of a parallel education system – what one French Minister has termed *'Le système d'enseignement bis'*.

In France, by September 1982, this will take on board some 160,000 youngsters and will involve both combined theoretical instruction with on-the-job training for a two-year period maximum. The third feature of these 'new structures' – though by no means of all – is the gradual replication inside them of tasks and aspects of education previously located inside school-based instruction. Whether one cares to call this affective development or the development of life or social skills, it is a reinforced form of socialization that, apparently, the school has failed to provide. [. . . The] arguments in favour of including elements of a general education either in a remedial capacity for the non-qualified, which is one justification, or because the essential purpose of such programmes is to impart an intellectual flexibility to meet widespread economic change which cannot exactly be foreseen in its finer details, may themselves be perfectly coherent. But, for all that, they mean that the part of general (or what would be known in Britain as academic or theoretical) education in the experience-based systems of instruction is increasing.

Arguably, this stems from the fact that much of the type of employment for which narrowly defined vocational training programmes prepared young people, is itself disappearing. [. . . In] the future, the types of skill required by an industry based on that new hope of the world – the new information technologies – are so broad that previous definitions of what is vocational and what is academic are becoming increasingly blurred. If one accepts this, then it is obvious to my mind that the adjustment to this new situation is being made less in the schools than in the parallel system itself. This leads me to my fourth point. This is less to do with the balance of the curriculum found in the experience-based sector than the fact that, being largely outside the school sector, it appears to be showing a far greater willingness to assimilate what would be seen as 'alternative' modes of presentation and innovative techniques than has yet been possible in the school.

[. . . It] is both amazing and a little disturbing that many of the utopias of self-directed learning, of group projects, of student-directed activity, have begun to put down roots as part of a regular system of education in the parallel experience-based system (McPherson and Neave, 1976). It will, not unreasonably, be pointed out that this innovative approach is necessary because for the greater part of the time, the young people for whom such programmes are intended are precisely those for whom the more rigorous or structured approach found in school has little appeal. Therefore, perforce, new techniques of presentation and new ways of imparting the growing range of what are deemed basic skills, whether literacy, numeracy, self-awareness or social comportment, are necessary.

But it is slightly disturbing that for this to be recognized on a basis other than experimental, requires a massive economic crisis and is introduced largely as a lesser of two evils, the other being the continued threat of social unrest amongst the disadvantaged young. I am not denying that good work in this direction is being done in schools. What I am saying is that in the short time that the experience-based sector has been functioning – since 1974 in Britain and since 1977 in France with the old *Pacte National de l'Emploi* – it has shown far greater willingness to take on board techniques and assumptions about learning that are still regarded as utopian, even perhaps heretical, in the school-based system.

What are the implications of this? Much depends, I think, on the particular relationship between the two sectors – school and experience-based education. In certain countries, mainly the Scandinavian ones, training programmes, guidance and counselling are still firmly located in the school. [. . . Even] if the young person has in fact left school, they are still the school's responsibility. In this pattern, the effects of changes in the balance of power between the two are relatively minor since education and training take place within a single framework of the school itself for the 16–19 age-range. In other countries, such as The Netherlands and Germany, it has been traditional to draw a rather rigid line between school-based and vocational education, though all school-leavers up to 18 are required to attend a system of compulsory day release up to that age. This dual system, split betwen academic and full-time technical education on the one hand and part-time vocational education on the other, is showing particular strain, even though it is precisely towards this model that the DES has currently turned its face. In the first place, since it comes under different administrative authorities and is segmented between different sector interests, it is perhaps less flexible than many would give it credence. The second thing that even the German employers themselves have recognized, is that it does not appear all that attractive to young people.

[. . . Attempts] to bring the two sectors closer together, mainly in the form of the tenth basic vocational training year, have not proven very successful. The reasons for this, however, are only partially within the realm of education. True, the feeling among those teachers identified with 'academic disciplines' is that it dilutes 'standards', but what is at stake here is not a question of standards so much as who is to teach what at which particular stage of the education system. And, on another level, there is the ever-present fear that any further extension of this system will involve increasing the power of the federal authorities in an area that, constitutionally, comes under the control of the 11 *Länder*.

If the German model of a parallel vocational training sector inside education (which frankly is not necessarily the same as an experience-based system *à la* MSC outside it) has appeal for the DES, there are at least two good reasons why this should be so. First, because almost since the turn of the century Britain, in various ways, most of which have been half-hearted, sought to emulate the German system. Second, and far more powerful, is the fact that responsibility appears to be slipping away from the DES for a sector that, because of the relatively high level of young people who emerge unqualified from education in this country, is proportionately more important in many regards than any of its Continental equivalents.

One of the crucial issues that underlies the development of the experience-based education system is to what extent the practices it develops may be assimilated into full-time school-based education? The danger is that because the former is regarded as a response primarily to youth unemployment with educational connotations in second position, because it may be cast as a programme either for the less able, the less motivated or less qualified, the lessons that are to be learned in the domain of restructuring the content of syllabuses and of the teaching techniques themselves will be ignored. Highly important in this is the fact that many of those who are actively engaged in 'teaching' or 'stimulating' young people in such programmes are not, formally speaking, qualified as teachers. Nor, as yet, is there a system for training those who will become such in the experience-based system. This is a very important point and one that will be of increasing interest to both central and local government the more it is realized that the system we have created in response to immediate needs is, in effect, becoming part of a structural framework, the role of which is to adapt to changing requirements. But there is another aspect as well. If the experience-based sector, call it YOP or whatever, is showing itself more attentive to different approaches, is it not acting as a species of reservation, where innovation may reign unmolested, that allows the continuation of the more traditional methods in school? In other words, the more the experience-based sector expands to meet the needs of the unqualified or what the Germans call the 'school weary', the greater the temptation to revert to time-honoured methods in schools because those young people who remain in school will be the less weary or the less unmotivated.

But it seems to me that without closer coordination between the dwindling school-based sector and the expanding experience-based sector, the benefits and efforts of the latter may well be lost on the former. By pushing large numbers of youngsters into the experience-based sector are we not, in fact, leaving the way open for the return of a species of elitism in the school sector?

References

Eurydice (1981) *The Impact of Demographic Change on Education Systems in the European Community*. Brussels, September 1981.

Hufner, Klaus (1982) Demography and higher education: some theoretical and empirical considerations on their relationships. *European Journal of Education*, vol. 16, nos. 3–4.

McPherson, Andrew and Neave, Guy (1976) *The Scottish Sixth: A Sociological Exploration of the Changing Relationship Between School and University in Scotland*. Windsor, NFER.

CHAPTER 3.4

THE IMPLEMENTATION OF MANPOWER-BASED PLANS FOR HIGHER EDUCATION*
O. FULTON, A. GORDON AND G. WILLIAMS

[. . .] The most widespread method of implementing manpower plans and of relating the social demand for places in higher education to employment opportunities is through the medium of vocational guidance and student counselling. One function of counselling is to try and ensure that educational provision based on the social demand for places will roughly correspond to society's needs for qualified manpower. These needs can of course be indicated either by manpower forecasting activities or by the trend of employment opportunities on the labour market. It might even be argued that full vocational guidance, based on accurate assessment of needs, would remove any contradiction between educational plans based on social demand and those based on manpower forecasts: there are, after all, few students in higher education who wish to be unemployed or misemployed after graduation.

This chapter discusses the arrangements which various countries make to facilitate vocational guidance and counselling and to implement policy-oriented manpower plans. It also examines the contention that the provision of information to students will by itself help to solve the problems of adjusting social demand to meet manpower requirements. Our starting point, however, is an examination of the difficulties caused by time-lags and rigidities in the operations of the labour market. Since market economies by

* *Higher Education and Manpower Planning*. Geneva: International Labour Office, 1982, Ch. 7, pp. 83–101. ©International Labour Organization, 1982. Oliver Fulton is a Lecturer at the Institute of Post-Compulsory Education, University of Lancaster. Alan Gordon is Research Fellow at the Institute of Manpower Studies, University of Sussex. Gareth Williams is Professor at the Institute of Post-Compulsory Education, University of Lancaster, and was Director of the Leverhulme programme of study into the future of higher education, 1981–1982.

their very nature rely to a great extent on market forces, which are believed to influence students, graduates, employed personnel and employers by means of remuneration and employment opportunities, provided information is available, these factors are of obvious importance.

The market mechanism – the economist's usual shorthand to depict the interdependency of the supply and demand for any goods or service is to focus on the relationship between demand as a negative function of price on the one hand, and supply as a positive function of price on the other. When applied to the labour market, *ceteris paribus*, these operations can be represented as:

Demand for qualified manpower (D) = negative f (price of
qualified
manpower)

Supply of qualified manpower (S) = positive f (price of
qualified
manpower).

The graphic representation of the labour market for qualified manpower in an equilibrium position is given in *Fig.* 6. The point at which demand (DD) and supply (SS) curves intersect gives the equilibrium price of qualified manpower. In this highly simplified example, the equilibrium price of highly qualified manpower is given as OX. At this price the number of highly qualified personnel prepared to offer their services on the labour market is equal to the number that employers are prepared to hire at this price (or salary level). This number is given by OY.

If the equilibrium position shown in *Fig.* 6 is disturbed for some reason, the speed with which adjustments take place to reach a new equilibrium is of obvious importance for the efficient allocation of resources. The equilibrium could be disturbed, for example, because of an increased demand by employers for highly qualified manpower due to economic growth, or because of a greater supply of personnel from universities. If, for instance, we assume an increase in supply because of expansion of higher education, the supply curve would shift to S1–S1 and the new equilibrium would be reached at a wage rate of OX1. If new graduates were reluctant to accept this fall in their relative earnings it would result in the number Y–Y1 being unemployed or at best under- or misemployed. The time-lag involved in the realignment of supply and demand needs to be as short as possible if market adjustments are going, by themselves, to be able to produce a satisfactory new equilibrium.

Figure 6 Supply and demand for qualified manpower in equilibrium.

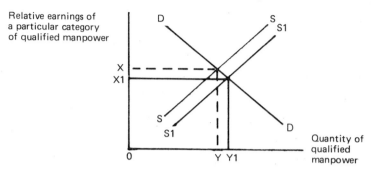

The concept of the 'cobweb cycle' illustrates one possible type of adjustment that has obvious economic and social disadvantages. Essentially the 'cobweb' is a graphical representation of the effects of time-lags on readjustments in supply and demand in the movement towards a new equilibrium. *Figure 7* shows that a new equilibrium position is eventually reached by a series of price fluctuations, each one of which causes employers or qualified personnel (or would-be students, depending on the time-lag involved) to overreact.

This model shows that under some assumptions about the operations of the labour market, it will be a long time before a new equilibrium is reached. In the intervening period there will be alternating shortages and surpluses of qualified manpower on the labour market. Empirical evidence from the United States of this type of adjustment for some categories of qualified manpower is given by Freeman (1971).

Figure 7 Cobweb cycle adjustments in supply and demand.

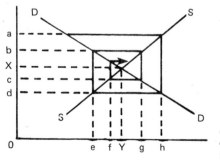

'Cobweb'-type adjustments in the market for highly qualified manpower occur when the time-lag between a decision to expand the supply of manpower and the time when new graduates are ready for employment is so long that changes in earnings may cause students or employers to over-react, so that shortages are turned into surpluses and earnings fluctuate wildly. Thus, for example, a shortage of accountants on the labour market, which is revealed by high earnings, rapid promotion, etc., may influence many students to enrol in accountancy courses, perhaps more than enough to compensate for the shortage. A situation of over-supply will then result. The situation is obviously made worse if students and potential students are responding to information that is some years out of date.

The question that has to be faced by any government that aims to regulate higher education in accordance with economic needs is whether it is more efficient to attempt to restore equilibrium through the use of manpower planning techniques or by other means. The point of disagreement between planners in favour of manpower forecasting and those against it is not whether the time-lags described above exist or not (clearly they do and are important: students, employers and educational planners generally base their own decisions on out-of-date information). Nor is there any disagreement about the need to remedy shortages or surpluses of manpower as quickly as possible so as to make the most efficient use of resources. The fundamental disagreement is about whether manpower forecasting and its implementation is an appropriate mechanism to remedy imbalances and to eliminate the uncertainty of time-lags. Those who favour manpower forecasting argue that the market is unable to remedy shortages and surpluses on its own, and a thorough assessment of the country's manpower requirements in the future, backed up by translation into places in higher education, is the only way to allocate scarce resources efficiently.

The view of economists who favour the free market is that there is not a rigid relationship between education and occupation, and that short-term adjustments are possible if the price mechanism encourages employers to substitute a category of labour in plentiful supply for one that is in short supply. Thus the effective time-lag between a disequilibrium appearing and the supply of labour reacting to it can be reduced, and the market turns out to be able to adjust itself without any severe disturbance.

Both views, however, rely to a large extent on good information, that is, on informing would-be students of career opportunities; even if the 'perfect' knowledge assumed in theoretical market economies is unattainable, some notion of likely outcomes must be present. We now turn, therefore, to examine the arrangements made for vocational guidance and counselling and graduate placement facilities in centrally planned and market economies. In the former, as we shall see, an attempt is made to orientate would-be students towards expected future manpower needs.

In the latter, whilst information concerning likely employment prospects is in many cases an important component of counselling and guidance, the information itself is less precise. Greater weight is placed on encouraging informed decision-making by students themselves, in the light of their own academic interests and the current labour market demand for various types of skills.

Guidance, counselling and job placement in the German Democratic Republic

In the German Democratic Republic the planned admission of students to university and the planned placement of graduates in employment is accomplished through a system of information, advice and guidance with a view to the harmonization of students' vocational preferences on the one hand, and the requirements of society on the other.

It is believed that detailed information on the needs of society, the encouragement of interest in needed disciplines and employment areas and the 'steering' of young people towards them are all necessary to coordinate individual preferences and societal needs. 'Any uncontrolled development leads to human disappointments and waste of societal resources if it is known from the start that no realistic possibilities of employment will be available' (Sachse, 1977).

The underlying theme of all vocational guidance in the German Democratic Republic is thus to attempt to bring the vocational aspirations of young people into line with the needs of society. Employment opportunities and opportunities in higher education derived from the prepared manpower plans are made known to young people, and they are encouraged to act in accordance with these social needs. The preparation and recruiting of applicants for higher education are part of the organized vocational guidance system. [. . .]

The orientation, preparation and guidance of young people prior to admission to higher education institutions can be considered in five stages:

1 Intensive vocational information and orientation begins at the start of the 11th grade of the extended secondary school (the matriculation

examination is taken after the 12th grade). The following material is available to students for information at this stage:

a. university and college guidebooks which describe occupations by content and employment opportunities;
b. the planned targets for admission of students to individual subject disciplines;
c. an 'orientation table' on the ratio of places in higher education to applicants in previous years. The idea is for students to draw their own conclusions on trends of shortages and surpluses of applicants for different disciplines.

[. . .] On the basis of this information, vocational guidance sessions are organized. In each province an institution of higher education has been established to carry out vocational guidance for all disciplines through the use of experts in each subject area.

2 At the next stage, students register their preferences for studying a certain discipline (a second choice may be indicated). General personal information is also submitted at this stage. As a result of these registrations, the first balance of students' choices and available places in higher education is drawn up by computer.

The long-term preparation for the admission of young people to higher education means that most would-be students are aware of the country's manpower requirements and the prospects of admission to higher education. 'The result is that individual preferences are, to a large extent, brought into harmony with the requirements of society' (Sachse, 1977).

There are, however, a number of matching problems: there are disciplines, for example, for which more young people regularly apply than there are places available and vice versa. In recent years those disciplines with more applicants than places include biology, psychology, pharmacy, construction, transport, architecture, medicine, veterinary medicine, law and journalism. Too few applicants have in recent years applied for mathematics, physics, polytechnical teaching and similar disciplines. The similarity to the proclaimed shortage of students in mathematically based science subjects in some Western European countries is striking.

3 At the third stage efforts are made to resolve such problems of over- and under-subscription to different disciplines. Fresh vocational guidance discussions take place with students and their parents, to try to shift applicants from overcrowded subject areas to those that are under-

subscribed. Experience in the German Democratic Republic has shown that such renewed counselling usually leads to closer harmony between student choice and manpower needs.

4 Students now submit actual applications for higher education by forwarding the required personal documents. To some extent the applications procedure is interwoven with actual admission. Schools are able to recommend strongly those applicants who receive the citation 'particularly suited for studies'. This procedure guarantees study places to the most able applicants and eases the pressure on selection by universities and colleges. Approximately 30 percent of all applicants are recommended in this way.

5 The fifth stage is the actual admission of applicants to universities and colleges. The numbers admitted are determined by each institution's plan of enrolments. For a high proportion of applicants, admission is determined immediately – those highly recommended by their schools and others with good matriculation marks. For a few disciplines separate admission examinations are arranged. All applicants not admitted to university or college are involved in discussions designed to orient them to vacant places on other courses and to determine their future careers.

In the planning of admissions, universities and colleges are given guidance on the number of graduates they should produce in each discipline. An appropriately larger number of applicants are admitted to the first year of study to make allowance for student wastage.

We have seen earlier how admission to university or college in the German Democratic Republic is closely related to employment opportunities for graduates. Each entrant to higher education has the guarantee that, subject to satisfactory performance in his studies, he will be offered a job upon graduation corresponding very closely to his qualifications. The first step in placing graduates in jobs consists of estimating the numbers expected to qualify in each discipline. They can then be 'steered' to the specific employment areas defined as having the most urgent need for their services. 'The steering of graduates . . . is materially and ideologically stimulated on the basis of the most effective method. Appropriate salary adjustments, recently also more and more measures for the provision of housing, child-care facilities and other benefits in working and living conditions, support planning so that in the end the targets can be attained' (Sachse, 1977).

The first stage in the process takes place two and a half years prior to graduation of the age-cohort concerned, and involves the elaboration by the Ministry of Higher Education of a preliminary balance in which the probable number of graduates available, by discipline and institution, is compared with the corresponding demands of manpower users. At this stage it is possible to identify subject areas where supply and demand are matched, as well as emerging problems of which notice has to be taken. Thus 'the problems and possible imbalances are sorted out and the programme for the placement of graduates is gradually worked out' (Sachse, 1977).

Eighteen months before students sit the state final examination, placement discussions commence. This enables the future graduate to conclude his employment contract a year before graduation and gives employing agencies advance information on the fulfilment of their own manpower plans. An important step towards the actual placement of graduates in employment is the preparation by employers of 'conditions of placement'. This document constitutes the offer made by the employer and contains information concerning the place of work, duties, remuneration, promotion possibilities and any social benefits. These placement conditions form the basis for recruitment. Suitable graduates are selected on the basis of personal discussion between university and college teachers and representatives of employing agencies, and employment contracts are concluded.

There has in the past been no difficulty in finding suitable employment for graduates. In 1971, for example, just over 50 percent of vacancies for university graduates were in fact filled by university graduates. The remainder of vacancies were filled by college graduates, technicians, etc. (Sachse, 1977). Thus, in these circumstances some vacancies for graduates have to be filled with personnel with lower educational qualifications. From 1970 to 1975 the number of graduates in the economy rose by some 50 percent. Some graduates are now being engaged for types of jobs which, owing to earlier shortages, were previously filled by personnel with lower qualifications. This change has caused difficulties in adjusting students' expectations and aspirations to match the new situation. These expectations have naturally been strongly influenced by the graduate employment opportunities of previous years: the filling of graduate level posts by non-graduates has led to some students regarding these positions as of inferior (non-graduate) status. This problem is one also experienced in the market economies of Western Europe.

Guidance, counselling and job placement in Poland

In Poland, as in the German Democratic Republic, 'the basic need for a rational link between manpower policy and educational policy arose from the strategy of full employment' (Kluczynski and Jozefowicz, 1977). The economic strategy of the centrally planned economies of Eastern Europe has as a basic doctrine a management of human resources to ensure full employment. It is not surprising, then, to find that considerable emphasis is put on the placement of graduates in suitable occupations as an integral part of manpower planning policy.

In the past in Poland there have been considerable discrepancies between education plans based on manpower forecasts and the implementation of these plans. The discrepancies can largely be accounted for by the repeated reforms of the educational system. These reforms were in a sense forced upon the authorities by the current needs of the economy and the demand for qualified manpower, or by the inability of the economy to always ensure the full and rational employment of young people.

One characteristic of the Polish situation which appears to contrast with the situation in the German Democratic Republic, is the relatively high proportion of graduates who do not take up employment in the field of their specialism. The long cycle of education, combined sometimes with the lack of early vocational guidance and orientation, as well as occasional errors in planning the targets for the education system, resulted in between 10 and 30 percent of graduates not taking up employment in the occupation for which they had been trained. It should be noted that in Western Europe a figure of over 70 percent of graduates taking up jobs closely related to their academic specialism would be considered remarkably high.

Although the attention which was given in the past to vocational guidance and orientation at the pre-university level is now regarded as inadequate (Kluczynski and Jozefowicz, 1977), considerable attention has been devoted for some time to the placement of university graduates in appropriate employment. The system of job placement was first introduced in Poland in 1950, with little reference to economic plans. Job placement at this time was performed mainly by administrative instruments of employment direction and allocation, assessed on the basis of an inflexible and often inaccurate perception of manpower requirements. This system was abolished in 1956 in favour of an employment service-operated job guidance and clearance system, which was kept in operation until 1963. The present system of the planned employment of graduates was adopted in a Parliament Act of February 1964, and operates within the following terms of reference:

– to determine which graduates should become eligible for employment placement, after first identifying the most important skills needed for set targets in Poland;

- graduates who obtain employment through this placement scheme must stay in their jobs for at least three years;
- graduates will be directed to their first employment by specially appointed representatives of the Labour Ministry who are assigned to individual institutions of higher education.

In the decade 1964 to 1974, just under 300,000 full-time students graduated from universities in Poland. Of these 220,000 graduated in the faculties covered by the Act of 1964. Ninety percent of this group were directed to jobs through the system of planned employment.

While the core components of the current preplanned graduate employment system bear some similarity to the systems in operation in the 1950s and early 1960s (i.e. allocation on the basis of anticipated manpower demand, the identification of crucial areas of job placement, and the obligation on graduates to stay for three years in the job to which they have been directed), the Act of 1964, together with its subsequent amendments, introduced more flexible and liberal procedures for graduate placement.

Three categories of prearranged job placement operate under the conditions of the 1964 Act. These are:

a. the industrial grant programme;

b. starting agreements;

c. employment direction.

The first category of prearranged placement is designed to attract, by means of economic incentives, the best specialists eligible to meet the vacancies of employing agencies. The grants available under the industrial grant programme are on average 20–30 percent higher than the stipends offered by the academic authorities. The regulations provide for certain sanctions to be applied in the event of the agreement being broken by either student or employer. Between 30 and 60 percent of graduates were placed in their first job under this form of sponsorship agreement in individual years of the last decade.

The 'starting agreement' procedure attracts the smallest proportion of graduates. These agreements are usually negotiated towards the end of a student's course of study by students who wish to obtain security against the risk of imbalances between employment opportunities and the number of qualified applicants for a given occupation. Under this procedure too, the employing agency gives financial aid to the student.

Graduates who have not received industrial grants or opted for 'starting agreements' receive 'employment directions' from the representative of the Ministry of Labour assigned to individual higher education institutions. These graduates are free to make their own choice of occupation from among those vacancies registered with their institutions.

Kluczynski and Jozefowicz (1977) identify a number of shortcomings in the present system of job placement. However, they recognize that the system in Poland, while attempting to implement manpower-based plans, allows a considerable margin of autonomy for the behaviour of individuals, educational institutions and employers. It may well be this autonomy that accounts for the main shortcomings which they outline. One problem has already been mentioned – the high proportion of graduates who take up jobs for which they have not been trained, in spite of the job placement schemes. It has also proved difficult to attract and settle specialists in areas of new development, owing to the inadequacy of suitable incentives, particularly in housing amenities. In addition, it is estimated that a significant proportion of the working time of graduates who are correctly placed is inefficiently used in performing tasks that could be delegated to less qualified staff. A further problem, not related to job placement, but which has to be taken notice of in implementing manpower plans, is the high level of student wastage in Polish higher education. It is estimated that dropout from intramural studies exceeds 20 percent of intake, while that from extramural studies exceeds 40 percent.

[. . .]

Guidance, counselling and job placement in Sweden

The relationship between higher education and the manpower needs of society was first studied in Sweden in the 1930s by the Wicksell–Jerneman Commission. Its brief was to investigate the growing difficulties experienced by university graduates in finding jobs in the 'intellectual professions'. In rejecting the notion of a limited intake to higher education tied to manpower forecasts, the Commission recommended better information for future students on labour market prospects, and educational and vocational guidance as methods of easing employment difficulties. This emphasis on social demand moderated by guidance services has remained the essential basis of higher education planning in Sweden since that time.

The National Labour Market Board has offered vocational guidance in upper-secondary schools since the early 1940s. In the early part of the period vocational counsellors visited these schools from time to time and gave students information about the relationship between subject disciplines and the labour market. In the 1950s careers teachers were introduced into the then experimental comprehensive schools, to help pupils make occupational choices. During this period university students were offered vocational guidance in the form of lectures by teachers and counsellors and through various social activities arranged by student organizations.

These rather ad hoc arrangements were systematized in 1964 as a by-product of the parliamentary reform of upper-secondary education. An integrated approach to counselling in the secondary school was then introduced. Counselling was provided that year on the basis of cooperation between the labour market authorities and the school. The school welfare officer was made responsible for the practical coordination of the system, and was given the task of assisting the careers adviser from the labour market authorities in providing vocational orientation and study guidance.

At the beginning of the enrolments explosion in Sweden in the 1960s, the first concerted efforts were made to create a system for counselling and guidance which would reach every student in primary, secondary and higher education, as well as to serve would-be adult students already in employment. By the mid-1970s the implementation of the new arrangements is complete as far as young people are concerned. It is anticipated that the next few years will witness the build-up of similar resources for information and outreach activities for adults in work or staying at home (Bergendal, 1977).

When in the early 1970s higher education graduates began to experience employment difficulties, the National Labour Market Board took a series of measures in an attempt to improve the situation. Within the employment agencies themselves more resources were devoted to a service geared to the needs of new graduates from universities and colleges. This was aimed both at graduates who were experiencing difficulties in finding employment corresponding to their qualifications, and at those whose subject specialism had a tenuous connection with employment. Personnel with specialized knowledge of the graduate labour market were posted to employment agencies in university towns. Although their main tasks were planning and information, there was a conscious effort on the part of the employment agencies to broaden the job horizons of student and graduate applicants towards considering new fields of employment.

One form of aid of which graduates avail themselves if they are unable to find jobs on their own or through the employment agencies is through a system of 'employment training'. In the past decade employment training has played an increasingly important part in Swedish employment policy. The state takes care of the costs of this form of occupational training and provides grants for students on the scheme. The training, which may range from a duration of two months to two years, has three main objectives:

a. to facilitate adjustment of the unemployed to new jobs and to provide individuals who may become unemployed in the near future with new skills;

b. to help groups who have difficulty finding employment, such as the handicapped;

c. to meet the need of the economy for trained manpower, particularly where technological or structural changes necessitate the acquisition of new skills.

Employment training in Sweden has been found to be an effective means of solving specific unemployment problems. Currently more than 2 percent of the labour force is taking such training every year. Among those taking part in employment training schemes are a high proportion of graduates: *Table 8* shows the numbers of graduates from universities and colleges who have undergone employment training since 1969.

Table 8 Number of graduates in employment training in Sweden

1969	1970	1971	1972	1973	1974
750	1100	1400	2200	2500	2500

Where there are no regular job opportunities and when employment training is not possible, measures may be taken to create employment opportunities. In recent years the aim has been to develop relief work projects in order to meet the demands of new categories of unemployed. Under this scheme a considerable number of new graduates have been offered temporary jobs, particularly in the administrative and service sector of the economy. The intention of the scheme is to give meaningful employment to those taking part, taking into account their previous educational and work experience. The scheme also serves the purpose of practice and further training as a preparation for the transfer into normal employment.

It can be seen that Sweden attacks the problems of the transition from full-time education to the labour market in a number of ways. The most comprehensive is the system of vocational counselling and guidance that pervades all levels of education and is soon to be fully extended to adults. In addition, through employment training schemes and temporary employment opportunities serious attempts are made to harmonize policies for the supply of qualified manpower with the available employment opportunities. This is done through the availability of information, training and retraining of graduates and non-graduates alike. In Sweden the use of *numerus clausus* at the entry point to higher education can also effectively limit student numbers in subject areas where employment difficulties are being experienced by graduates.

The role of counselling

'It is the task of the counsellor in schools and universities to help the student to analyse his own situation, his aptitudes, interests and requirements, and to assess his situation in the light of the requirements and of the opportunities offered by different courses of education and different tasks in working life' (Bergendal, 1977).

While this claim is applicable to all the counselling systems surveyed in this chapter, it is evident from the review of experience that some countries take counselling a step further. For instance, it is debatable whether a counsellor should have a directive or non-directive function. Policy-makers in different countries have given different answers to this. Many argue that the counsellor's role is to propose to the individual student a set of alternatives according to his or her ability, choice of studies, interests and so on but not to give advice on which might be best for the student in the light of either his attributes or the needs of the economy. Others maintain that, in order to be effective, it is necessary not only to provide information in a neutral way, but actively to advise, guide and 'orientate' the student with regard to possible alternatives. The debate becomes sharper when counselling attempts to harmonize individual aspirations and the manpower requirements of the economy.

Some planners have expressed the hope that accurate information to students and prospective students will prove to be an adequate method of achieving a reasonable balance between graduate output and the needs of the economy. According to this view, restricted admission to educational institutions could then be phased out since students would act in a rational way. However, it is evident that choices and preferences between various educational options are determined by a combination of rational and more or less irrational factors. In Hungary, grossly oversubscribed departments continue to attract highly qualified school-leavers who stand little chance of gaining admission, while other subject areas could accommodate them. In the German Democratic Republic, prospective students are aware of the relative difficulties in gaining a place in different departments but may still have to be reorientated towards less popular areas at the second stage of the application process. The same overapplication occurs in the *numerus clausus* faculties of the Federal Republic of Germany and The Netherlands. It may be claimed in the market economies concerned that more resources invested in information and guidance could mitigate the situation; but this does not appear altogether likely. There are convincing theoretical arguments to support a pessimistic view of the efficiency of information and guidance as a regulator of the overall relationship between education and the economy. This is so, especially in the market economies that rely primarily on social demand as the basis for the provision of publicly subsidized higher education. Given the lack of overall coordination, prospective students in the market economies who learn of a forecast shortage or oversupply in a particular occupation cannot, as individual decision-makers, anticipate the simultaneous decisions of all the other prospective students who must make similar choices; nor can individual counsellors help them. The centrally planned economies are at least able to coordinate entry to higher education, but it is evident that this does not resolve all difficulties.

The graduates themselves are confronted by a variety of job placement and counselling schemes in the different countries surveyed. These schemes can be regarded as a continuum from, at one extreme, early job placement of students before graduation, coupled with guarantees of full employment; to, at the other extreme, optional counselling and advice facilities if students and graduates wish to avail themselves of the service. [. . .] The actual system in operation will reflect the sociopolitical framework within which the higher education system operates. In spite of this basic constraint, there are few who would argue with Bergendal's (1977) observation on the objectives of counselling and guidance:

> The purpose of educational and vocational orientation and guidance is to give information on educational and occupational opportunities, and to help the individual to make a choice whose realization corresponds to his or her aspirations and potential. Thus guidance has to take into account both the individual's qualifications and wishes, society's foreseeable needs and the restrictions on educational capacity.

References

Bergendal, G. (1977) *Higher Education and Manpower Planning in Sweden*. Geneva/Bucharest, ILO/CEPES.

Freeman, R.B. (1971) *The Market for College-Trained Manpower: A Study in the Economics of Career Choice*. Cambridge (Mass.), Harvard University Press.

Kluczynski, J. and Jozefowicz, A. (1977) *Higher Education and Manpower Planning in Poland*. Geneva/Bucharest, ILO/CEPES.

Sachse, E. (1977) *Higher Education and Manpower Planning in the German Democratic Republic*. Geneva/Bucharest, ILO/CEPES.

CHAPTER 3.5

PAST FAILURE AND THE IMPERATIVE FOR CHANGE*
GERALD FOWLER

A failure to plan

The Robbins Report did one great disservice to the development of higher education in Britain, namely the establishment of the 'Robbins principle' that places should be provided in higher education for all those qualified for and seeking them. As a result much discussion of the future of higher education has been demography-led, especially in official publications. Thus a peaking of the 18-year-old age-group in the early 1980s, followed by a decline in the late 1980s and early 1990s, suggests a series of alternative strategies, one of which is 'tunnelling through the hump', and another is the attraction of new client groups, [. . .] not proposed by government as an end in itself, but rather as a means of utilizing effectively the resources already provided within the system to cope with a larger 18-year-old age-group.

The weakness of basing planning on the Robbins principle, at a time when the age participation rate is failing to increase, is apparent; Britain will remain the Western developed country with the lowest participation rate in higher education apart from Portugal and Ireland for the foreseeable future, and may be passed by them before too long. That may be right, or it may be wrong; the case has to be argued. It may be that there is no connection between educational investment provision for higher education in Britain and the country's poor economic performance. That too is a proposition which remains to be demonstrated, and which, in the light of complaints

* *Agenda for Institutional Change in Higher Education*, edited by L. Wagner. Guildford, SRHE, 1982. © SRHE. Gerald Fowler is Director of North East London Polytechnic, and a former Labour Junior Minister of Education.

about shortages of skilled manpower even at a time of high unemployment, seems implausible.

The Robbins principle always had several inherent weaknesses. First, there was no coherent definition of what counted as higher education, and hence of what qualified a student to partake in it. It is conventional to define higher education courses by their terminal point – taking that to be a point more advanced than GCE A-Level. That tells us precisely nothing about the starting point. [. . .] For degree-level education, there is not the slightest evidence that five passes in the General Certificate of Education, of which two shall be at A-Level, are either a necessary or a sufficient condition of success. Students without this level of qualification, albeit of more mature years, succeed; some students with this level of qualification fail; and in some subjects there appears to be no clear correlation between A-Level grades and the class of final degree. Further, the establishment of this as the basic level of qualification seems to have led to a social downgrading of courses, with a lower entry requirement, but nevertheless at higher educa- tion level. Numbers on Higher Diploma courses have showed even less buoyancy in Britain in the 1970s than those on degree courses; yet in the United States and in Europe these areas of work continue to develop, and it is arguable that we in Britain have a shortage of technicians.

Worse, the maintenance of the Robbins principle has become an article of faith to which the academic community attaches more weight than succes- sive governments. It was tacitly abandoned by government a decade ago, when the 1971 PAR Study of Higher Education stated that the then projections would require a level of 210,000–225,000 under-21s entering higher education in 1981, but that to provide places for 200,000 entrants would not 'wholly deny the principle' (whatever that could conceivably mean). Similarly, the 1975 Public Expenditure White Paper made financial provision for a lower number of students in 1981 than strict observance of the Robbins principle would have suggested. [. . .] The Robbins principle has now been finally abandoned, with cash rather than qualified demand being the sole determinant of the number of places to be provided. [. . .]

The principle was always more observed in the breach than in its mainte- nance, if one looks to the *balance* of provision within higher education. In 1976 a Prime Minister complained that there were 30,000 unfilled places in science and technology. No one ever explained the figure, but if accurate, it reflected governmental policy over the previous decade. [. . .] Planning took place on the 'carrot' principle: if places were provided in particular disciplines, young people would come forward to claim those places. They did not, and in consequence were censured by politicians seeking a scapegoat for their own mistakes. For a long time the expanding teacher education system was the cushion which absorbed the shock of governmental planning errors, taking up students qualified for study in the arts and social sciences for whom there were no places on degree courses. Its decline means that it can no longer be so. Compensation has come in the form of new arts or 'general' degrees in the colleges of higher education formed largely from the old colleges of education, but [. . .] any match between the places available in higher education and the qualified demand is partly an accident.

In this context, planning for the development of higher education in Britain can be seen to have become increasingly schizophrenic. Government consultative documents assume the utilization of spare capacity in further and higher education in exactly those areas where there is little evidence of increasing student demand. On the other hand there is an implicit assumption that the ability to profit from higher education is usually, although not always, to be measured by the level of achievement in an examination set for 16- and 18-year-olds, which is itself designed (and here enters an element of circularity) to permit the successful achievement of a degree in one discipline or a combination of 2–3 disciplines in 3–4 years, with favourable staff:student ratios and (by international standards) intensive teaching. The success of the Open University suggests that this is not a sensible planning assumption.

Also implicit in the planning of higher education in Britain is the belief that it must rest upon the existence of a large number of institutions which are 'autonomous', not only in the sense of freedom from direction by the state, but also in their ability to operate independently of their peer institutions. The universities are the model; the polytechnics and the CHEs have sought to follow it. We have the problem that the individual autonomy of institutions leads to a questioning of their collective autonomy. It is the failure of the institutions to plan their provision collectively which is likely to provoke intervention by the state. [. . .] The irony is that individual autonomy of institutions is a hollow façade, in that in respect of full-time courses, at least, each institution apes its equals or betters. We can detect here the influence of validating bodies, staff from the academic community, academic peer-groups in particular disciplines, and governmental 'arms-length' agencies largely staffed by academics. [. . .]

We thus have a system of higher education which is based upon a principle which is no longer observed, was incomprehensible when first stated, was always denied by governments in their desire to secure an accretion to the stock of qualified scientific and technological manpower, and which runs counter to the principle of the individual autonomy of institutions. That of itself suggests that a new approach may be required.

The fallacy of separate sectors

Successive governments have mistakenly perceived the problem as one of the financing and control of institutions. Hence they have attempted to establish new sectors of higher education, separate from the universities. Yet, it is alleged, these institutions always become mini-universities, in defiance of the intentions of government. The history of the CATs, which did become universities, is the best example of 'academic drift'. They rapidly shed part-time and subdegree work, and in their provision tried to achieve an academic subject balance, which denied their purpose of providing applied and vocational courses. It is in part the growth within them of traditional non-applied studies, perhaps less well done than in some older universities, which led the UGC in 1981 to single out some of them for discriminatorily harsh financial treatment.

The CATs having been received into the bosom of the UGC, the then government went back to the starting point, and set out again along exactly the same road, with the creation of the polytechnics. This time, however, they were to be denied permanently the prospect of university status. Despite this, they too have been charged with 'academic drift'. Worst of all, many of the new CHEs of the 1970s, formed from colleges of education which have little expertise in the physical or applied sciences, have diversified into 'general' higher education [. . .].

This has happened because government has grasped the wrong levers of control. The positive argument for this view is that, whatever the dicta in White Papers about the need for applied studies or 'relevant' work, the actions of government on more detailed technical matters have a precisely opposite orientation. Thus, the Woolwich speech which delineated the polytechnics was made in 1965,* but it was not until a decade later that the law was changed to ensure mandatory grants for HND students. The DES Permanent Secretary of the time argued strongly against this move, on the grounds that to extend the mandatory principle to any course which did not have an entry requirement of two A-Levels was to 'set one's foot upon the top of a slippery slope'. Thus, mandatory awards for DipHE students were

---

* Speech by the Rt. Hon. C.A.R. Crosland at Woolwich Polytechnic on 27 April 1965.

acceptable, although it was already obvious that few DipHE courses would have an applied or vocational bias, but they were not acceptable for HND students, and certainly not for those taking any other form of subdegree vocational qualification. There has been no further extension of the mandatory principle. Similarly, within the public sector, part-time students are converted into full-time equivalents by a formula which downgrades part-time courses. Government expresses an interest in the development of resource-based learning, including distance learning, yet pure distance learning students within the system are non-persons, having no FTE equivalent at all. [. . .] The student qualified to enter a full-time degree course has no incentive to begin his higher education with part-time study, for which he will receive no financial support from public sources, or with a subdegree qualification; it remains impossible, save in a few instances, to carry credit forward from subdegree study at higher education level to a degree course. Even the Open University mysteriously awards only one credit for a HND, normally deemed to be only a year's work short of a degree [. . .].

The negative side of the argument is best illustrated by the weakness of the reasons adduced by Crosland in support of local authority control of the polytechnics, said to be designed to ensure 'social responsiveness'. He suggested that the universities could not meet the rapidly rising demand and need for vocational, professional and industrially based courses of higher education, some of them at below-degree level and some part-time. The argument is clearly valid if he meant that the *existing* universities could not meet that demand. But it is not obvious why 30 institutions, given a charter which precisely specified their objectives, and financed in accordance with those objectives, could not meet them just as well as 30 institutions under the control of local authorities.

Crosland went on to argue that to remove from further education all degree-giving institutions must depress morale in the further education system. Again, it is unclear why morale in a local FE college should be more depressed if the degree-giving institution along the road is a university rather than a polytechnic under the control of the same LEA. [. . .] Nor did Crosland show clearly why 'social control', designed to ensure 'social responsiveness', must mean local authority control.

In this context, Crosland claimed that 'it is further desirable that local government, responsible for the schools and having started and built up so many institutions of higher education, should maintain a reasonable stake in higher education'. This sentence is to me incomprehensible. The responsibility of LEAs for the schools seems to be quite irrelevant, not least because the principal qualification offered by the schools – the GCE – is validated by the universities and not by any public-sector institution. The schools have been the subject of repeated charges that they do not prepare pupils well enough for the demands of industry and commerce – that is, that their work is biased towards theory rather than practice and application. Further, we must ask what is a 'reasonable' stake for the LEAs? That local education authorities should be responsible for higher education courses meeting a purely *local* need (mainly part-time) does indeed seem reasonable. Beyond that, it is impossible to attach any sensible meaning to the word. [. . .] I assume that Crosland's argument was purely political. Some LEAs had been offended by Circular 10/65 on comprehensive secondary education, others had been offended by the transfer of the CATs to direct-grant status in 1962, and others again were about to be offended by the Weaver Report on the government of colleges of education, which weakened direct local authority control of these institutions [. . .]. To remove all regional colleges of further education, and some area colleges, from LEA control would thus have been too much. Further, there existed no national or regional mechanism of control for the new institutions: to create one was more difficult than to leave them with the LEAs.

There thus never was any coherent justification for local control of institutions offering courses serving a regional, national or international need. Initiatives have come from the institutions themselves, not from their LEAs, and LEA control has in general been purely negative – sometimes (but rarely) refusing to give an imprimatur to proposed new course development, or in recent years restricting or reducing the finances of the institution, under pressure from central government. The UGC has been able to encourage developments in universities, and to back them with finance. In so far as anyone has performed this role in the public sector, it has been Her Majesty's Inspectorate. It is no criticism of HMI to point out that very few of them have themselves direct experience of teaching in or administering higher education. Nor do they have access to any blueprint for meeting national manpower requirements which is not available to the institutions themselves.

The central problem lies in the very phrase, 'the public sector'. It suggests that there are sectors with distinct purposes, which are served by distinct methods of funding and control. It is indeed possible to categorize institutions of higher education by their functions. But the division between universities, polytechnics and other colleges of higher education in the

English/Welsh system does not correspond to any such categorization. The government suggests that public-sector higher education should have a 'vocational' bias. There are two weaknesses in this. First, many university courses have a vocational bias (e.g. medicine, law, etc.). Second, vocationalism is in part, like beauty, in the eye of the beholder; whether a course is vocational or not depends upon the use to which the individual student subsequently puts it. If we were to ask which course, historically, had been the vocational preparation for senior administrators in the Civil Service, we should have to answer Greats at Oxford. It is certainly not obvious that, for example, the University of Bath has a less vocational orientation than Bristol Polytechnic. [. . .] Some CHEs, which still have teacher education as their main concern, are heavily vocational; others, which have diversified widely, are among the least vocational institutions within the higher education system.

We must therefore ask whether it makes sense to maintain separate *sectors* of higher education, as opposed to funding a diverse range of institutions, each with its own defined function, with public financial support for the performance of that function. [. . .] That Oxford University, Preston Polytechnic and Bulmershe CHE should not have the same purposes and the same pattern of courses is right and proper. It is not clear that the first should be funded through one mechanism of national control, and the other two, which are quite as different from each other as they are from it, should be funded through another.

We are back to the fundamental question of determining by what mechanism government can ensure that institutions or groups of institutions perform the functions assigned to them by government on the basis of strong evidence, weak evidence or no evidence of national need. This has little to do with the ownership of institutions, or the mechanisms through which public funds are channelled to them. It has a great deal to do with the value accorded by government to particular types of course, particular modes of learning, to part-time as opposed to full-time study, to subdegree as opposed to degree and postgraduate work, to research as opposed to (or as complementary to) teaching, and to credit transfer. It is therefore to these questions that I turn in the next section of this chapter.

Breaking the mould

If any reformed system of higher education is to operate efficiently, as well as in an innovatory manner, then institutions must be trusted adequately to perform the tasks laid upon them by their funding and managing bodies. Funding bodies must base their decisions about what to support and what not to support upon an evaluation of the academic and educational value of existing or proposed activities. There can be no place for a permanent split between funding agencies and validating agencies. At present the UGC decides in what areas each university is, in its view, competent, providing that for which there is a national need; the university is then free to provide it, the shape of the package being in accordance with the academic judgement of its members. In the public sector, by contrast, HMI may suggest the provision of a course, an institution may propose it, the Regional Advisory Council may approve it and so may the DES, and validation may then be refused by the CNAA, or by TEC or BEC or some other external body. The problem is further compounded by the judgement of the professional bodies in respect of 'vocational' courses; it is in their interest to restrict entry to the professions in order to maintain shortages of specific types of highly qualified manpower, and thus salary differentials. It is not in the national interest. Thus a course approved regionally and nationally, and validated by the CNAA, may not be accredited by a body which is accountable to nobody save its own existing membership. Both rational planning and innovation thus become doubly difficult to achieve.

The membership of a national body, for the funding and management of public-sector higher education, whose members are appointed by virtue of their expertise in higher education, or their knowledge of industry, commerce or other sectors of employment must logically be indistinguishable in character from that of the CNAA, as well as overlapping that of the UGC. Its task will be to distribute funds according to its own judgement of national need and institutional capability. It would therefore seem to be a work of supererogation for the CNAA, or other validating bodies, to do its job for it all over again, in respect of the validation of new or revised course proposals which fall within the basic framework established by the validating body in question. One could even have the embarrassment of the same person making different judgements when wearing different hats, through his membership of more than one body. In short, while existing roles may be maintained in respect of the provision of courses designed to meet local needs at what are locally oriented institutions, those institutions falling within the remit of any new national body must become essentially self-validating. [. . .]

Such a system clearly demands that recognized institutions of higher education should collectively determine what credit weighting to attach to each other's offerings, which may be parts of courses as well as whole courses. We return here to the thesis of collective autonomy rather than individual autonomy as the key to change within the system. This seems to me to be a matter for institutions themselves, although it may well be that there will be little movement, not least from the universities, without governmental pressure. The American analogy certainly suggests that institutions should collectively organize their own credit transfer arrangements, rather than look to some public body. [. . .] Once such a system were established, there would be no good reason why any institution offering courses at higher education level, even if purely on a part-time basis to a local clientele, should not join the credit transfer consortium. [. . .]

[. . .] In Britain such proposals are regarded as dangerously innovatory. That is because of the view, normally unstated but almost universally held in Britain, that it is the single unified course which is the keystone of higher education. The autonomy of the course is more important than the autonomy of the institution.

This doctrine clearly has more than one root. One is the belief that higher education is an activity undertaken in youth, and designed in some sense to qualify the partaker for a specific place in employment and life. It must therefore beam in on a narrow focus, with each element of the course a linear extension of what has gone before. Indeed, the same is true of courses which lead to qualification for entry to higher education, which are perceived as preparatory to degree courses. The *General* Certificate of Education is nothing of the kind. To my knowledge, no credit is given for expertise in plumbing, or in electrical maintenance. Students who wish to work in these areas should take CGLI or TEC courses – their qualifications then going unrecognized by most universities. Yet there is no evidence whatsoever that a student who has 'majored' in English literature at school, and has studied as a subsidiary plumbing and electrical maintenance, would be a worse student of English literature at degree level than one whose subsidiary work was in history or in French. He might incidentally be a better householder, husband and citizen, but those are questions which we normally disregard in education.

Another root of the dominance of the coherent single-subject course is the belief that the structure of academic disciplines reflects the 'real' world. This view has been widely questioned in recent years. The only impeccable defence of the traditional single-subject Honours degree is that it has no vocational value, but is a training of the mind through exercise in the intricacies of a single academic discipline. This is of course a denial of the vocational relevance of any course. Yet the demands of mature students reveal that vocational relevance must be different for each individual – the principal manifestation of this phenomenon being degrees by independent study. The areas of study chosen by mature students in their final year of work for such a degree normally reflect their work experience hitherto, and their expectation of the demands of work thereafter. The government now accepts that mature continuing education students may require a different type of course and a different mode of teaching from the conventional undergraduate, and no one any longer questions the validity of the Open University credit-based degree. The pattern of 18-year-old teaching remains, however, essentially unchanged.

A further root of the difficulty lies in the belief that the three-year Honours degree is the 'normal' mode of higher education, although peculiar to the United Kingdom and not even to all parts of that (granted the Scottish system). Institutions offering two-year qualifications are common in other countries. Four-year systems of two + two are implemented in other countries. In Britain, an attempt to introduce a general two-year course of higher education (as opposed to the vocational HND) was the DipHE. It was determined that it should have the same entry requirement as that of a degree course, and it was thus killed stone-dead, except as a dropout course for those who could not succeed on a degree whatever their initial qualifications, or in institutions which manifestly 'misused' the new course and abused the DES-determined rule. Further, the reorganization of the colleges of education in Britain into CHEs was carried through on the principle that they should become mini-universities, offering the same range of courses without the same range of academic expertise. They were the models of what might have been two-year institutions, and most of them should become so, within a system which through credit transfer permits the progression of their students to other institutions and higher qualifications.

How do we effect this change? This is a serious question, since it is not obvious that either HMI (with most of their experience outside higher education) or administrators within the DES (normally with no experience whatsoever of teaching in or administering higher education) could exercise informed judgement. Decision must therefore be left to an appointed body, largely composed of experts in the field. It cannot, however, sensibly be left to two separate bodies – the UGC and a new national body for public-sector higher education. In any event, initiative must come largely from the institutions themselves. There seems no good reason why a single national body should not invite proposals from all institutions as to their own future, with a verdict given upon them within a three-year period. Equally, it is hard to see why it should not offer to institutions the option of running two-year courses with a lower entry qualification than that currently demanded for degree courses, although if this were to be done sensibly it would demand a reform of 16–19 education. Nor is there a convincing argument why proposed schemes should not include the merger of existing institutions, or the establishment of consortia formed from several existing institutions, or collaboration between institutions, with some serving as 'feeder' colleges to others. The alternative, if traditional patterns persist, must be the closure of colleges; to share a declining number of students among the same number of competing institutions can make neither economic nor academic sense. [. . .]

In short, it seems to me desirable that we should move to a pattern of two- and three-year institutions, three- and four-year institutions and four-year-plus institutions, on a principle of voluntarism, each institution pro- posing its own role, with a single national body ratifying that role and providing appropriate finance.

Within that system there can be no financial discrimination between types of institution, except as is appropriate to the expense of varying activities. At present such discrimination occurs not only between univer- sities and other institutions, in respect of background support for research, but also between departments within institutions (the 'level' of work) and between individual members of staff. Within the present system reward is not directly related to the perceptions of utility which the organs of govern- ment have, judging by their stated priorities, less than coherent though these may be. In the end it is they and the public they represent who pay the piper. This is the hub of all the problems facing higher education in the 1980s. It is of course about value for money. But it is also about money for changing social values, and their embodiment in institutional activities. Only a varied, flexible and perhaps constantly changing pattern of institu- tions, and of educational enterprises within them, can guarantee continued and ungrudging financial support.

The validity of this argument is clearest if we look at the relationship between course patterns and their varying entrance requirements, and institutional structures and the grading of staff within institutions. Here the universities are liberated, in the proper sense of the word. But in the public sector a department which concentrates upon part-time and subdegree work has less opportunities for promotion, whatever the excellence of its staff, than one whose teaching record is less than good but which conducts a substantial amount of postgraduate work. If it be national policy that certain subdegree courses should run in the national interest (the HC or HD), then it cannot make sense that those teaching them should be paid less than those teaching postgraduate students, merely by virtue of the 'level' of work. The national interest is indivisible. It is time that the higher education system came to terms with this.

The national interest and perceptions of it change from time to time. New arrangements for the funding of higher education must therefore avoid the danger that the system might take on a new shape, but then ossify in it. [. . .] This danger may be avoided if there is, and is expected to be, a continuing dialogue between individual institutions and the national body (or bodies). It is not steady evolution which is the enemy of excellence in higher education, but the imposition from above of half-planned but far-reaching change at irregular intervals. While the academic grass is not always greener on the other side of the Atlantic, the American system of higher education does have the virtue that some part of it is always in a state of Heraclitan flux, responding to new need and demand. Contrast Europe: the French post-1968 'reforms', the German attempts to create comprehensive universities and even the Swedish reforms of the last decade all suggest that an imposed once-for-all change of direction brings in its wake unforeseen difficulties and undesired consequences, as well as predictable resentment. In America, evolution comes largely, though not wholly, in response to 'market forces'. In Britain, the dominance of government as the source of finance means that steady change can only be achieved if there is constant dialogue between the centre and the periphery, as well as between institutions and their potential clients. This cannot eliminate problems, but at least it can ease their handling.

Change is difficult: revolution impossible

Lest this chapter appear starry-eyed, I must summarize briefly the obstacles to the reform of our system of higher education.

1 Central government has a poor record of imposing change on the system, except either by addition to it (the creation of the polytechnics, etc.), or where it or its agencies or local government is/are the sole employer (the foundation of new medical schools, the contraction of teacher education), or where it has provided a positive financial incentive to change.

2 The internal politics of institutions, where power normally resides with elites based on existing structures, inhibit change.

3 The system of academic tenure and the absence of any comprehensive exchange/retraining facilities, stemming from the independence (autonomy) of each institution of higher education, frustrate the redeployment of staff [. . .].

4 The diffusion of power between several levels of control in the British higher education system has a conservative effect, because of the tension between the several organs of control. The best instance of this problem in recent years is the failure to resolve the problem of the control and funding of public-sector higher education [. . .].

5 The links of the academic community, and especially of the universities, with Whitehall and the political parties also favour conservatism, although the higher education lobby is now weak by comparison with the 1960s.

6 'Academic drift' blunts the edge of innovatory schemes [. . .].

7 Economic recession and the tight control of public expenditure restrict the introduction of innovatory schemes which are initially expensive [. . .].

8 The autonomy of individual institutions and the autonomy of the teacher (sometimes called 'academic freedom') also inhibit innovation – such as the spread of credit transfer, the supplementation of examinations by student transcripts, or the collective development and use of resource-based learning materials, and hence both the optimization of resource use throughout the system and a shift in the age-pattern of students in favour of adults. Again, collective or collaborative autonomy (the freedom of institutions and of those teaching within them from direction by the state) may seem more important than individual autonomy, but that is not the tradition of the British system.

The need for systemic change

The reform of higher education is impossible without a reform of the educational system as a whole. Thus, attempts to extend the participation of under-represented client groups in higher education raise fundamental questions about the relationship of higher education institutions to the rest of the educational system (entry requirements, selection mechanisms, and the pattern of examinations/assessment/credit), and the financing of school, further and higher education institutions (funding cannot be divorced from control, nor the character of institutions from client demand, in a system where the client provides any substantial part of institutional finance). It is not the purpose of this chapter to discuss these questions. Nevertheless, proposals for changes in the system, in the character of institutions, or in the pattern of courses cannot be divorced from them. The reform of higher education made little progress in the 1970s precisely because no one envisaged the need for systemic change. In the 1980s reform must be comprehensive if it is to be reform at all.

CHAPTER 3.6

SYSTEM, DIVERSITY AND CHAOS*
HAROLD SILVER

In times of growth or even vague optimism the extension of the frontiers of higher education looked like increased diversity or flexibility. Not to everyone, of course, since the new, the enlarged, the wider definition of what constituted higher education also looked like a threat to the old, the established. That conflict has been historically close to the centre of decision-making processes in and for higher education. What to do about the new 'university colleges' in the late nineteenth century? How to handle the higher aspirations of the technical or art college? Where to situate the increasingly higher status forms of training – of teachers, for example, or social workers? Through what channels to finance and control the institutions invented or promoted to educate the increased numbers of students resulting from pressures for more manpower or democracy? Questions like this have surfaced internationally [. . .].

All British discussions of what constitutes a higher education have had to confront the traditions of Oxbridge – announcing established criteria of what constitutes good learning, standards, academic respectability. Traditions elsewhere have adapted, resisted, but at least taken notice. British discussion has had to reconcile Oxbridge traditions with others – the different assumptions and style of the Scottish universities, of London and the provincial universities, of the 1960s new wave, of the different demands and controlling influences of new professional groups and institutions – in industry, technology, commerce, the public and social services.

The result has been mounting complexity [. . .]. The complexity has

---

* *Times Higher Educational Supplement*, 15 October 1982. Dr. Harold Silver is Principal of Bulmershe College, Reading.

increasingly become one of practices and ideologies of control as well as one of institutional difference. A higher education which includes colleges built on nineteenth- and twentieth-century traditions of technology or training for school teaching, management or the caring professions, alongside ones with medieval or nineteenth-century roots in European processes, has offered a ground on which multiple battles take place. The battle for definition – who belongs to the inner or outer clubs of higher education, the mainstream or the periphery, with their confused rules about what constitutes a liberal or a vocational education? The battle for resources – for students, for status, for prestige. And the battle for control. The different historical routes to acceptance in higher education have left institutions and their controllers or paymasters subject to endless warfare about mastery. The wars looked more like after-dinner games as long as there was reasonable hope of increased resources, and therefore of constantly renegotiated ceasefires. New, partial, sector-specific machineries and agencies were created or adapted at different times: the University Grants Committee, Regional Advisory Councils and the National Advisory Body (NAB). [. . .] National committees and commissions proposed and altered the pattern of technological, teacher, art and university education. Shapes of control were modified and solidified accordingly. The ideologies of university and 'maintained sector' drew the binary line between historically different forms of finance and control, as well as between vaguely and inaccurately defined differences of curriculum and purpose.

Increasingly in the late 1970s and early 1980s, diversity was seen to be chaos, not differences amongst institutions so much as confusion about and amongst the battalions of decision-makers, real and would-be. The lines of battle were in one sense characteristically British – a search for a remodelled machinery of control or decision-making (primarily in the 'maintained' sector) which avoided the excesses of centralization (we have been avoiding those since we first heard of Prussia and some other parts of Europe) and the anarchy of the market-place (which we have been avoiding since the Americans discovered it). [. . .] The lines of battle were in another sense international. Economic recession and declining birthrates revealed tensions everywhere as only recently created universities in Denmark or Australia saw themselves threatened with extinction; as prestigious private colleges in America faced bankruptcy; as Germany and Britain took decisions pointing towards amalgamations and closures. Above all, what Britain shared with countries around the world was the loss of the expansive framework within which ceasefires had been negotiable. The United States, for example, was faced with the new dilemma of a higher education of the most diverse kind, priding itself on its competitive dependence on the market-place, but suddenly revealed as having become massively more dependent on federal and state funding, and subject to intricate regulation, during the years of expansion. The consequences suddenly looked different in conditions of contraction and uncertainty. Increased federal regulation of many kinds, national pressures for a more responsive or accountable system, demands for greater public or governmental influence or control over the distribution of resources, and therefore over the shape and balance of the curriculum, sent profound shudders through the whole system. [. . .] The rhetoric remained the need for flexibility, the preservation of diversity, the capacity to respond sensitively to local and national, industrial and technological, community and social, needs and changes. What Britain shared in the early 1980s with America and Australia was conservative governments which, ideologically committed to decentralization, to getting government off the backs of the people, found themselves more and more managing centralized decision-making in order to achieve reduced scale and expenditure.

In Britain, the need to produce new management for the system aroused old enmities. The universities, the polytechnics, the colleges and institutes of higher education defended themselves by silent suspicion and competition for reduced resources, against cuts and redundancies, even for survival. The most vocal activity was the declaration of who was being worst treated. Attempts to find a new national body to plan or supervise or coordinate or control (the difference between the verbs was of fundamental importance) public or maintained or local authority higher education provoked conflicts between local authorities and central government, and the definition of frontiers aroused hostilities between the 1960s-designated polytechnics and the 1970s-designated colleges and institutes of higher education. [. . .] Local authorities were largely reluctant to give up their traditional control. Government and the DES were reluctant to abandon the opportunity to plan nationally. The universities were reluctant to join in the planning of new national or regional controlling or coordinating machineries for all or some of their activities, and thereby lose all or part of their traditional autonomy. Colleges and polytechnics could not agree (and did not consult) about their preference for the interminable uncertainties of shifts in local authority control and policy and often irrational decisions, or the certainties of government central planning and rational surgery and execution. [. . .] Centralized UGC decisions about finance and centralized DES decisions about teacher training were not necessarily more rational than the local varieties.

Who, then, was left competing for a share in decision-making and higher education shaping? Ministers had assumed a more interventionist role than ever before. The DES had assumed greater powers for directing the affairs of higher education – directly for the voluntary colleges, and through the UGC for the universities – both of which had lost the protective covering of autonomy they had enjoyed for over 60 years. Responsibility for the maintained colleges, institutes and polytechnics lay with the local authorities, exercised through governing bodies, and attempts to develop a national machinery had zigzagged inconclusively until the creation (temporarily, it was alleged) of the NAB, sitting uncertainly between the local education authority, DES and the government, and uncertain of the direction of its efforts and future powers. Standing on and across various frontiers was the Council for National Academic Awards, academic guardian of the polytechnics and sharing that function with some universities in the case of the colleges and institutes of higher education. Roles were being learned or rewritten, by the NAB, local authority politicians and officers, national bodies such as the Association of County Councils, interest groups and representative bodies like the Standing Conference of Principals and Directors of Colleges and Institutes of Higher Education or the Committee of Directors of Polytechnics.

New roles were being thrust on the institutions themselves. Unpopular and unpleasant decisions were in Britain, as elsewhere, recasting the power balances within institutions, overturning important principles established in the long-gone days of the 1960s and 1970s. Staff willing to be elected to share in planning expansion were less willing to declare one another redundant. The excision of courses and departments could be a focus of student protest, but not easily of staff and student codecision with administration. Diffused and unhappy discussion about reduced resources, redundancy terms, course provision, rationalization, became inevitably paralleled by the need for a stronger central, administrative hold on decisions, and a weakening in practice of democratic bodies. [. . .] Alliances, enmities, suspicions were seen to be fluid, often beyond serious control, and crucial.

For reasons only partly connected with these complexities, plans began to be advanced for reviewing and remodelling the structure and control of higher education. The creation of the NAB for one sector, and the more exposed role of the UGC for another, have led to more than conversations about national and regional coordination. Political parties with uncompleted past agendas and future elections in mind, have begun to bid for the policy vacuum [. . .]. In searching for the principles on which to base future approaches to access, to teaching and learning, to student recruitment to the relationship of higher education to the economy, Leverhulme-sponsored seminars and others have advanced to the gates of discussion about management and control, about the future of the binary distinction, about the future involvement of local authorities, but they have not been able to take bold steps beyond. There are many reasons for reticence, but two are perhaps most important.

The first is financial. For local authorities the balance of gain and loss in one or another national solution is primarily and inevitably financial, as long as economic forecasts are as gloomy as they are. Local authority thinking about institutions [. . .] can be overwhelmingly dominated by financial calculations. The long-term calculations are, however, extraordinarily difficult to make [. . .]. In addition, finance has to be coupled with power and prestige, with relative considerations of many kinds. In the search for national solutions the local authorities have, therefore, a better record for avoiding or preventing solutions than for proposing and encouraging them.

Local authorities, with institutions on their hands vastly changed from the technical colleges and teacher training colleges or whatever else they were [. . .] have to decide whether they wish to remain controllers, and, in kaleidoscopic economics, what kind of control, or co-control, they are prepared to accept. They are having to count costs, weigh local government powers and balance them in terms of decisions about colleges – decisions which have become increasingly complex and elusive, and which tail off into discussions about the relative powers of the NAB, the UGC, the DES.

The second reason for reticence is the massive uncertainty of the institutions themselves. Where to run for cover? When the government, through the UGC, is on the attack, is it best to run towards the polytechnics, themselves under the same threat, through different channels, or away from them? When maintained-sector finance is being cut through the mechanism of the 'pool', should polytechnics, under the same threat as the colleges and institutions of higher education, run towards or away from them? [. . .] When is the maintaining local authority a bulwark against damaging decisions by the DES and when is national reason or mystification an obstacle to local eccentricity? There is no answer to such questions, [. . .] and there is no rational basis of choice. All masters are suspect. Yet things cannot stay as they are. The outcome of present fragmentation may yet be seen by reluctant partners to be maximum national damage, maximum local eccentricity, maximum institutional decline. [. . .]

The future of higher education has still to be discussed at many levels, [. . .] diverse access to more diverse higher education, satisfying more diverse needs; sensitivity to the needs of its supportive and expectant society; flexible structures which enable the various constituencies inside and outside institutions to play a meaningful part in debate. Argument will continue about courses and curricula, teaching and research, participation rates and standards, the degree package and continuing education . . . but issues of control remain pressing. The solution of some American commentators for their situation, maximum decentralization, maximum return to the market-place, is neither feasible nor desirable in Britain. Such a move, in American terms, means reaching for flexibility especially through the survival value of high-prestige private colleges and universities. In Britain it would mean, if anything, intense and irrational competition for the same resources within different arms of the same publicly funded system.

The way ahead in the British situation lies in systematizing the system. Regional and national coordination of all the disparate parts may be more palatable in the immediate future than total unification of the present binary system. Osmosis through the UGC and the NAB may become feasible and acceptable. [. . .] Whatever the solution, it has needs to serve and dangers to avoid and avert. For the institutions, their staffs and students, their administrators, and governing bodies and councils, a crucial need is the systematization of dialogue, the establishment of a forum or forums within which friends and foes can be adequately identified. The worst chaos is that in which alliances can be based neither on firm evidence nor on perceptions of the real future shape of educational politics. If there is to be genuine flexibility and responsiveness, capacity for change and negotiation to permit it, the possibility of changing sides as well as ground or direction becomes important. The isolated institution is likely to become more isolated, more vulnerable, more inflexible. [. . .] The present chaos does not permit realignments, and in fact prevents them. The universities, with their institution–UGC model, have given priority to the preservation of their autonomous purity, and have not escaped significant damage to their institutions and their principles. The polytechnics, colleges and institutes of higher education, fighting for their elusive definitions and space in the system, have dithered between the local authorities and models of national finance and control, dreams of self-governing charters and determination to be different, and have been no less damaged.

In the way of decent dialogue and negotiation, therefore, lie traditional statuses, nice financial calculations, the politics of local and national power,

and institutional prides and jealousies. The continued divisions and reluc-
tances mean continued chaos within which solutions can be increasingly
imposed. It is this chaos which, in the British situation, means conformity
and stagnation. To systematize the system means to promote decent debate,
real negotiation, and alliances based not on self-protecting fears, but negotiated action [. . .]. We may never have the right masters, or allies, or
solutions. But without a national system that deserves the name, none of us
– in any part of the present scatter of systems – can put up a decent fight, or
look forward to anything but futures more and more embattled, isolated
and conformist.

CHAPTER 3.7

COMPREHENSIVES AND COLLEGES*
WILLIAM REID AND JANE FILBY

[. . .] The failure in the post-Crowther† period to move towards more flexible curricular patterns, coupled with the broadening of the intake to sixth forms, meant that the costs of 16–19 provision escalated rapidly. This provided an economic impetus towards a style of sixth-form organization which had, on other grounds, already been implemented in some areas – the sixth-form college.

The first serious proposal for a sixth-form college had been put forward in Croydon in 1954 and had raised a storm of protest because it struck at one of the basic assumptions of the sixth-form ideology – that sixth-formers should stand in an authority relationship to younger pupils. This had been central to the original Arnoldian conception and remained an article of faith for many heads and teachers, as well as for a wider public.[1] The sixth-form college also implied an extension of the mixed sixth form, which many were quick to resist, and carried an implication that the notion of the 'continuous course' from 11–18 was a mere façade, since a break of institution at 16 was held to be tolerable, if not positively beneficial. All of these widely publicized objections, which made their appearance in letters to the press and statements from teacher associations, related to those moral qualities which had, from the outset, characterized the sixth form. [. . .]

[. . . However,] because of the problems posed by the persistence of the

* *The Sixth: An Essay in Education and Democracy*. Lewes, The Falmer Press, 1982, pp. 179–180, 184–197. Jane Filby is an administrative assistant at the University of Aston Management Centre. Dr Reid is a senior lecturer in the Faculty of Education, University of Birmingham.
† The Crowther Report – Central Advisory Council for Education (England) (1959) *15 to 18*. London, HMSO.

traditional A-Level curriculum, the idea of colleges did have strong economic attractions [. . .]. They allowed the scarce resources of books and equipment needed for advanced teaching to be concentrated on one site instead of being scattered over several; and, if the colleges were purpose-built, teaching spaces could be rationalized to allow for a combination of small and large groups which was impossible in most secondary schools. But more compelling from the point of view of local authorities and rate-payers were the economic advantages which related to the major cost of a labour-intensive system of education – staffing. [. . .] In spite of the expansion in sixth-form numbers, the persistence of the curriculum model endorsed by Crowther meant that economies of scale were slight as long as sixth forms remained as part of the 11–18 secondary school. As groups in the more popular subjects grew larger in the grammar schools, this benefit to staffing costs was offset by the introduction of new subjects (economics, Russian, modern maths), the decline of subjects which were dropping out of favour (Greek, Latin), and the arrival of new and underpopulated sixth forms in comprehensive schools. Thus, national figures for 1978–1979 reveal that just over half the secondary schools with sixth forms failed to enrol more than 100 students in them, and that the average group size for sixth-form classes in comprehensive schools was still below 10 (DES, 1980, Table 10).

Even the most impervious ideology has difficulty sustaining itself in the face of figures like these and, from the beginning of the 1970s, the trickle of schemes for sixth-form colleges, which had begun in the mid-1960s with Luton and Mexborough, became a flood. They were of all types. Some involved the use of existing buildings and some were set up in new premises. Some concentrated on traditional A-Level courses, some aimed at a wider spectrum of students. A few, generally referred to as 'tertiary colleges', combined sixth-form provision with facilities for taking further education courses. By 1972, 14 colleges had been opened and a further 43 were planned. At this stage the schemes were confined to areas which had not reorganized their secondary provision and opted for colleges as part of a plan for 'going comprehensive'. The peak of this phase was reached in 1974, when 25 colleges were opened, and by 1977 the total number had passed 100, enrolling over 50,000 students. In most of the authorities concerned, there was resistance to the introduction of the break at age 16 based on claims that it was being done for 'merely economic' reasons and not on good educational grounds. But these reactions became progressively more muted as the realization grew that comprehensives of the size needed to sustain viable, let alone economic, sixth forms presented their own problems of curriculum and organization for teachers, especially where they could be created only by the use of split sites. Moreover, such large schools were difficult to justify in terms of educational advantage to students. In fact, ideological antipathy towards colleges could hardly fail to be associated with a distaste for large comprehensives since they were just as remote from the traditional image of the 'community of scholars'. As long as the choice had been, or had seemed to be, between the grammar school sixth and the college, it had not been a choice between evils. But by the early 1970s there were enough practical examples around for it to be plain what the real alternatives were – colleges as against comprehensives of 1000–2000 students – and some who would have been bitterly opposed to colleges a few years before were now not so sure, especially if, as was often the case, the plan involved forming the college out of an existing grammar school. Others, however, softened their attitudes to comprehensives as it became apparent that these might be the only hope for the preservation of a sixth form integrated into the secondary school.

In terms of the character of sixth-form education as it was practically exemplified, the period from 1965 to 1975 represented a revolution, in which the colleges were of even greater significance than the comprehensives – though, as we have seen, the one cannot be understood without the other. But the revolution was an even greater one in terms of its general impact on the thinking of the public, the professions and the politicians about 16–19 education. Ideologies are undermined not by theories, but by realities. By the mid-1970s real manifestations of alternative ways of organizing the education of sixth-formers were abundant, and significant not just for what they were, but also for what they implied about possible future developments. Sixth forms in comprehensive schools represented a new *species* rather than a new *genus*: some were growing up where no sixth form had existed before and, much as the incipient sixths of new grammar schools after 1902, could be seen as evolving towards the archetypal form; others took over an unbroken tradition from an established grammar school sixth. In most cases, rivalry with neighbouring schools ensured that the tendency was to preserve the traditional trappings of captains, prefects and uniforms. Everywhere the comprehensive sixth was an organic part of the whole secondary school. Typically, it was small and of low prestige compared to the sixths of the grammar and public schools and, locked into the traditional and unyielding pattern of the academic curriculum, there was no road it could follow which would take it very far from the path of orthodoxy.

The colleges were a different matter altogether. Even where they grew out of the grammar schools and were guided by heads and teachers whose sympathies were more with the old than the new, the possibilities for change were potent.

Shorn of the lower school, college sixth-formers became democratized; the symbols of leadership and status lost their meaning. Arguments that dress and conduct must be regulated 'to set an example' to the less mature students became irrelevant. Evolution towards a less hierarchical and more relaxed kind of society was inevitable, especially since all but one of the 100 colleges open by 1977 were mixed. But, with heads and teachers who shared Wearing King's positive vision of what the college could offer to its students, quite bold courses could be steered.* The colleges were usually large and without competition in their immediate area. They could set fashion rather than follow it. In the case of Solihull College, for example, which was set up in 1974 in an area where there had been very strong support for the traditional grammar schools, uniform was abolished, students were permitted to be off the premises when they were not scheduled for teaching and important areas of decision-making on policy and finance were handed over to them. The fact that the building was a new one also permitted some innovation in teaching method through the use of tutorial suites and large lecture theatres. Colleges like this moved rapidly and purposefully towards a realization of King's vision:

> This then is the concept: a collegiate institution taking pupils who have passed the fifth-form stage, at whatever age, and providing for them in a more adult atmosphere than is possible in a school; not tied to the school day; not using the prefectorial and disciplinary methods of a school; and taking the pupils through a professionally planned syllabus, giving them responsibility not for the conduct of their juniors but for their own educational advance; with individual time-tables and the tutorial method as well as lectures and seminars superseding the idea of a class or form. (King, 1968, p. 69.)

Beyond that, the colleges posed in a very clear way the question of the relationship between sixth forms and the technical and vocational courses offered in colleges of further education. From the beginning of the sixth-form college movement there were those who saw the institution of a break at 16 as an opportunity to bridge over the division between the 'academic' students and the student looking forward to qualifying for entry to a specific

---

* *Editors' footnote*: Wearing King, Chief Education Officer of Croydon, instigated the 1954 Croydon sixth-form college scheme mentioned earlier.

trade. In thinly populated areas there was an extra incentive to look into such possibilities, and as early as 1970, the first tertiary college combining sixth-form and FE provision was set up in Exeter. In the following years the idea was copied in other areas, and in some which had originally stuck to a traditional definition of the sixth-form student the attraction of the more broadly defined college began to assert itself.

From the mid-1970s, colleges were numerous, popular and visibly successful. Wearing King's claim that, where A-Level success was concerned, more was better seemed to be amply borne out. Parents who had been disconcerted by the move away from the conventional apparatus of the grammar school sixth were considerably mollified when they found that the new institutions were delivering academic success even more predictably than the old regime had. And gloomy forecasts that the break of school at 16 would deter students from staying in full-time education were nowhere confirmed in practice. For every student who could not face an unfamiliar sixth, there was at least one more who welcomed the chance of a fresh start in a college where he or she brought no reputation other than public examination results.[2]

Thus, a new *genus* was established which shared some characteristics of the old, but was also interestingly different. As far as the basic curriculum was concerned, the colleges, like all other sixth forms, were constrained by the unvarying diet of advanced specialist work enforced just as surely by inaction on the part of the central authority as it would have been if established by decree. To some extent they could experiment with new teaching methods though, since the majority of establishments had inherited existing buildings, the scope for this was limited. Their high levels of enrolment – the average of 97 colleges in 1979–1980 was 501 (DES, 1980; Table 4) – enabled them, if they wished, to go further than most schools could in providing complementary or 'general studies' courses. But most colleges concentrated on the traditional A-Level courses, which were wanted on average by about 80 percent of their clientele, and taught them in the time-honoured way – through factual, transmission teaching which, much as it might be deplored by educational theorists, was not in the least resented by the majority of the students.[3] In their successful teaching of the A-Level curriculum, the colleges preserved and embodied Crowther's first three 'marks of a sixth form' – '(A) close link with the university', 'subject-mindedness' and 'independent work'. Solihull College, for example, in 1975–1977 enrolled all of its students in A-Level courses, achieved pass rates of over 80 percent in most subjects (against a national average of about 70 percent), sent about 60 percent of its leavers on to higher educa-tion, and made special efforts to foster private study. This, one might have thought, would have met with near universal approval – from those who were inclined against sixth-form colleges as well as those who naturally favoured them. In fact, many people found it worrying. For the first time, the platonic chain of approximations to the ideal sixth form was broken. The conception had been born in the public schools, passed on to the reviving grammar schools and transmitted to the nascent LEA secondary schools. In the mid-1960s this hierarchy still persisted: if you wanted to know what a sixth form *should* be like you looked to the leading independent schools; the grammar schools struggled to follow them, and the comprehen-sives struggled to draw themselves after the grammar schools. All was in its proper place. Colleges like Solihuli challenged the natural order; not only were they bidding to become as academically successful as the independent schools, they were actually attracting students away from them. Boys who would not have contemplated leaving Solihull School for a maintained grammar school were finding in the sixth-form college a real and preferable alternative to their public-school sixth. This was deeply disturbing to anyone with an ideological commitment to the idea of the sixth form. Worse, however, was the colleges' neglect of 'marks' four and five – intellectual discipleship and social responsibility.

In what way, it might be wondered, were the colleges transgressing in terms of 'intellectual discipleship'? Surely, the preservation of the A-Level curriculum guaranteed that there would continue to be a close relationship between teacher and taught? The groups were, from the point of view of both economy and good teaching, satisfyingly larger than those found in comprehensive schools which traditionalists attacked for lacking 'the stimulus that comes from competition', but the average size was still only 11 or 12 (DES, 1980, Table 10). Moreover, the colleges were attractive pre-cisely to those teachers who were well qualified in and committed to their subjects. What, then, was the difficulty? Crowther discusses discipleship only in terms of time spent in the sixth – though the Report refers to 'frequent contact between a teacher and a small group of pupils over several years'. But separation of the sixth from the lower school affects the teacher–student relationship in a quite fundamental way. To understand how this comes about, it is necessary to consider the notion of 'sponsorship'.

Sociologists have distinguished two types of elite linked to educational systems: 'sponsored' and 'contest'.[4] Schooling aimed at producing a 'con-test' elite sets out to retain as many students as possible in a common system of education up to a final point at which an objective criterion of achievement is applied to determine who is qualified for entry to the elite and who is not. The 'sponsored' elite model depends on the idea that there is no need to operate a common system because elite qualities are identifiable when children are quite young. What is required is a system involving parallel types of schooling and continuous selection. In principle, this kind of education could also make use of objective tests of achievement but, since the difference between the systems is one of philosophy as well as of practice, something else is added to or substituted for examination: a support system for pupils identified as 'elite material'. This ensures that the arbitrary nature of early selection is disguised, and that the system is one of self-fulfilling prophecy rather than trial and error.

These descriptions are of 'ideal types' which nowhere exist; different education systems approximate to them more or less. The traditional sixth form approaches the 'sponsorship' model. [. . .]

Viewed in one way, the 'discipleship' of the sixth form marked a weaning-away from teacher dependence and towards self-directed learning; viewed in another, it was a process which ensured that the self-direction occurred within approved limits and that the sixth-former saw his status as something collectively established and protected (comparisons could be made with initiation into professions). This, of course, was the vision of sponsorship rather than the reality. Not every sixth-form teacher saw his role in this way, or had his teaching organized in a way to make it possible. Often they might have little contact with the lower school. But ideologues do not ask whether what they believe to exist actually does exist; they look for reassurance that nothing in the prevailing circumstances rules out the possibility of it being the case. Where the sixth-form college was concerned, it was plain that the teachers *could not* have known their 'disciples' before they entered the sixth; moreover, the lack of any previous contact tending to set up the dependency relationship would inevitably mean that teachers and students would meet on a level of greater equality than would be the case in the school. Thus the duality of status of the sixth-former as independent learner *and* pupil, to which so much importance was attached, would be broken down. At root, what was involved here was the same concern as was raised by the colleges' most obvious and serious departure from the conventional 'marks' – social responsibility. In the conventional ideology, this was narrowly defined as the exercise of authority over younger children. Plainly, no argument could be made that social responsibility defined in this way was being exercised by college sixth-formers. Indeed, it was an article of faith among their supporters that this was one of the outstanding virtues of colleges – they allowed students to create their own adult society, untrammelled by the need to adjust to and regulate a younger age-group.

It is worth pausing at this point to consider why the 'social responsibility' issue should assume such a central significance in the traditionalist arguments against sixth-form colleges. The obvious answer is that the separation of the sixth from the lower school produced an institution with a built-in tendency towards openness, equality, flexibility and pragmatism. This movement away from the notion of the sixth as fixed, as linked to differentiation and hierarchy, and as controllable, presented two related and equally distasteful possibilities of development for those attached to the traditional ideology of the sixth. On the one hand, it moved the conception of the sixth away from the small world of the community of scholars [. . .]. On the other hand, it provided a context within which democratization seemed inevitable. Even the preservation of the A-Level curriculum was no guarantee of the security of hierarchy.

Democratization was already taking place both within the academic curriculum and across its boundary. Comprehensive schools operated quite effectively as instruments of exclusion at the level of the academic sixth form; not because they intended to, but because the effort of staffing an open-choice, specialist curriculum stretched their resources and, unless they were schools which built on an existing grammar tradition, they found it hard to create sixth forms large enough to generate confidence and enthusiasm in the face of a school of over 1000 pupils which was drawn towards different conceptions of education. Sixth-formers were often a beleaguered minority pursuing courses which seemed fairly meaningless in terms of the ethos of the schools as a whole. Colleges, on the other hand, even those that claimed titles like 'open' or 'comprehensive', had a firm centre of gravity in A-Level work with good specialist teachers and substantial classes. Here the student who would have been 'marginal' in the comprehensive sixth could be readily coopted into the academic curriculum. Except in some areas where the grammar school tradition had itself been weak, colleges found less problem than the comprehensives with the 'new sixth' former. The public schools had been showing for years that students of modest ability could cope with a curriculum that was supposedly for the academic 'high flyers';[5] grammar schools, with their selective entry, had never really had to face up to the problem. Now the colleges were beginning to show that, given the right kind of institution, the maintained sector could generate the kind of expectation and commitment which can expand enrolments even in apparently 'exclusive' courses.

Moreover, entry to the A-Level curriculum was cutting across the sponsorship system. With the break at 16 giving students an opportunity to think seriously about what they wanted to do instead of simply following their teachers' expectations, leavers from grammar schools began to choose vocational courses in further education, and some from secondary moderns preferred to aim at A-Level. [. . .] With no history of lower school careers shared between students, no experience of the effects of sponsorship or its reverse, or differential relationships with juniors to divide them, students began to shape communities where each was valued for himself and for what he brought to a fellowship of equals. The notion of a level of perfection against which the sixth-former was measured in terms of how near he approached it, or how far he fell short of it, was being lost. What is more, in the tertiary colleges the distinction between academic and vocationally oriented students was being eroded. The tradition of 'knowledge as an end in itself' was in danger of being confounded with the baser one of knowledge 'as a means to some cheaply utilitarian end' (Norwood and Hope, 1909). Such developments were obviously not welcome to the supporters of the traditional ideology of the sixth. Yet perhaps they do not in themselves go to the heart of the matter. In any sponsorship system, it is boundaries which are of prime importance. From the beginning, the sixth, and the route to the sixth, were marked by ritualized transitions, so we should suspect that the 'break at 16' might have a significance which goes beyond what is obvious to the casual observer. This idea is strengthened when we contrast the opposition mounted in some quarters to the idea of the sixth-form college with the strong advocacy, from the same quarters, that, two years later, the academic student should enter a university course involving residence away from home – enrolment in a 'home' university being looked on as a poor alternative. What is it that distinguishes the one situation so clearly from the other?

We would suggest that what makes the sixth form special is that it is marked at its beginning by a curricular boundary without an institutional one, and at its end by an institutional boundary which is not curricular. The rhetoric of sixth-form ideology emphasizes continuity of curriculum – the sixth as the natural continuation and crown of what has gone before – and discontinuity in the social role of the sixth-former – the attainment of a status involving personal responsibility and a changed relationship with teachers. Both claims are misleading. As far as the curriculum is concerned, the A-Level student moves from a general curriculum of 8–10 subjects with only marginal choice available (though it may be very significant for the career of the individual) and followed in conventional classes with probably no free time, to a specialist one entailing commitment to three or so subjects studied in a depth and detail that in many countries would be associated with university-level work, and based on small-group tutoring and extensive private study. But this happens within a familiar environment and in the company of well-known teachers and a stable cohort of contemporaries. In their new situation, students have a different role but are still defined as being in a state of dependence because their 'sponsors' emphasize both the novelty of the work, which passes beyond common knowledge, and also the responsibility of the sixth-formers towards younger students. The state of being in unfamiliar territory with familiar superiors is calculated to produce command of the environment, but in such a way that it seems to arise from guidance, not initiative. The means of achieving success is experienced as a kind of talisman inherited from others, rather than as a developed capacity of the individual. When the break of institution comes, and the sixth-former is sent out into the world, as all neophytes must be, however long their period of tutelage, the rules of success will work, more or less, because the task is a familiar one.[6] And, by the time the break comes, there can be some assurance that those destined for high places will not be easily weaned from the philosophy of education they have imbibed. There can be practically double assurance that this will be the case for the next generation of heads and teachers who, almost without exception, come from the ranks of sixth-formers. They are unlikely to return to the place of their initiation in order to dismantle it. And that is what traditionalists most need to feel comfortable about.

Viewed against this background, then, the challenge of the new *genus* was a very serious one. A fresh institution was being created which bore the name of sixth form and performed the core curricular work of sixth forms, but which, contrary to the character of the long-established school sixth forms, had inherent propensities towards universalism and democratization, both in a social and an academic sense. By undermining the initiatory function of the sixth the colleges were threatening that peculiar freedom of which Norwood (1929) had been such a strong advocate: 'the boy is taught to choose what he ought to choose and that is the real freedom; not the pseudo-freedom of many-headed uneducated democracy'.[7] It was not surprising that, in the context of a revival of hard-line political conservatism, the colleges were to become, in the early 1980s, the battle ground *par excellence* of competing visions of sixth-form education, and of competing visions of the meaning of British democracy in the nation as a whole.

Notes

1 An account of the origins of the Croydon scheme, and the reasoning behind it, is given in King (1968). [. . .]

2 'There is support from work by HMI and analysis of DES statistics that its (separate post-16-provision) establishment tends to increase participation in post-compulsory education' (DES, 1980, p. 30).

3 This was the finding of our own study of three West Midland colleges through observation, questionnaire surveys and interviews with staff and students, 1975–1977 (Reid and Filby, 1978, p. 66).

4 See, for example, Turner (1961). The 'sponsored' model aims at early selection, a concentration of resources on 'those who can benefit', and stresses *esprit de corps* and intellectual values. The elite presents a unified front, while the masses are trained to regard themselves as unfitted for positions of responsibility. The 'contest' model delays selection as long as possible, and emphasizes social adjustment training and the practical benefits of education.

5 On success rates at A-Level in public schools, see Kalton (1966).

6 We say 'more or less' because success depends on the character of the individual coupled with the nature of the university to which he transfers. [. . .]

7 Compare Friedrich Engels, 'Freedom is the appreciation of necessity'.

References

Department of Education and Science (DES) (1980) *Education for 16–19 Year Olds*. DES/CLEA. London, HMSO.

Kalton, G. (1966) *The Public Schools: A Factual Survey*. London, Longman.

King, R. Wearing (1968) *The English Sixth-Form College: An Educational Concept*. Oxford, Pergamon Press.

Norwood, Cyril (1929) *The English Tradition of Education*. London, John Murray, p. 79.

Norwood, Cyril and Hope, Arthur H. (eds) (1909) *The Higher Education of Boys in England*. London, John Murray, p. 300.

Reid, W.A. and Filby, J.L. (1978) *The Organisation and Curriculum of Three Sixth Form Colleges*. Final Report to the Department of Education and Science. Teaching Research Unit, University of Birmingham, April 1978.

Turner, R.H. (1961) In: Halsey, A.H., Floud, J. and Anderson, C.A., *Education, Economy and Society*. New York, Free Press.

SECTION 4

INSTITUTIONAL POLICY-MAKING AND LEADERSHIP

CHAPTER 4.1

MANAGEMENT OF HIGHER EDUCATION INSTITUTIONS IN A PERIOD OF CONTRACTION AND UNCERTAINTY*
JOHN L. DAVIES AND ANTHONY W. MORGAN

Varieties of unstable and contracting environments

The landscape of institutional environments is highly variable and reflective of the historical development of the institution, differing attitudes of local political support, the financial climate of localities, differential treatment of institutions by funding bodies, shifts in student demand and so forth. Added to these conditions is an unusually high degree of uncertainty and potential decline facing higher education. While some measure of uncertainty has always been present, the high degree of uncertainty now surrounding enrolments and budgetary levels is in sharp contrast with the relatively stable environment of the past two decades.

Levine (1978) outlines varying causes of decline in public organizations and emphasizes that an understanding of the causes of particular situations is vital to any formulation of appropriate organizational responses. Levine divides the causes of decline along two dimensions: (1) whether the causes are primarily the result of conditions external or internal to the organization, and (2) whether they are principally a product of political or economic technical conditions.

Organizational decline in institutions of higher education can logically derive from any of the four loci mentioned by Levine, or combinations thereof. The strategies and politics of institutional change and adaptation will vary somewhat depending upon the cause(s). For example, if the cause

---

* Based on a research study and paper presented to the Leverhulme seminar series by Anthony W. Morgan, executive assistant to the President, University of Utah, USA, and John L. Davies, Assistant Dean (Academic Planning and International Affairs), Anglian Regional Management Centre, North East London Polytechnic.

of decline is due primarily to 'organizational entropy' or a declining level of organizational performance, staff development and technological innovation strategies, with the attendant politics of innovation, seem appropriate.

Table 9 attempts to categorize types of unstable or contracting environments that institutions of higher education might face. While some institutions may evolve through the four categories identified, most cases reviewed did not move from category 2 to 3; in other words, institutions tend to experience various combinations of environments over time. The categorization scheme does not therefore necessarily represent a characterization of phases on the road to long-term decline. Categories 1–3 do, however, represent an increasing degree of severity of decline over a relatively short period of time.

Category 1 is a set of experiences now commonly found in many nations including the UK and US. The causes of such decline tend most commonly to be external and political or environmental entropy in terms of the Levine typology of causes. British and American institutions generally experienced category 1 types of 'decline' during the 1970s as the aggregate demand and revenue growth for higher education slowed. This is reflected in the institution's perceived inability to realize planned academic expansion – the agony of lowering expectations. A suppression of expectations was accompanied in the US and the UK by actual declines in enrolment growth rates, and higher education expenditures as a percentage of GNP also slowed during the 1970s. The category 1 experience in the UK is widespread and represents both a slowing-down of demand and of financial support.

The most common response to the slowed growth conditions of the 1970s among American and British institutions has been twofold: (1) stimulation of demand through increased marketing devices, and (2) efficiency measures to cope with reduced rates of revenue growth.

Category 2 represents situations induced primarily by short-term financial problems, for example governmental revenue shortfalls necessitating mid-year budget cuts or political mandates which result in budgetary cutbacks.

Institutional responses in these cases are heavily influenced by the time available to make the necessary budget cuts. When retrenchment occurred at mid-year or late in the budget cycle, characteristic responses include across-the-board reductions, although certain non-personnel budget categories are vulnerable (e.g. travel, utility costs, maintenance). In both the US and the UK, in those systems where formula-based budgeting or unit cost-based resource allocation plays a dominant role, existing formulas

Table 9 Varieties of contraction

Category	Most common causes	Characteristic institutional response
1. Slowed institutional growth; possibility of contraction	Externally imposed fiscal constraints, e.g. recession, government spending limits Stable enrolments or decline in enrolment growth rate Inflation above rate of budget increase	Efficiency measures Deferral of planned programmes and buildings Institutional self-study Increased student marketing efforts Increased fund-raising activities
2. Moderate, 'temporary' contraction	Externally imposed budget cuts High rates of inflation Decline in enrolment	Intensified efficiency and productivity measures Some staff development/redeployment Deferral of certain types of expenditure (principally one-time cuts) Programme reviews as basis for selective cuts Intensified student marketing and fund-raising activities Early retirement policies
3. Substantial contraction over relatively short time	Fiscal crisis, e.g. severe recession or depression or fiscal solvency Sharp decline in enrolments Reorganization/merger of institutions	Crisis personnel policies; redundancies; redeployment Suspension of capital expenditures Intensive mission/programme studies Closure of units and courses Explicit personnel and resourcing policies
4. Long-term contraction	Permanent state of uncertainty surrounding institutional viability Organizational, political or economic entropy	Programme closures Heavy focus on personnel policies Planned disposal of assets

have been influential in reducing budgets (e.g. Wisconsin, the National Advisory Body).

The British polytechnic sector cases also demonstrate the immediate pressures, namely time and political, for large across-the-board or at least arbitrary reductions. While not necessarily across-the-board in their impact, arbitrary reductions fall in areas where savings can be made at that particular time, for example early retirement or job vacancies in subject areas which may or may not bear any relationship to an overall academic development plan. To develop and implement a more rational pattern of reductions would require several years.

Category 3 encompasses those situations where an institution encounters severe contraction necessitating large-scale personnel and expenditure reductions, or even closure. Cases here include the closure or merger of many colleges of education in the UK during the mid-1970s, some small private colleges in the US, or the City University of New York (CUNY). There are many cases of 'threats' of major contraction, which induced certain types of contingency responses on the part of institutions.

Characteristic institutional responses to category 3-type situations vary tremendously, depending upon whether the financial crisis is commonly perceived and widely believed or viewed primarily as a short-term political and adversarial situation.

Staff reductions are part and parcel of most institutions' response since a large portion of an institution's budget is tied up in personnel costs. Characteristic institutional strategies for staff reductions, reported by the Sprenger and Schultz survey (1974) in the US, include the following (in order of frequency reported): (a) not filling vacancies; (b) terminating non-tenured faculty; (c) terminating part-time faculty; (d) terminating teaching assistants; (e) early retirement; (f) seniority of tenured faculty; (g) reassignment; and (h) performance appraisal. Though the incidence of this problem in the UK has occurred later, the same broad strategies may be observed, though the battle over tenure is in the early stages in the UK.

Recent British experience under government-imposed budget reductions confirms the prevalence of 'efficiency' and 'income maximization' responses, for example trimming down administrative costs, increasing student–staff ratios and maximizing other sources of income. In the polytechnic sector, it can also be observed that (1) several local authorities are making extra payments to polytechnics in order to soften the effect of government capping of pooling funds (an income maximization strategy), and (2) some polytechnics are attempting to increase less expensive full-time undergraduate programmes and reducing more costly part-time, post-experience courses. The latter response is of course prompted by incentives built into or at least perceived as being built into present funding arrangements.

Category 4 represents a situation often cited as characteristic of the next two decades for higher education, given the declining size of the pool of traditional college attenders. Experience to date would indicate that this is common with teacher training institutions in the US and the UK and in many private institutions in the US. These and other institutions struggling for survival over a long period of time offer cases of strategic regrouping through curtailment of programmes and services offered, or indeed through institutional mergers with more buoyant institutions (Mingle, 1981).

However, a more pervasive long-term condition confronting many institutions of higher education in the 1980s is what Rubin has called the 'permanence of uncertainty' surrounding decline (Rubin, 1980); in other words, an institution may have encountered environments described by categories 1, 2 and/or 3 over the entire decade of the 1970s and may be facing substantial uncertainty as to where it may find itself in the years to come. The seeming permanence of uncertainty surrounding contraction fosters an institutional environment with significant barriers to institutional change, namely the difficulty of achieving organizational consensus as to the probable level of environmental support, a reluctance of administrators to make long-term commitments and the general difficulty of carrying out serious, long-range planning.

It is important for institutions to recognize in which of these categories they apparently are; which they may be going towards; and thus, what strategies ought to be before senates and academic boards.

Institutions of higher education as organizations

The foregoing analysis of institutional responses to unstable and contracting environments has largely focused on policy questions, but we have to consider the dynamics of the organization in which these policies are generated. This is a critical factor in determining the character of the policies. As Richman and Farmer (1974) observe, 'top management, in the final analysis, is responsible for getting an adequate mesh between what the outside world wants, needs and expects from a given institution in terms of its goals, priorities and programmes, what the internal constituencies want, need and expect, and what the faculty is capable of delivering'. Scarce resources, coupled with the issue of goals, are at the heart of the problem of institutional decision-making. It follows that the perceptions of the workings of the institution held by the various participants in decision-making is a critical factor, especially whether those perceptions are normative, descriptive, explanatory or predictive.

There appear to be four main organizational models of the higher education institution. The *bureaucratic model* assumes that the institution comprises a formal organizational structure, with specified roles, clear hierarchies and chains of command, predetermined procedures and regulations. It is assumed that people behave and the organization works according to the formal structure (Weber, 1947). Richman and Farmer (1974) and Becher and Kogan (1980) observe that institutions are much less predictable than this prescription, because of the many social, psychological and self-actualization needs unfulfilled in the model; the increasing number of issues which have no precedent and venture solution; and the fact that the head does not exercise unequivocal managerial authority.

The *collegial model* (Millett, 1962) assumes a fraternity of scholars seeking individual and collective fulfilment, through full participation in decision-making. In this model, consensus decision-making by academics does not admit of an influential administrative role. The model does tend to ignore the existence of academic hierarchy and academic ritual, and assumes, often wrongly, a genuine spirit of cooperation, deep commitment to the institution, similar shared values and abundant resources.

The *political model* (Baldridge, 1971a, b) takes conflict as the natural state of academic affairs, and focuses on the issues created by interest groups with different goals, values, styles of operation and methods of generating and pursuing policy preferences. Participation is fluid, decisions are normally negotiated compromises, achieved informally and processed through legitimate decision-making arenas which translate pressures into policy. While a helpful explanation of current phenomena, it clearly does not apply to all institutional conditions.

The *organized anarchy model* (Cohen and March, 1974; Olsen and March, 1974) posed the problem of the institution being caught in an 'anarchy trap' as a result of ambiguous goals, ambiguous means–ends relationships, ambiguous systems of rewards and sanctions, high autonomy of subordinates with strong extra-institutional affiliations, and weak market feedback mechanisms. Decentralization is necessary because leaders and administrators are not sufficiently knowledgeable in all disciplines to be able to make informal decisions (Corson, 1973; Parsons and Platt, 1973). Cohen and

March (1974) believe that decision processes in institutions are not so much mechanisms for solving problems, but more for participants to air grievances and pose preferences which may have but passing relevance to the issue ostensibly under discussion. Their conclusion is that the institution head needs to develop tactical responses in order to influence decisions. Unlike Enderud (1977), Cohen and March are not so much interested in strategic policy generation – a significant limitation – and somewhat underplay the extent to which institutions can be managed.

None of these types, of course, are pure forms. Becher and Kogan (1980) indicate the linkages which occur because of the functioning of individual managers such as vice-chancellors, directors, registrars, deans and heads of department. They operate both within the hierarchy and the collegium, through executive offices, committees and informal political arenas. Richman and Farmer (1974) develop a more comprehensive open systems approach, with a view to prescription and prediction, coupled with a strong contingency element. Enderud (1977) locates the four models outlined above in a phased evolution of policy decisions, where each has a role to play at a particular time in the delivery of effective policy. However, the incidence of contraction inevitably generates more insecurity and thus, more conflict and politicization than in times of plenty or even steady state. In general, therefore, the political and organized anarchy models seem to have more affinity with the current situation in higher education.

The contemporary external pressures for institutions to develop corporate policies for the internal management of programmes, personnel, finance and space are clearly very considerable. We therefore have widespread plans for senior management to develop rational and imaginative policies which are academically sound, financially viable and politically acceptable, both internally and externally. In this case, many highly intelligent institutional heads would tend to adopt systematic approaches of generating policy; these incorporate a definition of desired outcomes, the identification and weighing of alternative solutions and options, the attribution of costs and benefits, a decision based on a mix of appropriate options, and a systematic evaluation of efficiency and effectiveness of the adopted policy mixes. Each of these activities is impregnated with potential conflict and disagreement, which clearly hinders satisfactory progress. We observed the following tendencies in the institutions we studied:

– joint policy decisions are slow and problematic to make;
– decisions which are carried through are usually partial, short range and based on compromise;

- policy decisions and criteria have to be attacked over and over again before a conventional wisdom gets established;
- more institutional bureaucracy is created, in the sense of more participant involvement, more requests for information to executives, more referrals of decision for subcommittee consideration, etc.;
- the academic finds himself in several concurrent dilemmas: he doesn't like meetings yet he must generate or attend them to preserve his interests and influence, the direction and substance of his plans; he does not wish to spend too much time himself on planning matters, yet he is reluctant to trust others, including administrators; he wishes to plan in the sense of having a stable framework in which to operate, yet he resents being constrained by a substantive plan; he wants a power fixer on whom he can rely to sort out difficult issues, yet he resents the growth of power centres which are beyond the effective control of himself and his colleagues;
- policy decisions, given the economic realities, environmental uncertainties and political context, may increasingly be concerned with the marginal decision consistent with a very broad loose framework rather than the grand fixed strategy of a development plan. Points of specificity in planning may be possible on particular issues, but this in itself does not remove the anarchy trap;
- difficulties with planning and policy-making originate with questions of reluctance and inability of participants to plan, namely to imagine the future of the institution as a whole. The role of the rector or central planner would thus seem to be as much concerned with creating an appropriate psychological climate in which participants can be creative, as with the more conventional technical aspects of information collection and analysis.

In this context, yearnings for corporate rationality may be illusory.

It becomes quite vital, therefore, for institutional leaders charged with the development of policy to have a very precise understanding of how their institutions behave or are likely to behave. If they assume collegiality where none exists and push decisions accordingly, they will very likely be disappointed. Both the policy-making process they develop, and the roles in policy formation which they play, need to be carefully attuned to the variables of the particular situation.

Perceptions, expectations and constraints

Institutional administrators, particularly those operating at a high policy level, perform an interface function, that is, they interact with key governmental bodies and other influential public bodies which are external to the institution (Thompson, 1967; Pfeffner and Salancik, 1978). In performing this role, administrators must interpret the direction and level of intensity of external pressures. Overreaction to transitory issues and pressures is therefore a charge often levied by academics against administrators. The Association of the University Teachers' response to the interim report of the Swinnerton–Dyer Committee illustrates this phenomenon: 'The committee . . . has taken the worst possible set of assumptions and then assumed that will inevitably happen. To project present trends for a period of nearly 10 years, as the committee has done, seems to us completely unrealistic' (*Times Higher Education Supplement*, 1981).

Academics, on the other hand, are in most cases marvellously insulated from pressures imposed by external sources; this does, however, create a barrier for the emergence of a common set of expectations. They tend to believe, at least during the initial stages of contraction, that budgetary cuts can be handled through centrally held funds, economies in non-academic and non-personnel categories of expenditures or that new funding will be forthcoming.

Prior to or in the initial stages of contraction, most individuals in an institution tend to believe that contraction will occur elsewhere (Glenny et al., 1976). As modest financial decline occurs, most people in an organization will initially believe that personnel cutbacks, other than a freeze on vacant posts, are not necessary (Behn, 1980). Administrative action beyond these expectations is commonly met with a high degree of distrust and suspicion reflected in charges of a 'hypothetical deficit' being used to 'rush through major academic changes' (language used in an internal document circulated among academics at a British polytechnic).

As contraction becomes more of an organizational reality, usually through widely publicized press coverage and visible signs of resource cuts in a person's work environment, differences in perceptions become more pronounced and are substantially influenced by actions being taken at other institutions. The accentuation of differences in perceptions is illustrated in the case of a British polytechnic where the governors and the directorate, who are close to the financial pressures from government and local authorities, assumed a policy stance of compulsory redundancies as being necessary to deal effectively with short- and longer-term financial conditions. The academics' union, on the other hand, took a strong position against compulsory redundancies opting instead for further non-personnel savings and a voluntary redundancy scheme. The union's case was bolstered by its reference to actions being taken at other institutions: '. . . other polytechnics . . . have managed to deal with similar financial circumstances in much less draconian ways'. Delay in a decision to proceed with compulsory redundancies provided sufficient time to identify a substantial number of voluntary redundancies and other savings which appeared to meet immediate financial deficit targets. (Whether this could continue indefinitely is another point!)

American and British institutions have been living with a considerable degree of uncertainty surrounding future enrolments and finances for nearly a decade now, and the level of uncertainty does not seem to be subsiding. On enrolments, for example, opinions and forecasts vary widely depending upon assumptions made as to traditional and non-traditional student participation rates, college retention rates and the effects of the job market on these rates. The types of formula and unit costing used as a basis for resource allocation create similar uncertainty on the supply side. With this range of variability in projections, it is not surprising that administrators have difficulty in developing consensus within their institutions as to a probable future equilibrium level.

Apart from the above differences in perception and uncertainties, Glenny and Bowen's case studies (1980) demonstrate that the time available to make budget cuts is the most pervasive constraint on institutional options. Selective programmatic cuts require substantial lead time for programme evaluation, consensus building and planning (Dougherty, 1978). Objectively, an institution should attempt to buy its own lead time by anticipating and targeting a certain level of contraction one or two years in advance and developing personnel and programme policies accordingly. One British university, through judicious and imaginative personnel policies, has been able to turn an operating deficit of around £500,000 into an operating surplus of £600,000 in two years.

Time as a constraint upon institutional change and adaptation is a two-edged sword. Lead time is needed to develop plans and internal political support for selective programmatic cuts. Such plans can, however, serve notice to external bodies that such cuts can be, and in fact are, anticipated. Moreover, the types of severe financial contraction which produce a widely perceived need for institutional contraction tend to come about without much advance notice. If notice were given, and not widely believed, serious programmatic plans for pruning are unlikely to emerge internally.

The final constraint on an institution's rational planning of contraction is the myriad of statutes, employment agreements, tenure provisions and other legal restrictions that play a central role in personnel dismissals. In the British context, universities and polytechnics have been reluctant to initiate a policy of compulsory redundancies because it would entail ground-breaking legal work in determining the level of redundancy payments to be made in testing the strength of individual contracts. However, this may well change as they run out of alternative ways of saving money.

The political nature of change in institutions of higher education

All kinds of power problems are implied in the discussion so far. Decision-making and change processes are basically reflective of the under-lying power structure and the environmental context of institutions (Clark, 1978). Institutions of higher education are built around a strong core of professionals who exercise considerable autonomy and influence over cen-tral institutional processes. Decision-making and change processes are therefore characterized by a substantial degree of bargaining, persuasion and manoeuvring, hence 'gamesmanship' or politics, among peers. Were educational and research outputs and 'production functions' more clearly understood and quantifiable, the degree of gamesmanship would be reduced although certainly not eliminated. But because decision-making in institutions of higher education is characterized by a wide distribution of power among numerous, semi-independent entities and by what has been described as the 'complexity of joint action' (Pressman and Wildavsky, 1973), any constructive change moving through the organization is subject to such 'political' forces as:

> the players involved; what they regard as the stakes; their strategies and tactics; their resources for playing; the rules of play (which stipulate the conditions for winning); the rules of 'fair' play (boundaries of acceptable play); nature of communications among players; and the degree of uncer-tainty surrounding the outcomes. (Bardach, 1978)

Institutional leaders have always had to contend with such forces, but the prevailing consensus or collegial norms, coupled with a certain respect for the authority of legitimate office-holders, was usually sufficient to sort out behavioural aberrations without too much fuss. Under conditions of expan-sion, the conflicting interests of organizational subgroups could most often be accommodated by giving partial funding now and the promise of future funds later. As long as powerful individuals and groups received what they perceived to be reasonable shares of expanding resources, the core organizational coalitions were maintained in relative harmony (Cyert and March, 1963). Those not receiving their fair share and who had marketability elsewhere often exercised that ultimate market sanction against deterioration in organizational performance – 'exit' (Hirschman, 1970).

The politics of institutional change under conditions of instability or contraction are different from those most commonly characteristic of expanding organizations in that they are more intense and 'defensive'. As resources to meet the policy commitments and funding demands of competing organizational groups have diminished, institutional administrators have experienced an increased level of conflict particularly as options to exit the organization have diminished, leaving what Hirschman (1970) terms 'voice' or the political response, as the only viable option for most members of the organization. In their study of 42 American institutions, Cohen and March (1974) confirm that financial adversity did result in a precipitous rise in conflict and in the time required to arrive at decisions. Richman and Farmer (1974) and Baldridge (1971a) observe that in many cases, none of the formal or informal ordinary mechanisms of power can cope. Noncompliance and the limited effect of traditional sanctions lead to increasing reliance on regulations, due process and sterile legalism.

Interest group politics and coalition politics

Bacharach and Lawler (1980) discuss four sources of authority and power – office, personal, expertise and opportunity – and argue that only the first is a prerogative of official institutional leaders. Other leaders of informal subgroups may wield much more effective authority or influence deriving from personality, expertise and control of information related to a particular issue, and the ability to create and exploit opportunities. Cohen and March (1974) illustrate the illusions in the role of the institution's head by attempting to demonstrate that his formal powers over recruitment, planning and the budget are only operative at the margin, and in any case he is mainly reactive to initiatives made elsewhere.

One can witness in many British institutions the interplay of interest groups as a manifestation of the apparent divisiveness which contraction or expected contraction induces. For example, high-cost faculties are pitted against low-cost faculties; high staff–student ratio faculties against low ones; younger faculty members against older ones; academic purists against those who are more market oriented; departments against the centre; unions against management. These tendencies are greatly exacerbated as a result of contraction, and intensified territorial defence is the result.

In each issue which comes to the institutional agenda, interest groups must decide whether to pursue the 'live and let live' mode of operation, which is typical of expansion, or to join with a coalition of interest groups in pursuit of a common goal. A distinction may thus be drawn between institutions dominated by interest group politics or coalition politics. Coalition politics are concerned with more than transient, issue-by-issue relationships and involve hard bargaining between groups on the content and price of areas of common agreement. Bacharach and Lawler (1980) suggest the conditions that either facilitate the emergence of coalitions (e.g. severe resource scarcity, specificity of issues) or reinforce the maintenance of interest group politics. *Table* 10 summarizes their conclusion. As yet, British higher education institutions do not display strong tendencies to lasting coalitions of interest groups, but more to interest-specific groups. The universities in our case studies appeared to be less coalition prone than the polytechnics, possibly because of the severity of the financial contraction in the latter at the time of the study. In one university, a suggested structural rationalization based on a large comprehensive faculty of social science was successfully resisted by an interest-specific grouping of lawyers and educationalists, on the grounds that the 'special' needs of professional schools would be lost in such a rationalization. A polytechnic example was of two separate faculties of business and management which had differed on most issues since their inception, suddenly finding unity against a proposal

Table 10   Relationship of ideology and functional goals to institutional politics (Bacharach and Lawler, 1980)

	Functional goals	
Ideology	**Convergent**	**Non-convergent**
Convergent	1 Coalition politics	2 Issue-specific outcomes
Non-convergent	3 Issue-specific outcomes	4 Interest group politics

to merge them! One could not imagine such grouping developing any permanency.

There are many implications in the above for institutional leaders. If, as Bardach (1978) says, implementation of change is an 'assembly process', that is, inducing or in some other way securing the assent or contributions of influential individuals or groups within the organization, it becomes critically important for the leader to develop a system of 'political mapping' of the institution. There are several means which may be used to do this (Bardach, 1978; Brosan, 1978; Davies, 1980b), but all rest on the assumption that he needs to know the nature of the political jungle, to develop appropriate tactics for stimulating alliances in favour of policies; to create incentives to secure the non-opposition of other groups and to use the most relevant arenas. The style and tactics which the head of an institution needs to adopt differ considerably depending on whether interest group politics or coalition politics are the dominant mode. The former do permit a certain degree of informal 'dividing and ruling', using the tactics recommended by Cohen and March (1974). The latter may be much more difficult to contend with, since the tactical sophistication developed by the coalition may be much higher than that of the institution head, especially in mobilizing external opinion.

Resistance of organizational subunits to the threat of contraction

Several recent studies indicate that academic units representing disciplines with a high degree of theoretical or 'paradigm' consensus, for example physics or engineering, command a disproportionate share of influence and resources within the institution (Hills and Mahony, 1978; Pfeffner and Moore, 1980). A separate but related stream of research suggests that the influence of organizational subunits is dependent upon the degree to which they can mitigate organizational uncertainty; in other words, in a highly unstable environment, the subunit(s) that copes best with uncertainty and provides the larger organization with an added measure of stability is likely to emerge as a powerful and influential group (Thompson, 1967; Hickson et al., 1971).

It follows that during a period of instability and contraction, those subunits which continue to attract outside research funding, student enrolments, and/or reduce uncertainty in other ways such as possession of information or external political influence, become even more influential. Our interviews with academics in various departments confirm that those who felt most secure were basing such expectations upon either research or other external funding resilience, externally and internally recognized reputations including widely recognized signs of high-quality programmes, and/or buoyant student demand. Those expressing the highest degree of confidence were strong in all three areas. Almost all units were actively soliciting student applications as a strategy of enhancing their security. In polytechnics and other non-university institutions, student demand as reflected in applications and actual enrolment levels constituted a far more important factor than it did in the university sector, but within the polytechnic sector, those departments with high, full-time, first-degree enrolments tended to be politically much less vulnerable than those with postgraduate, part-time or short-course emphases. The effects of this on the long-term mission of the institution are profound, in terms of possible academic drift, imbalance between overseas and domestic students, etc.

Departmental size was also used as a criterion by those considering selective as opposed to across-the-board cuts. Small departments or research service units, often relatively new and not fully developed, whose potential for fiscal savings could be added to one or two other small units, were most often considered in programme closure discussion. To close these types of unit, as opposed to large, well-established departments, was considered easier both in terms of rationale and politics. As one pro-vice-chancellor indicated, it is easier 'to cut than weed'. Cutting selected small units is usually justified on the basis of partial development and little prospect for future full development. Selection of personnel to be made redundant (or assisted to depart) is made easier by discontinuing the whole programme. Politically such small developing units have often not had time to build up important symbols of an academic reputation or a large and influential clientele to advocate on their behalf.

Cutting into large and influential departments poses a more difficult change strategy for the administrator. Selective personnel 'weeding' requires a well-established and well-documented evaluation system in order to make a reasonable and legally defensible case. Across-the-board cuts, often decried as an irrational institutional response, can be used to force large departments into 'weeding'. The danger is that the department will not weed within any systematic context based on programme need, but instead will tend to be governed by factors such as tenure or eligibility for premature or early retirement schemes.

Another important factor is clearly the political strength of the department within the university community. Such factors as memberships of key committees, access to information and chairmanships, as well as a range of more informal factors come into play.

The factors discussed pose another range of political problems and constraints for the leader in his attempts to find solutions which are rationally sound, yet politically acceptable.

Decision criteria

In the formulation of policy to cope with contraction, the political 'crunch' issue is how to decide which departments grow, which remain in steady state, which contract, and which are to be immediately cut, or progressively phased out. The search for appropriate decision criteria becomes a matter of considerable interest.

The balance between 'political' and 'rational' or universalistic decision criteria shifts towards the political when resources are scarce. Hills and Mahony's empirical study (1978) of the University of Minnesota confirms that (1) rational decision criteria are a significant influence only during times of abundant resources, and (2) the relative political power of organizational subunits is more significant at a time of resource scarcity.

There was evidence that several institutions did strive to develop 'rational' decision criteria. Those used by one university included the numbers of undergraduate applications, taking account of competition; postgraduate taught courses; research students; studentships; percentage of completions; staff–student ratio; research grants; publications; general contributions to the higher education system internally or externally. On this basis, several departments were recommended for closure, but the recommendations were rejected by senate. Sizer (1981) outlines a highly systematic means of balancing internal and external criteria in a decision matrix. In the polytechnic sector, one organizational unit within North East London Polytechnic, for example, was initially earmarked for a loss of some 12 academic staff positions on one method of calculating workload. The director recommended no loss of positions and the governors compromised on three. We also found an increased level of interest among all academic subunits in the methods of calculating workload with the participants in the debate well aware of funding and bargaining implications. What constitutes an FTE student, whether a polytechnic should use pooling committee, NAB norms or its own versions for internal evaluation and resource allocation or disallocation is clearly not just a philosophical question. Technical questions become political totems. The debate is not really about whether

0.5 for a part-time MSc really represents the true resource consumption or the academic status of an MSc vis-à-vis a BEd: it is about jobs.

We did not find that 'educational' criteria were missing in the debates on contraction. Lancaster University, for example, decided to protect an innovative independent study programme even though workload and cost criteria would have targeted it for probable elimination. Aberdeen University's controversial decision to fill a chair in classics on the basis of a minimum core of academic staff needed in that subject area was criticized by those departments with high workloads. The latter example demonstrates how differing perceptions of what constitutes 'educational' criteria can easily form the basis of a political or coalition form of decision-making.

However, senates and academic boards find it difficult to grapple with a systematic array of indicators and criteria which encompass input, process, response and impact considerations. The absence of absolute standards enhances the ambiguity already referred to, and thus opens the door to political power-play. This in itself is provoking acute tensions in the institutions studied between non-traditional departments, which advance conventional academic criteria of performance, and those departments with a considerable market orientation (e.g. business/management), which advocate criteria related to market penetration, income generation, etc., and moreover, may demand the operational independence to be entrepreneurial. This, incidentally, creates an interesting clash between the control metaphor associated with contraction and accountability and the market metaphor associated with a form of academic free enterprise.

The process of generating effective policy

Alternative views of policy formation

So far it has been argued that there are many mutually reinforcing factors within and without the contemporary higher education institution, which place severe limits on the extent to which it can be managed with any degree of certainty. Yet the situation imperatives are invariably for clear, firm guidelines as soon as possible to allay fears and solve problems. So what avenues are open to senior management to develop effective policies to cope with contraction and its attendant issues? At a conceptual level, Enderud (1977) postulates three possible courses of action:

1 To straighten out the ambiguities by increasing the degree of

rationality and structure in decision-making. This may involve:

- increasing the degree of structure and formality in organizational charts, regulations and procedures related to planning (highly unlikely to succeed, since non-compliance and informal bypassing of formal structures are likely to increase; as a result, information overload will create reactions against more clarification);
- increasing coercion by the hierarchy (unlikely to succeed, given the increasing democratization of institutions and the shortage of sanctions to enforce the coercion);
- applying radical shocks to the system, through controlling key elements which influence academics' job satisfaction – validation, monitoring and evaluation of research; control of monies; manipulating balance of teaching, research and administration time (possible, but requires the existence of a steady state or contraction, and a stable coalition of appropriately strong institutional interest groups, to make it last);
- actively seeking to manipulate and control all the variables which go to create the ambiguities. If these factors are responsible for creating the bulk of our planning difficulties in the first place, it would appear to be logical to try to remove them, if they hinder the effectiveness of the institution. (This would seem to be well beyond the reasonable capabilities of institutional administrations.)

2   To accept the ambiguities of the situation as inevitable, and use a 'muddling-through' style of planning process – non-interventionist and procedural.

If this course is followed, it may rest on the assumption that it is highly desirable to maintain the ambiguity in order consciously to limit the influence of macro-policy matters, and to protect the essential characteristics of academic autonomy. It is a matter of judgement whether external agencies would enable this stance to be taken, what the costs to the institution would be, and whether the problems associated with the contraction would ever be resolved.

3   To evolve a policy/planning process which recognizes the existence of ambiguities at certain points, but uses them positively and consciously to arrive at workable decisions. This would seem to require a fusion of the explicit elements of Lindblom's theory of muddling through, and Enderud's four-phase model (1977). The assumptions would seem to be that:

– any planning system which attempts to create a massive and fundamental rethink and recasting of the nature of the institution and a considerable switching of resources across the board over a short time-scale is most unlikely to succeed. A planning system which encourages and facilitates shifts at the margin on a continuing and incremental basis is likely to succeed;
– the opportunity must be seized within the planning process to ensure that relatively small-scale changes have maximum pay-off in psychological impact and practical effect, particularly to undermine historical relics and create precedents;
– such successful planning decisions will need to create internal commitment to the means of achieving an end, without necessarily having widespread agreement to the end itself, which is likely to be the subject of value differences;
– successful planning decisions may be more opportunist than cyclical in their timing and incidence. They may not necessarily coincide with particular stages in the budget process, but do not have to be ad hoc or uncoordinated in intent as a result of this;
– such a planning process may call for more political/behavioural skills than technical skills (enhanced sensitivities to the realities of others' beliefs, preferences and modes of action);
– a firm and stable coalition needs to exist over the period of the genesis and implementation of the decision, consisting of key groups of people who, to collaborate, need incentives, which may be provided by the administration. Furthermore, they must be determined to use the formal structure to effect their desired changes, but in ways best suited to their particular purpose.

A model of policy formation for conditions of politicization and ambiguity

Figure 8 is an extension by Davies (1980) of Enderud's four-phase model of policy formation. Policy here is concerned with the non-routine, non-programmed decisions of high visibility and potential conflict. The essence of the model lies in the following:

1 The sequence is based on a gradual evolution of the planning decision, to ensure that there is a proper allowance for an essentially high ambiguous period (phase 1); a political period (phase 2); a collegial period (phase 3); and an implementation/executive period (phase 4). To miss any phase, or to allow insufficient time for it, is to invite problems subse-

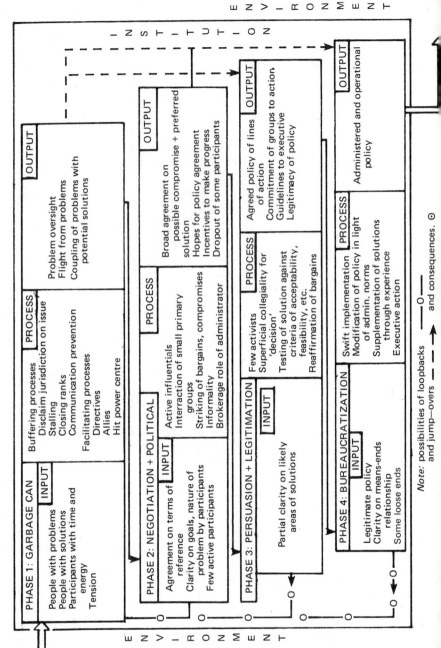

Figure 8 A four-phase political systems model of policy formation. (After Enderud, 1977)

PHASE 1: GARBAGE CAN

INPUT
People with problems
People with solutions
Participants with time and energy
Tension

PROCESS
Buffering processes
Disclaim jurisdiction on issue
Stalling
Closing ranks
Communication prevention
Facilitating processes
Directives
Allies
Hit power centre

OUTPUT
Problem oversight
Flight from problems
Coupling of problems with potential solutions

PHASE 2: NEGOTIATION + POLITICAL

INPUT
Agreement on terms of reference
Clarity on goals, nature of problem by participants
Few active participants

PROCESS
Active influentials
Interaction of small primary groups
Striking of bargains, compromises
Informality
Brokerage role of administrator

OUTPUT
Broad agreement on possible compromise + preferred solution
Hopes for policy agreement
Incentives to make progress
Dropout of some participants

PHASE 3: PERSUASION + LEGITIMATION

INPUT
Partial clarity on likely areas of solutions

PROCESS
Few activists
Superficial collegiality for 'decision'
Testing of solution against criteria of acceptability, feasibility, etc.
Reaffirmation of bargains

OUTPUT
Agreed policy of lines of action
Commitment of groups to action
Guidelines to executive
Legitimacy of policy

PHASE 4: BUREAUCRATIZATION

INPUT
Legitimate policy
Clarity on means-ends relationship
Some loose ends

PROCESS
Swift implementation
Modification of policy in light of admin. norms
Supplementation of solutions through experience
Executive action

OUTPUT
Administered and operational policy

ENVIRONMENT

INSTITUTION

Note: possibilities of loopbacks and jump-overs ——O—— ◀— — — and consequences. ⊙

quently, since one may find that, for example, the wrong participants have been coupled (phase 1); or that one comes to phase 4 without having tested a key group's support of the proposition. Jumping over one phase may well create the necessity of a loopback; thus, if one is in phase 4, which is clearly not working, a return to phase 1 may be necessary to redefine the problem, or to phase 2 to build a workable coalition of interests; or to phase 3 to use additional validation criteria in respect of the proposal. The loopback may be a decision of the sensitive vice-chancellor who realizes the necessary foundations have not been laid; on the other hand (and less desirably!), it may be forced on him by hostile groups who are just not happy with having a possibly ill-conceived and partially tested decision thrust upon them.

2   While one may have a specific planning strategy in mind to cope with a series of problems, one does not start by exposing this in its fullest glories! On the contrary, the starting point is a close definition of the dimensions of the problem to which one's plan is related in terms which (a) appeal to people from various positions on the power spectrum and (b) are internally consistent with any preferred solution one may have. The administrator then has the considerable advantage of being in the business of identifying problems rather than indiscriminately peddling bright ideas which may be perceived as irrelevant or threatening. Planning in this context thus has a very strong element of problem diagnosis.

3   The university head has a significant role of creating communication links and dialogues between parties who may have the capability of developing perspectives on a planning problem. They may be part of some formal structure or key members of an informal group which nevertheless has something positive to offer. At its most sophisticated, the vice-chancellor's or administrator's role involves coalition building between potentially like-minded groups.

4   The administrator will soon recognize that there are many arenas in which to act in any of the four phases. Enderud indeed makes the point that the formal phase 3, which gives ostensible legitimacy to the planning proposal or document, is likely to be the emptiest in terms of real argument and contribution. Other avenues are likely to be informal (the bar, the common room, the golf club) – ones which are appropriate to the needs of the particular phase concerned; ones which make most sense to the participants one is trying to involve; and ones which take the pressure off the administrator. Those left holding the baby of a particular problem or specific solution are easily turned on or deserted when hard choices are needed. Using the four-phase processes to share the ownership of a problem

or solution with others, therefore, is important.

5   The plan or proposal itself has the opportunity of evolving through the phases not only as an increasingly complex and detailed guide to subsequent action, but as an increasingly acceptable political, educational and resource package. Consequently, the model is one which facilitates close attention to task and process concurrently – one of the perpetual problems of organizational theorists and practitioners (Blake et al., 1981).

Applications of the model

When the model shown in *Fig.* 8 is applied to the British cases studied by the authors, some very interesting perspectives begin to emerge. The tentative conclusions (at the time of writing) are:

1   There are few cases where agreed policy requiring contraction has been delivered at the end of phase 3 in order to be implemented at phase 4. Senates or academic boards have very often referred back executive proposals for departmental rationalization encompassed in a 'grand strategy' type of document, thus creating a loopback, usually to phase 1, for a redefinition of the problem.

2   The reasons why proposals have foundered eventually at phase 3 are normally to be found in the neglect or failure of critical processes in the preceding phases 1 and 2, for example:

- failure to appreciate the magnitude and dynamics of political feeling generated by proposals;
- neglect of informal action by senior administrators (especially phases 1 and 2) and an undue reliance on the ability of senates to process controversial proposals;
- reluctance of top management to get involved in bargains and incentives to develop support for policy packages (phases 2 and 3);
- unwillingness of top management to play a brokerage function between interest groups, particularly in the passage of vital information (phases 1 and 2);
- neglect of the vital function of building alliances in support of proposals, even when potential opposition groups had not yet crystallized their joint preferences, and were still disorganized.

3   In all cases, the head of the institution staked his personal reputation as chairman of a steering committee/working party/development committee, to produce strategies for contraction, thus jeopardizing his subsequent

freedom of manoeuvre, especially in full senate meetings.

4   The working party concept, whilst a time-honoured device of collegial contemplation, has tended in places to act as a closed system collecting 'objective' information and presenting it cold to senates without prior political preparations.

5   Grand strategy documents give the distinct impression of being ultimate statements, rather than snapshots on the way to an evolving solution. Consequently, in full senate debates, they tend to polarize positions into 'winners' and 'losers': in general, this is not a good strategy for managing change.

6   The grand strategy mode of operation is clearly very vulnerable, especially when all the critical information on the performance of departments underlying such analyses is not made publicly available. This is usually for admirably civilized reasons of not wishing to expose too cruelly the weaknesses of colleagues' departmental leadership. Senates have interesting ways of reacting to disturbing tidings, not the least being the almost intuitive formation of negative coalitions; the collegium defending itself against the bureaucracy!

7   Some institutions which have undergone the harrowing experience of having policies defeated have learned a great deal about the process of managing change; there is considerable evidence that some of the tactics used once will not be used again – or will be substantially modified.

Consensus building

Consensus building is seen here as the development of commonly held values and beliefs which can be used to deliver subsequently a range of policies, which have a chance of being implemented by general consent and goodwill. In Enderud's terms, it would be a means of recognizing and working with the ambiguities. It has very much to do with organizational climate, and can be seen to be an essential element in effective corporate strategy, and in reducing conflict levels and ambiguity. However, consensus building, like other key change processes, is permeated and substantially influenced by the general characteristic of periods of contraction, namely a high degree of environmental uncertainty and consequent differences in perceptions as to the duration and extent of enrolment and budgetary contraction. Consensus building, by its very definition, is highly dependent upon a reasonable number of commonly held expectations as to future conditions. In the cases reviewed, those institutions exhibiting a relatively high degree of consensus under conditions described earlier as category 1 (slowed growth) and 2 (moderate contraction) types of environment, were those which had: (1) anticipated a period of instability or contraction and initiated a serious 'programme review' or 'corporate strategy' exercise while normal levels of trust and confidence existed within the institution; (2) built over time a widely held consensus as to what constitutes the institutional 'core'; or (3) chosen to present a strong, if not temporary, stand ('stonewalling') against any threatened or possible external constraints.

Programme review

The first approach, that of anticipatory rethinking as a basis for corporate strategy, normally requires considerable lead time in institutions of higher education because of the existence of strong norms for widespread consultation and peer review, whether internal or external.

Lead time may not be sufficient to initiate this type of comprehensive, consultative, peer review-based programme review mode of consensus building, and certainly British institutions do not have the convention of using external colleagues to assist in this process. (CNAA is about course validation, not the above.) Given a shorter time-frame and a more politicized environment, many institutions have used the small, carefully chosen committee appointed to examine institutional priorities as a mechanism to compensate for lack of time and consultation. Lancaster, Southampton and Sussex Universities, as well as the Swinnerton–Dyer Committee at London University, illustrate this mode, with limited initial success. Consensus is more difficult to achieve under these circumstances, and the initial negative reaction of academic staff to reports issued was an accusation of premature and precipitate action on the part of the administration. In each case, however, an educative function has been served by raising the level of awareness as to the problems facing the university and serving as a powerful agenda-setting mechanism for further discussions.

The select committee mode of consensus building relies heavily upon the credibility and legitimacy of its membership, the importance of being able to initiate and set the agenda, and the rationale used in recommending major changes (the definition of quality and its recognition in parts of the institution is an important element); for example, the Swinnerton–Dyer Committee's interim report which placed the London School of Economics and Imperial College on the top of its 'untouchables' list.

The case of North East London Polytechnic (NELP) illustrates how the failure to build on membership credibility and a rationale coinciding with widely perceived reputations of quality can work against the select committee method of consensus generation. In February 1980 a small group of governors and members of the administration proposed closing programmes in sociology, applied economics, humanities and mathematics as well as substantial reductions in many administrative support areas. The initial report was very brief and appeared to rely primarily upon loosely constructed references to national manpower needs as a rationale. Several of the academic units identified for elimination responded vigorously and cited relatively high student demand, high student–staff ratios, reputations of quality and their tendency to be identified with unpopular political activity as a rationale for defence. The response of NELP's academic board, joined by an increasingly strong union, was a broad-based coalition opposing the proposed cuts and eventually turning back the proposals altogether. Subsequent attempts at the same institution have used quite different criteria – resulting in different candidates for contraction.

Attempting to build consensus on academic programme priorities through a carefully developed programme review mechanism encounters increasing difficulty as the amount of lead time diminishes and the magnitude of the contraction increases. Academics interviewed at NELP, for example, unanimously confirmed that any programme review efforts mounted, regardless of who initiated them, would be highly suspect for hidden agendas. Behn (1980) also cautions against the use of the 'study panel' technique because 'the committee might recommend cuts which conflict with the manager's corporate strategy'.

Conducting evaluations and reviews in a highly charged political environment gives rise to both offensive and defensive evaluation strategies and tactics (Davies, 1980). The former may include shrewd appointments of key evaluators, control of circulation of reports and sophisticated use of media relations. Those on the defensive may challenge the validity of the conceptualizations, methodologies and statistics in a review in an attempt to discredit it.

'Core' values and programmes

Some institutions may not need a formal programme review process for arriving at a consensus on institutional priorities. Research by Clark (1972) suggests that some institutions have developed a relatively cohesive set of publicly expressed beliefs and values, rooted in the institution's history and its unique accomplishments, which provides a means of organizational unity around which priorities form.

As Clark points out, however, a crisis period does offer an opportune time for a major change in the organizational saga. In a survival atmosphere, an organization may

> . . . relinquish the leadership to one promising a plan that promises revival and later strength . . . Deep crisis in the established organization thus creates some of the conditions of a new organization. It suspends past practice, forces some bordering groups to stand back or even to turn their backs on failure of the organization, and it tends to catch the attention of the reformer looking for an opportunity.

Many institutions are thus ripe for the type of non-incremental change that Clark describes, but many emergent institutions, including new universities and polytechnics, have often been caught at a stage of partial institutional development before a saga has really been formed. Contraction or steady state has come at an awkward time in the institution's history, in many cases preventing the development of a 'proper' balance among disciplines, and forcing a re-evaluation of previously planned evolutionary development.

Cases reviewed also suggest that a weakly held organizational saga quickly disintegrates as the contracting environment moves from category 1 through category 2. A strongly held organizational saga, on the other hand, appears in other cases to be one of the most important variables in determining institutional response, particularly in category 1 and 2 types of environment.

The use of incentives

Consensus building cannot be viewed solely as the generation of common views about a series of phenomena in institutions; it is also very much about whether people subsequently behave as if there were common views. In the task, therefore, of trying to generate some sort of basic agreement about the shape of an institution and its academic and other policies, the role which incentives play at present, or could play in the future, is likely to be significant.

Why would academics, in particular, change their behaviour and performance just because a document encompasses a desired institutional change? Such a comment may be regarded as distasteful by custodians of public accountability (who would argue a legal basis for compliance), by proponents of rational planning processes (who may not admit the possibility!) and by the professional academic community (who would argue that the concept of a collegium embraces dedication, professional standards and doing the right thing in the interests of the institution). However, because of the manifestations of conflict, the rapidly increasing visibility of collective bargaining schemes and the onset of steady state, it cannot be denied that certain types of reward and incentives may (1) contribute to a complex set of motivations, and (2) be necessary in the future.

In the case studies of British universities, there was not much evidence of senior administrators admitting to think about explicit incentives as a means of delivering policy agreement. (This was less so in the polytechnics we visited.) It may be because such an admission would be perceived as somehow unprofessional. Yet, if institutions are trying to become increasingly explicit about policies, this in itself may necessitate more formal incentive structures to translate these goals into work expectations and faculty behaviour. Three immediate examples of such corporate policies frequently mentioned in the context of the next five years are:

1   the movement towards recurrent/community/non-traditional education, given the declining birthrate in many countries;

2   the attempt to get more academic staff to engage in research in some British polytechnics; to be more immediately competitive with universities in the battles to come;

3   the attempt to encourage many research-oriented academics in universities to improve their teaching performance or become involved in new teaching programmes, to be in a better position to cope with polytechnic challenges;

4   the attempt to persuade academics to retire early, leave the institution temporarily or permanently, thus saving money.

Let us conjecture what incentive structure an institution would need to move its members in these directions. It can certainly be said that such movement depends on (a) the degree to which institutional goals are well formed and articulated; (b) the degree to which faculty behaviour in support of organizational goals is evaluated and rewarded.

It is clear that the incentive structures in some institutions are stacked against the implementation of such policies. In the case of movements to recurrent/community education, for instance, the necessity of creating highly flexible programme structures, modes of study and attendance patterns may be thwarted by strong disincentives consisting of the bother of inventing new fee structures, low FTE weightings for part-time students; absence of time-off in lieu for working unsociable hours, and the low academic status often accorded to such work in most institutions. If, in the case of the British polytechnics, few members of the academic staff choose to participate in further research programmes, it is because research-related policies do not coincide with teaching-related incentive structures. If the production of extensive publications and the acquisition of research money do not result in any career advancement because promotions are based on administrative roles, this policy will find it hard to survive in fact. On the other hand, there is evidence that imaginative vice-chancellors and directors are being reasonably successful in encouraging staff mobility by arranging transfers to other institutions, visiting professorships/sabbaticals overseas, fractional appointments, work sharing, etc.

Incentives design is an area of activity which does not rest happily within bureaucratic or collegial modes of institution, but has far more affinity with political models and the behaviour associated with them. However, there is little hard-researched evidence on the effect which the use of incentives to operate consensus has on the ethos of the organization, particularly in times of contraction. One suspects, from the polytechnics visited, that consensus thus generated would tend to be relatively shortlived – but this may be because of the particular politics of the institution rather than the inherent characteristics of the incentives themselves.

Although most heads of institutions in the case studies were of the view that consensus was a quality to be sought and nurtured, they fully recognized (1) the tendencies to divisiveness in the contemporary scene, and (2) that swift executive action as a response to urgent problems might be increasingly necessary. The interrelationship of these factors could have serious effects on their success in building consensus.

Institutional leadership

Running through the previous discussion are a number of threads related to the roles of institutional leadership. These now need some synthesis.

Centralization

An increased degree of centralization is a commonly observed tendency in decision-making during periods of organizational stress and contraction (Trow, 1975). The review of cases undertaken by the authors confirms, at least in some general respects, the validity of this assumption, particularly when moderate and substantial financial contraction occurs suddenly. Governing bodies, and councils, by virtue of their legal responsibilities alone, are necessarily more involved in personnel policies and actions and in most cases take a much more active and directive role in financial decisions. Central administrators, too, have a more active role under conditions of decline for similar reasons and by virtue of the fact that they are normally in the position of proposing policies for response by governing bodies and internal constituents. Since financial criteria tend to dominate policy formulation under contraction, those in possession of financial information and controls – the administration and governing body – naturally become more proactive. This logical chain of events and distribution of formal responsibilities can be misleading, however, in the simplicity of its conclusion. Indeed, some argue that the organizational conditions created by contraction necessitate not only centralized decision-making but abandoning the traditional, unobtrusive style of organizational change in favour of a highly directive and 'intrusive' style (Behn, 1980).

The thesis of centralized decision-making requires qualification when applied to institutions of higher education. Our review of cases suggests that a strong top-down, corporate strategy approach to contraction decisions results in substantial political conflict within the institution and an erosion of trust and confidence between top administrative personnel and affected academics and staff. How serious or permanent the erosion is depends upon the style used and the level of the existing stock of trust and confidence.

In the case of North East London Polytechnic, the erosion was widely perceived as serious and was cited by the first director in his letter of resignation. The University of Lancaster's plan, although similarly voted down by the senate, was developed in a more consultative and representative style and the administration generally enjoyed a higher level of trust and confidence among academic staff. In the cases reviewed, then, central administrative initiative was not as much at issue as the manner and style in which it was carried out. Managers are expected to manage!

Leadership and participation

In 'normal' times organizational members tend to be 'fluid' participants in the decision-making process; in other words, an individual may be actively involved for a short time on a particular issue but in general is not highly active across many issues. We found that this characteristic of 'fluid participation' generally held for slowed-growth environments and that as institutions encountered contraction, only moderate increases in participation levels were experienced. Academics were more generally aware of circumstances and policies and were found to be more active in seeking up-to-date information. Active participation in decision-making or in lobbying decision-makers was still left, by and large, to those representing faculty interests, for example union officials, department heads. Regular attendance at union meetings, with the exception of a 'crisis' issue meeting, has not appreciably changed although union membership at our case-study institutions has. However, despite continuing levels of relatively low direct participation, academics' expectations for involvement in decision-making were higher than before slow growth or moderate contraction affected the institution. Expected modes of involvement most commonly mentioned were early consultation with respect to changes in the environment and alternative policy responses. High levels of environmental uncertainty induce considerable stress among organizational members who may not actively seek direct participatory roles but who have a heightened sense of a 'need to know'. The four-phase model analysed earlier makes it clear that 'participation' is by no means to be equated with 'representation' or 'committees'. There are many arenas, formal and informal, where participation, access, consultation and information can take place, and if senior administrators are to cope successfully with ambiguity, it appears that more systematic and wide-ranging strategies for involving staff are needed.

Using the opportunities afforded by instability

The conditions created by instability and contraction could be viewed as critical yet ideal periods for effecting creative, programmatic and institutional mission changes that would prove difficult under other circumstances. Given the natural tendency of higher education organizations to resist change, many theorists as well as politicians view a heavy dose of external inducements and directives as necessary to effect any significant change (Pfeffner and Salancik, 1978). Contraction provides such inducements.

Reformulation of an institution's role or mission or even more marginal changes such as programme 'rationalization', however, requires time and some idea of what new level of financial equilibrium might be expected.

Governments caught in recessionary times, with the attendant difficulties of predicting revenues, may well have difficulty in providing assurances of new equilibrium levels. Governments committed to inducing new equilibrium levels as a matter of policy, on the other hand, may misjudge the viability of the levels set and/or the time required to achieve those levels with an acceptable level of rationality.

One of the key tasks of higher education leaders is, therefore, to develop mutual understandings with government as to probable financial equilibrium levels over a period of time. Once reasonably stable parameters have been established, and assuming that they provide both pressures for change and sources of stability, educational leaders in concert with their faculties can proceed to develop long-range plans.

The difficulty of achieving this type of mutual understanding between government and higher education leaders is twofold. First, the British and American political systems do not necessarily lend themselves to stability of policy, that is, short-term, election-relevant actions tend to be pursued. Government leaders may therefore find it 'politically irrational' to give higher education a greater measure of support and stability than they enjoy themselves or in fact can provide. The second difficulty emerges from the fact that institutional leaders are, by the very nature of their roles, advocates for their particular institution, genuinely believing in the need for and value of programmes offered by their institution. They are naturally reluctant to agree to any 'equilibrium' that might undermine the viability of these programmes. Yet without some reasonable estimate of resources available it is difficult to engage in positive planning efforts; in other words, goals are dependent upon resources.

Creating a positive institutional climate

Another set of major tasks of institutional leadership under conditions of instability and contraction concerns maintaining a positive climate in which to work. The first element in this set of tasks seems to us to be a sense of institutional initiative or 'master of our own destiny' feeling within the institution. This may take the form of institutionally initiated 'programme rationalization' or pruning, or a united stance against contraction pressures. Whatever the particular response, the general psychological benefit is one of a proactive attitude. Another key element, closely related to the first, is to avert a paralysis of action by the institution. One of the well-recognized deficiencies of widely distributed patterns of influence, such as those found in institutions of higher education, is a tendency to paralyse action altogether (Banfield, 1961). Carefully formulated initiatives guided through the thickets of academic environment by a leadership which was sensitive to genuine consultation and to political gamesmanship were rare phenomena in the cases studied.

In formulating such initiatives, institutional leaders need to balance political feasibility with educationally sound strategies. There are, for example, strong pressures for uniformity of treatment both in the context of institutions vis-à-vis the government and subunits within the institution. This tendency towards uniformity derives from (1) political pressures of equity, and (2) the uncertainty of doing otherwise, but may be unhelpful in any institutional reshaping.

The use of 'policy portfolios'

Davies (1979) in discussing the evolution of policy appropriate to contraction in school systems in the US, uses the term 'policy portfolio' to describe the range of necessary policies. Strategic policies are concerned with the desired shape and size of the institution. Substantive (or 'bread and butter') policies are concerned with precise plans for curriculum and research development, personnel, space allocation, cost effectiveness, student services, etc. Climatic policies are concerned with creating a collaborative mood in the organization, where people are prepared to be open and confront problems. They include, for instance, openness of information (for staff), secondment and staff development possibilities, rewards and incentives. Interest groups are rarely mobilized by lofty strategic thoughts, but they are activated by the substantive policies which affect them directly. It is desirable that climatic policies should be operational before leaders start pushing strategic and substantive policies through, otherwise the 'loopbacks' described earlier will surely occur, and it is much more difficult to resurrect a good climate once it has disappeared.

Leadership at various levels

We have tended to talk of the vice-chancellor or institutional head as the 'change-agent'. Yet it emerges from the cases studied that it is not a good thing for him to be the 'front man', leading his troops into battle on a white charger. Defeats (and there will be some) weaken his position. It appears to be far more effective to develop a strong senior leadership team to share the load. In this case functional specialisms may develop within the team.

Collectively they stand a greater chance of participating across the whole range of discussions and meetings throughout the institution to assist in problem clarification, information dissemination, the sowing of seeds and the proposal of solutions. This view is strongly confirmed by Mayhew (1979) and by Enderud (1977) in the various phases of his four-phase model. However, this needs to be balanced and supported by a broad-based alliance of people in different parts and at different levels of the organization. Davies (1979) also refers to the role of central-planning and service organs as agents of change, rather than as hatchet men. In this sense, they would need to consider colleagues in the departments as clients needing specific assistance to overcome problems associated with contraction. With the exception of certain curriculum and educational technology units, we did not get the impression that those in central units saw themselves as providing help or giving a service: they were in the business of maintenance and control rather than organizational development. If contraction is about institutional change, then it follows that those in key staff positions need to develop capabilities in this area to supplement their technical expertise, and personally act in a low-key, informal influencing role. Kipnis et al. (1980) have observed the techniques used by administrators in a variety of organizations to influence superiors, subordinates and peers. It appears that they use quite different tactics, depending on the benefit sought from the target person, the power and amount of resistance shown by the target person, the size of the work unit, the presence or otherwise of unions, and their own level in the organization. This field of influencing tactics is one about which we found administrators in our cases reluctant to be too specific, perhaps understandably! Yet, in some ways, it is one of the most crucial aspects of the whole exercise. When Sizer (1981) speaks of managers of change, it is surely the considerations represented in this chapter which represent the qualities he has in mind, both in terms of executive leadership and staff roles.

The other level of leadership is that of middle management, which seems to be in a most difficult position. For example, the role of dean is ambiguous, and usually part-time for a limited period ('Buggins' turn). It is not a position which, in universities, gives appreciable financial reward, immense job satisfaction or great career prospects. The amount of autonomy and authority a dean has will be determined by the degree of centralization in the university, the latitude allowed him by heads of departments, and his own style and personality. In polytechnics, there is a growing tendency to appoint full-time permanent deans, and in some larger institutions they may also double up as assistant directors with a functional responsibility across the institution. If the phenomenon of contraction necessitates middle management which can anticipate cutbacks through meaningful contingency planning, establish priorities in a calm rather than crisis setting, develop faculty-wide consensus, enhance the external fund-raising capability of the faculty and deal with the considerable number of personnel problems likely to emerge, it is not at all clear at present what type of dean is likely to be the most effective. One is not searching for administrative skills, nor scholarship alone, but a rare combination of expertise.

Political will

Finally, it has been suggested to us that institutions and their leaders lack the political will to make the decisions associated with contraction, because of the personal unpleasantness involved, the ethical questions raised by butchering one's colleagues or the shortage of rational or political skills. It has been widely noted that a much more proactive UGC or NAB role of specifying precisely what should go or stay in individual institutions would meet with some sighs of relief from vice-chancellors and directors. The evidence collected in our cases does not confirm this view. Even when early attempts had been unsuccessful, we observed a determination to get things right but in ways which made sense in terms of the historical development and character of the institution. Considerable learning and adaptation have taken place in a relatively short period. Nonetheless we come back to the point of viewing problems as opportunities – a trite phrase in many ways, yet one which ought to encapsulate a managerial philosophy for the 1980s in higher education.

References

Bacharach, S.B. and Lawler, E.J. (1980) *Power and Politics in Organisations*. San Francisco, Jossey-Bass.

Baldridge, J.V. (1971a) *Power and Conflict in the University*. New York, Wiley.

Baldridge, J.V. (1971b) *Academic Governance*. Berkeley, Calif., McCutchan.

Banfield, E.C. (1961) *Political Influence*. New York, The Free Press.

Bardach, E. (1978) *The Implementation Game*. Cambridge, Mass., Institute of Technology.

Becher, T. and Kogan, M. (1980) *Process and Structure in Higher Education*. London, Heinemann.

Behn, R.D. (1980) Leadership for cut-back management. *Public Administration*

Review, November/December, pp. 613–620.

Blake, R., Mouton, J.S. and Williams, M.S. (1981) *The Academic Administrator Grid*. San Francisco, Jossey-Bass.

Bowen, F.M. and Glenny, L.A. (1980) *University in Public Higher Education: Response to Stress at Ten Californian Colleges and Universities*. Sacramento, Calif., The California Post Secondary Education Commission.

Brosan, G.S. (1978) *Models of Management in Education*. Paper presented to Second European Higher Education Management Programme. London, Anglian Regional Management Centre.

Clark, B.R. (1972) The organisational saga in higher education. *Administrative Science Quarterly*, June, pp. 178–184.

Clark, B.R. (1978) Academic power: concepts, modes and perspectives. In: Van de Graaff, J.H. et. al. (eds) *Academic Power*. New York, Praeger

Cohen, M. and March, J.G. (1974) *Leadership and Ambiguity*. New York, McGraw-Hill.

Corson, J.J. (1973) Perspectives on the university compared with other organizations. In: Perkins, J.A. (ed.) *The University as an Organisation*. New York, McGraw-Hill, pp. 156–169.

Cyert, R.M. and March, J.G. (1963) *A Behavioural Theory of the Firm*. Englewood Cliffs, N.J., Prentice Hall.

Davies, J.L. (1979) *Declining Enrolments, Conflict and Ambiguity: The Search for an Appropriate Policy Formation Process*. Paper presented to British Education Management and Administration Society Annual Conference, Sheffield, September 1979.

Davies, J.L. (1980) The role of the university rector in policy formation in the contemporary context of steady state and uncertainty. *CRE New Series*, no. 51, hind quarter.

Dougherty, F.A. (1978) *What is the Most Effective Way to Handle Program Discontinuance? Case Studies from Ten Campuses*. Paper presented to the American Association of Higher Education, April 1978.

Enderud, H.G. (1977) *Four Faces of Leadership in the Academic Organisation*. Copenhagen, Nyt. Nordisk Forlag.

Glenny, L.A. and Bowen, F.M. (1980) *Signals for Change: Stress Indicators for Colleges and Universities*. Report to the California Post Secondary Education Commission, Sacramento, California.

Glenny, L.A. et al. (1976) *Presidents Confront Reality*. San Francisco, Jossey-Bass.

Hickson, D.J., Hinings, C.R., Lee, C.A., Schneck, R.E. and Pennings, J.M. (1971) A strategic contingencies theory of interorganisational power. *Administrative Science Quarterly*, June, pp. 216–229.

Hills, F.S. and Mahony, T.A. (1978) University budgets and organisational decision making. *Administrative Science Quarterly*, September, pp. 454–465.

Hirschman, A.O. (1970) *Exit, Voice and Loyalty Responses to Decline in Firms, Organizations, and States*. Cambridge, Mass., Harvard University Press.

Kipnis, D., Schmidt, S.M. and Wilkinson, I. (1980) *Intraorganisational Influence Tactics*. Faculty Working Papers, School of Business Administration, Temple University, Philadelphia.

Levine, C.H. (1978) Organizational decline and cutback management. *Public Administration Review*, July/August, pp. 316–325.

Mayhew, L.B. (1979) *Surviving the Eighties*. San Francisco, Jossey-Bass.

Millett, J. (1962) *The Academic Community*. New York, McGraw-Hill.

Mingle, J.C. (1981) *The Challenge of Retrenchment*. San Francisco, Jossey-Bass.

Olsen, J.P. and March, J.G. (1974) *Ambiguity and Choice in Organisations*. Bergen Universitetsforlaget.

Parsons, T. and Platt, G.M. (1973) *The American University*. Cambridge, Mass., Harvard University Press.

Pfeffner, J. and Moore, W. (1980) Power in university budgeting: a replication and extension. *Administrative Science Quarterly*, December, pp. 637–653.

Pfeffner, J. and Salancik, G.R. (1978) *The External Control of Organizations*. New York, Harper & Row.

Pressman, J.L. and Wildavsky, A. (1973) *Implementation*. Berkeley, University of California Press.

Richman, B.M. and Farmer, R.N. (1974) *Leadership, Goals and Power in Higher Education*. San Francisco, Jossey-Bass.

Rubin, I. (1980) Universities in stress: decision making under conditions of reduced resources. In: Levine, Charles H. (ed.) *Managing Fiscal Stress*. Chatham, N.J., Chatham House Publishers, Inc.

Sizer, J. (1981) *Institutional Performance Assessment, Adaptation and Change*. Paper delivered to Leverhulme Seminar on Institutional Adaptation and Change, Bristol, September 1981.

Sprenger, J.M. and Schultz, R.E. (1974) Staff reduction policies. *College Management*, May, pp. 22–23, 36.

Thompson, J.D. (1967) *Organisations in Action*. New York, McGraw-Hill.

Times Higher Education Supplement (1981) 1 May 1981.

Trow, M. (1975) The public and private lives of higher education. *Daedalus*, Winter, pp. 113–127.

Weber, M. (1947) *The Theory of Social and Economic Organisation*. New York, Free Press.

CHAPTER 4.2

A SYSTEMS APPROACH TO COLLEGE MANAGEMENT*
JACK LATCHAM AND ROB CUTHBERT

This paper is written for managers in further education. It aims to stimulate the reader's thinking about management, and thereby to help him or her to manage better.

Although it would be convenient, it is difficult to begin with a definition of 'management'. In one sense all teachers are managers – they manage students and they manage learning processes. Management is a flexible concept and it sometimes helps to give it such a broad meaning, but for the purposes of this paper we will regard management as a process which goes on in organizations, involves getting things done through people, and involves some special responsibility for the oversight of one or more aspects of college work. It is important at all times to remember that how we manage depends on our assumptions about what management is. This paper suggests one approach which seems to have particular merit for many further education situations. It does not offer a panacea, for there is none.

[. . .] The 'systems approach' to college management is the application of a few general concepts which help us to think about how college objectives and college resources are related.

Chambers' Dictionary defines a system as 'a set of things which together form a connected whole'. Clearly we can think of a college as a system in this sense. The first step in developing this idea is to recognize that the various parts of the system interact in a dynamic way. This interaction may be formally structured – as in a meeting of the college academic board – or informal – as in a chance conversation in a corridor between two heads of

* *Coombe Lodge Reports*, 1979, vol. 11, no. 14, pp. 589–593. © The Further Education Staff College, 1979. Jack Latcham is Associate Tutor, and Rob Cuthbert is a Staff Tutor, both at the Further Education Staff College.

department. Any organizational process can be regarded as the interaction of different parts of the organization. The 'parts' we choose to recognize may well vary according to the process we are considering. Each part will itself have the characteristics of a system, and in general any system may be regarded on the one hand as made up of several subsystems, and on the other hand as itself part of a wider (supra-) system. Our recognition of any one system as a distinctive whole depends on our seeing a certain coherence or unity in the processes of that system. The unity of the college comes, in part, from the common aim of providing educational programmes for a particular clientele. Unity, in other words, comes from our attributing certain objectives to the system as a whole. For the purposes of this paper the terms 'objective', 'goal', 'aim' and 'purpose' will be used more or less interchangeably in this general sense.

The ideas of systemic unity and systemic objectives are inextricably linked with the idea of a system boundary. Boundaries may be geographical (the college gates), temporal (end of term), sociological (the class) or mental constructs (the course), and are usually a mixture of these. In principle, boundaries are lines drawn for analytical convenience. Are employers and parents part of the college system? The answer will vary according to the problem we are trying to solve.

Drawing a boundary not only defines the extent of the system, it also defines that system's environment. We then become particularly interested in transactions across the boundary. If there is none, then the system is said to be closed – nothing enters or leaves. All man-made systems, however, are open systems. There are transactions between the system and its environment. We can distinguish between inputs to the system and outputs from the system.

How do we regard students within this framework? If we take students to be an input, then the 'qualified' student can be regarded as the system's main output. For the college it will usually be convenient to regard resources – staff, equipment, buildings, money – as inputs. We might draw our college boundary to exclude students and regard college output as courses, or, more generally, learning opportunities. In this case we tend to highlight the problem of take-up of the opportunities provided.

In summary, then, we define a system in terms of purpose, boundary, process, inputs and outputs. We recognize the college as a system, with a boundary which we can mentally redraw to suit a particular problem. The college is itself part of wider systems, notably the local and national FE systems. The college itself contains subsystems – departments, sections, courses, trade union branches, the library, the administration, etc. Any particular system is partly constrained by the wider system of which it is part, and partly free to exercise self-control. The college, for example, may be constrained to operate within a fixed budget and subject, perhaps, to certain student–staff ratio norms, but often has discretion in the deployment of staff to courses.

What does this mean for the individual manager? It suggests one way of dealing with managerial problems. The first step is to identify the problem; then and only then is it possible to decide on suitable systems parameters for handling that problem:

- Where do I draw the boundary?
- What shall I regard as inputs and outputs?
- What subsystems and suprasystems shall I recognize?
- What are the objectives of the system vis-à-vis this problem?

Of course, the answers to these questions do to a large extent identify the problem; what matters is avoiding automatic assumptions about, say, boundaries, which might lead to distortion.

Using these concepts can give us a clearer picture of what we mean by 'good' management, by forcing us to think systematically about what it means to be effective. What are the inputs and outputs? What is their interrelationship?

We may also have to consider what are the most important constituent parts of the college. If we start at college level and work down, we will usually identify departments as important units, then perhaps sections within departments, courses, years within courses and so on. This will tend to give us a picture in which teaching is the central process. For a different picture it may be easier to start at the level of the individual course.

If we look on the course as a system (*Fig.* 9) we might assume that the central process is learning, and that the course boundary is drawn so as to include the learning experiences of a specified group of students. Students and resources can be regarded as inputs, and 'qualified' students are the major output. The overall course aim is to facilitate student learning of certain kinds, and syllabuses may be written in terms which make the objectives of student learning explicit. Thus effectiveness can be defined in fairly precise terms. Once objectives are fixed it is possible to monitor progress and to feed back corrections to the learning process as required. The course manager may in practice be more concerned with effectiveness than efficiency, since the amounts of resource input may well be prescribed

Figure 9   The individual course seen as a system.

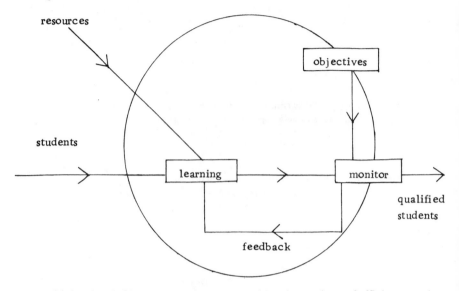

at a higher level. However, at departmental level questions of efficiency and effectiveness each require careful consideration.

Learning may remain the central process, but the head of department is, as manager, at one or more removes from this central process. The boundary of the department may be drawn according to student experience, or according to staff membership, or both. Objectives for the department will probably go beyond individual students' learning objectives. The department as a whole may be conceived as serving a particular local industrial or other community. Inputs then become the wishes of that community, and outputs are actions and programmes to meet those wishes – new courses, research, consultancy, information and so on. The head of department will also be concerned to maintain and develop his system's major resource – the staff. At the same time the head must ensure that the continuing work of the department is progressing satisfactorily, and needs to establish some sort of monitoring system for all the work of the department. Performance criteria must relate to effectiveness or efficiency, or more likely to both, and measures may be qualitative or quantitative. Commonly used criteria include total student numbers, examination results, wastage rates, class size, staff–student ratios, room utilization rates and so on. Rather more subtle qualitative assessments of, say, staff satisfaction, or the satisfaction of local employers, may be equally important. Most of these criteria depend on the assumption that the central process to be managed is teaching, rather than learning.

At college level the problems may often be similar, but one stage further removed from the 'chalkface'. There is also a new set of problems concerning the place of the college in wider systems – the local community, the local FE system, the local education system, the national FE system and so on. The principal and the college governors stand very much at the boundary of the college system and need to face both inward and outward. *Figure* 10 suggests just some possible inputs, outputs and processes which may need to be taken into account. Good management, particularly at college level, becomes increasingly a matter of striking a desirable balance between these different activities.

Figure 10   Inputs, outputs and processes of the college system.

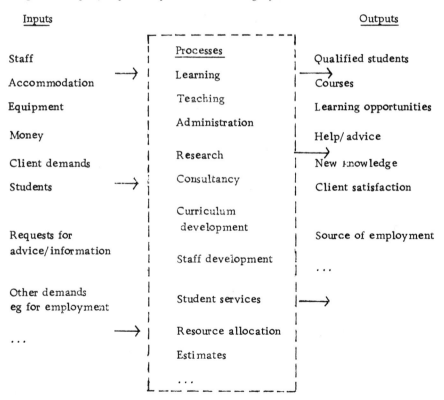

[. . .] Two caveats are necessary. The first is that analysis is useless without action. This paper suggests one mode of analysis, but it has nothing to say about the interpersonal skills which the manager needs if he is to act on his analysis. The second, and related point is that it can be dangerous to assume, as this paper assumes, that there are such things as systemic objectives. There may be some issues, such as student discipline, for example, where different protagonists hold such different views about institutional purposes that reasoned debate become difficult (for want of common ground) and a systems approach becomes worse than useless – because it assumes a consensus where none exists. Faced with an intractable problem, the manager must always be ready to take one step further back and question the assumptions which create the intractability. Those assumptions may rest on unshakeable values which indeed make the problem intractable, but a systematic analysis of the situation will at least have replaced seat-of-the-pants management with a more systematic and disciplined intuition.

CHAPTER 4.3

LEADERSHIP AND AMBIGUITY*
MICHAEL D. COHEN AND JAMES G. MARCH

The basic ideas

When we look at universities as they struggle with the problems of reorganization, reform, choice and survival, we are struck by one quite consistent theme: decision opportunities are fundamentally ambiguous stimuli (Cohen et al., 1972).[1] Although organizations can often be viewed as vehicles for solving well-defined problems and as structures within which conflict is resolved through bargaining, they are also sets of procedures through which organizational participants arrive at an interpretation of what they are doing and what they have done while doing it. From this point of view, an organization is a collection of choices looking for problems, issues and feelings looking for decision situations in which they might be aired, solutions looking for issues to which they might be the answer, and decision-makers looking for work.

Such a view of organizational choice focuses attention on the ways in which the meaning of choice changes over time. It calls attention to the strategic effects of timing (in the introduction of choices and problems), the time pattern of available energy and the impact of organizational structure on these.

A key to understanding the processes within organizations is to view a choice opportunity[2] as a garbage can into which various problems and solutions are dumped by participants. The mix of garbage in a single can

---

* *Leadership and Ambiguity: The American College President*. New York, McGraw-Hill, 1974. © The Carnegie Foundation for the Advancement of Teaching, 1974. Reprinted with permission. James G. March is the Fred H. Merrill Professor of Management at the Graduate School of Business, Stanford University.

depends partly on the labels attached to the alternative cans; but it also depends on what garbage is being produced at the moment, on the mix of cans available and on the speed with which garbage is collected and removed from the scene.

Although we may imagine that choice opportunities lead first to the generation of decision alternatives, then to an examination of the consequences of those alternatives, then to an examination of the consequences in terms of objectives, and finally to a decision, such a model is often a poor description of what actually happens. In a garbage can situation, a decision is an outcome (or an interpretation) of several relatively independent 'streams' within an organization.

We will limit our attention to the interrelations among four such streams:

1 *Problems.* Problems are the concern of people inside and outside the organization. They arise over issues of lifestyle; family; frustrations of work; careers; group relations within the organization; distribution of status, jobs and money; ideology; or current crises of mankind as interpreted by the mass media or the next door neighbour. All require attention. Problems are, however, distinct from choices; and they may not be resolved when choices are made.

2 *Solutions.* A solution is somebody's product. A computer is not just a solution to a problem in payroll management, discovered when needed. It is an answer actively looking for a question. The creation of need is not a curiosity of the market in consumer products; it is a general phenomenon of processes of choice. Despite the dictum that you cannot find the answer until you have formulated the question well, you often do not know what the question is in organizational problem-solving until you know the answer.

3 *Participants.* Participants come and go. Since every entrance is an exit somewhere else, the distribution of entrances depends on the attributes of the choice being left as much as it does on the attributes of the new choice. Substantial variation in participation stems from other demands on the participants' time (rather than from features of the decision under study).

4 *Choice opportunities.* These are occasions when an organization is expected to produce behaviour that can be called a decision. Opportunities arise regularly, and any organization has ways of declaring an occasion for choice. Contracts must be signed; people hired, promoted or fired; money spent; and responsibilities allocated.

Although not completely independent of each other, each of the streams can be viewed as independent and exogenous to the system. Attention will be concentrated here on examining the consequences of different rates and patterns of flow in each of the streams and different procedures for relating them.

The properties of universities as organized anarchies make the garbage can ideas particularly appropriate to an understanding of organizational choice within higher education. Although a college or university operates within the metaphor of a political system or a hierarchical bureaucracy, the actual operation of either is considerably attenuated by the ambiguity of college goals, by the lack of clarity in educational technology and by the transient character of many participants. Insofar as a college is correctly described as an organized anarchy, a college president needs to understand the consequences of a garbage can decision process.

Implications of the ideas

Elsewhere (Cohen et al., 1972) we have detailed the development of these basic ideas into a computer simulation model that has been run under conditions simulating a variety of different organizational structures. This garbage can model of choice operates under each of the hypothesized organization structures to assign problems and decision-makers to choices, to determine the energy required and effective energy applied to choices, to make such choices and resolve such problems as the assignments and energies indicate are feasible.

For each run of the model we have computed five simple summary statistics to describe the process:

1   Decision style. Within a garbage can process, decisions are made in three different ways:

a.   By *oversight*. If a choice is activated when problems are attached to other choices and if there is energy available to make the new choice quickly, it will be made without any attention to existing problems and with a minimum of time and energy.

b.   By *flight*. In some cases, choices are associated with problems (unsuccessfully) for some time until a choice 'more attractive' to the problems comes along. The problems leave the choice, and thereby make it possible to make the decision. The decision resolves no problems (they having now attached themselves to a new choice).

c.   *By resolution.* Some choices resolve problems after some period of working on them. The length of time may vary greatly (depending on the number of problems). This is the familiar case that is implicit in most discussion of choice within organizations.

Some choices involve both flight and resolution (i.e., some problems leave, the remainder are solved). We have defined these as resolution, thus slightly exaggerating the importance of that style. As a result of that convention, the three styles are mutually exclusive and exhaustive with respect to any one choice; but the same organization may use any one of them on different choices. Thus, we can describe the decision-making style of the organization by specifying the proportion of completed choices that are made in each of these three ways.

2   Problem activity. We wish to find some measure of the degree to which problems are active within the organization. Such a measure should reflect something like the degree of conflict within the organization or the degree of articulation of problems. We have taken the number of time periods that each problem is active and attached to some choice, and added them together to obtain the total time periods for all problems.

3   Problem latency. A problem may be active but not attached to any choice. It may be recognized and accepted by some part of the organization but may not be considered germane to any available choice. Presumably an organization with relatively high problem latency will exhibit somewhat different symptoms from one with low latency. We have measured problem latency by taking the total number of periods that each problem is active but not attached to a choice and added them together to obtain the total time periods for all problems.

4   Decision-maker activity. To measure the degree of decision-maker activity in the system, we require some measure that reflects decision-maker energy expenditure, movement and persistence. We have computed the total number of times that any decision-maker shifts from one choice to another.

5   Decision difficulty. We want to be able to characterize the ease with which a system makes decisions. Because of the way in which decisions can be made in the system (see the above discussion of decision style), that is not the same as the level of problem activity. We have used, as a measure, the total number of periods that each choice is active, and we added them together to obtain the total number of periods for all choices.

These summary statistics,[3] along with a more intensive look at the individual histories of the simulations, reveal eight major properties of garbage can decision processes.

First, resolution of problems is not the most common style for making decisions except under conditions where flight is severely restricted or under a few conditions of light load. [. . .]

Second, the process is thoroughly and generally sensitive to variations in load. An increase in the net energy load on the system generally increases problem activity, decision-maker activity, decision difficulty and the uses of flight and oversight. Problems are less likely to be solved, decision-makers are likely to shift from one problem to another more frequently, choices are likely to take longer to make and to be less likely to resolve problems.

Third, decision-makers and problems tend to *track* each other through choices. Both decision-makers and problems tend to move together from choice to choice. As a result, decision-makers may be expected to feel that they are always working on the same problems in somewhat different contexts, mostly without results. Problems, in a similar fashion, meet the same people wherever they go with the same result.

Fourth, there are some important interconnections among three key aspects of the 'efficiency' of the decision processes we have specified. The first of these is problem activity – the amount of time unresolved problems are actively attached to choice situations. Problem activity is a rough measure of potential for decision conflict in the organization. It assesses the degree of involvement of problems in choices. The second aspect is problem latency – the amount of time that problems spend activated but not linked to choices. The third aspect is decision time – the persistence of choices. Presumably, a good organizational structure would keep both problem activity and problem latency low through rapid problem solution in its choices. In the garbage can process we never observe this. Some structures reduce the number of unresolved problems active in the organization but at the cost of increasing the latency period of problems and (in most cases) the time devoted to reaching decisions. Other structures decrease problem latency, but at the cost of increasing problem activity and decision time.

Fifth, the decision-making process is frequently sharply interactive. Although some phenomena associated with the garbage can are regular and flow through nearly all the cases (for example, the effect of overall load), other phenomena are much more dependent on the particular combination of structures involved. In fact, the process is one that often looks capricious to an observer. Many of the outcomes are produced by distinct consequences of the particular time phasing of choices, problems and participant availability.

Sixth, important problems are more likely to be solved than unimportant ones. Early-arriving problems are more likely to be resolved than later ones. The system, in effect, produces a queue of problems in terms of their importance – to the strong disadvantage of late-arriving, relatively unimportant problems, particularly when load is heavy. This queue is the result of the operation of the model. It was not imposed as a direct assumption.

Seventh, important choices are much *less* likely to resolve problems than are unimportant choices. Important choices are made by oversight and flight. Unimportant choices are made by resolution. The differences are substantial. Moreover, they are not connected to the entry times of the choices. We believe this property of important choices in a garbage can decision process can be naturally and directly related to the phenomenon in complex organizations of 'important' choices that often appear to just 'happen'.

Eighth, although a large proportion of the choices are made, the choice failures that do occur are concentrated among the most important and least important choices. Choices of intermediate importance are virtually always made.

In a broad sense, these features of the decision-making process provide some clues to how organizations survive when they do not know what they are doing. Much of the process violates standard notions of how decisions ought to be made. But most of those notions are built on assumptions that cannot be met under the conditions we have specified. When objectives and technologies are unclear, organizations are charged to discover some alternative decision procedures that permit them to proceed without doing violence to the domains of participants or to their model of an organization. It is a difficult charge, to which the process we have described is a partial response.

At the same time, the details of the outcomes clearly depend on features of the organizational structure. The same garbage can process results in different behavioural symptoms under different levels of load on the system or different designs of the structure of the organization. These differences raise the possibility of predicting variations in decision behaviour in different organizations. In the next section we consider one possible application of such an approach to the domain of higher education.

Garbage cans and universities

Although there is great variability among colleges and universities, we think the model's major attributes have fairly general relevance to decision-making in higher education. University decision-making frequently does not 'resolve' problems. Choices are likely to be made by flight or oversight. University decision processes appear to be sensitive to changes in load. Active decision-makers and problems seem often to track one another through a series of choices without appreciable progress in solving problems. Important choices seem particularly likely not to solve problems.

What we see, both in the model and in actual observations of universities, are decisions whose interpretations continually change during the process of resolution. Problems, choices and decision-makers arrange and re-arrange themselves. In the course of these arrangements the meaning of a choice can change several times – if the 'meaning' of a choice is understood as the mix of problems that are discussed in the context of that choice.

Problems are often solved, but rarely by the choice to which they are first attached. A choice that might, under some circumstances, be made with little effort becomes an arena for many problems. As a result, it becomes almost impossible to make – until the problems drift off to another arena. The matching of problems, choices and decision-makers is partly controlled by content, 'relevance' and competence; but it is also quite sensitive to timing, the particular combinations of current garbage cans and the overall load on the system.

[. . .]

Conclusion

We have tried to translate a set of observations made in the study of some university organizations into a model of decision-making in what we have called organized anarchies – that is, in situations which do not meet the conditions for more classical models of decision-making in some or all of three important ways: preferences are problematic, technology is unclear or participation is fluid. The garbage can process, as it has been observed, is one in which problems, solutions and participants move from one choice opportunity to another in such a way that the nature of the choice, the time it takes and the problems it solves all depend on a relatively complicated intermeshing of the mix of choices available at any one time, the mix of problems that have access to the organization, the mix of solutions looking for problems and the outside demands on the decision-makers.

A major feature of the garbage can process is the partial decoupling of problems and choices. Although we think of decision-making as a process for solving problems, that is often not what happens. Problems are worked upon in the context of some choice, but choices are made only when the shifting combinations of problems, solutions and decision-makers happen to make action possible. Quite commonly this is after problems have left a given choice arena or before they have discovered it (decisions by flight or oversight).

Though the specification of the model is quite simple, the interaction within it is rather complex, so that investigation of the probable behaviour of a system fully characterized by the garbage can process and our specifications requires computer simulation. We acknowledge immediately that no real system can be fully characterized in this way. Nonetheless, the simulated organizations exhibit behaviours that can be observed some of the time in almost all organizations and frequently in some, such as universities. The garbage can model is a possible step towards seeing the systematic inter-relatedness of organizational phenomena that are familiar, even common, but that have generally been regarded as isolated and pathological. Measured against a conventional normative model of rational choice, the garbage can process does seem pathological, but such standards are not really appropriate since the process occurs precisely when the preconditions of more 'normal' rational models are not met.

It is clear that the garbage can process does not do a particularly good job of resolving problems. But it does enable choices to be made and problems sometimes to be resolved even when the organization is plagued with goal ambiguity and conflict, with poorly understood problems that wander in and out of the system, with a variable environment and with decision-makers who may have other things on their minds. This is no mean achievement.

We would argue that there is a large class of significant situations within universities in which the preconditions of the garbage can process probably cannot be eliminated. Indeed in some, such as pure research, they should not be eliminated. The great advantage of trying to see garbage can phenomena together as a process is the possibility that that process can be understood, that organization design and decision-making can take account of its existence, and that, to some extent, it can be managed.

Notes

1   This chapter draws heavily on work we have done jointly with Johan Olsen.
2   Choice opportunity may be defined as an occasion on which an organization is expected to produce a decision.
3   For a discussion of alternative measures, see Cohen et al. (1972).

Reference

Cohen, M.D., March, J.G. and Olsen, J.P. (1972) A garbage can model of organizational choice. *Administrative Science Quarterly*, 17(1), pp. 1–25.

CHAPTER 4.4

TERTIARY COLLEGES: SOME ORGANIZATIONAL ISSUES*
MARGARET PREEDY

This chapter examines three aspects of tertiary college provision: (1) the characteristics which distinguish this form of provision from other types of institution serving the 16–19 age-group; (2) the constraints within which the tertiary college operates; and (3) the management and organizational issues confronting these colleges in the light of (1) and (2) above. The paper is based on evidence from 11 of the oldest-established colleges, in the form of policy documents and staff and student comments.[1]

Characteristics of the tertiary college

The tertiary colleges are responsible for all full- and part-time non-advanced education for the post-16 age-group in the areas which they serve. (Some also have some advanced work.) Unlike sixth-form colleges, they operate under further education regulations. The colleges thus combine all provision which elsewhere is separately administered in school sixth forms/sixth-form colleges and FE establishments. In 1982 there were 20 colleges in operation and a number of others at the planning stage (e.g. in Croydon and Sheffield). A tertiary college system enables economies of scale in concentrating staff, technical, library, sports and social facilities, and other resources in one institution, rather than spreading them across an FE college and several school sixth forms or sixth-form colleges.

With respect to the educational and social possibilities of this institutional

* Section 3 of this chapter draws on some material in Preedy, M. (1981) Tertiary colleges: some research issues. In: Ribbins, P. and Thomas, H. (eds) *Research in Educational Administration*. Proceedings of the Second BEMAS/SSRC Research Seminar, University of Birmingham. Margaret Preedy is a Research Assistant at the Open University.

form, some proponents have made fairly limited claims, suggesting that the colleges could provide under one roof a wide curricular choice for all ability- and age-groups in non-advanced post-compulsory education (see, for example, Mumford, 1970; Alexander, 1969). Some advocates of this system make more extended claims in arguing that it also provides an opportunity to break down the traditional barriers between 'academic' and 'vocational' education, enabling cross-disciplinary curricular developments, the chance for students to combine GCE and vocationally oriented elements in their programmes of study, and the development of a degree of integration between staff from all areas of work and between full- and part-time students with a wide range of course and social backgrounds and ability levels (see, for example, Janes and Miles, 1978; Pedley, 1973; ACFHE, 1981). Thus, it is suggested, the tertiary college would not be merely a bilateral institution serving the needs of 'sixth-form' and 'further education' students as separate categories, but rather could provide individual course programmes to meet the needs of each student according to his/her abilities.

In drawing a broad distinction between the 'limited' and 'extended' approaches to the potential of tertiary colleges outlined above, it is useful to apply Daunt's (1975) concept of the two views of comprehensive educa- tion.[2] The 'first view' or 'limited' approach stresses meritocratic aims and high standards of performance, combining flexibility with the potential for social mobility. The second more 'extended' view emphasizes the develop- ment of the potential of each individual child and parity of esteem between different curricular routes and varying ability levels – 'the education of all children is held to be intrinsically of equal value' (Daunt, 1975, p. 16).

The third section of this chapter examines the day-to-day management and organizational issues facing the colleges in the context of these two broad approaches. First, it is necessary to take into account another condi- tioning factor in the development of the colleges – the constraints, both external and internal, under which they operate.

Constraints

External environmental factors

The colleges operate within a network of competing demands and expec- tations from a wide range of institutions, agencies, groups and individuals. These include the LEA, DES, government legislation and initiatives, the MSC, employers, exam boards, HE institutions and parents. Thus, for example, parents of students aiming at three A-Levels in preparation for higher education will expect an emphasis on academic performance, expert guidance on HE applications and so on. Employers, on the other hand, will expect a programme of training in job-related skills by staff with industrial experience backed up by up-to-date technical equipment. The requirements of local employers for specific skill training in a particular industrial process may clash with national government imperatives, under the auspices of the MSC, for Youth Training Service (YTS) provision stressing the development of broad generic and transferable skills. (See Gleeson and Mardle, 1980, for a discussion of the 'mismatch' between the demands of local industry and government in the FE sector.)

Economic factors

Financial restraints have, of course, increasingly affected the whole of the post-compulsory education sector since the mid-1970s. As a consequence the profile of provision of the tertiary colleges has not, in general, developed in the ways that were envisaged in the more propitious economic climate of the early 1970s. In particular, with a few exceptions, the adult and community education role of the colleges and provision for the handicapped have not expanded as expected. Since most LEAs now require that leisure/recreational course provision should be self-financing, this area has been particularly hard hit. At the same time resources have been increasingly available for YOP/UVP and later YTS work, thus tilting the balance of provision further towards the 16–19 client group.

Heterogeneity of clients

The colleges cater for the needs of a student body which is probably more heterogeneous than that in most other types of educational institution. Their students are drawn from all of the 16–19 client groups discussed in the Macfarlane Report (see Chapter 2.2), as well as a diverse group of adults whose needs range from GCE provision for late/mature aspirants to higher education, to retraining for the redundant and unemployed, to leisure and recreational classes. This diversity has considerable implications for the determination of curricular priorities.

Heterogeneity of staff

As Tipton (1973) has noted, FE sector institutions, as compared with schools and higher education, are characterized by particular diversity among staff in terms of social background, education, prior career paths, and attitudes and approaches to teaching. Gleeson and Mardle (1980) similarly note the 'two distinct cultures' in their case-study college. They contrast the 'liberal', 'academic' approach of the usually graduate general studies staff with the practical, industry-oriented attitudes and perspectives of staff in technical/vocational studies departments. Most of the latter group have had considerable experience in industry, gaining qualifications by part-time study, and regard professional colleagues in industry as their main reference group. These separate cultures tend to be reinforced by the interdepartmental insularity of many FE colleges (see Morgan and Parkes, 1976). While ex-FE staff bring with them a wide range of professional/vocational identities and perspectives, ex-school staff joining the tertiary college (usually sixth-form/sixth-form college teachers) have a background in a form of professional socialization, system of values and an institutional ethos markedly different from those of the FE sector. In King's (1976) terms the attitudes and ideologies of schools and FE staff can be characterized dichotomously as 'community' oriented (stressing expressive values, group consensus and loyalty) as opposed to 'associationist' (emphasizing instrumental concerns, the development of useful skills and a voluntarist approach).

Physical factors

Some of the colleges operate under considerable restraints in terms of buildings and accommodation. Of the colleges operating in 1982, two have substantial amounts of purpose-built accommodation, while most continue to use former FE college buildings. Though some of these premises are relatively modern, most colleges have a number of annexes on separate sites, often several miles from the main building. In addition to lack of space for teaching and technical equipment, many lack adequate facilities for staff and student common rooms and sports activities.

Historical factors

This category covers local circumstances and attitudes pertaining prior to and during the reorganization process, which can have a long-term impact on the operation of the new institutions and local attitudes towards them. It includes such variables as the reputation of the pre-existing institutions, the degree of local support for/opposition to reorganization, the attitudes of the local press and the way in which the reorganization process has been managed by the LEA.

Management and organizational issues

We shall now examine some of the main organizational and management issues in the establishment and development of the tertiary colleges in the context of the factors discussed above. The discussion focuses on the following task areas: (1) staffing, (2) organization structures, (3) curriculum, (4) pastoral provision, (5) student response.

Staffing

Nearly all of the existing tertiary colleges have been formed by combining the *provision* and staff of a pre-existing FE college and local school sixth forms or sixth-form colleges. In cases where 11/12–18 schools are involved, their sixth forms become part of the new college and the schools are redesignated as 11–16 institutions. The process inevitably involves considerable uncertainty and disruption for staff in all the institutions involved. The reorganization process therefore entails careful planning and negotiation of the transition with the various bodies and individuals involved; creating a framework for the smooth transfer of staff and students to the new institution; and achieving integration of ex-school and ex-FE staff in the college as it develops.

LEAs have approached the transition in a variety of ways. Some have left the CFE staff in their existing posts, and asked staff in the relevant schools to apply for posts either in the college (for teachers who have had sixth-form experience) or in the redesignated 11–16 schools. Other authorities have created an entirely new structure of posts in all the institutions involved, asking all the staff to reapply. In either case, a lengthy consultation procedure, with staff, unions, governors, parents, etc., has been necessary. The principal of Strode College describes the management of the process in his LEA:

> The LEA preparation had included a thorough information-giving activity to secondary and further education teachers about respective conditions of service and about the objectives of the new schools and the new college. The LEA had given a guarantee to all full-time teachers that no one would lose his/her job as a result of the reorganization. Every serving teacher was provided with detailed lists of all posts in the new schools and the new college and had an opportunity to indicate his/her first, second and third preference

for posts within the total new system.

This staffing exercise was carried out with considerable care and justifiably absorbed a great deal of time. It produced a high degree of satisfaction amongst the staff in the sense that 75% of full-time teachers in all the institutions concerned were offered their first choice posts in the new structure, while 20% were appointed to posts in accordance with their second preference. The number of seriously dissatisfied teachers was no more than one or two.

Authorities have also eased the transition by such means as allowing school staff to transfer to the new college on protected schools salaries where appropriate, and by balancing ex-school and ex-FE staff in senior appointments to the college. Some LEAs have also been fairly generous in their allocation of promoted posts in the new establishment. However, while many staff have benefited in salary terms, there is an inevitable loss of status for some, especially in areas such as GCE work and general/liberal studies, where there is considerable overlap between the work of the pre-existing schools and FE college. Thus there will be many aspirants for posts such as head of department of maths and science, and for section leader positions in these areas. By contrast, staff in the more vocationally orientated areas such as business studies and engineering are less affected by competition. Indeed, in some colleges whole departments, which have not been reorganized and continue to provide for the same clients, have felt very little impact from the change to a tertiary college system.

In larger reorganization schemes it has been difficult to achieve such a high degree of staff satisfaction as that reported by the principal of Strode College. In such situations, traces of a 'them and us' attitude can linger on between ex-school and ex-FE staff, especially among those who feel that they have lost out in terms of status or promotion prospects as a result of the reorganization.

The initial problems of adjustment are probably greater for staff from schools since they are moving to new terms and conditions of service and a different institutional ethos. Most, however, welcome the change, and regard themselves as considerably better off than they were in schools, with respect to class-contact hours, technical and clerical support, equipment and resources, and in teaching only voluntary participants in the 16–19 age-group, as opposed to sixth-formers *and* younger pupils. Many ex-school staff also enjoy the additional stimulus of teaching part-time and adult students.

In the colleges which have been established for some time, there are now large numbers of staff who have joined the college post-reorganization, from a variety of institutions, and hence the composition of the original staff groupings has been considerably modified. Staff therefore tend to distinguish themselves not as 'ex-school' or 'ex-FE' but by departmental area or by what they teach, and status differences are usually those between GCE and vocational work. Staff note that A-Level work tends to hold higher prestige than BTEC options, both among many of the staff, and in the eyes of students, parents and governors, reflecting the high esteem of A-Level in society at large and its status as the main qualifying route for higher education. In these circumstances it is difficult to develop parity of esteem for vocationally oriented options.

Many staff adopt the 'limited' model of their college's role as outlined earlier, and continue to work with colleagues, curricula and client groups with which they are familiar from their former schools or FE colleges. Others take a more college-wide perspective and welcome the opportunity to work with students from a variety of backgrounds and to interact with colleagues from other departments in curricular developments and socially. They note, however, that the more limited approach must take priority and, in particular, the development of high standards in the various areas of the college's work; the development of a more extended approach is seen as a longer-term goal.

Principals have used various means to avoid barriers between different groups of staff and to promote integration. These include cross-departmental servicing for maths, English, communications, etc.; spreading GCE work across a number of departments, or developing matrix organizational structures. Other colleges have mixed staff workrooms, shared by staff from a variety of subject and discipline areas. In smaller colleges, staff from all departments/teaching areas tend to mix in the staff common room. In larger colleges there is often less integration. In many cases staff spend break- and lunchtimes in their departmental/subject-area staff workrooms (cf. Tipton, 1973, on interdepartmental divisions in a CFE).

Organization structures

A central concern for the colleges has been to devise an appropriate organization structure which provides an effective and efficient means of administration; allows both ex-school and ex-FE staff transferring to the new institution to adapt rapidly and work cooperatively; and enables the development of the 'comprehensive' potential of the college as discussed earlier. Consideration of these factors and the appropriate balance between them has led to the adaptation of a variety of patterns of organization – ranging from conventional FE departmental structures to matrix systems drawing on organizational models from the secondary school sector.

Some colleges have developed a fairly orthodox FE department structure, adopting the organization system of the pre-existing CFE to accommodate the increase in GCE provision. It is claimed that this approach entails the minimum of disruption, especially for areas of work which are relatively little affected by the reorganization. This structure can be very efficient in administrative terms but it promotes a 'limited' model of the college's potential and tends to encourage rather than erode divisions between 'academic' and 'vocational' and 'school' and 'FE' areas of work.

For this reason other colleges have adopted a modified form of departmental organization, with the centralization of some functions; these include student admissions, counselling and careers guidance, as well as staff development, and resource centres for audiovisual aids and other equipment. A centralized admissions system, operating in coordination with heads of department, provides a means of preventing possible competition between departments in recruiting students. In some cases the director of studies, vice-principal or principal takes responsibility for the initial interviews of students who are doubtful about their course choice, especially where their possible options are based in more than one department. Similarly, several principals have a policy of ensuring that departments are kept roughly equal in size, to avoid the expansionist tendencies associated with traditional FE departments (see, for example, Tipton, 1973).

The main reasons for adopting a departmental system can be summarized as follows:

1 It provides an effective and convenient means for administration.

2 It acts as a useful 'first base' in curricular and social terms for both students and staff to relate to in a relatively large and complex organization.

3 Such a system does not necessarily promote competition between departments. It is argued that it is not a departmental structure per se which encourages divisive attitudes, but rather the manner in which it is often operated. Given effective coordination by senior staff and openness of resource allocation between departments, they can work in cooperation.

4 A departmental system does not necessarily encourage a division between 'sixth-form' and 'FE' elements of the institution, since in most cases GCE work is spread over a number of departments and many students and staff work in more than one department.

5 It is argued that a departmental system allows for clear lines of responsibility and efficient delegation of tasks. In a matrix system, on the other hand, teachers are responsible to at least two separate senior staff (i.e. as tutors and subject/course lecturers). This may be confusing for both staff and students and can lead to problems of communication and large amounts of paperwork.

Other colleges have completely abandoned the departmental system and opted for a matrix form of organization which divides functions and tasks into a grid system of interrelated horizontal and vertical lines of responsibility – often incorporating elements of models used in secondary schools. Thus, for example, the principal of Yeovil College describes the college's matrix system as follows:

> There are two arms of the matrix. One of these comprises the teaching staff organized in 15 teams, called Schools, each under its own Head whose brief is to work with the team in having regard first and foremost to quality in teaching and in the efficient and effective use of all its resources in meeting the needs of the students of the college . . . Schools resemble secondary departments, differing from the conventional FE departments in that they do not have 'their own' students or 'their own' courses. In the FE sense of the word, each School is a *servicing* agent . . . The co-ordination of the work of these teams is the responsibility of the Director of Resources (Associate Vice-Principal).
>
> The second arm of the axis is under the control of the Vice-Principal who as Director of Studies works with six Deans of Studies (Burnham FE Heads of Department for pay and rations) to provide the curriculum and educational guidance of the students. Each Dean has two major responsibilities, the care of students and the oversight of an area of curriculum . . . contributing courses in his field to the college timetable and commissioning the necessary teaching from appropriate Schools. Teaching staff also in their capacity as Tutors work with the Deans in the care of students. Deans may be compared with secondary Year Heads or House Heads, tutors with Form Masters or Mistresses.

A matrix system can involve a number of problems. Thus, for example at Yeovil College, where it generally works well, the principal comments that it took some time to get used to the system. This was a greater problem for staff who had transferred from the old technical college, with its orthodox

FE structure, than for ex-school staff. It is sometimes difficult to create a balance between the two axes of the matrix which can therefore tend to revert to a more hierarchical form. Also, of course, there may well be problems of communication and role conflict, particularly in a larger college (see point 5 above), and the introduction of a matrix system involves considerable negotiation of new roles as staff adjust.

The main reasons put forward by principals for adopting a matrix system are:

1   that the traditional FE departmental system tends to promote an entrepreneurial and empire-building approach. Departments tend to operate as semi-autonomous subunits, hence making it difficult to develop cross-college cooperation in mounting courses and reducing flexibility of students' programmes of study;

2   since the status and grading of departments and the grades and salaries of their staff depend to a considerable extent on their volume of staff and student hours (as well as levels of work), there is a tendency to competition for staff and students, rather than a coordinated cross-college approach to meeting student needs;

3   for these reasons, a matrix system is argued to encourage more cooperative attitudes and to provide a more effective means for promoting curricular flexibility, adequate pastoral provision for students and closer integration between the various areas of the college's work;

4   it is suggested that the organization structure should reflect the fact that the tertiary college is a new type of institution, and that a substantial modification of the orthodox FE organization system is necessary to demonstrate to staff, students and parents that the college is not merely a continuation of the pre-existing technical college with the incorporation of the sixth-form element, operating as bilateral subunits under one roof;

5   such a system enables a larger number of staff to participate in decision-making and administrative responsibility.

In either type of organization system a number of other variables are also very important. These include the size of the college, the nature of its accommodation and the number of sites on which it operates (some of the colleges have as many as six–eight sites spread across a wide area). Thus a large college operating on a number of sites might find it difficult to operate an effective matrix system. Similarly the design and location of accommodation can exercise powerful constraints on organization. Thus, for example, Leigh College has two main sites, one of which was designed and built as a sixth-form college before control of the LEA changed hands. This has made it difficult to operate as an integrated tertiary college, as the accommodation on the newer site is designed as classroom and laboratory space for GCE work, with no technical and practical facilities for vocational subjects, which therefore continue to operate in the old technical college building about three-quarters of a mile away. There is, however, some movement of staff and students between sites, and the separation has been reduced with the completion of an additional building on the newer site to house business studies and commercial subjects. Senior staff comment that in situations where some courses or even whole departments are located in substandard buildings several miles from the main site, it is very difficult to persuade staff and students that the principle of parity of esteem is actively upheld by the college.

The management style of the principal and senior staff also plays a major role in the effective operation of the organization system. Research evidence has shown that teaching staff in general like to have reasonable access to the principal and senior staff (see, for example, Hughes, 1977; Nias, 1980). An 'open door' policy can be operated equally with either matrix or departmental forms of organization. Likewise, in both systems vice-principals or other senior staff can act as 'gatekeepers' standing between the principal and junior staff. Effective formal and informal lines of communication are also crucial to the college's operation and ethos. Split sites again often produce difficulties with the relative isolation of staff and students who are based away from the main site. In some colleges, to alleviate this problem the vice-principal/director of studies and/or Chief Administrative Officer are located on a subsidiary site.

Curriculum

The tertiary colleges can claim to offer a comprehensive range of courses in that they provide for all ability levels, offering a wider choice than other types of institution catering for the age-group. As well as the range of full- and part-time vocational and pre-employment courses usually found in a CFE, they also offer a large number of A- and O-Level subjects. Thus, for example Strode, which is one of the smallest colleges (group 3), offers 18 A-Levels and a similar number of O-Levels; W.R. Tuson, one of the largest colleges (group 7), offers over 30 A- and O-Level subjects. There is also evidence of a degree of flexibility in offering appropriate individual programmes of study, mentioned in the discussion of the 'extended' model in the first section of this chapter. The timetables of GCE students show considerable diversity in subject combinations. For O- and A-Levels, the majority of colleges operate a timetable grid spanning most departments/teaching areas of the college. Thus it is possible for students to combine GCEs with, for example, TEC units or a typing/shorthand option. Also, since there are large numbers of students involved, popular subjects can be offered in several option blocks, giving great flexibility in availability of subjects. (For most vocationally oriented options, of course, the demands of the syllabus entail that students follow a largely prestructured programme for most of the timetable.)

South East Derbyshire College's 'continuous curriculum' is designed to provide for both full- and part-time students at a variety of entry and ability levels (ranging from ESN(M) to Oxbridge), and to enable maximum flexibility for progression from one programme to another, as students develop their interests and abilities. A timetable blocking system enables students to combine a broad range of options, for example A- or O-Levels plus BTEC/secretarial studies. An important element of this approach is that it allows students to combine 'academic' and 'vocational' components as appropriate in their individual programmes of study. When tertiary colleges were first established, some proponents argued that the opportunity for such 'mixed economy' courses was an important curricular development which would be valuable for many students. South East Derbyshire College has gone further than other tertiary colleges in offering this opportunity – in the 1981–1982 session some 330 of a total of 1020 full-time students were following mixed economy courses. Most other colleges provide for a combination of A- and O-Levels with a typing or secretarial option (as do many CFEs); some offer pre-professional courses which include O-/A-Levels with vocational subjects in such fields as nursing, community services, engineering, secretarial or agricultural studies.

However, on the whole mixed economy courses have developed very little in the tertiary colleges, and certainly less than was expected. Staff comment that the main constraints are the entry demands of HE institutions and employers, attitudes of exam boards, timetabling problems and the preference of many young people and their parents for either a wholly academic or a wholly vocational course. Some colleges and staff also oppose the idea of 'mixed' courses. It is argued that to combine, say, a BEC course with A-Level(s) can lead to the devaluing of the vocational element, in the eyes of the students, parents and employers, by implying that it cannot stand in its own right. The Business Education Council itself also has preferred that its courses should not be studied with other options.

Student and parental attitudes also operate to maintain the popularity of GCE courses and the high esteem in which they are held, despite the range of vocational and prevocational options offered by the colleges. Staff note that such alternatives as BTEC courses may often be more appropriate than the discouraging repetition of O-Levels or the achievement of a couple of A-Levels with modest grades. They also may often provide a better basis for gaining employment. It is sometimes difficult to persuade students that this is the case, and the status and the prestige of GCE continue to lure a number of students who have little chance of success.

However, there is evidence to suggest that the broad range of alternatives to GCE offered by the colleges is having a significant effect on students' course choices. As the principal of one of the colleges notes, nationally, in schools and further education, 80 percent of full-time 16–19-year-old students on exam courses are aiming at GCE, and 20 percent at a vocational qualification. In tertiary colleges the respective figures are 54 and 46 percent (Austin, 1982).

General studies and sports/recreational activities provide an opportunity for the development of a more 'extended' model of the college's provision, in enabling students to develop their abilities and interests beyond the confines of exam work and to mix with students from other courses. Most colleges stress the importance of general/complementary studies as an essential component in student programmes and sports/recreational activities as an optional element – a very wide range of cultural, practical and sporting options is offered. Colleges use various means to integrate general studies into the curriculum and to counter the frequent student claim that this area of work is irrelevant and a waste of time (see, for example, Dean et al., 1979). Thus, for instance, at Exeter College, A-Level students choose one of their A-Levels as a 'key subject'. Students are allocated to tutor groups on the basis of their key subject, which is taught to them by their personal tutor. Extra time on the timetable is allocated to the key subject in order to go beyond the exam syllabus, making connections with other disciplines.

In general, however, students have a keenly instrumental approach towards their work in college and it is difficult to convince them of the importance of non-examination work in the curriculum. (Some colleges encourage students to enter for the A-Level in general studies offered by several of the exam boards.) Unless attendance is monitored, and this can be difficult when several options are run concurrently, many students fail to attend general studies classes or sports activities. General studies work is, of course, prescribed by the exam boards as a compulsory element of many vocational courses and is often resented by day-release students who argue that they would prefer a shorter college day instead.

An important curricular development has been the growth of a substantial amount of vocational preparation and MSC-sponsored work. While the issues raised by this are faced by all institutions providing for 16–19-year-olds, the new area of work has interesting implications for the tertiary colleges in the light of the factors discussed in the earlier sections of this chapter. Provision for a new client group which has not traditionally participated in any form of education post-16 represents a move to greater 'comprehensivization' of the colleges in providing for a wider ability range. It has considerable implications for the balance of provision between GCE, vocational and 'voc prep' work, the determination of curricular and accommodation priorities and the integration of the new area of work with the rest of the college. Some staff are concerned that the development of YTS work may have an adverse effect on the attitudes and motivation of students on traditional courses, particularly as MSC trainees are paid while students on full-time LEA-funded courses are not. This financial disparity also tends to increase differentiation among the student body rather than to promote integration. Some argue that YTS and 'voc prep' work should be incorporated within the mainstream of the college and located, where possible, on the main site. Others suggest that youngsters on these courses respond better to a more sheltered and work-oriented environment away from the rest of the college.

Pastoral care and guidance

Another important policy issue for the colleges has been the development of pastoral and guidance provision. Critics have argued that the colleges, as institutions operating under FE regulations and with substantial numbers of part-time and adult students, might well find it difficult to achieve the close contact between staff and students and the concern for the personal and educational guidance of pupils which form an important element of the sixth form, but are not strong traditions in the FE sector. It might be observed that this argument reflects a somewhat outdated view of FE colleges, since many of them, especially those with large numbers of full-time students, have paid considerable attention to this aspect of their provision in recent years. However, since most tertiary college clients remain in the institution for only one or two years, and are faced with a potentially daunting range of options on entry, effective means for student guidance and for coordination with feeder schools prior to students' entry to college are of crucial importance.

Most colleges have a personal tutor system. The use of tutorial time and the commitment of individual members of staff to this aspect of their work varies widely within, as well as between, colleges. Some staff and students are doubtful about the usefulness of having formal tutorial sessions. In some cases part of this time is used for careers guidance – talks from outside speakers, help with UCCA procedures and so on. Several colleges are considering the development of a more structured programme for tutor groups, based on schemes used in secondary schools.

Tutors are also usually responsible for monitoring the academic progress of students and are notified by course tutors about any problems relating to work or attendance. In most cases tutors conduct a weekly check on class attendance by members of their group in order to identify and deter absenteeism. Irregular attendance can be a problem, especially with A- and O-Level students whose attendance is more difficult to check on than it is, for instance, with BEC students who spend most of their time in the same group. Some colleges have developed elaborate procedures for monitoring attendance, for example producing computer print-outs of each student's weekly attendance record. Such schemes are cumbersome and not always effective.

The colleges usually have centralized careers guidance systems, though in a few cases this work is organized on a departmental basis. The larger colleges have a full-time careers officer, sometimes assisted by other staff with a few hours' remission for this function. In smaller colleges the careers programme is usually run by a member of the teaching staff with some remission; such staff argue that more staff time needs to be devoted to careers guidance. Large colleges, such as Exeter, have an elaborate pro-gramme of weekly careers activities including lectures, group discussions, visits to higher education institutions and industry, guidance on UCCA and polytechnic applications, etc. In some cases careers staff work closely with tutors, providing packs of careers guidance material for use in tutorial sessions. Careers interviews are usually arranged by self- or tutor-referral, and some careers staff feel that there may be a number of students who need advice but fail to seek it. The LEA careers service usually also has an office housed on the college site. LEA staff tend to deal with job placements, rather than HE guidance, though sometimes college staff play a part in finding employment for students, and this can be an area of boundary conflict between the two agencies.

Another important issue is the guidance of students on course choice prior to college entry, and the development of close links with feeder schools in order to facilitate this. Most colleges seek to provide advice and information to school pupils and their parents from the stage of third-year option choice onwards. However, this is not always possible, and the extent of cooperation shown by the schools varies very considerably, with respect to both pupil guidance on course choice by the colleges and the information on intending students which they provide to the colleges. For this reason, some colleges have schools liaison staff who visit schools regularly in order to develop close links and effective coordination on pupil transfer.

A further consideration is curricular liaison with feeder schools as regards syllabuses, examination boards for O-Level/CSE, teaching methods and curriculum development. In most cases there are subject panels for particular discipline areas, comprising relevant college and schools staff. However, these panels tend to be not very well supported, meeting infrequently and sometimes lapsing altogether. In some LEAs school–college liaison is organized on a more formal basis, as, for example, in Devon, which has a system of joint academic boards covering most curricular areas. These meet regularly with formal minutes and are attended by senior staff from college and schools as well as LEA staff. Curriculum liaison is a sensitive area, and college staff are very anxious to avoid appearing to dictate to the schools on matters regarding the curriculum. In some discipline areas, such as French and maths, the lack of a common basis of skills among students entering college can cause particular problems in developing college syllabuses and teaching programmes. However, given the problems involved, it seems unlikely that it will be possible to develop the use of common examination boards and syllabuses by a college and all its feeder schools.[3] Also, of course, as some staff argue, complete curricular continuity for all students is virtually impossible since an increasing number of students are entering the colleges from the private sector (up to 25 percent of the full-time intake in some cases).

Student response

Student response to the tertiary colleges is in general very favourable.

Students appreciate the adult atmosphere of the colleges, the informal relationships with staff and the absence of petty rules and regulations. They suggest that, since they are expected to behave and work as responsible individuals without constant prodding from staff, they are more 'mature' in their outlook than friends attending school sixth forms.

The participation rate gives an indication of the colleges' popularity with students. It has been argued that students may be deterred from continuing in full-time education if they are required to transfer to a new institution at 16+. However, annual admission figures from the older colleges, which are now available for a period of over five years, indicate a distinct rise in the participation rate as compared with staying-on rates prior to reorganization and in other areas. (Though other variables are also important here, of course – for example local levels of youth unemployment.) The findings of Dean et al. (1979) also tend to support the view that provision of separate post-16 institutions may actually help to encourage an increase in participation.

While students express general satisfaction with their life at college, many would prefer more guidance and advice on their work and progress in college and, in particular, on career opportunities. This latter factor is probably linked to students' awareness of the high level of unemployment among young people in their age-group. Some students also note that they found the change from fifth form to college a fairly abrupt one at first, given the much larger size of the college and the very different atmosphere and approach to work. Students transferring from the private sector have particular problems in settling down and making friends at first, because students from the main feeder schools tend to stick together in their school friendship groups for the first few weeks; it is very difficult for 'outsiders' to enter these cliques.

Students welcome being given a large degree of responsibility for their work, progress and social life at college. However, during the early stages of their college careers, some students miss the stricter discipline of school and feel that they would like to be made to work harder at college. Certainly the need to organize the efficient use of private study time and develop effective learning techniques makes heavy demands on some 16-year-olds, and adjustment takes time. While students on vocationally oriented courses have a relatively structured timetable, some students, especially those studying A-Levels, have large amounts of private study time which can often be wasted during the first few months.

As noted in the first section of this chapter, a potential advantage of providing for all post-16s in one institution, rather than separate school/sixth-form college and FE routes, is that it offers the opportunity for a degree of social integration between students of all ages, abilities and social backgrounds. Opportunities for social mixing between students on various types of courses occur in student common rooms and refectory facilities, in sports and recreational events and through student union activities. Some of the colleges have taken particular steps to encourage social integration among students by, for example, timetable blocking for sports and recreation, and sometimes general studies, enabling students from most full-time courses to take part together. One college, Cricklade, has extended this approach to tutorial groups – students are allocated to these on a mixed basis so that each group contains students from several courses. While the principal notes that this can be administratively time consuming and may lead to problems of communication, it is felt to be worthwhile in order to develop student and staff relationships across course boundaries.

However, in general, there is not a great deal of social mixing among students on different courses. Students, like staff, are aware of the relative statuses ascribed to various courses, and tend to socialize within these groups. Perhaps inevitably, there is very little evidence of social integration between full- and part-time students, since the latter spend only a small proportion of their time at college and have a full programme of classes, leaving little opportunity for social activity with other students.

The colleges have taken steps to encourage extracurricular activities, such as student-run clubs and societies, drama productions, concerts and so on. While musical and dramatic productions achieve a degree of success, student-run clubs and societies show less vitality. A minority of students participate in these and in running the students' union, but the majority of students do not take part. Two of the factors which may account for the lack of involvement in extracurricular activities are that students are not required to attend college when they do not have classes, and that the colleges tend to have large catchment areas with long travelling distances for students.

Conclusion

The tertiary college is a relatively new institutional form and it is therefore too early to draw firm conclusions about its development. Evidence available so far, however, suggests that in terms of the 'limited' model outlined earlier such colleges are achieving a considerable degree of success.

Exam results in both GCE and vocational courses are very satisfactory and, in many cases, well above the national average, indicating that the colleges can achieve standards of performance as high as, or better than, more traditional forms of provision (see also Dean et al., 1979). The colleges are also moving towards some degree of coordination between the various areas of their work. They are attempting to increase cross-disciplinary curricular development and to promote a measure of interaction among disparate groups of students and staff. At the moment, though, the colleges in many respects reflect Daunt's (1975) 'first view' rather than the 'extended' one. Development towards the latter approach is likely to be a slow and incremental process.

The reasons for this can be found in the constraints outlined earlier. The colleges are pluralist institutions serving heterogeneous groups of clients and external interest groups. As Cuthbert (1984) argues, such institutions are characterized by diverse and often competing goals and missions. The demands of exam boards, HE entrance requirements, employers and other agencies exercise strong restraints on the development of an 'extended' approach. For instance, employers' expectations that their apprentices and trainees undertake 'a full day's work' at college, for which the employer pays them, militates against social integration of these students with full-timers in social and recreational activities.

Attitudes, both within and outside the colleges, are also slow to change. Staff with approaches and perspectives which have been shaped in King's (1976) contrasting school and FE cultures take time to develop a degree of interdisciplinary understanding and cooperation. (See also Hewton's (1982) discussion of the strength of subject cultures and the difficulties in overcoming their differing approaches when developing interdisciplinary courses.)

Research by King (1973) and Ford (1969) indicates the powerful influence of cultural and social norms in shaping perspectives and approaches within educational institutions. Ford argues that comprehensive schools are unable to ascribe equal value to all pupils and curricular routes since 'it is through the educational system that selection and differential training for major adult roles are effected . . . While the different academic streams are "feeding" different occupational rivers, prestige and resources will be diverted accordingly . . . and the hoped for consequences of comprehensivization cannot . . . be achieved' (pp. 134–135). Viewed in these terms, the development of parity of esteem and closer integration between different areas of work in tertiary colleges, as in comprehensive schools, may be unduly unrealistic. Nonetheless the tertiary college, in combining provision for the whole of the 16–19 age-group and adult students, does provide at least the potential for a closer degree of understanding and interaction among disparate clients, curricular routes and discipline areas. The considerable achievements of the colleges so far, in terms of such criteria as examination pass rates, range and flexibility of course choice, curricular development and favourable student response, suggest that this potential may well be realized as the colleges evolve.

Notes

1   Grateful acknowledgement is made to the principals, staff and students of the colleges for their help and cooperation.

2   See also Marsden's (1969) discussion of the two philosophies of comprehensive education.

3   Problems of curricular and pastoral continuity are often used as arguments in favour of the retention of school sixth forms. See Reid and Filby (Chapter 3.7) for a critique of the case for continuity.

References

Alexander, W. (1969) *Towards a New Education Act*. London, Councils and Education Press.

Association of Colleges for Further and Higher Education (ACFHE) (1981) *16–19: The Tertiary College in Practice*. Sheffield, ACFHE.

Austin, G.M. (1982) Something suitable for everyone? *Education*, 15 October 1982.

Cuthbert, R. (1984) E324 Block III, Part 2, The Open University.

Daunt, P.E. (1975) *Comprehensive Values*. London, Heinemann.

Dean, J. et al. (1979) *The Sixth Form and its Alternatives*. Slough, NFER.

Ford, J. (1969) *Social Class and the Comprehensive School*. London, Routledge & Kegan Paul.

Gleeson, D. and Mardle, G. (1980) *Further Education or Training?* London, Routledge & Kegan Paul.

Hewton, E. (1982) Inside knowledge. In: *Rethinking Educational Change*. Guildford, SRHE.

Hughes, M. (1977) Consensus and conflict about the role of the secondary school head. *British Journal of Educational Studies*, vol. 25, no. 1, February 1977.

Janes, F. and Miles, J. (1978) *Tertiary Colleges*. Bridgwater College.

King, R. (1973) *School Organization and Pupil Involvement*. London, Routledge & Kegan Paul.

King, R. (1976) *School and College*. London, Routledge & Kegan Paul.

Marsden, D. (1969) Which comprehensive principle? *Comprehensive Education*, no. 13, autumn 1969.

Mumford, D. (1970) *Comprehensive Reorganization and the Junior College*. ACFHE.

Morgan, C. and Parkes, D. (1976) E321, Unit 12, The Open University.

Nias, J. (1980) Leadership styles and job satisfaction in primary schools. In: Bush, T. et al. (eds.) *Approaches to School Management*. London, Harper & Row.

Pedley, R. (1973) School or college? *Education and Training*, no. 15.

Tipton, B.F.A. (1973) *Conflict and Change in a Technical College*. London, Hutchinson.

Various unpublished college documents.

CHAPTER 4.5

ROLE STRAIN IN THE FURTHER EDUCATION COLLEGE*
GRAHAM PEEKE

Introduction

The purpose of this article is to discuss the use of the concept of role strain in aiding the understanding of organizational behaviour in the further education college. There are those who believe the concept of role to be a redundant one (Coulson, 1972), but many of the criticisms levelled at role theory stem from its development within the Functionalist school in sociology. Interactionist and, more recently, interpretative (Bowey, 1976) conceptions of role go a long way towards abrogating such criticisms.

If we accept that in joining any organization we enter the role system of that organization (although obviously commitments vary) then it is useful to conceive of each role as subject to three separate sets of perceptions. One set is characterized by the perceptions of the 'organization' in that the role is an ascribed role, with a set of behaviours often identified in a job description and locating the role within a hierarchy of accountability. Regardless of whether one accepts that organizations exist as independent entities with 'needs' of their own, the existence of ascribed roles is indisputable: needless to say, any analysis of organizational behaviour in these terms alone would be sorely impoverished. Another set is identified by the perceptions of those who interact with the occupants of roles. A lecturer in a college never acts strictly in accordance with the behaviour laid down in his job description (if he has one!). He brings to his role experiences gained both outside and inside the organization and these are bound to influence behaviour. Col-

* Role strain in the further education college. *The Vocational Aspects of Education*, 1980, vol. XXXII, no. 83, pp. 77–80. Graham Peeke is Senior Lecturer in the Department of Health and Community Studies, Norwich City College of Further and Higher Education.

leagues react to the behaviour they observe and not just the behaviour they expect from a person occupying a role in a hierarchy. Following Turner (1962), it is likely that the ascribed role acts as a device to set the 'real' role in motion, for individuals are, at least, partially free to reinterpret their roles through interaction with others. The third set of perceptions are those of the occupant of the role: we are not merely the sum of the perceptions of others, but are motivated by our own phenomenological constructions.

Role strain

A useful concept in role theory is role strain and this concept is valuable in a discussion of the behaviour of lecturers and students in further education. Central to the concept of role strain is the idea of role expectations. Expectations are those ideas about role behaviour held in common by all actors in the role system. The validity of these expectations is generally reinforced in the everyday behaviour of actors, in that they conform to these expectations. Role strain occurs when expectations are contradicted or actors do not hold expectations in common. Readers will observe that such concepts as expectations and strain rely heavily on the second set of perceptions discussed above. This locates the concepts of role expectations and role strain within the interactionist perspective. It is the writer's view that the various approaches to the study of roles (characterized by the three sets of perceptions) are not contradictory, but complementary in that they address themselves to different questions.

Hargreaves (1972) identifies eight sources of role strain that are worth listing in full.

1 Where an actor simultaneously occupies two positions whose roles are incompatible.
2 Where there is a lack of consensus amongst the occupants of a position about the content of the role.
3 Where there is a lack of consensus amongst the occupants of one of the complementary role positions.
4 Where an actor's conception of his role conflicts with the expectation of a role partner.
5 Where various role partners have conflicting expectations.
6 Where a single role partner has incompatible expectations.
7 Where role expectations are unclear.

8 Where an actor lacks basic qualities required for adequate role performance.

Even a cursory glance through this, at first sight repetitive, list is enough to confirm that scenarios for role strain exist in all aspects of life and certainly in further education. A lack of goal planning or agreement over departmental and college goals, lack of discussion over priorities, poor staff recruitment, appraisal and development policies, will all provide ample situations in which role strain can develop; as will the existence within further education organizations of those who have not decided which role is the most appropriate for them, e.g. professional engineer or professional teacher.

With so many opportunities for role strain to develop, it is legitimate to ask why actors or lecturers are not constantly subject to it and its dysfunctional consequences. To be aware that one is suffering from role strain needs an awareness of the nature of the theory and of role strain itself. Most such strain is probably rationalized as the normal stress associated with teaching. This is an unsatisfactory diagnosis because if role strain is not recognized as such, it is rarely resolved satisfactorily and consequently many problems within an organization are caused or ignored.

Role strain in the college

The incidence of role strain in colleges can be usefully discussed under three headings. These three headings are the level of the social system, the individual personality level and the cultural level. These levels are originally derived from the work of Parsons (1951) and are elaborated in Secord and Backman (1964).

The social system

At this level it is the social system that the actors are involved in (e.g. the college) that influences the roles the actors fulfil. At the level of the social system several causes of role strain exist. One of the most common is where the expectations of groups or individuals are unclear. A newly appointed lecturer may be unclear about his role as a teacher and bring inappropriate expectations to it. Newly appointed staff with established role expectations in different organizations, in industry for example, may also be unclear about role expectations in their new situation. This difficulty can be compounded where the new appointee is not teacher trained. Students who have not previously studied in further education may be unclear as to their role, perhaps in respect of motivation for self-learning. Newly created roles in further education, such as counsellors or handicapped students' specialists (arising our of the recommendations of the Warnock Report), have a particular problem and suffer a lack of clarity, leading to underuse and frustration.

Another problem at social system level is that of incompatible and competing expectations. Incompatible expectations arise when roles require behaviour inconsistent with other expectations the actor holds. A lecturer with commitment to a political perspective may find it difficult to reconcile his expectations with the expectations of neutrality traditionally ascribed to teachers or with the social construction of knowledge he perceives in the curriculum. Competing expectations arise when an actor cannot perform all his expectations, due to restrictions of time for example. The inflexibility of the class-contact hours system in further education could mean inadequate teaching and poor administrative standards due to pressures of time. Time and energy left to devote to pastoral functions can be severely restricted in a syllabus-dominated environment. Students also are subject to incompatible and competing expectations, a factor which could account for high rates of wastage amongst day-release students.

The social system itself can be an important source of strain. Perhaps the organization has failed to keep the actors satisfied by not awarding sufficient rights or rewards to motivate teachers and students to carry out their roles. Roles can sometimes be related in such a way that one actor may interfere with the goal achievement of another. This could account for the ambiguous situation of the liberal studies teacher who may often find his aims and methods at variance with those of his vocational colleagues. The social system may also permit interpersonal manoeuvring that blocks the goal achievement of other actors.

Individual personality

This level is that at which individual personal characteristics may encourage the role strain. There are three main sources at this level. The first is that an individual attribute may affect the production of expected role behaviour. Expected role behaviour of students (expected by lecturers) is that they exhibit a desire to learn. It seems that some students display personality characteristics that mitigate against this. In the same sense some lecturers seem unsuited to meeting the needs of their students (however they are defined) due to inflexibility, authoritarianism, lack of interest or other unsuitable attributes.

Role enactment may also result in strain if the role expectations of the actor are incompatible with the actor's self-concept. Students who see themselves as a destructive influence in the classroom and sense that this gives them a certain status in the eyes of their peers will experience role strain as will a lecturer who sees himself as caring and student-centred yet finds he cannot 'control' his class in order that learning takes place. Other teachers may be quick to criticize attempts to 'liberalize' classroom activities, thus intensifying role strain and perhaps adding to the conflict at the social system level.

The third source of strain at this level is that where a role which a person occupies is within his capabilities, but not suited to his needs. This raises questions like: is this lecturer teaching on the right courses? the correct subject? in the appropriate organization? In the present economic situation, it is not unusual to find opportunities for personal development restricted, personal changes incompatible with 'organizational' requirements and poor job and promotion opportunities. Considerable role strain can result where a lecturer feels the need to be challenged by work of a different nature, yet this is not possible to arrange. Students suffer as a result of poor careers guidance or insistence by their employers to study certain courses; this means they may be studying on courses entirely unsuited to their needs or interests.

Cultural level

The cultural level is that where the ideology of actors may be contrary to the role.expectations of the position. The major source of strain is thus a conflict of ideology. This can occur when the ideology of the professional (the lecturer) comes into conflict with the role expectations of administrators or other professionals. The strain between the demands of the administration and those of professional standards is an important one because a commitment to professional standards can make an employee more critical of his employers and less apt to conform to established administrative procedures. The administrative system in further education ensures that there are ample opportunities for conflict here.

The conflict between the ideology of the professions (engineers, scientists, social workers) and the professional lecturer can also be an important source of role strain for those susceptible to both. This is a particular characteristic of further education.

Resolution of role strain

With so many potential sources of role strain it is no surprise that many techniques of resolution exist, most of which are automatically applied. Examples include committees, codes of operation, induction and training courses, methods of facilitating communication and elaborate selection procedures for both staff and students. Colleges also generally develop a clear hierarchy of obligations that ensures that certain actions take precedence. Spatial and temporal separations of roles are also practised and special roles that may be particularly vulnerable to sources of role strain (perhaps that of the liberal studies lecturer for example) can be protected by being set up as autonomous departments or sections less subject to control from other sources.

Individuals also establish their own hierarchies of values and rely on techniques like rationalization, displacement and fantasy to allow them to restructure situations. They may also leave the organization if the strain becomes too great. Most roles are subject to some role bargaining which may resolve conflict when an individual accepts a role more fully by receiving some form of compensation or exchange. At the cultural level a shared set of common beliefs usually develops which leads to gradual modification of conflicting role expectations as actors become reconciled to them. This often occurs because professionals and administrators or related professionals share a common problem.

Role strain and educational change

The concept of role has often been recognized as useful in understanding educational change (Gross et al., 1971) Reluctance to adopt a new role model with changed expectations or becoming subject to role strain when innovations change the nature of roles and role relationships can account for individual reluctance to embrace innovations. This problem is compounded by organizational reluctance to allocate time and resources to assisting lecturers in modifying roles. Recent innovations in further education necessitating the adoption of new role models for lecturers have been those of the Business Education Council (BEC). Taking changes at BEC national level, for example, the new role model is made up from the following shifts in the nature of a lecturer's role as a business studies teacher.

1 A shift from a specialist role to a generalist one. A move from teaching

economics or law to contributing to a theme called 'The organization in its environment'. (I am not suggesting that this is not educationally desirable, but that it necessitates role changes, the consequences of which have not been fully considered. The problem can be complicated further when the shift is only necessary for part of a timetable.)

2 A shift from didactic teaching to student-centred learning through the medium of work related assignments. This involves a change in the lecturer's conception of the educational process and in the role of student.

3 A shift towards team teaching and subject integration due to the inclusion of cross-modular assignments in the course programme.

4 A shift from summative assessment to continuous assessment on the basis of assignment performance.

Together these constitute considerable changes in lecturers' roles. To consider that such changes are not problematical and can be achieved overnight is simplistic and insensitive. At the social system level the new role model will be subject to lack of clarity and competing expectations. At the individual level the new role may well be incompatible with lecturers' existing conceptions of how students should be taught and business skills developed. They may also find the defence of the autonomy of their particular specialism best suited to their current needs. At the cultural level conflict can develop between lecturers, whose main concern is with teaching, and BEC, whose interests centre on the administrative functions of assessment and moderation. They may also resent the implied criticism of their ability to produce effective business students, inherent in any innovation that seeks to revise existing practices.

In conclusion

The concept of role strain is useful in highlighting sources of stress and dissatisfaction and conceptualizing them in a manner amenable to discussion and resolution. The continuing development of role theory and such concepts as role distance, role embracement (Goffman, 1961), and role relationships (Bowey, 1976), together with role strain, provide a useful model for the examination of individual behaviour in further education organizations. This is a valuable goal for, to paraphrase Silverman (1970), it is individuals not organizations that respond to events and any valid understanding of behaviour in further education organizations must come through the interpretations which individuals in the organization place upon their behaviour and the behaviour of others.

References

Bowey, A.M. (1976) *The Sociology of Organisations*. London, Hodder & Stoughton, pp. 70–73, 205–208.

Coulson, M. (1972) Role, a redundant concept in sociology. In: Jackson, J.A. (ed.) *Role*. Cambridge University Press.

Goffman, E. (1961) *Encounters: 2 Studies of the Sociology of Interaction*. Indianapolis, The Bobbs-Merrill Co. Inc.

Gross, M., Giaquinta, J.B. and Bernstein, M. (1971) *Implementing Organisational Innovations*. London, Harper & Row.

Hargreaves, D.H. (1972) *Interpersonal Relations and Education*. London, Routledge & Kegan Paul, p. 81.

Parsons, T. (1951) *The Social System*. New York, Free Press.

Secord, P.F. and Backman, C.W. (1964) *Social Psychology*. New York, McGraw-Hill, pt. 4, ch. 14, 15 & 16.

Silverman, D.A. (1970) *The Theory of Organisations*. London, Heinemann.

Turner, R. (1962) Role-taking. Process vs conformity. In: Rose, A. (ed.) *Human Nature and Social Processes*. Boston, Houghton-Mifflin.

CHAPTER 4.6

PROBLEMS FACING HEADS OF DEPARTMENT*
ROBERT OXTOBY

If the growth in the literature is anything to go by, the urge to apply management concepts and techniques to educational activities of all kinds has increased dramatically during the past 10 to 15 years. In particular, approaches based on management by objectives (MbO) are strongly advocated, especially in relation to institutions of further and higher education (see, for example, Baron, 1978). This probably stems in large measure from developments in industrial management, despite the fact that hardly any attempts have been made to review 'the elements of management which might be regarded as of primary relevance by industry and which it might be reasonable to compare with those of the educational institutions' (Bailey, 1977, p. 96). Objectives for individual managers in industry and commerce are usually expressed in terms of performance standards to be reached within specified time limits. Management by results is the watchword. No such claims can be made for educational institutions and, partly because of this, it is almost impossible to identify the skills and qualities which their managers require in order to perform effectively.

Since virtually all colleges have departments, all of which seem to have heads who are accepted quite naturally as being an essential part of the management structure of the college, it ought to be relatively easy to understand and describe the work and managerial role of a head of department (HoD). Yet, as Tolley (1972, pp. 12–16) points out, the task is curiously difficult, not least because there is no defined set of problems or issues which are common to all departments. HoDs doubtless share certain common responsibilities (e.g. for students, staff, equipment, courses and

---

* *Journal of Further and Higher Education*, spring 1979, vol. 3, no. 1, pp. 46–59. Dr Robert Oxtoby is Deputy Director of Luton College of Higher Education.

teaching) which, to a greater or lesser degree, they are all required to fulfil. But even when these responsibilities are spelled out in some detail, we are often none the wiser about what HoDs actually do and how effectively they do it. We know very little about the problems which HoDs face and the alternative courses of action that are available to solve these problems.

There are a number of reasons why we need a better understanding of HoDs and their work – selection and training are perhaps the most important – and there are at least five areas to which we must turn our attention in order to facilitate this understanding. In the first place, we are more or less totally ignorant about *differences* between HoDs, whether these be differences between HoDs in the same college or between HoDs in different colleges; the few attempts which have been made to describe the job of an HoD concentrate on the common features of jobs rather than on their differences.[1] Secondly, we still have very little detailed information about what HoDs are called upon to do, the pressures that they work under and the demands made by the job. Thirdly, we need to know more about the kinds of choices offered by the job and the sorts of constraints within which it operates; to what extent is the HoD free to shape his own activities? Management styles and effectiveness also depend on the attitudes and personal qualities of the individual manager and so, fourthly, we should be inquiring as to whether there are particular attitudes and personal characteristics which an HoD must have in order to perform effectively. Finally, and underlying each of the other areas, we have to face the fact that traditional methods for analysing managerial jobs are fairly rudimentary. There is a need for new techniques and approaches.[2]

The study reported here is an exploratory attempt to illuminate some of these issues and was designed primarily to pave the way for subsequent, more detailed investigations. It draws on data derived from the published details of advertised HoD posts and the responses to a short questionnaire circulated to a random sample of 240 HoDs.[3]

Job descriptions and specifications

It is more or less axiomatic nowadays that college staff should have a clear idea as to what is expected of them. The introduction of even the most unsophisticated management approaches usually involves an assessment of the work which staff do and the preparation of some sort of job description or specification. A job *description* can be defined as a statement of the main duties and responsibilities which a job entails, whereas a job or man *specification* is a list of criteria in terms of the skills, knowledge, experience and personal qualities deemed necessary for successful job performance. Now, the preparation of job descriptions and specifications is frequently difficult and time consuming, especially for professional or managerial jobs. In the case of a college, therefore, 'it will not be easy to secure agreement on job descriptions for staff who are both managers and professionals . . .' (Baron, 1978, p. 38).

Not surprisingly, job descriptions and specifications for HoDs are relatively hard to come by.[4] Even when they are available, their value is sometimes open to question, since they are probably based on little more than subjective views and personal hunches. Ideally, of course, job descriptions should be based on what is *actually* done and not on what somebody in authority thinks is done. Job descriptions and specifications are only as good as the information on which they are based.

The first formal indications which an HoD has about the duties and responsibilities associated with his post – and in some cases the only indications – are usually those given in the advanced details for the job and the 'further particulars' which accompany the advertisement. As far as schools are concerned, even these indications are by no means always available. A recent study of vacancies for heads of mathematics in secondary schools, for example, showed that only about 50 percent of advertisements offered 'further particulars' and only about three-quarters of these actually produced details of a job description or specification (Hall and Thomas, 1978). The situation in further education is a good deal more satisfactory. A survey was carried out of all HoD posts advertised in the *Times Educational Supplement* during the six-month period April–September 1976; all except one of the advertisements (N=52) offered 'further particulars'. The comments which follow are based on an analysis of the particulars associated with 30 of these vacancies.[5]

All of the 'further particulars' gave some information about the college or institution concerned, as well as about the courses offered by the particular department and the number of staff in the department. The amount of such information varied widely. In one instance, the college managed to supply all the details in a total of 170 words, of which 50 were devoted to the price of houses and the joys of the surrounding countryside; in another, the details occupied more than 1500 words and a college prospectus was also included. Rather more than half of the particulars outlined the duties and responsibilities of the post. Descriptions varied in length from carefully collated lists of 10–15 items to little more than a sentence or two; for example, 'The head of department controls and is responsible to the Principal for the internal organisation, management and discipline within his department and exercises supervision over the work of teaching and non-teaching staff'. No clear differences emerged between descriptions in terms of subject specialisms, although, interestingly enough, there were no job descriptions for two-thirds of the posts in business and management studies.

Just over one-third of the 'further particulars' mentioned something about the kind of qualifications and qualities needed to carry out the job, including three cases where there was no description of the duties and responsibilities associated with the post. These specifications were always brief, typically one or two sentences; for example, '. . . it is hoped to appoint a person with sound academic qualifications in at least one of the fields covered by the department, who has had substantial teaching experience and some responsibility for organisation, preferably in further education . . . (I)ndustrial or commercial experience, together with a teacher training qualification, will be an advantage'. Despite this brevity, however, the range of characteristics mentioned was fairly extensive. Out of 20 or so counted, perhaps the most dominant were those relating to initiative and ability ('be a person with the ability and enthusiasm to develop the work of the department', 'have the necessary initiative and ability to inspire confidence within and outside the college'); sympathy with the aims of further education ('have a thorough understanding of the further education system, sympathy with its basic objectives and an understanding of the needs and aspirations of students at all academic levels'); ability to fit into existing management structures ('demonstrate the capacity to function as a member of the senior management team, in circumstances where the aspirations and problems of particular departments must be considered within the context of those of the institution as a whole'); and overall breadth of experience ('have a broad background, preferably including both teaching and industrial experience', 'possess the capacity to grasp and firmly understand a broad range of disciplines').

Colleges expend a considerable amount of time and energy on the recruitment and selection of staff. The main purpose of advertising is presumably to attract applications only from those who are aware of what is required of them, who are genuinely interested in the job and capable of carrying it out successfully. Judging from 'further particulars', it seems as though applicants for most HoD posts should be able to obtain a reasonable idea of the general duties and responsibilities associated with the job and of some of the qualities thought necessary for its performance. Equally, however, particulars are rarely detailed enough to enable selection committees to match personal characteristics, qualifications and experience with the likely requirements of the job. Work activities are certainly not specified in a manner that would make it possible to monitor and assess the effectiveness of HoDs. Can it be that this arises partly because nobody knows what HoDs actually *do*? Before we can begin to talk seriously about *priorities* in relation to the roles and functions of HoDs, it seems as though we need a series of job analysis exercises to 'reveal the tasks already being performed so that decisions can then be taken whether they are relevant to the achievement of college and departmental objectives' (Baron, 1978, p. 38).

Analysing work activities

Job analysis is a 'process of investigation into the activities of work and the demands made upon workers, irrespective of the type or level of employment (Livy, 1975). In other words, it is a means of identifying the duties or *responsibilities* which a job involves, the *tasks* with which these responsibilities are associated and the *demands* which they make on the worker's behaviour. It is not, of course, an end in itself and can be undertaken for a wide variety of purposes. The preparation of realistic job descriptions and specifications is simply a convenient starting-point for looking at a whole range of organizational and personnel management problems.

As far as colleges and HoDs are concerned, job analysis seems likely to be particularly valuable in relation to:

1 Recruitment and selection. Some of the shortcomings inherent in existing recruitment and selection practices have been referred to above, notably the lack of detail in job descriptions and specifications. Job analysis clearly has a part to play here in helping to define tasks and responsibilities. The more sophisticated forms of job analysis might also be useful in identifying those personal qualities or traits which are desirable if HoDs are to carry out their jobs effectively. Having said this, however, it must be accepted that the prospects for major improvements are strictly limited. Not only is the literature on personnel testing extensive and complex, but relatively little of it refers to professional occupations. Such evidence as there is, suggests that only a minority of British firms use formal job descriptions and specifications in recruiting and selecting managers.[6]

2 Identification of training needs. Determining training needs and developing training programmes are presumably dependent in large

measure on a comprehensive knowledge of jobs and occupations. But there seem to be very few recorded instances where job analysis has been used to draw up training schemes for senior staff in education. This arises partly because job analysis as currently performed is too limited in scope to be truly satisfactory. There is a need to transfer the emphasis from task analysis to job *behaviour*: 'most work problems are not caused by acts of God, but by people or groups of people failing to take appropriate action . . . The need, therefore, is to identify the important work problems and identify which individuals or groups could affect them significantly. The next step is to determine what these individuals or groups need to learn in order to solve the problem' (Singer and Ramsden, 1972; see also Youngman, 1975). This approach is the antithesis of the conventional training needs analysis, with its flavour of 'doing things to people' to make them better. It underlines the value of knowing more about HoDs' work activities and the kinds of problems which they face.

3 Job design and organizational development. Training is by no means the only way to help people to improve their performance. Organizational changes can also have major influences on individual and group achievement. Similarly, changes in the work content and methods of jobs can also be fruitful, especially if geared towards improving job satisfaction as well as towards engendering greater efficiency. Many colleges have grown in size and become more complex in recent years, sometimes as a result of mergers between institutions. Redesigning the jobs of HoDs and modifying organizational structures have thus emerged as fairly common occurrences. Conceivably, however, the roles of many HoDs have become more ambiguous as a result and this might have produced lower levels of job satisfaction. Part of the, as yet, untapped potential of job analysis, therefore, lies in its relevance for wide-ranging studies of the relationships between work activities, job satisfaction and organizational structures.

In parallel with these uses of job analysis is its application in terms of encouraging HoDs to be more aware of the ways in which they employ their time. There is, claims Tolley (1972), 'no more urgent task for any head than that of reviewing the use of his time and redeploying his activities more effectively' (p. 16). An HoD who cannot organize his own time to good effect is perhaps unlikely to be an efficient organizer of other resources. Managers who have analysed their use of time point to the following as being some of the ways in which they have benefited (Rendell, 1977): a better understanding of their own job; improved cooperation with superiors/subordinates/peers; ability to use time more effectively; greater self-confidence; increased awareness of other people's functions; greater ability to delegate and to create discretionary time in order to concentrate on problems appropriate to their own position in the organization. How, then, can an HoD attempt to find out how his time is spent? How can he sift the key aspects of his job from the trivial ones? How can he set about determining priorities and ensuring that he spends time on the problems that really matter?

Analysing work activities can be approached from many different points of view and several useful summaries of these approaches are available in the literature (see, for example, Stewart, 1976; Youngman et al., 1978). Some methods are not capable of being used by HoDs to monitor their own activities, for example interviews, observation and activity sampling, questionnaires and checklists. More appropriate methods are those which rely on written activity records of one kind or another, such as diaries, critical incident reports, problem portfolios. The use of a job diary is perhaps the most simply and widely accepted way of finding out how time is spent. But self-recording can be inaccurate – many of the shorter episodes tend to get omitted – and compiling a detailed diary is usually a tiresome and onerous business. Although it is undoubtedly valuable in terms of enabling people to make more effective use of their time, a diary does not provide much reliable information about the skills or qualities deployed. Moreover, the prospect of using diaries to compare differences between large numbers of staff and their jobs is extremely daunting, if only because of the difficulties involved in handling the data. There are snags, therefore, in employing job diaries to analyse the diversity of HoD activities.

The critical incident technique is an attempt to identify the more 'noteworthy' aspects of job behaviour and is based on the assumption that jobs are composed of critical and non-critical tasks.[7] For example, a critical task might be defined as one which makes the difference between success and failure in carrying out important parts of the job. The idea is to collect reports as to what people do that is particularly effective or ineffective in contributing to good performance and then to scale the incidents in order of difficulty, frequency and importance to the job as a whole. The technique scores over the use of diaries in that it is centred on specific happenings and on what is judged to be effective behaviour. But it is still laborious and does not lend itself to objective quantification.

An even more flexible and productive approach for colleges and HoDs is possibly that due to Marples (1967), who suggests that one measure of a manager's ability may be expressed in terms of the number and duration of 'issues' or *problems* being tackled at any one time. He advocates the compilation of 'problem portfolios', recording information about how each problem arose, methods used to solve it, difficulties encountered and so on. Such an analysis also raises questions about the job incumbent's use of time: what proportion of his time is occupied in checking; in handling problems given to him by others; on self-generated problems; on 'top priority' problems; on minor issues? Unfortunately, there is very little published work based on this approach and so it is difficult to be sure of its limitations. One of the aims of the exploratory study reported here was to clarify some of these possible limitations.

Difficult tasks and situations

In November 1976, a short questionnaire was sent to a random sample of 240 HoDs in FE colleges in England and Wales. The sample was representative of four main subject areas: business and management studies, food and fashion, engineering, general studies and humanities.[8] Interest was focused largely on a question which asked: 'What was the most difficult task or situation with which you had to deal during the past two–three days?' Replies were received from 201 people, 191 of which contained usable information (80 percent response).

Two hundred and twenty incidents were identified in the replies and edited versions of these were presented independently to three judges – an HoD, an educational researcher and a teacher of educational management – who were asked to group the incidents into an arbitrary number of discrete categories and to label the categories. The three different versions were then discussed with each of the judges and agreement reached on 14 categories which it was thought would cover the 220 incidents adequately. A further six judges were then asked to place each of the incidents into *one* of the 14 categories. On the assumption that agreement by at least four of the six judges represents a satisfactory criterion of consensus, allocation of the 220 incidents is as set out in *Table* 11. As can be seen, in broad terms roughly half of the incidents relate directly to staff and students. The remainder are concerned with curriculum planning, accommodation and resources, external relations, record-keeping, and a series of miscellaneous problems which appear to fall outside the 14 selected categories, for example:

> Dealing with a series of thefts from students' changing rooms. The real point at issue is the question of who is going to pay for the replacement of the missing items should they fail to be recovered.

Table 11   Allocation of incidents

	%	Rank order
A. Planning, development and monitoring of courses	5.9	7
B. Advising *individual students* with academic and/or personal problems	8.2	3
C. Recruitment, appointment and promotion of teaching staff, including procedures for staff development	5.0	8
D. Supervision of secretarial, technical and ancillary staff	2.3	12
E. Liaison with the principal, other HoDs and senior staff	3.2	10
F. Timetabling and deployment of staff	15.4	1
G. Recruitment, selection and enrolment of students	1.4	13
H. Mediating in *student–student* conflicts	1.4	13
I. Allocation of financial resources, accommodation, equipment and materials	8.2	3
J. Advising *individual staff* with personal and/or work-related problems	9.4	2
K. Mediating in *staff–staff* conflicts	5.0	8
L. Relations with other colleges and outside agencies (employers, parents, schools, etc.)	6.4	6
M. Compilation of records, statistics and related information	3.2	10
N. Mediating in *staff–student* conflicts (including complaints about teaching)	7.3	5
Other (i.e. not covered by any one of the above, or covered by more than one category)	17.7	

Contentious discussion with caretaker over a broken chair – he maintains that it has been vandalised ('It's the Engineers again'), whereas I suggest that it is possibly fatigued.

The surfeit of paper work and the hundreds of minor decisions that are required detracts seriously from work and thought on the basic philosophy for the department's future development.

Approximately one-third of the problems were described as being ones which cropped up no more than once or twice a year. A further 20 percent apparently arose at least once a week. Problems in different categories occurred in much the same sort of frequency pattern, but it is interesting to note that, whereas more than half of the incidents relating to staff appointments, external relations and staff–staff conflicts were said to happen only once or twice a year, a similar proportion of incidents relating to accommodation and resources arose at least once a week. As one HoD put it: 'I could write a book on the subject. Financial aspects of the work in my department require constant vetting . . . and to make matters worse we always seem to be short of classroom space'.

As shown in *Table* 12, possible differences between subject areas are accounted for mainly in terms of six categories (B, I, J, K, L, N). As expected, incidents relating to resources are more common in departments which make a lot of use of specialized equipment and materials (e.g. catering, engineering) than in other departments. Not so clear is why staff–student conflicts should figure more prominently in the incidents described by heads of business and management studies than in those described by other heads, and why staff–staff conflicts appear to be especially prevalent in food and fashion departments. A possible link here is that three-quarters of the business and management departments were grade IV–VI departments, compared with only one-quarter of the food and fashion departments. The same factor might also be important in relation to the two incident categories mentioned most frequently by respondents – timetabling and advising individual staff. Sixty-six percent of the incidents relating to timetabling and staff deployment, and 72 percent of those associated with advising individual staff, were mentioned by grade IV–VI heads; only 53 percent of incidents in the remaining categories could be so attributed. Further, all of the problems associated with the compilation of records and statistics stemmed from grade IV–VI heads, and it is only in the case of mediating in staff–staff conflicts that grade I–III heads score more

Table 12   Selected categories of incident by subject area (% in each category)

Category	Business and management studies	Food and fashion	Engineering	General studies and humanities
Advising individual students	7.8	14.6	2.3	15.5
Staff–student conflicts	15.7	7.3	6.8	4.4
Advising individual staff	15.7	4.9	9.1	15.5
Staff–staff conflicts	2.0	14.6	4.5	4.4
Resources	7.8	14.6	13.6	4.4
External relations	3.9	7.3	13.6	6.7
All other categories	47.1	36.7	50.1	49.1

heavily than their higher graded counterparts.

Inevitably, these findings and tentative conclusions are all highly speculative. No attempt is made to measure the amount of time which HoDs spend on different kinds of problems and the survey relates to only a small number of incidents. A further limitation is that the survey concentrates on a particular month in the college year; problems in the spring and summer are likely to differ from those in November. It is sometimes hard to define a problem and one or two respondents indicated that they had found it almost impossible to identify the most difficult task or situation which they had encountered during the past 2–3 days: 'Easily my most difficult task has been to complete your questionnaire and to select the most difficult task from among so many possibilities'. Similarly, the approach tends to focus on isolated current problems, rather than on more general 'background' problems. This possibly helps to explain why so few of the incidents appear to stem from self-generated problems concerned with, for example, planning new courses, fostering close relations with industry and commerce, keeping abreast of the general educational scene.

To summarize, therefore, HoDs seem to be preoccupied with day-to-day problems that are more closely allied to checking and routine maintenance functions than to monitoring and future planning. The great majority of these problems are probably raised by subordinate staff and students rather than by peers or superiors. Fewer than 4 percent of the 220 incidents discussed above mention the principal or vice-principal. What the survey reported here does not do is tell us whether HoDs are really concentrating on the sorts of problem which they ought to be concentrating on; whether, to use Tolley's words, they are 'over-busy rather than over-worked' (1972, p. 16).

What the survey does do is illustrate that the job of an HoD is much less tidy, straightforward and easily defined than might be supposed simply by looking at specimen job descriptions. There seems little doubt that a much more comprehensive approach to the study of HoDs' work activities is needed. This will require a methodology that integrates 'time-spending' models based on diaries, structured observations, etc., with 'problem-solving' models based on critical incidents, problem portfolios and the like. It must be capable of exploring distinctions between isolated 'day-to-day' problems and general 'background' problems, of identifying the ways in which these are generated, the manner and extent to which they interact, the time which they occupy and their relative importance in terms of judging the effectiveness of HoDs.

HoD: academic, administrator or manager?

Up until the 1950s, FE colleges were small monolithic organizations with relatively unsophisticated administrative arrangements. Superficially, at any rate, the job of an HoD was fairly simple. In little more than 20 years, however, the situation has changed dramatically. The number of colleges has decreased, but there has been a sixfold increase in the number of full-time staff (from just over 12,000 in 1956 to more than 76,000 in 1976); the range of courses has widened considerably. Colleges are now large, complex organizations and, whatever else it is, the job of an HoD is no longer simple.

Innovation has become established as a more-or-less permanent feature of the educational scene. There is a superabundance of examples, models and perspectives (see, for example, Bolam, 1974). Despite this, not a lot is known with certainty about the different circumstances which give rise to change and, more importantly, there is a dearth of evidence concerning factors which govern the success or otherwise of particular strategies for implementing change. Not only is there no accepted framework for the study of educational innovation, but there are precious few guidelines to assist policy-makers and practitioners. The absence of such guidelines is of special significance for further education, if only because it seems to be characterized by rapid change to an extent even greater than that in other sectors: 'Further education remains the Heraclitan sector of British education in which flux is the natural state and stability is transient or illusory. There is rarely a moment when at least one major change is not in the course of execution and when no national committee is considering further reform' (Fowler, 1973).

Amongst many recent changes affecting further education, special mention can be made of the impact of the Manpower Services Commission and provision for unemployed youth; mergers between neighbouring colleges and existence of many more split-site institutions; curriculum changes and the setting up of new validating bodies like TEC and BEC; a rapid growth in the number of full-time students, coupled with an influx of students with a wider range of abilities, interests and aspirations than previously; additional constraints and external controls, not least economic stringencies and policies of 'nil growth'; increasing overlap with other sectors of the educational system, including the emergence of new types of institutions such as colleges of higher education and tertiary colleges. Against this kind of background, it would be very surprising indeed if the problems facing

HoDs did not increase. Moreover, the fact that much of the impetus for change in further education tends to lie *outside* the colleges probably makes it more difficult for HoDs to come to terms with these problems.

In trying to pull together the main themes of the argument, it is difficult to escape the conclusion that much of the uncertainty surrounding HoDs and their problems centres on questions about roles and functions, organizational control and leadership. Are HoDs clearly aware of their duties and responsibilities? Do they share a common pattern of beliefs as to what they should or should not be doing? Do the demands of the job vary from one college to another and how do these variations affect what HoDs actually do? To what extent can HoDs determine for themselves what they actually do? Do they have enough authority to carry out their job? What expectations do other people (e.g. principals, lecturers) have about the roles and functions of HoDs? How are these expectations perceived by HoDs themselves? What effects do role ambiguities and conflicts have on job satisfaction and job effectiveness? The situation is perhaps best illustrated by considering what seems to have happened as a result of DES Circular 7/70 and the setting up of academic boards. Many HoDs now feel themselves to be sandwiched between members of staff who wish to participate more in decision-making and a principal who is eager to retain as much authority and control as possible. 'The increased workload to the head of department as a result of his membership of an academic board and its committee is considerable. Not only has his role changed from mainly administrative with a bit of teaching, to more academic with responsibility for course content, etc.; he now has to add a political dimension . . . (O)ne of the problems facing colleges in successfully operating their academic boards is that many heads do not accept the redefined role' (Morgan and Parkes, 1977).

Managerial functions are usually said to be the same – creating, planning, organizing, motivating, communicating, controlling – regardless of the type of organization, managerial level or pattern of work activities (Hicks and Gullett, 1976). In this sense, HoDs have always been called upon to fulfil a managerial role; as colleges and departments have become larger, heads have probably become increasingly remote from teaching (Charlton et al., 1971).[9] But Circular 7/70 appears to give HoDs greater responsibility for planning academic developments and for maintaining and improving standards of teaching. The managerial role of an HoD might be expected to change from one involving mainly *administration* ('management with minimum disturbance') to one involving considerable academic *leadership* ('management with the likelihood of change'). With the advent of agencies like TEC and BEC, new patterns of leadership are developing which tend to emphasize 'professional' authority rather than simply 'organizational' authority. It is the member of staff who is respected by his fellow *academics* who becomes the acknowledged leader in matters of curriculum design and development; sometimes this is the HoD, frequently it is not. For both head and academic leader, however, 'the importance of the acquisition of the subtle skills of staff motivation, team leadership and communication completely outweigh the more pragmatic administrative functions of allocation of rooms, ordering of equipment and so on, which had for too long been seen as fundamental in the head's role (Bailey, 1977, pp. 99–100).

The possible tensions created by these role ambiguities and conflicts might be regarded as good reason for separating out the academic and administrative functions of HoDs, perhaps appointing different people in respect of each function. Alternatively, the present system of permanent appointments to departmental headships might usefully be reappraised.[10] Either way, we need to know more about the problems facing HoDs: what these problems are, how they arise and how they might be resolved. There is an abundant literature on innovation in education, organizational theory, managerial behaviour and effectiveness. Whatever the implications of a knowledge of HoDs' problems for recruitment and selection, identification of training needs, job design and organizational development, ways must be found of bridging the gap between theory and practice.

Notes

1   See, for example, Brosan (1965) and Leveson (1961). For an interesting study of different types of managerial jobs, see Stewart (1976).

2   The argument is developed further in Youngman et al. (1978).

3   I am greatly indebted to the many respondents who found time to complete and return the questionnaire. I am also grateful to a number of colleagues in the Faculty of Education, Huddersfield Polytechnic, who helped to categorize the responses.

4   An example of a 'job specification' for a head of department is given in ACFHE/APTI (1973).

5   The vacancies were at different colleges drawn from different LEAs. They were all at grade III or IV level and represented four main groups of subjects: construction, engineering and science (10), general education, humanities and general studies (8), business, management and secretarial studies (6), catering, health and community studies (6).

6   Out of 179 firms which participated in a recent survey, fewer than 60 percent used a formal job description on a regular basis and only 35 percent used an appropriate job (or man) specification. See Kingston (1971).

7   The technique owes its origins to Flanagan (1954). It has been used recently to derive a

model of an 'excellent' college or university teacher: see Truex (1975).

8 The sample of HoDs was drawn from the 590 or so FE colleges listed in *The Education Authorities Directory and Annual* (1976). A table of random numbers was used to select the 60 departments from each of the four main subject areas.

9 See also 'A head of his time', in *College Management – Readings and Cases, vol. 1*, ed. D.D. Simmons, Coombe Lodge, 1971. ORG 14–100.

10 Some commentators suggest that we might be able to dispense with HoDs altogether. See Davis (1978).

References

ACFHE/APTI (1973) *Staff Development in Further Education*, pp. 35–37.

Bailey, R. (1977) Management of education – An industrial comparison. *Journal of Further and Higher Education*, vol. 1, no. 3.

Baron, G. (1978) *The Managerial Approach to Tertiary Education. Studies in Education, No. 7*. London, University of London Institute of Education.

Bolam, R. (1974) *Planned Educational Change: Theory and Practice*. Bristol, University of Bristol, School of Education Research Unit.

Brosan, G.S. (1965) The head of department and his work. *Technical Education and Industrial Training*, vol. 7, pp. 158–159.

Charlton D., Gent W. and Scammells, B. (1971) *The Administration of Technical Colleges*. Manchester, Manchester University Press, pp. 46–47.

Davis, M. (1978) Who needs heads of department in FE colleges? *Times Higher Education Supplement*, 21 July 1978, p. 10.

Flanagan, J.C. (1954) The critical incident technique. *Psychological Bulletin*, vol. 51, pp. 327–358.

Fowler, G. (1973) Further education. In: Bell, R., Fowler, G. and Little, K. (eds) *Education in Great Britain and Ireland – A Source Book*. London, Routledge & Kegan Paul/Open University, p. 187.

Hall, J.C. and Thomas, J.B. (1978) Role specification for applicants for heads of mathematics departments in schools. *Educational Review*, vol. 30, pp. 35–40.

Hicks, H.G. and Gullett, C.R. (1976) *The Management of Organisations*, 3rd ed. New York, McGraw-Hill.

Kingston, N. (1971) *Selecting Managers*. London, British Institute of Management.

Leveson, J.H. (1961) The head of department in a technical college. *Vocational Aspect*, vol. 13, pp. 105–112.

Livy, B. (1975) *Job Evaluation*. London, Allen and Unwin, p. 45.

Marples, D.L. (1967) Studies of managers – A fresh start. *Journal of Management Studies*, vol. 4, pp. 282–299.

Morgan, C. and Parkes, D. (1977) *Management and the Academic Board in Further Education Colleges*, Unit 12, E321. *Management in Education* (Educational Studies: A Third Level Course). Milton Keynes, Open University Press.

Rendell, J. (1977) How to manage time. *Management Today*, November, pp. 129–136.

Singer, E.J. and Ramsden, J. (1972) *Human Resources: Obtaining Results from People at Work*. New York, McGraw-Hill, p. 87.

Stewart, R. (1976) *Contrasts in Management*. New York, McGraw-Hill.

Tolley, G. (1972) The managerial role of a head of department. *Technical Journal*, vol. 10, no. 3.

Truex, N.H. (1975) Factors critical to college teaching success or failure. *Improving College and University Teaching*, vol. 23, pp. 236–240.

Youngman, M.B. (1975) Structuring work for training purposes. *Vocational Aspect*, vol. 27, pp. 77–86.

Youngman, M., Monk, J.D., Oxtoby, R. and Heywood, J. (1978) *Analysing Jobs*. Farnborough, Gower Press.

CHAPTER 4.7

THE ORGANIZATIONS OF CONSENT*
CHARLES B. HANDY

'Universities,' I said, 'are the prototypes of the organizations of tomorrow.' 'If that be so,' said a Professor standing near, 'then God help us all!'

Behind my remark, however, was the suggestion that universities, rather like voluntary societies, theatrical groups or mountain climbing teams, have to be managed to be effective, but have to be managed by consent. There seem to be good grounds for supposing that this is the way of the future for all organizations, that the organization managed by consent will be as common and as necessary in the city or the factory as it is in the theatre. If this be so, then we had best begin to learn how to manage such organizations rather better than we do today.

What do we mean by the organizations of consent? Why do they seem to be on the increase? Perhaps we should explore these questions before looking at the management practices required and the implications of such organizations for society as a whole.

What is involved in an organization of consent?

The psychological contract between individual and organization has a different slant in an organization of consent. The psychological contract is implicit. In the average run of organizations the contract would run something like this:

* *The Changing University*, edited by David Warren Piper and Ron Glatter. Slough, NFER, 1977. © D. Warren Piper and R. Glatter, 1977. Charles B. Handy is visiting Professor of Management Development at the London Business School and Warden of St George's House in Windsor Castle.

The individual is there because he has a particular talent or skill or aptitude or just a pair of hands, he is lending this resource to the organization in return for some mixture of money, facilities, excitement, or just the chance to participate in something in which he believes.

If the organization violates this implicit contract, if, for instance, it offers increased excitement when all the individual wants is money, then it runs into difficulties.

In the organization of consent the contract goes beyond this. For one thing, it has a very individual slant. The individual tends to see himself as a valuable resource which the organization ought to cherish. Secondly, he is very much an individual with a personality and with individual rights and must be so regarded. Thirdly, the contract includes some deep beliefs about the way people should relate to each other. Hierarchy is bad. Argument is good. All men, and women, are essentially equal.

The flavour of the organization of consent can best be conveyed by some short anecdotes:

I was talking with some friends who belong to such an organization and happened to remark how interesting it was that one person could make such a difference to one's life and work if that one person was one's boss. 'How odd,' they said, 'that you think of yourself as having a boss.'

In attempting to manage one bit of an organization of consent I was trying to discuss why my instructions had not been carried out by a colleague that I thought of as subordinate to me. 'You cannot *tell* me to do something,' he explained gently, 'you can only *ask* me.' 'On the other hand,' he went on, rubbing salt into the wound, '*I* don't ask *you* if I'm going to do something, I *tell* you.'

A friend, moving into an organization of consent from a traditional hierarchical business organization, was dismayed to find that his circular memoranda and his published requirements of his associates produced absolutely no result at all, not even rebellion, just silence. 'Would you believe it?' he said, 'I've had to go along and make an individual personal contract with each one of them.'

To the outsider these anecdotes would seem unbelievable, the attitudes described intolerable. How can organizations work, he would say, without rules and procedures? There must be some decision-making procedure, some delegation of responsibility, some way in which A has the right to require B to do so and so. And of course he would be correct. No organization can survive for long without the apportionment of responsibility and the concomitant authority.

The friend who ran afoul of the organization of consent got into further difficulties when he assumed that since his associates rejected his assumption of decision-making powers they wanted to take all decisions themselves. Not so. 'That's your job,' they said, 'we have other and better things to do than to help you take your decisions.' He had confused the questioning of *his* authority with the questioning of authority as a principle.

For the distinction between the organization of consent and the traditional hierarchical organization is that authority in the former is granted by those below whereas in the hierarchical state authority is conferred by those above. Your official role in the organization of consent gives you little effective power – that is only won by the consent of those you seek to manage. Nor does this consent, once given, hold good for all time or for all circumstances. It needs constant ratification.

This process of the ratification of authority does not mean that everyone must be involved in everything. The organization of consent is not a consensus organization. Far from it. The manager in an organization of consent is meant to manage, to take decisions, set up information systems, plan and organize. Each individual, it is felt, has his own proper and valuable role to play and no one wants to do anyone else's work for him. *But* the important decisions, the right to institute procedures, must be exposed to possible dissent before implementation. The individual may not want to be involved but he does want to be consulted. He wants to be unfettered but not unnoticed. The minority report may never be implemented but it has a right to be heard.

Ratification of authority proceeds therefore by exposure to dissent. It is consultative management, not participative management. Committees and meetings in these organizations will be large but they will not be decision-making forums. They will be rather the testing grounds of decisions, the platforms for dissenters.

It is when the management confuses the need to be consulted with the need to participate, or feels that a minority's desire to be heard means a wish to veto, that the organization of consent becomes a bog of talk and inertia.

It is when a management, un-understanding, infringes the psychological contract by assuming unratified authority that morale is lowered, secrecy and subversion mount, energy and commitment reduce. Lonely and anxious, management then too often responds with more controls and checks, more assumed rights. Self-fulfilling, the organization begins to respond only to whips and spurs and everyone wonders what went wrong.

Factors heralding the organizations of consent

These are the most difficult of organizations to manage. Why, one may well ask, should one tolerate them or encourage their existence? Unfortunately, the choice is not ours. There is a range of trends in our society which makes it likely that all organizations will one day have to be managed by consent, whether we will it or not. How one might go about this management task will be discussed in the next section. First, let us briefly look at two major forces at work in organizations.

Management as a semi-profession

The principal advantage of a profession to its practitioners, namely protected entry and its corollaries of catchment areas, agreed fee scales and effective tenure, is never likely to become available to managers. Instead, as it gradually assumes the societal status of a profession, management and the manager may be acquiring only the difficult cut of the deal.

Leaving aside the union-like aspects of professionalism the other concomitants of a professional status for one's work are:

1   Work becomes a major source of identity. If you cease to describe yourself in terms of where you live, or of your ancestry, but in terms of your occupation, then the nature and style of that occupation become increasingly important to you. Work is no longer instrumental, it is central to your identity. You therefore look for opportunities to express and develop your identity at work instead of outside your work.

2   Skill-related earnings. A professional, like a craftsman, is paid for his skill. If the skill deteriorates or is no longer required, then the earnings diminish or cease. Redundant blacksmiths received no income from their previous users when these switched from horses to cars. Professional managers, like mercenaries, will be well paid when their skills are needed but cannot expect employment for old times sake. The idea of an organization owing a man a career is disappearing with the growth of professionalism. The professional manager will therefore be concerned to ply his skill to his maximum advantage. His commitment will be to himself first, his profession next, his organization third.

3   Mobility and self-development. Professionals are mobile. Their reference group spreads across organizations. If organizations are less committed to them so are they to organizations. If they are good they can move when they want to. Since their career will not necessarily be with the

same organization they cannot expect the organization to invest too much in their long-term development. They must take responsibility for their own development. Mobility is one good way of doing this.

Organizations will find that their good men have to be handled gently or they will disappear. Effectively the good professionals have tenure. It is only the poor and the mediocre who can be ordered around.

Organizations used to view themselves as twentieth-century squire-archies, with managers and workers as their agents and tenants. The emergence of the manager as a professional has meant the abandonment of this conception of the organization. An organization, at the managerial level, is becoming more and more a partnership of mobile professionals. Such organizations can only be managed by consent.

The spread of matrism

Gordon Rattray Taylor in his latest book *Rethink* has drawn attention to the difference between what he terms 'patrism' and 'matrism' in our society. The values and attitudes of patrism might be called traditional, or tough, as opposed to radical or tender. Patrism believes in order and discipline, wishes to maintain the traditions of the past, respect for authority, values self-control and rational behaviour, distinguishes male and female roles, puts more faith in experience than insight, age than youth. Matrism, on the other hand, is optimistic about the future, decries the past, believes in openness and likes emotions, makes little distinction between the sexes, wants discussion rather than orders, places reliance on expertise rather than experience, values youth and imagination more than age.

We can debate whether Rattray Taylor is right in attributing the swing towards matrism to changes in child-rearing practices. But the dimension he is describing seems real enough and there are indisputable signs that the younger generation have more matrist values. If this is so, then organizations will not be able to buck the trend. Management style is neither ultimately right or ultimately wrong, it is only culturally appropriate. The hierarchical style of management may well have been appropriate to a Britain reared by Victorians and Georgians. For the new Elizabethans it seems very probable that the culturally appropriate style is going to be management by consent.

How does one manage by consent?

There are certain principles that seem to apply. Like all principles they are easier to describe than to practise. Perhaps at least they will provide a manager in an organization of consent with a checklist of desiderata.

1   *Recognize the right to disagree.*
In these organizations John Stuart Mill's dictum that truth proceeds from argument is a widely held belief. To be invited to disagree is everyone's prerogative but this does not imply that they have the right to take the decision, that right belongs to him to whom they have consigned the responsibility.

2   *Control by planning not by checking.*
In these organizations it is legitimate to plan and to replan or change plans. It is not legitimate to check what others are doing unless their specific agreement has been obtained. Information for planning is willingly vouchsafed, information for monitoring less willingly. The manager therefore has to work with a variety of planning cycles and be clearly seen to use past information as a base for future planning.

3   *Manage by reciprocal trust.*
Trust and control displace each other. If you are seen to control someone you are seen not to trust them. If you cannot control them you must trust them. Similarly they must trust you. Reciprocal trust is hard to establish and is not self-maintaining. It is easier to trust those whom you yourself have chosen than those you are landed with. Tenure, at least for managerial positions, must be on its way out since it reduces a top manager's freedom to choose his own colleagues.

4   *Manage by platoons.*
Individuals find it easier to identify with smaller groups. They also perceive themselves to have greater influence the smaller their primary group. Trust is easier to create, the smaller the group. The concept of platoons, the ten group in Antony Jay's analogy, has served the army well and must be one of the buttresses in an organization of consent. The platoon concept should be allowed to override other ways of organizing work which may look more rational but involve a larger primary group. Individuals may be individuals but they need a group to identify with. Everyone should therefore be a member of at least one platoon.

5   *Be yourself.*
Organizations of consent are personal rather than impersonal. You cannot trust a façade. Openness and frankness and sincerity are

valued. To act a role is to disappear as a person. Whatever your idiosyncracies or habits or values, let them be visible. Your sense of your identity and purpose gives identity and purpose to your part of the organization. These organizations are tolerant of unimportant differences, but place great emphasis on the concept of 'mission' or 'purpose'.

6   *Husband your energy.*
    The managerial role in these organizations is exhausting. To treat individuals as individuals, to welcome disagreement, to tolerate dissent, to listen more than talk, to be true to oneself as well as others – all these requirements require a deal of energy. When energy fails we fall back on routines and general principles, we listen less and dictate more. Fatigue should not be a battle honour in these organizations, it should be a crime. Protect what Toffler calls 'stability zones', the places of retreat, the times of withdrawal, and you will protect your colleagues.

The implications for society

Organizations built on consent sound exciting, sound democratic and in tune with modern ideals. In fact they look to be dragging a train of undesired consequences behind them:

1   *Managerial burn out.* The energy requirements of managers in these organizations is so high that in years to come it will be the exception when a man of over 50 will be appointed to a top managerial job.

In all probability skill-related earnings will increasingly contain a high proportion of provision for the future – in the form of pensions, stock options, etc. It will no longer be necessary to work till 65 to provide for lifetime earnings. But financial viability does not guarantee psychological satisfaction. Society will find itself with a glut of economically self-sufficient unemployed managers in their fifties. Seen as a resource for other sectors of society this vision is optimistic. There is however a real danger that they become a resource for the psychoanalyst.

2   *Professional obsolescence.* In a profession with no control over entry the good will prosper and the bad perish. Change, we are constantly reminded, is changing ever faster. To survive in the new self-responsible world the individual will have to maintain a constant investment in his own development. A heady prospect for adult education perhaps, but there will

be many who will forget to provide for the future in the trauma of the present. Will society provide a safety net?

3 *The globule society.* If the middle classes become increasingly professional and self-oriented, if mobility increases, if the successful prosper and the failures perish, one can see a society made up of small globules which constantly change their shape. Homes, families and friendship groups will be temporary and changing. Loyalty will become an outmoded virtue. Society will be divided into interest groups, force increasingly used as a mediator, stress the modern epidemic.

It is not a pleasant picture. If one takes a look into the future, a fashionable and low-risk pastime, an ironic possibility emerges. The organization of consent will prove too demanding and too threatening to most of society. We shall see the emergence, as a form of self-protection, of modular man, the individual who gets only part of his identity from his work. The job will become instrumental once again, individuals will become less committed to the organization but will expect less of it. Economic growth will slow down, but non-economic activities will flourish. Mobility will decrease as individuals develop other ties than their work. Society will be more stable, less rich, perhaps more fun.

Perhaps, after all, the organization of consent will be only a temporary phenomenon. But of this I am sure, it will dominate us for a time, and we in the management of universities are already tasting its pleasures and its pains.

CHAPTER 4.8

INSIDE KNOWLEDGE*
ERIC HEWTON

Culture is, according to Tylor (1871), 'that complex whole which includes knowledge, belief, art, law, morals, custom and any other capabilities and habits acquired by man as a member of society'. Culture is usually associated with society as a whole but subcultures within society have for long been recognized and the concept is transferable to other contexts. Here it will be applied to educational organizations and to insider groups or units, such as academic departments.

Culture offers a unifying concept, in so far as it assumes certain similarities and a degree of consensus between members of a particular group, but, at the same time, it indicates the diversity which can be found between groups. For the outsider culture offers some preliminary insights into a number of questions which will be of concern in deciding policy and strategy. For instance, if faced with an attempt to introduce change, might a technical college react differently to say a college of education or a university? Or, might the approach needed to ensure the cooperation of a physics department in a polytechnic be different to that needed for, say, a law or history department? Or might the procedures and results which an electrical engineering department would expect from allowing outsiders to evaluate their courses or introduce changes into their teaching or courses differ from those expected by say a sociology or an English department?

A cultural perspective offers only a partial answer to such questions but it opens some windows on the insiders' world and identifies certain patterns of thinking and acting which may have some explanatory power when the outsiders – assuming the role of diplomats – approach the culture with a

* *Rethinking Educational Change*. Guildford, SRHE, 1982. Eric Hewton is a lecturer in Education at the University of Sussex.

view to negotiating change. The topic is dealt with under two headings – organization and subject discipline: both are major factors in shaping the practices of insider groups.

Organizations

The idea that there are different 'styles' of organization, which profoundly affect atmosphere, morale, communications, efficiency, adaptiveness and innovativeness within an institution, is far from new, and there is a growing body of literature on this theme. Although much of the writing is concerned with industrial organizations it is relevant to educational institutions.

A useful starting point is Harrison's (1972) rather simplified, but conceptually helpful notion of organizational character. He was initially struck by the extent to which many of the problems which surround organizational change are based upon conflicting attitudes which individuals, from different styles of organization, bring to a discussion. He cites the following example in support of his argument.

During the setting up of an American factory in a foreign country it became clear that there were considerable differences between the Americans and the nationals with regard to decision-making.

> The Americans tended to operate within a task-oriented ideology. In problem-solving meetings they believed that everyone who had relevant ideas or information should contribute to the debate, and that in reaching a decision the greatest weight should be given to the best-informed and most knowledgeable people. They strove, moreover, for a clear-cut decision; and once the decision was made, they usually were committed to it even if they did not completely agree with it.

> Some of the nationals, however, came to the project from very authoritarian organizations and tended to operate from a power-oriented ideological base. . . . Each individual seemed to be trying to exert as much control as possible and to accept as little influence from others as he could. If he was in a position of authority, he seemed to ignore the ideas of juniors and the advice of staff experts. If he was not in a position of authority, he kept rather quiet in meetings and seemed almost happy when there was an unclear decision or no decision at all. He would then proceed the way he had wanted to all along.

> The task-oriented people regarded the foregoing behaviour as uncooperative and, sometimes, as devious or dishonest. The power-oriented people, however, interpreted the task-oriented individuals' emphasis on communication and co-operation as evidence of softness and fear of taking responsibility.

> Each group was engaging in what it regarded as normal and appropriate

practice and tended to regard the other as difficult to work with or just plain wrong. The fact that the differences were ideological was dimly realized only by the more thoughtful participants. The remainder tended to react to each other as wrongheaded *individuals*, rather than as adherents of a self-consistent and internally logical way of thinking and explaining their organizational world. (p. 120)

This provides an important illustration of the need to know the other culture. For an educational adviser it indicates the need to be aware of and sensitive to the problems which may arise through misunderstanding where parties to a discussion remain ignorant of the cultural background of those with whom they are negotiating.

Harrison suggests that there are four main styles of organization and calls them *power*, *role*, *task* and *person*. These categories have since been adopted and developed by Handy (1976), who maintains

In organizations there are deep seated beliefs about the way work should be organized, the way authority should be exercised, people rewarded, people controlled. What are the degrees of formalization required? How much planning and how far ahead? What combination of obedience and initiative is looked for in subordinates? Do work hours matter, or dress, or personal eccentricities? . . . Do committees control or individuals? Are there rules and procedures or only results? These are all parts of the culture of an organization. (p. 177)

They are also matters which should be of concern to an outsider intent upon introducing change into a culture. Each culture offers to the outsider different kinds of opportunity and different forms of resistance.

Handy compares the *role culture* to a Greek temple (*Fig. 11*). The pillars represent specialist units (usually departments) which are coordinated and controlled by a narrow band of senior management in the pediment. In this form of organization the role, or job description, is more important than the individual who occupies the position. Position power (the power which

Figure 11 The Greek temple representing the role culture.

stems from the role description) is the major source of authority and clearly defined rules and procedures relating to job specification, limits of authority, settlement of disputes, etc. are the major form of influence.

The *task culture* has a dominant value system which emphasizes getting the job done. Roles are not so clearly defined and power is more related to personal expertise and influence than to the formal authority of an office. Influence is therefore more widely dispersed than in the role culture and tends to shift according to the job in hand. The organization seeks to bring together the appropriate resources at the right time in order to complete a specific task or project. People are more likely to work in teams and the task culture 'utilizes the unifying power of the group to improve efficiency and to identify the individual with the objectives of the organization'. This culture is represented by a net (*Fig.* 12). Some of the strands are thicker than the others and power and influence are located at the interstices of the net.

Figure 12   The net representing the task culture.

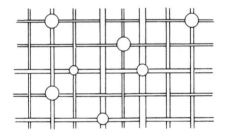

The main difference between the two cultures lies in the tendency of the former to stress formal procedures and impersonality and the latter to be concerned with people and their relationships. Both seek to direct individuals and groups towards the achievement of organizational goals but the former uses formal rules and authority whilst the latter relies more upon communities within the organization created and directed by individuals themselves. A similar distinction between organizational styles is made by Burns and Stalker (1966) in their analysis of two types of industrial firm which they refer to as 'mechanistic' and 'organismic'.

The remaining two cultures are called person orientated and power orientated and they represent significant alternatives to the role and task cultures.

The *person culture*, according to Handy, is one in which the individual provides the central point of interest and whatever structure there is exists only to serve those within it. It comes into being when a group of individuals band together to follow their own goals or ideas in their own way but, at the same time, seek some common facilities and the support of others to assist them. It is depicted as a cluster (*Fig.* 13).

Figure 13   The cluster representing the person culture.

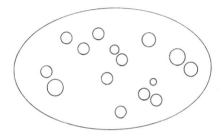

As the organization is meant to exist only for those within it, it has no overriding objective. Handy suggests as examples: barristers' chambers, architects' partnerships and some small consultancy firms. He also suggests that some academics in universities use the organization as if it were a person culture. Members of these organizations are normally professionals who, although having considerable autonomy of action vis-à-vis their firm, may well still be bound by strict rules and procedures imposed by their professional body. In such organizations influence is generally shared and based upon expertise. Individuals do what they are good at and are listened to on appropriate topics. They are free to give up their membership but the organization seldom has the power to evict them.

Finally the *power culture* is depicted by a web (*Fig.* 14). There are few rules and procedures. Control is exercised by a powerful group at the centre through key individuals dispersed at strategic points in the web. Decisions are taken largely on the outcome of power struggles rather than on purely 'rational' grounds. Resource power is the major power base in this culture, with some elements of personal (charismatic) power at the centre. Emphasis is upon results and the means are less important. The culture therefore has a tough and abrasive side which creates a highly competitive atmosphere. There will be concern for the individual only in so far as he produces results. Such organizations may well suffer low morale and high turnover.

The four cultures outlined above represent organizational stereotypes

Figure 14   The web representing the power culture.

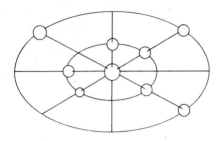

unlikely to be found, in pure form, in practice. But a tendency towards one style or another is probable and it is important for the outsider involved in educational change to recognize this. There are, for instance, *some* technical colleges which clearly operate on the lines of a role culture with a definite hierarchy of authority, pronounced specialization into functionally separate departments, and an abundance of formal rules and procedures. By contrast there are *some* universities which appear to be more like a task culture, adopting a collegial approach to their work and relying more on personal expertise and influence than on formal authority, rules and procedures.

But, within any organization, departments may develop their own cultural style. For instance, some clerical and accounts departments, which adopt standardized procedures, will lean towards a role culture. Academic departments, however, may evolve quite differently and, depending upon a number of factors such as size, the personalities of the leading members, research interests, etc. may move closer to any one of the four organizational styles – role, task, person or power.

There are no firm guidelines to suggest that one type of institution – college, polytechnic or university – or any one kind of department can be linked to a particular culture. Each case has to be treated separately and the possibility of mixed cultures and contrasting subcultures within an organization must be carefully examined. Despite this, the notion of organizational cultures, and particularly dominant cultures, within an institution, or within a department, is a useful way of clarifying the complex mixture of factors which together give rise to a 'normal' way of doing things and offer some clue as to the reaction which might be expected to attempts by outsiders to introduce change. The importance of this to the adviser in working towards a strategy for change is clear. The kind of strategy he must choose, or not choose, will be determined, in part at least, by the kind of culture he is dealing with.

Assume, for instance, that the adviser identifies what seems to be a predominantly 'role' culture characterized by formal structure, a clearly defined hierarchy of authority, impersonal position power and centralized control exercised by senior management. If change is to be introduced, it is to those formally charged with responsibility for the functioning of particular parts of the organization that the outsider will turn. The assumption is that once top or middle management is persuaded that the change is in the interests of a particular department then implementation becomes a fairly formal matter. This is not to say that others, further down the hierarchy, will not require information and explanation, nor that there will not be problems, but that the flow of information is down the hierarchy and is dependent upon acceptance of a policy, plan or decision at the top. The likelihood is that in these circumstances the adviser will be attracted towards an empirical-rational strategy and will attempt to convince senior management of the measurable effects of the change for the organization as a whole or for specific parts of it.

This approach, which Tichy (1975) calls 'analysis from the top', lies at the root of management philosophy in the role culture. It contains the assumption that most problems can eventually be solved by analysis and every attempt should be made to predict and prepare to deal with future uncertainties. Research and development should be an ongoing and essential part of the enterprise and results, whether concerned with new technology, markets, management systems, organizational structures or staff development, should be effectively incorporated into the overall decision-making process. Management consultancy thrives in this culture and it is here that outsiders, either employed by the host culture or hired from specialized agencies, play their part. Systems analysis, information technology, automation and standardization techniques are tools of the trade. Studies will be made of organization structures and how they might be more effectively integrated and improved. There will be attention to: the analysis of tasks; the addition or elimination of certain roles or units; the appropriateness of spans of control and number of hierarchical levels; and alternative reward structures and how they might be more effectively integrated and improved.

The language used to explain approaches to change in this category is usually formal, and the methodology deductive. The procedures follow a logical and systematic pathway and emphasis is laid upon specific rigour and protocol. It is assumed that an optimum solution can be found; if it is not, then it is the procedure which is at fault and must be changed.

But an empirical/rational approach would be less suited to a predominantly task culture. Here the prevailing norms focus members' attention less upon structure, formal authority, systematic relationships, functional differentiation, etc. and more upon how people see their situation; how they work in groups; how they operate in situations of uncertainty which demand of them flexibility and creativity; how power and authority are continually shifting as different kinds of expertise are needed.

In this situation there can normally be no straightforward imposition of change from above; most members are considered experts in their own right; the culture demands consultation and collaboration; informal networks and personal relationships are important and cannot be bypassed. Organizations, viewed from this standpoint, are places where people, dealing with their own frustrations, insecurities and personal needs and ambitions, interact with each other – often in situations which create conflict. Such people act according to their reading of a situation. They form alliances and cliques which may have little in common with formal organization structures. Along with others in their task or social groups they negotiate and construct their own view of reality and their own social order. For those concerned to bring about change, the choice of strategy must take into account this view of organization. Information, ideas, new ways of working, new attitudes, etc. must penetrate and be accepted into this 'informal' world. Individuals and groups, who are responsible for, and uphold this world, must themselves be identified and changed, perhaps through the use of a normative re-educative change strategy.

If the outsider is perceptive in identifying dominant cultural styles he will be in a better position to predict the kinds of attitudes and behaviours insiders will expect of each other and of outsiders who become involved in their affairs. But the matter is further complicated in educational institutions by the influence of subject disciplines.

[. . .]

Subject disciplines and culture

The problem raised by differing disciplinary cultures is particularly apparent when attempts are made to bring subjects together to create interdisciplinary courses. A great many such courses were introduced into universities and polytechnics in the 1970s and their progress and problems provided a focus of study for the Nuffield Group for Research and Innovation in Higher Education. Several case studies indicated just how difficult it was to overcome the cultural distinctions between disciplines which affect all aspects of interdisciplinary curriculum development (GRIHE, 1975).

What then are the implications for an educational adviser of disciplinary differentiation of the kind suggested above? Perhaps the most important lesson that will be learned from a study of disciplinary cultures is that each department will tend to regard the outsider in a different light, to expect different things from him and to react differently to the things that are said or done by the outsider group. The diplomatic outsider will learn the value of applying different approaches, at different times, of 'tuning in' to the unspoken norms of a particular group, and of using a language which is understandable by and acceptable to the 'client'. But the problems of cultural differentiation are sometimes accentuated when the outsider is called upon to work with several cultures at the same time.

Bligh (1978), faced with the problem of providing courses on teaching for university lecturers, became acutely aware of the different expectations and assumptions held by those from different disciplines. The physical and applied sciences, he maintains, generally work within paradigms of high mathematical content, accepted facts and theories and clearly defined structure; the biological medical subjects rely upon a great deal of factual information but have less theory than the physical sciences to synthesize it; the social sciences involve large bodies of information and abound in theories, many of which are untested or untestable, but there is a general expectation that philosophical underpinnings will be the subject of much critical analysis; and in most arts subjects subjective opinions are encouraged, there is emphasis upon linguistic expression rather than mathematical calculation, and lecturers are used to stimulating imagination rather than presenting established truths.

Broad as these generalizations are, they do point to the possibility of considerable variation in what different audiences will find acceptable as evidence, what will convince and what will lead to rethinking and change. To illustrate the problem faced by an adviser charged with the task of helping lecturers improve their teaching, Bligh draws two stereotypes of participants in a new faculty introductory course.

> Mr Martin has been appointed as a lecturer in a literary subject. It is a basic assumption of his discipline that the written or spoken word can stimulate emotive reactions. The authors and works he has studied do this pre-eminently. . . . His contributions to discussion at a course for new lecturers rely on appeals to common experience.
>
> He diverts discussion with untestable generalisation, and when challenged,

raises new hares to be chased. He is unpractised numerically and distrusts statistics because he cannot understand them, but articulately defends the rationalisation invented to cover his fear. Hence at the introductory course for new lecturers he is predisposed to reject empirical findings in education which may conflict with his presuppositions. (p. 24)

Dr Johnson is a new lecturer in one of the dogmatic sciences. . . . He expects educational issues to have a more clearly defined structure than they have. Consequently he is prone to think that he is getting very little out of a course for new lecturers and that 'Education is a load of waffle'. In sharp contrast to Mr Martin, he looks for truth external to himself, but he is unlikely to accept any 'truths' offered when he is unfamiliar with the method by which they have been obtained. He is unhappy with the uncertainty of education, and unsettled by the absence of any agreed paradigm of inquiry.

. . . Unlike Mr Martin who despises teaching factual information, Dr Johnson sees this as his job and feels he is expected to know all aspects of his subject . . . he now focuses on the quantitative data given in the new lecturers' course, regardless of its educational implications and importance. (p. 25)

The assumptions and expectations illustrated in the above examples stem from the influence of disciplinary cultures. They are related to the way in which members of subject groupings see things and do things. There are many such cultures, and for the outsider to communicate with the separate groups successfully (that is, in a way which will make educational change possible) he must, in Bligh's words, 'learn to speak with many tongues. . . . The same sentence given to a mixed audience will mean different things to different members'.

So far the examples provided depict disciplines as relatively unified cultures exhibiting certain predictable traits. To the extent that this is true, it is valuable information for the adviser. But it will sometimes be found that as well as unifying factors there are also internal divisions. It is not, simply, that some departments are made up of representatives of several subcultures (archaeology, for instance, may well have historians, geologists, chemists and statisticians working alongside each other) but that seemingly unitary disciplines are themselves divided according to specialism. Startup (1979), following a study of four university departments, points to some of the differences which arise from this basic division in the sciences:

Therefore, the research components of the academic role of the two types of scientist are necessarily different. In particular there must be some influence upon the activity of the applied scientists flowing from social relationships which link him to the practical activity of society generally. Though the academic pure scientist is made independent of the external world (and is thus, in a sense, parasitical upon it), the academic applied scientist is essentially dependent upon the external world (and he is thus inevitably a creature of it). (p. 91)

The differentiation, however, is not merely a division between, say, engineering subjects and so-called pure science subjects: it extends into the subjects themselves. Becher (1981), analysing physics as a disciplinary culture, points to major divisions stemming from a theoretical as opposed to an experimental orientation.

Within any particular branch of the subject, the two groups may be closely interdependent, accepting the same underlying principles. Nevertheless, they are trained differently, work in different ways and have divergent interests. . . . There is often a sense of mutual rivalry (illustrated in the comment that the experimentalists 'have to produce the meat which the theoreticians then pick'). There are further differences within each broad category. The design of experiments may call for very different talents from the exploitation of apparatus. Again, axiom theorists, working at a level of abstraction far removed from experimental results, can be clearly distinguished from phenomenologists, who start with the experimental data and try to fit mathematical formulae to them, so generating plausible hypotheses for further theoretical or experimental investigation. (p. 2)

Hudson (1980), examining the position of psychology as a discipline, maintains that much of the real excitement in the subject lies at the boundary rather than the heartland of the discipline. The discipline, he continues, will tend to become a polyglot with:

those facing one particular part of the boundary having much more in common, intellectually, with outsiders who work just on the far side of it than they do with other insiders whose energies are addressed elsewhere. (p. 11)

This segmentation of disciplines offers an important clue to the outsider seeking to understand groups of insiders. In many discipline areas he will find one or more splits separating academics into distinct and sometimes hostile camps. Such divisions can clearly be seen in economics, psychology, history, sociology, social anthropology, geography, etc., as well as in the science subjects referred to by Startup (1979) and Becher (1981).

Bucher and Strauss (1961), following a study of specialisms in the medical profession, suggest that segmentation owes a great deal not only to the focus of interest but also to ways of viewing problems and the methodological approaches adopted for solving them. In other words the unity which is provided by common field of study or subject area may be divided by differences in the way those associated with the subject define and approach the problems involved.

This suggests that there may be other factors operating which provide a common perspective for certain groups and that a discipline may contain one or more such perspectives. But what are those perspectives and how are they derived? Are they based purely upon methodological approaches or are the methodologies in turn dependent upon underlying values? Clearly these are not straightforward questions but the outsider who seeks to understand and influence groups who adhere to particular ways of seeing and doing things cannot afford to ignore them. [. . .]

Summary

An outsider intent on bringing about change will have to operate at various levels in seeking to understand the culture into which he seeks to introduce change. Overall, the organization with which he is concerned may tend towards the acceptance of a certain kind of management style which affects the way in which control over members is exercised and the way in which they are formally required to relate to each other. But there may also be variations in management styles between departments which have different functions – administration and teaching units representing one obvious division.

In educational institutions the matter is further complicated by the fact that subject disciplines tend to create their own cultures. At one level the nature of the subject itself engenders a set of ideas and methods, the adoption of which causes subject specialists to think and act in relatively similar ways. But disciplines are continuously evolving and they themselves segment, and spawn separate groups which develop their own identities.

A single department within an institution may, through a deliberate policy of selection, have only one (or, at least, only one dominant) culture or it may have several. Chemistry for instance, may, at first sight, appear a unitary culture but further study may well indicate different orientations between those concerned with organic and those concerned with inorganic chemistry. The adviser must be aware of these internal divisions and of allegiances to other professional groups which some specialists may have outside their own disciplinary cultures.

Overall, there are many interrelated factors which contribute towards the making of a culture. The adviser can rarely hope to understand them all but that is not what he seeks to do. His main concern is to identify those aspects of the culture which will enable him to devise the most appropriate change strategy.

References

Becher, R.A. (1981) *Physicists on Physics and Historians on History.* Unpublished paper, University of Sussex.

Bligh, D.A. (1978) *Policies of Acceptance within Universities.* Unpublished paper included in *Forum 78,* a collection of working papers of the conference of the Coordinating Committee for the Training of University Teachers, University of Aston, 1978.

Bucher, R. and Strauss, A. (1961) Professions in process. *The American Journal of Sociology,* 66, pp. 325–334.

Burns, T. and Stalker, G.M. (1966) *The Management of Innovation.* London, Tavistock.

Burkhead, J., Fox, T.G. and Holland, J.W. (1967) *Input and Output in Large-City High Schools.* New York, Syracuse University Press.

GRIHE (1975) *Case-Studies in Interdisciplinarity* (Group for Research and Innovation in Higher Education). London, Nuffield Foundation.

Handy, C. (1976) *Understanding Organizations.* Harmondsworth, Penguin.

Harrison, R. (1972) Understanding your organization character. *Harvard Business Review,* May–June 1972.

Hudson, L. (1980) The octopus, the telephone exchange and the ivory tower. *The Times Higher Education Supplement,* 26 September.

Startup, R. (1979) *The University Teacher and His World.* Farnborough, Saxon House.

Tichy, N. (1975) How different types of change agents diagnose organizations. *Human Relations,* 28, pp. 771–789.

Tylor (1871) Quoted in Kroeber, A.L. and Kluckholm, C. (1963) *Culture: a Critical Review of Concepts and Definitions.* New York, Vintage Books.

SECTION 5

CURRICULUM POLICY AND CONTROL

CHAPTER 5.1

THE IMPLICATIONS AND PROCESSES OF QUALITY CONTROL IN FURTHER AND HIGHER EDUCATION*
GORDON WHEELER

[. . .] Those of us who manage education have to ensure particular standards of quality. This implies that we must hypothesize some particular process by which quality can be achieved. It further implies that we must organize ourselves to bring about a statement of quality and the control of activities to achieve that quality.

Our main problem here is one of definition. We have no British Standard for education. In education we have many definitions of quality, not a single one. The education process is participative rather than regulative. We have a teacher-based concept of quality, that is, what the skilled teacher believes is good. We have a concept of agencies as regulators of standards, for example TEC and BEC. We have processes of external validation. We try to bring these differing concepts of standards together.

Up to further education at 16 we may follow the Plowden Report (CACE, 1967):

> We have considered whether we can lay down standards that should be achieved by the end of the primary school, but consider that this is not possible. It is not possible to describe a standard of attainment that should be reached by all, or indeed most children. Any set standard would seriously limit the bright children and be impossibly high for the dull. What could be achieved in one school might be impossible in another.

I suggest that we have adopted a Plowden-like approach to much of further education and, indeed, a good deal of higher education.

Although we have attempted quality definitions, I suggest that we are a

* *Coombe Lodge Report*, 1982, vol. 15, no. 5, pp. 179–183. Gordon Wheeler is Director of the Further Education Staff College.

long way from setting any absolute quality standards. One of the fascinating discussions at CNAA is the attempt to establish some equality between, say, a new Masters degree in education management and the much older Masters degree in, perhaps, one of the sciences, and relate this still further to a Masters degree in a university. The same is true at first-degree level and those of us concerned with TEC courses may contemplate how far one TEC unit equates with another at standards 1, 2, 3, 4 and 5.

The concept of quality standards has some philosophical foundation. We can distinguish between what might be called absolute standards and relative standards. The absolute standards of 22-carat gold or pure water can be defined with precision. But the relative standards concerned with such matters as social purpose, life skills, how much a person knows about, say, economics, are very different.

We are concerned too with the difference between value and facts. Are we thinking in quality terms of particular value systems and the achievement of those systems – whether it be democracy, honesty, participation or whatever – or are we concerned with quality in the knowledge and use of facts?

Are we also concerned with universality versus locality? Is the particular FE process in a particular place, for a particular group of students, something for which we are trying to achieve a quality standard? Or are we trying to think of some universal standard? For example, the *Report on Transferable Credits* (DES, 1980) raises some of the problems of trying to achieve universality in the statement of credit between institutions of education in this country. If you widen the credit problem and consider the possibility of a degree taken partly in Hong Kong, or India, or Germany and partly in Britain, you begin to see how very difficult the problem of universality is.

We can adopt the evaluation approach to quality in which we attempt to state some criteria by which we judge what is going on. The criteria may be the experience of the staff, the equipment being used, the size of the library, the experiences of the students. The criteria may have to do with teaching method rather than teaching content, for example whether case studies are used, the type of science equipment being used and how experiments are conducted.

Alternatively we may adopt an objectives approach, as many validating bodies have done, and ask whether the education we are providing meets certain objectives. If it is possible to state objectives and to measure achievement against them, we have something with which we can at least feel managerially confident.

We may adopt what we could call the 'returns' approach to quality – the rate of return on investment in a particular educative process as measured by outputs. Typical of this is a study of HND a few years ago which indicated that the best investment in British education in terms of the rate of return to the student was an HND. If we adopt this approach we must ask what educational level is most profitable? How do we measure the rate of return on education as against the rate of return on social services or the rate of return on industrial activity, or indeed the rate of return on non-specific investment?

We then have the criterion of human versus physical investment. Is it more profitable to put money into teachers, technicians, administrative staff or into physical capital? This kind of exploration of economic returns to education was very popular in the early 1970s. I quote from *Returns to Education* by George Psacharopoulos and Keith Hinchcliffe (1973):

> The most recent profitability evidence of investment in education in Great Britain has been provided by Maurice Zidderman, 1971, using a 1968 earning sample of almost 2,500 people with post-secondary qualification. Social rates of return were estimated for both full time formal education up to the Doctorate level and also for qualifications based upon part time education. The important results were that, whereas a first degree earned unadjusted return of 10.8 percent and a Doctorate earned 1.6 percent, the highest part-time qualification resulted in a return of over 20 percent.

That is one approach to quality management, but we must look at quality in terms of what the presumed market activity of the student is when that future market cannot be forecast.

There is also the question of whether the quality of the service we provide is a factor of the curriculum or the client group for whom the curriculum is provided. Without considering the client group, arguments about curriculum quality are sterile.

Quality as determined by indicators is another approach. How many enrolments have we? How many finishers? What educational opportunities does a particular programme lead to? How many students take two or three languages? How many acquire two A-Levels or two O-Levels? For example, the state of Iowa in the USA publishes a massive volume on educational achievement which can be contrasted with the Association of County Councils' thin published volume on statistics of education, which lists achievement of economy in cost per student rather than any suggestion of output or other measures.

Some of us adopt the peripheral approach to quality. We note how clean the college is – since cleanliness reflects care – and say this must be a caring institution because it is clean. We note the amount of graffiti and interpret it either as a student-centred environment or anarchic. We count the number of gold medals achieved in City and Guilds courses, and if two have been awarded we think the general standard of all students must be high since two have managed to do very well. We notice social or student life and judge it to be good if, for example, more than 50 percent of staff attend the social at Christmas willingly.

I have traversed a very large field along a footpath which is well trodden by problems. Quality in education is not really definable. The industrial/ commercial approach which is commended to us is too simple. It implies a controlled input of raw materials (in our case, people) and a clear standard of output. It leads to concepts of contract in which there is a guarantee that if a particular product or process does not have a predicted outcome you get your money back. We issue no such guarantee in further education.

If we attempt quality control in education we are altering the nature of the educative process in a number of ways. We are accepting the concept of open criticism to a far greater extent than is now accepted. We are probably accepting the impact of market forces to a greater extent than at present.

We do have management of quality in further and higher education. For example, the DES carries out quality management through its inspection and assessment processes. Major curriculum agencies – BEC, TEC and CNAA – validate much of the work that is done and assume that they can invent quality standards to justify their validation. The examining bodies – City and Guilds and the university boards – state quality standards by their examinations and the way they mark them. [. . .] But overall we have a decentralized, localized, fragmented educational system and we cannot hope that within that system we are going to have universally accepted quality standards. Nor are we going to be able to create a system which will enable us to identify good quality, have it nationally agreed, and invent mechanisms for achieving it.

References

Central Advisory Council for Education (CACE) (1967) *The Plowden Report*. London, HMSO.

Department of Education and Science (DES) (1980) *Report on Transferable Credits*. London, HMSO.

Psacharopoulos, George and Hinchcliffe, Keith (1973) *Returns to Education*. Amsterdam, Elsevier.

CHAPTER 5.2

THE PRODUCTION MODEL OF QUALITY CONTROL AND ITS APPLICATION TO HUMAN RESOURCES IN EDUCATION*
DEREK MARSH

[. . .]

Too many educationalists have for too long believed that education is somehow different from any other organizational process and has to be treated idiosyncratically. As Taylor (1981) says, the language of education is esoteric; but is it definable only 'in its own terms'? New language, such as that provided by the production model of quality control, offers new perspectives and provides a base from which to explore, to rethink stereotyped or irrationally held views. Is education really not 'production'? Are we not changing basic materials into something else? Granted that further education starts with a kind of product and not raw material and can be seen as a value-added process, but does that difference necessarily cause a rejection of any product-based model? Granted, too, that there are semantic problems in talking about education in production terms; but problems can be seen as opportunities. Exploring production models can, in my view, help us to be consciously more systematic in approaching the problem of quality provision in education by at least trying to transfer key words and concepts from one model to another. In trying to do so, we may see that quality is an implicit process within education. Much of what we do is effective quality control, although we may not recognize it as such.

The basic production model

The basic model, or conceptual map, is the systems model of input,

---

* *Coombe Lodge Report*, 1982, vol. 15, no. 5, pp. 184–192. Derek Marsh is Staff Tutor at the Further Education Staff College.

process, and output, not unfamiliar in its application to further and higher education (Cuthbert and Latcham, 1979).

The conceptual focus of the scientific model of quality control is concerned with cybernetics, the study of the control of systems, generally via feedback (Emery, 1978). The cybernetic loop model adds four key processes in the loop (*Fig.* 15). Inputs are of two kinds: controllable and uncontrollable. The feedback loop is generally concerned with the controllable elements of input and consists of monitoring the output, taking a sample of that output and examining it. The information acquired, both qualitative and quantitative, is interpreted and related to standards laid down. At the comparison stage the actual output is compared against the standard. In the event of any discrepancy, a decision has to be made on what appropriate actions will eliminate that discrepancy, followed by adjusting the input by carrying out those necessary actions. The loop consists therefore of two phases: a *static* one (sample, interpret, compare) and a *dynamic* one (decide, adjust).

Figure 15   The cybernetic loop model.

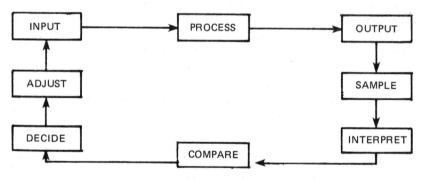

Control systems in the production model generally include elemental subsystems labelled: quality, production, materials, progress, cost, wages and labour. 'Quality control' is therefore only one of seven necessary control components. 'Quality control' is primarily *action* which adjusts operations to predetermined standards and its basis is *information* in the hands of managers. A map, therefore, of general organizational control would be as shown in *Fig.* 16.

The production model also distinguishes between *quality* and *reliability*.

Figure 16 Managerial control.

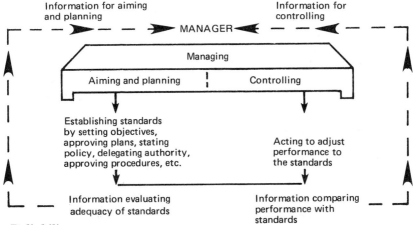

Reliability

Reliability is the extent to which the product can be relied upon to perform its intended duties effectively over a given period of time. Four main tests are applied to ascertain reliability:

a. 100 percent inspection of the product;

b. Sampling of the product (regularly or at random);

c. Life tests (i.e. testing until the product is destroyed);

d. Operating tests (i.e. testing the product in its proper use).

Quality

Quality is the product's fitness for purpose according to the required standard. Three main tests of quality are applied:

a. 100 percent inspection;

b. Sampling;

c. Key trouble areas (KTA) (e.g. fault frequencies are recorded).

Tests (a) and (b) are achieved by three forms of control:

i. Process control (on-the-spot checks by production people);

ii. Acceptance control (sampling a batch delivered);

iii. Statistical control (sampling by variables, attributes).

This is the model which is generally seen to be inapplicable to education. However, simply replacing words such as 'product', 'batch', by 'student' or 'teacher' suggests that many of the stages of the cybernetic loop are implicit in managing educational processes. For example, student and staff monitoring processes and qualitative and quantitative information processing are well established (Birch, 1978a). Nevertheless, there are difficulties in using the model as an exact template. The major problem is arriving at a clear, homogeneous definition of quality: quality in the educational process (curricula, learning–teaching methods), in student performance, institutional management and staff performance.

Applying the production model

The three static phases of sample, interpret and compare are already reasonably well represented in college processes. Students are *sampled* on 100 percent inspection basis through assignments, tests and examinations. We also evaluate the learner product on a number of other bases – random sampling, stratified random sampling, cluster sampling and matrix sampling. These tell us something about the quality of student learning, although at the back of our minds we have an absolute norm of the ideal (the 100 percent pass mark or the grade A). These figures tell us little about the quality of the educational experience students have undergone, although tools such as student self-evaluation exist together with those designed to evaluate student peer and staff relationships and student morale (which are too infrequently used). Information concerning student pass rate, retention rate and dropout rate is also collated, but little attempt is made to measure student productivity, that is, measuring student achievement against the resources used. The failure is to *interpret* this information because we cannot be certain what that information is telling us. This is largely due to the lack of any strong cause–effect relationship in education (how much of the learning is directly attributable to a teacher, to the institution?). Without vigorous pre- and post-learning assessments we can neither identify nor measure the value-added element as a result of learning. We therefore rely on other bits of information which are deemed to be useful and accurate: staff–student ratios, average student taught hours, average class size, average lecturer teaching hours, room hours, man days, actual student numbers, etc. (Marsh, 1979a).

When it comes to defining costs (quality is a function of what people are prepared to spend) the problems of variable, fixed, recurring and non-recurring costs are enormous. Nor have we defined 'costs' adequately –

average, marginal, ex-post, avoidable, economic, opportunity, value-added, etc. (Birch, 1978b; Cuthbert, 1979).

The third step in the cybernetic loop – *compare* – concerns the measurement and provision of quality which education has consistently failed to take with any firmness. It is easy to measure the actual; comparison is difficult because there is no standard against which to compare the actual. The generation of standards remains a key problem area. Education is as unwilling to take the 100/100 approach of training as a standard as it was to adopt a behavioural objectives approach to curriculum design. Similarly, as far as staff performance is concerned, the unwillingness to develop appraisal systems has largely enabled marginal performance to become institutionalized. When the standards required are imprecisely stated, 'quality' becomes impossible to define and hence to attain.

The dynamic parts of the loop – decision and adjustment – are relatively simple to achieve. Given the appropriate decision-making processes (and taking into account the prescribed rules and regulations) adjustment is largely a matter of choosing the most effective course of action and possessing the appropriate skills to carry it out (in educational institutions these skills are going to be basically interpersonal and leadership skills).

Applying the model: a staff quality control process

All writers on quality control agree that quality begins on the production line with an increased awareness on the part of the production line workers. (Indeed, the Japanese measure of 'quality circles' being adopted in British industry [Hutchins, 1981; Rendell and Mager, 1980] is based on this principle.) In education this places the real quality control of the product in the classroom during the interface between student and teacher. If we have to start somewhere in improving the quality of educational provision, this is obviously the most effective point of entry. Let us follow the production model's loop:

1 Output.
   The outputs we are concerned with include:
   a. *Student* Academic achievement
             Learning
             Motivation
             Productivity
             Quality
             Reliability
             Job placement (or entry to higher education).

   b. *Staff*   Quality
              Reliability
              Productivity
              Performance
              Motivation
              Student achievement (student output).

2 Sample.
   (Staff) We can sample staff output in a number of ways:

   a. Evaluating lessons (by superior, subordinate, peers, students);
   b. Evaluating student output.

3 Interpret
   We need quantitative and qualitative information before moving to
   the next stage. We need therefore a formative (not summative) evaluation process with the primary objective of professional improvement
   and development and with the underlying principle that what happens to the student in the classroom is what is meant by 'quality'. A
   wide range of information-collecting processes is available:

   a. Student evaluation (based on some agreed definitions of 'good'
      teaching);
   b. Classroom visits (by individuals or groups);
   c. Systematic observations (e.g. by using Flanders Interaction
      Analysis);
   d. Teaching materials (analysis of hand-outs, outlines, tests, exams,
      student papers returned);
   e. Teaching procedures evaluation (the evaluation of the mechanics
      of classroom management);
   f. Special incidents analysis (both positive and negative incidents);
   g. Teacher self-evaluation;
   h. Teaching performance tests (e.g. mini lessons with given objec-
      tives);
   j. Student testing (pre- and post-criterion referenced tests to evaluate
      total learning);
   k. Contract plan (teacher negotiates a contract with evaluator about
      kinds of public performance to be raised and measured.

   The literature of evaluation is full of such measures. Since there are no
   reliable and valid measures of teachers' instructional prowess – (h)

and (j) above seem to offer most opportunities for useful information – the solution is to opt for multiple indicators of teachers' skills. Teaching may, however, be only one process; most teachers also have managerial responsibilities which have to be sampled and interpreted. As with classroom performance, several techniques are available:

a. Management by objectives approach (including total coverage of all aspects of the job, selected key activity areas, and key effectiveness areas and training needs analysis).

   Linked with teaching performance evaluation this forms what has been called an 'educational accountability plan' (Stenning, 1981).

b. Management style analysis (to identify a need to change from one style to another (Blake and Monton, 1969).

c. Productivity (achievements, as specified, measured against resources used).

d. A measure of student–staff relationships, staff morale, expectations and perceptions (Bradley and Silverleaf, 1978).

4 Compare.
   As far as staff are concerned, internal control is simply the observation of actual performance of duties as against the assigned duties (as specified in a job description, analysis or contract via MBO), and action to correct deviations of the actual from the assigned. Unless the assigned duties are clear, this step cannot be undertaken. It has, moreover, to be continuous, after-the-fact, and corrective in its effect (Russell, 1977; Marsh, 1979b).

5 Decide.
   The decision-making process is as effective as the information available and the executive power of the decision-making organization. Most colleges use academic boards to deal with staff development. This may not be the most appropriate way in which to make decisions leading to action to improve quality of performance. The decision-making process should also take into account a number of possible options, such as tighten standards of performance; raise, improve or decrease 'tolerances' (since we can usually only identify the 5 percent on either side of the acceptable in the performance continuum,

tolerances of teachers' duties is a difficult area which has to be negotiated); widen or narrow specifications of the product (student).

6   Adjust.

To achieve the desired quality, inputs have to be adjusted. In terms of staff performance the implications are frequently for remedial, supportive staff development with an emphasis on pedagogic or managerial training for specific tasks. Hoping that quality will improve by the normal staff development programme can prove to be a false hope.

When the production model is applied, weaknesses and strengths are readily identifiable. The model offers an opportunity for valuable institutional self-evaluation of the approach to quality and its control.

References

Blake, R. and Monton, J.S. (1969) *Building a Dynamic Corporation through Good Organisational Development*. London, Addison-Wesley. (Tests and inventories published by Telemetrics (UK) Limited, Old Orchard, Bickley Road, Bickley, Kent, BR1 2NE.)

Bradley, J. and Silverleaf, J. (1978) *Making the Grade*. Slough, NFER.

Birch, D.W. (1978a) *An Overview of Management Information Systems in Educational Institutions* (Information Bank Paper 1275). Coombe Lodge.

Birch, D.W. (1978b) *An Outline of the Nature and Problems of Educational Costing* (Information Bank Paper 1284). Coombe Lodge.

Cuthbert, R.E. (1979) *An Introduction to Costing in Further and Higher Education* (Information Bank Paper 1419). Coombe Lodge.

Cuthbert, R.E. and Latcham, J.L. (1979) *Systems Approach to Management in Further Education* (Information Bank Paper 1419). Coombe Lodge.

Emery, F.E. (ed.) (1978) *Systems Thinking: Selected Readings*. Harmondsworth, Penguin Books.

Hutchins, D. (1981) Ringing the bell with quality circles. *Management Review and Digest*, vol. 8, no. 1.

Marsh, D.T. (1979a) *The Management of Educational Output* (Information Bank Paper 1352). Coombe Lodge.

Marsh, D.T. (1979b) *Role Clarification* (Information Bank Paper 1350). Coombe Lodge.

Rendell, E. and Mager, M. (1980) Using quality control. *Journal of European Industrial Training*, vol. 4, no. 6.

Russell, T.J. (1977) *Job Descriptions* (Information Bank Paper 1101). Coombe Lodge.

Stenning, R. (1981) *Quality Control in Education. Proceedings of the 9th Annual*

Conference of the British Educational Management and Administration Society, vol. 9, no. 2.

Taylor, W. (1981) *Quality Control in Education. Proceedings of the 9th Annual Conference of the British Educational Management and Administration Society*, vol. 9, no. 2.

CHAPTER 5.3

EVALUATION, VALIDATION AND ACCOUNTABILITY*
CLEM ADELMAN AND ROBIN ALEXANDER

What is evaluation?

This chapter is about formal evaluation in and of educational institutions. By 'educational evaluation' we mean *the making of judgements about the worth and effectiveness of educational intentions, processes and outcomes; about the relationships between these; and about the resource, planning and implementation frameworks for such ventures.*

An educational institution's inhabitants are engaged in a more or less constant process of evaluation: every decision demands it, from matters of overall policy to a teacher's decisions about what to say or do at a particular point in time in the process of classroom events and relationships. Much of this evaluation is an extension into the everyday work of educators of those continuous appraisals of conditions and events on the basis of which humans act and interrelate. At this level, the evaluative process remains largely idiosyncratic and private, though none the less valid, and as far as the quality of educational experiences available to the student is concerned, this level of evaluation is probably the most potent. So one way of characterizing the range of evaluation processes is to place such appraisal at one end of a continuum ranging from 'informal' to 'formal', with evaluation programmes set up for specific purposes as a part of institutional policy at the other. However, informal evaluation contributes to formal evaluation in a variety of subtle and significant ways to the extent that whatever our professional determination to produce 'objective' judgements on students,

* *The Self-Evaluating Institution*. London, Methuen, 1982, pp. 5–27. Clem Adelman is Research Co-ordinator, Bulmershe College, Reading. Robin Alexander is a lecturer in Education at the University of Leeds.

courses or other educational or institutional phenomena, it is virtually impossible for such judgements to escape its influence. Informal evaluations may be the product of attributes, behaviours and values which are as much 'personal' as 'professional', and these influences can and do play a significant part at all levels of evaluation, regardless of the appearance of detachment and objectivity which many 'formal' evaluation procedures have or at least claim.

'Formal' evaluation, therefore, is distinct from 'informal' not so much in terms of judgemental process itself as by virtue of the *accessibility* of that process, the intentions which lie behind it and the uses to which it is put. By formal educational evaluation we mean the making of judgements of the worth and effectiveness of educational endeavours at a *public* level, sometimes as a matter of *deliberate institutional policy*. These judgements are ostensibly informed by criteria and methods which are to some degree open to scrutiny and appraisal in order that the judgements may reasonably claim to be valid and fair.

[. . .]

Evaluation and institutional life

In theory *all* formal evaluations in an educational institution have in some way to do with furthering the stated educational purposes of the institution. However, for most staff certain evaluations are more obviously tied to these purposes than are others, and for this reason it is convenient to distinguish between evaluations made as a basis for *institutional* decision-making and policy formulation in general and those made as a basis for *educational* decision-making in particular. In the latter category we would distinguish three distinct sorts of formal evaluation common in educational institutions:

1 The appraisal of the quality and feasibility of course proposals or curriculum packages and the intentions and aspirations embodied within them. Where such appraisal leads to a decision about whether a proposal may be translated into action, we term it *validation*, and it can be undertaken by agents internal or external to the institution. (See Church, 1982.)

2 The appraisal of student performance on a course, especially, but not essentially, in relation to intended learning outcomes. This we term *assessment*. (See Heywood, 1977; Bloom et al., 1971.)

3   The appraisal of a course's organization and teaching–learning processes in action, and its various outcomes (in addition to student
learning). This is the usual sense in which *course* or *curriculum evaluation* is used. The most familiar form of course evaluation is the
'student feedback' approach, or survey of customer reaction (Dressell, 1976; Kemmis et al., 1978; Flood-Page, 1977.)

Three points should be immediately apparent from this analysis. The first is
that as formal processes *validation* and *assessment* are much more familiar
forms of evaluation in institutions than is *course evaluation* (and in universities student assessment may be the *only* formal appraisal of a department's
educational activities which takes place). The second is that the three are
equally necessary and complementary elements in a comprehensive
approach to institutional self-appraisal since one focuses mainly on intentions, another mainly on processes and another mainly on outcomes. Conceptually it would seem strange to try to make a case for only one or even two
of these, rather than all three, to constitute an adequate basis for educational
decision-making, yet in practice this is exactly what tends to happen: a
college or polytechnic may be permitted under CNAA regulations to run a
new course for five years purely on the basis of 'evaluations' of the adequacy
of the claims made for it in advance; the same course may eventually be
'evaluated' on the basis of students' marks in examinations. In neither case
is evidence sought about what *actually happens* on the course, about the
interactions and processes central to learning.

The third point is that institutionally these three complementary parts of
the evaluation process usually have separate and independent existences:
this separation is both *organizational* in that there may be distinct bodies and
procedures to deal with each (e.g. internal validation committees, course
development groups, assessment/examination boards, evaluation units)
and *temporal* in that they almost invariably follow a particular sequence –
first plan, next validate, then teach, then assess, and finally evaluate. In the
case of validation and assessment, the sequence is to some extent inevitable,
but a justification for tacking course evaluation on at the end of the process
of course development is hard to find. In practical terms it tends to ensure
that data from one sort of evaluation are used only in relation to their
immediate context (e.g. assessment data in relation to assessment procedures rather than, say, as commentary on teaching processes or course
goals) and that the cross fertilization of judgements on proposals, student
learning and courses in action can be very restricted. Decisions will then

tend to be tied similarly to the immediate experiences of context, and the further separation of the elements as distinct and unrelated areas of institutional life will be exacerbated: decisions on planning, on assessment, on teaching methods, etc. may be taken without significant reference to each other. Moreover, the extent to which these three facets of formal educational evaluation are institutionally and organizationally distinct may well reflect the demands for certain sorts of information, or for evidence that such information is being gathered, from external agencies to which an institution justifies its practices. In LEA sector higher education the character of internal institutional evaluation will reflect, in part at least, the requirements of validating bodies like the CNAA, and in this chapter we shall be concerned at certain points with what we see as a critical relationship between such external requirements and internal institutional responses in terms of policy and action.

Institutional self-evaluation is both *in* and *of* institutions. It is institutionally located and thus has a relationship to the complex network of norms, roles, values and relationships which make up the culture of an institution. And it is *of* institutions in that however particular the judgement – whether it is of a student, a course, a teacher or an educational proposal – it is in the end a judgement *of an institution's collective endeavour* to achieve the purposes for which it has been established. It is a conscious attempt to appraise this institutional endeavour and if it has any critical bite it will naturally produce reactions both positive and negative from individuals and groups involved or implicated.

Thus in the phrase 'institutional evaluation' the *institutional* dimension is as significant as the matter of *evaluation* techniques and criteria. In this chapter we shall reflect therefore not only on the latter but also on those key areas of institutional life to which they relate: curriculum innovation and institutional management. It is our assumption that improvements in these areas are unlikely without commitment to formal evaluation as a matter of policy. But we also believe, conversely, that the quality and usefulness of formal educational evaluations are very much dependent on the strategies and procedures for innovation and management. Consequently, it is necessary to explore the relationship between educational evaluation and other sorts of educational and institutional action.

Moreover, the ubiquitousness of public and private, formal and informal evaluations as elements in the life of educational institutions suggests strongly that the starting-point for the development of institutional evaluation policy must be *the explication and analysis of existing evaluation practices*,

rather than a grafting of new evaluation procedures onto an institutional culture whose existing evaluative processes remain unexplored and with which new policy and practice may prove incongruent. In certain instances it could well be that the most appropriate evaluation policy is an extension and integration of existing practices rather than additional arrangements.
[. . .]

Evaluation and validation: the significance of the CNAA

However, what to us seems particularly significant for the development of coherent approaches to evaluation in higher education institutions is the influence on ideas and practices of the Council for National Academic Awards as the main validating body. Until recently, for institutions running CNAA-validated courses, there has been a clear distinction between 'internal' and 'external' validation. The latter is the activity undertaken by the CNAA whereby a course proposal and its staffing, resource and management contexts are assessed and, if found to meet certain criteria, are deemed 'validated' for a given period of time, thus enabling the course proposal to be translated into living educational events and relationships. (See Alexander and Wormald (1982) for a comparison of CNAA and university validation styles and criteria.) Internal validation is a process, controlled and conducted by and within the institution, of 'vetting' a proposal before forwarding it in its polished form to an external validating agency (in the case of LEA maintained-sector institutions) or to enable it to be put into operation (e.g. in a university, where, of course, all validation is 'internal'). In the latter case validation may be no more than a rubber-stamping formality at faculty or senate level which ensures that the outward forms of a proposal – title, syllabus and examination arrangements – are consistent with prevailing practice. In the former case something considerably more extensive is involved, and colleges may have systems for internally appraising proposals which are as rigorous as anything offered by an external body (Alexander and Gent, 1982). However, internal validation procedures may tend to exist not so much because they are seen as educationally desirable but because they are a proven device for maximizing the chances of successful *external* validation. This may distort the judgemental criteria so that they are less about the educational quality of the proposal than about its chances of being externally validated. Internal validation becomes a dummy-run for the 'real' validation rather than a process of appraisal deemed valuable in its own right. Moreover, the style of internal validations, being modelled on the real thing, tends to repeat the inadequacies of external validation. Thus they may display disproportionate concern with documents and claims (rather than actions), and the ability to present a convincing case: performance and pre-packaging skills (Alexander, 1979) may count for more than the case itself. What we have yet to see in higher education is a genuinely comprehensive procedure for appraising course documents and statements of intent comparable to those developed in connection with school curriculum materials (e.g. Eraut et al., 1975).

For maintained-sector institutions of higher education this model of validation is now in the process of modification, following the publication of the CNAA's most recent *Partnership in Validation* proposals which introduce a greater measure of flexibility into the validation process and place greater reliance on institutions' internal procedures, both for the initial validation of courses and for their subsequent monitoring and evaluation (CNAA, 1975, 1979). Course approval will now be for indefinite periods, subject to regular reviews at five-yearly intervals, and reviews will consider not merely course proposals but also internal procedures for validating and evaluating such proposals (Kerr et al., 1980). It is not yet clear what criteria or methods the CNAA will use for appraising the adequacy of these internal validation/evaluation procedures: at the time of writing colleges are being encouraged to bring forward their own suggestions for implementing the idea of 'partnership' to contribute to discussion within the CNAA. Since the publication of *Partnership in Validation* and *Developments in Partnership in Validation*, the CNAA has become closely concerned with the conduct and problems of 'institutional review', presumably as a consequence of its experience of visits to institutions and the responses that institutions have made to CNAA reports about their organization, staffing and curriculum. The CNAA's influence is substantial: it has power to withdraw validation of courses; its recommendations on how programmes might be administered and on appropriate organization and staffing are usually heeded by institutions. However, although the CNAA – like the DES – may issue recommendations for practice, both acknowledge that the institution knows more about itself than any outside body. Some go rather further and argue that it is 'impractical, unreal, impertinent and unprofessional' for the CNAA to expect to be able to make a valid judgement about the quality of an institution on the basis of its current procedures (Ball, 1981); it is partly in response to such criticisms that the CNAA has placed greater emphasis on institutional *self*-evaluation.

However, how much more 'valid' can be the institution's appraisal of itself? Requests for information about registry statistics, budgeting, formal organization and aspirations are familiar foci for external appraisal, but most institutions have limited knowledge, and this usually of an unsystematic kind, about the qualities of their programmes and courses as experienced by their students, and the problems and successes of teaching these courses as experienced by their staff. Although a considerable volume of opinion may be voiced in committees, senior common rooms and staff rooms, there are few occasions when systematic attempts are made to collect information which would allow the institution to debate the worth of particular pedagogic practices, courses and programmes.

The CNAA has now begun to work towards specifying the *criteria* that it will use to judge whether its validated institutions are able to make an appropriate 'self-analysis' (CNAA usage) of their practices, and this development seems highly significant not merely for the institutions directly affected, but – given the paucity of alternative models – for the theory and practice of institutional evaluation generally. Rather than concentrating on content and teaching the focus appears to be on management and resources (CNAA, 1980, 1981). This is significant, as in our view the way in which management is conducted determines the 'health' (CNAA usage) of the institution as much as do the quality and adventurousness of the teaching. The crucial question is whether the way in which management is conducted is appropriate and/or effective in fostering the educational practices of the institutions. (This presupposes that management and teaching are manifest and acceptable as a division of labour.) Here the CNAA might concede that industrial management by objectives and the bureaucratization of small institutions with a diversity of programmes have not necessarily been conducive to the fostering of educational qualities. In the criteria under the 'Objectives' section of *Notes for the Guidance of Institutions* (CNAA, 1980), the Committee for Institutions refers only to resources and management.

Given these requirements, what criteria will heads of department, deans or directors of courses use to justify their endeavours? Those appropriate to profit-making organizations, or to the consumer base of education institutions? If the CNAA wishes to assure itself that the institution is 'healthy', what set of managerial phenomena will be taken as symptomatic of any disease? But, more significantly for self-accounting, does the institution have any ideas about the aetiology? The 'healthy' institution, on CNAA management criteria, will presumably be one that is capable of mounting courses of consistent quality.

It is not difficult to envisage the managers in many institutions trying to justify their endeavours by criteria such as efficiency of resource distribution and staff allocation. But that would not be sufficient for the CNAA as the managers would also need to demonstrate evidence. Yet the request that managers give accounts of their practices places them in positions of vulnerability in their own institutions if their accounts go beyond CNAA readership.

What can be evaluated, what is accessible and releasable, may be subject to the control of 'gatekeepers' (Barnes, 1979; Adelman, 1980; Alexander and Wormald, 1982), usually managers and committees. There are few institutions that allow the process of evaluation to open all the 'books' and release all reports [. . .], and it would be naïve for an institution not to be wary of the consequences of such release of information (MacDonald, 1976). There are no institutions without some conflict, usually factional, and the report that pleases one will not please another (Becker, 1970), even if the evaluation encompasses multiple realities and attempts to be just and fair. Differentials in power over other peoples' lives in institutions will continue to make institutional evaluation difficult to conduct.

An institution that conducted self-appraisal as an ordinary rather than a quinquennial activity would be pioneering in British higher education; though several higher education institutions in Sweden are currently exploring the possibilities of 'activity evaluation' (Furumark, 1979), while Braskamp (1980), Rippey (1975) and Dressel (1976) chart the sometimes substantial developments in faculty evaluation in the USA, using self-evaluation, peer evaluation and student ratings [. . .]. However, as Becher and Kogan (1980) state, 'formal evaluation is only a marginal aspect not an inherent feature of British higher education . . . higher education is as poor in impersonal evaluation as it is rich in personal judgement'. We consider that Becher and Kogan's statement 'institutions are not as knowledgeable about the specialisms which they collectively provide . . . academic judgement which an institution has to make in its basic units is made in a position of comparative ignorance' is both accurate as a commentary on current practice and disturbing when set in the context of the contraction of higher education now under way. On what evidence about the educational activities of departments are judgements and decisions about selective cuts to be based, given the paucity and superficiality of current knowledge?

The above discussion of the CNAA may seem somewhat parochial in a chapter aimed at a wider audience. However, the CNAA's significance in evaluation matters is not restricted to CNAA-validated institutions. Rather it is because in the absence of any significant tradition in higher education of explicit 'formal' course evaluation, the styles of evaluation engendered as a result of 'partnership' could provide the only available operational model for all manner of institutions at a time when internal evaluation seems the appropriate response to accountability pressures and budget cuts. It has frequently been suggested, for instance, that the quality of some university courses would be greatly improved if they were subject to CNAA-style validation (a suggestion emanating from within the universities – see Ball (1981) and Alexander (1979) – not merely from disgruntled victims of university members of CNAA validation panels). There are also suggestions that the CNAA's 'model' of validation could be translated into schools as a form of institutional self-evaluation to offset pressures for public accountability. Both these seem to us to rest on a serious failure to take account of the considerable limitations of the CNAA validation model (Alexander, 1979; Ball, 1981) and erroneously characterize CNAA validation as being a device for appraising both educational processes and products, whereas it is pre-eminently a means for appraising *intentions*, only marginally (through external examiners' reports) a means of appraising products, and hardly at all a means of appraising processes. The 'CNAA model' would offer, as it stands, an extremely restricted basis for institutional self-evaluation.

Thus we would see the contribution of the CNAA's proposals as one to be welcomed in that they may encourage debate about institutional self-evaluation, but also as needing to be treated with caution because they may limit the extent of such debate. There is always the danger that the unique initiative may become a conceptual straitjacket; that the one available model may gain a monopoly. This has happened in the evaluation field before, most notably in the way the conceptual framework for evaluation has been dominated by the experiences of external consultancy project evaluations along Schools Council lines. Similarly, it is easy to assume only one available operationalization for 'validation'. Elsewhere it can mean something rather more extensive than intention appraisal: in British Forces establishments, for example, it connotes the approval of courses *which have demonstrated their success in action* over a trial period and have had the 'wrinkles' ironed out: something more akin, in fact, to what is termed in mainstream curriculum parlance 'summative evaluation'.

[. . .]

Accountability and the control of institutional evaluation

We argue that those devising programmes and procedures for institutional evaluation need to devote at least as much attention to the character of their institution as to the methods by which its work might be evaluated. The extent to which one sees the institutional context as problematic for evaluation depends on one's analysis of institutional reality. We tend to conceive of educational institutions as places characterized by conflict and plurality, whatever impressions of order and consensus they might manage to give to outsiders or even to some of their own members. Rarely, we suggest, can one find a higher education institution having the unity of purpose and commitment implied by the encapsulating term 'institution', and in any case the strongly hierarchical structures of such institutions guarantee the existence of competing interests. This being so, 'institutional evaluation' cannot in any practical, comprehensive sense mean 'evaluation by an institution of itself and its activities' but rather it is generally a matter of *one part* of an institution evaluating *a limited range* of these activities.

Exactly what the activities are, and how they are evaluated, depends on who controls the evaluation. And since it is another basic premise of this chapter that, given the choice, most people would prefer not to have their professional work subjected to the public scrutiny implied by 'institutional evaluation', we infer further that control of the evaluation process is something to be prized, not least as a means of deflecting attention away from one's own activities.

What, more specifically, do we mean by control of evaluation? We see evaluation as encompassing a number of related decisions, as follows:

1 Decisions about *goals*. What is an evaluation for? What purpose is it to serve?

2 Decisions about *focus*. What aspects of institutional life, of courses, teaching, learning, administration, etc. are to be evaluated?

3 Decisions about *methods*. By what means is information to be gathered on the basis of which evaluative judgements and possibly subsequent policy decisions are to be made?

4 Decisions about *criteria*. What will be the nature and source of the criteria to be used for judging the worth and/or effectiveness of the aspects of institutional life studied?

5 Decisions about *organization*. Who will undertake the evaluation?

What resources will be available? How will the programme be organized?

6   Decisions about *dissemination*. To whom will the findings of evaluation studies be made available? What will be the extent of openness or confidentiality?

7   Decisions about *application*. To what use will evaluation studies be put? By what process will they feed into institutional decision-making?

Control of evaluation, then, is multi-faceted. However, our case-study experience showed that not all these decisions and questions are perceived as being equally significant to all parties. To the 'Charlesford' evaluation committee and the 'Enlands' evaluators attention to *methods* and *criteria* was essential to preserve the integrity and the credibility of the process. To course managers what mattered more than these was control of *focus*, *dissemination* and *application*, of what to evaluate (and, especially, what to avoid evaluating), whom to make findings available to and what action to take in the light of such findings. In the Charlesford evaluation, control of all the decisions was invested by the constitution in the college academic board which, having agreed on focus and a standard dissemination policy, left the details of methods, criteria and organization to the evaluation committee. But the final decision, about application, was delegated to the course management committees and they thereby retained a substantial measure of control of the entire process since without tangible applications to policy an evaluation programme soon loses its credibility.

Individual self-evaluation is a process of finding out about and judging one's own activities for one's own purposes. *Institutional* self-evaluation is the means by which individuals and groups find out about and judge their own and each other's activities as these contribute to the institution's collective endeavours. It is the tool of accountability. Now, conventionally, discussion of accountability tends to focus on extra-institutional relationships, on the 'public' accountability of whole institutions to outside bodies who have a claim to know how well they are performing. Indeed, much institutional evaluation is devised to meet demands for such public accountability. But the process of institutional evaluation throws into sharp relief the issue of *internal* accountability, of who should be answerable to whom for what actions. We would suggest that control of the central evaluation decisions listed above is a vital means of determining the direction of the accountability relationship. Whoever controls the evaluation can control de facto this relationship regardless of the formalized de jure accounting relationships worked out for the institution – faculty boards, academic boards and the like. Thus, to take just one evaluation decision, a policy of confidentiality on the dissemination decision effectively ensures that those who are the subjects of an evaluation report become accountable to the limited few who are permitted to read that report rather than vice versa, and a policy of open dissemination to some extent ensures that there is greater likelihood of individuals and groups demonstrating accountability to each other. However, this in turn depends on control of the focus decision, for an open dissemination policy is effectively neutralized if only certain aspects of institutional life are studied and the work of some groups and individuals escapes scrutiny. Thus the focus decision in its way becomes as crucial as the application decision and the (wholly natural) tendency of bodies controlling evaluation is to avoid at all costs having their own work appraised.

So there need to be consistent procedures on control for all seven evaluation decisions, to ensure that none is invalidated by others, and that the accountability relationship is in reality what it is claimed to be. [. . .]

Models of accountability

The following 'ideal types' of accountability (adapted from Alexander, 1980) reflect assumptions and practices currently obtaining in educational institutions and show how the accountability relationship is related to the location of control of the central evaluation decisions listed above.

1   *Professional autonomy*. This model reflects the assumption that what goes on in a particular educational institution, course or classroom is the responsibility of each of the professionals concerned. It rests on a view of the individual – whether teacher, manager or administrator – as professionally competent over the full range of activities he undertakes, and this competence includes the necessary knowledge and skills to make or seek insightful and valid appraisals of his work and to act on those appraisals. His status as 'professional' is a guarantee of the integrity of such evaluation. The professional retains control over the key evaluation decisions of what to evaluate, how, to whom to disseminate findings and what action to take in the light of them. We see this view as particularly pervasive at the departmental level of British universities, as ideology, if not always as practice, and to some extent as an assumption underpinning teaching at all points in our educational system. However, despite its pervasiveness, it is not properly a model

for *institutional* self-evaluation since it is essentially the antithesis of that collective sense on which the latter depends.

2   *Managerial*. This model reflects the assumption that the individual is formally accountable to those who administer and control the course or institution to which he contributes and who allocate human and other resources to his work. What goes on in his classroom or office, therefore, is of legitimate concern to such 'managers' and control of the key evaluation decisions is vested in them as a function of their designated responsibility. This view, or its modified version which follows, appears particularly dominant in the further education/technical strand of non-university higher education (especially in the polytechnics).

3   *Consultative*. This model reflects the view that, as professionals, individuals in an institutional hierarchy have a right to be involved in discussions about their work but that the form of such involvement and the control of evaluation decisions still rests with 'managers'. It is the version of 'democratic' decision-making operated in many educational institutions and is a familiar response at local and national government levels to pressure for public 'participation' in decision-making.

4   *Mutual culpability*. This model reflects the view that all who participate in a particular educational activity have a legitimate interest in its quality and progress, that such quality and progress are the result of the particular contribution which each participating group or individual makes, and that, therefore, participants should account to each other for their various contributions. Being the most public and open form it is some distance from 'professional autonomy' at the individual teacher level, though in fact it is essentially a model for professional autonomy at the whole institution level. It does not necessarily incorporate any particular structural view of institutional decision-making (e.g. 'open' or 'participatory' in the sense of non-hierarchical); it allows for continued role and status differentiation, such as is probably inevitable in both schools and higher education institutions. It is egalitarian only in the sense that it requires that all participants, regardless of role or status, see themselves as equally accountable to each other for their particular contributions to the educational process. Control of the evaluation decisions rests with the participants, and in organizational terms steps have to be taken to prevent the domination of one group's definition of what is problematic, what is evaluation-worthy, or what are the 'facts' about the activities being evaluated. We see this model as likely to be reflected not so much in practices as in *aspirations* or *climate* in educational institutions.

5 *Proletarian*. This is the exact reverse of managerial accountability in that the accounting relationship is downwards from those given managerial responsibility to the 'workers'. At the same time it is neither a 'professional autonomy' model (since it is collectivist rather than individualist) nor 'mutual culpability' (since the accountability is one-way only). This, since it implies student and/or grass-roots staff control, is the least likely in the British educational context, but it is a theoretical possibility, and of course, like all the other models it has its counterpart, as a working out of the relationship of the individual to the state, in national political systems.

Note that no accountability model implies a particular organizational form for evaluation, except – probably – 'professional autonomy' which implies private self-evaluation and is therefore not a model for institutional self-study as such, however important it is to professional development at the deeper level. But even 'professional autonomy' could involve others: an individual could invite a colleague to observe and comment on his teaching, or could distribute a feedback questionnaire to students. What matters is that *he controls the key evaluation decisions* and so if his colleague or the questionnaire come up with unpalatable conclusions about his teaching he is not obliged to act on them or to divulge them to anyone else.

[. . .]

References

Adelman, C. (1980) Some dilemmas of institutional evaluation and their relation-ship to pre-conditions and procedures. *Studies in Educational Evaluation, vol. 6.* Oxford, Pergamon, pp. 165–183.

Alexander, R.J. (1979) What is a course? Curriculum models and CNAA validation. *Journal of Further and Higher Education*, vol. 5, no. 1.

Alexander, R.J. (1980) The evaluation of advanced in-service courses for teachers: the challenge to providers. *British Journal of Teacher Education*, vol. 6, no. 3.

Alexander, R.J. and Gent, B. (1982) Internal validation in higher education institu-tions: characteristics, problems and justifications. In: Church, C.H. (ed.) *Practice and Perspectives in Validation*. Guildford, SRHE.

Alexander, R.J. and Wormald, E. (1982) Validation in teacher education: expecta-tions, criteria and processes. In: Church, C.H. (ed.) *Practice and Perspectives in Validation*. Guildford, SRHE.

Ball, C.J.E. (1981) *The Advancement of Education, Learning and the Arts.* Thames Polytechnic Annual Lecture, June 1981 (mimeo).

Barnes, J.A. (1979) *Who Shall Know What?* London, Penguin.

Becher, A.R. and Kogan, M. (1980) *Process and Structure in Higher Education*. London, Heinemann Educational.

Becher, A.R. and Maclure, S. (1978) *Accountability in Education*. Slough, NFER.

Becker, H.S. (1970) *Sociological Work: Method and Substance*. Chicago, Aldine.

Bloom, B.S., Hastings, J.T. and Madaus, G.F. (1971) *Handbook of Formative and Summative Evaluation of Student Learning*. New York, McGraw Hill.

Braskamp, L.A. (1980) The role of evaluation in faculty development. *Studies in Higher Education*, vol. 5, no. 1.

Church, C.H. (ed.) (1982) *Practice and Perspectives in Validation*. Guildford, SRHE.

Council for National Academic Awards (1975) *Partnership in Validation*. Guildford, SRHE.

Council for National Academic Awards (1979) *Developments in Partnership in Validation*. London, CNAA.

Council for National Academic Awards (1980) *Institutional Reviews: Notes for the Guidance of Institutions*. London, CNAA (mimeo).

Council for National Academic Awards (1981) *A Note of Guidance on Critical Appraisal of Courses*. London, CNAA (mimeo).

Dressell, P. (1976) *Handbook of Academic Evaluation*. San Francisco, Jossey-Bass.

Eraut, M., Goad, L. and Smith, G. (1975) *The Analysis of Curriculum Materials*. Education Area Occasional Paper no. 2, University of Sussex.

Flood-Page, C. (1977) *Student Evaluation of Teaching: The American Experience*. Guildford, SRHE.

Furumark, A.M. (1979) *Institutional Self-evaluation in Sweden*. Paper presented at the Fifth General Conference of OECD Programme on Institutional Management in Higher Education, Paris (mimeo).

Heywood, J. (1977) *Assessment in Higher Education*. London, Wiley.

Kemmis, S., Atkin, R. and Wright, E. (1978) *How do Students Learn?* CARE Occasional Paper no. 5. University of East Anglia.

Kerr, E., Billing, D.E., Bethel, D., Gent, B.B., Webster, H., Wyatt, J.F. and Oakeshott, A.M. (1980) CNAA validation and course evaluation: implications of the Partnership in Validation proposals. *Evaluation Newsletter*, vol. 4, no. 1.

MacDonald, B. (1976) Who's afraid of evaluation? *Education*, 3–13.

MacDonald, B. (1981) *Mandarines and Lemons – The Executive Investment in Program Evaluation*. Paper presented at AERA symposium, Los Angeles (mimeo).

Rippey, R. (1975) Student evaluations of professors: are they of value? *Journal of Medical Education*, vol. 30, no. 10.

CHAPTER 5.4

CURRICULUM CONTROL IN FE: THE 'CENTRAL BODIES'*
T.J. RUSSELL

[. . .] The definition of the curriculum used in this report is that the real curriculum is the learning that students achieve as a result of interaction with teachers. Most teaching in colleges takes place against a background in which the teacher is aware of the presence of a single central curriculum body.† These bodies try to influence the curriculum in the series of interactive social processes between them and the students. Their style of operation, that is, their approach to curriculum design, varies. In summary the model of curriculum design and development processes used in this analysis is that the varying styles of curriculum design and development are the variations in the networks of decisions whereby the curriculum comes about. The curriculum decisions can be most fruitfully classified as being located within a nine-box grid (*Fig.* 17).

Within each box of the grid one might reasonably ask the questions:
a. Who is taking the decisions?

b. Subject to what external validation?

c. Subject to what external monitoring?

d. Under what structures of advice?

e. Under what patterns of influence?

* *Curriculum Control: A Review of Major Styles of Curriculum Design in FE*. London, Further Education Curriculum Review and Development Unit, 1981, pp. 89–94. T.J. Russell is Staff Tutor at the Further Education Staff College.
† Editors' footnote: This research looked at 10 'central bodies': City and Guilds of London Institute, Council for National Academic Awards, Technician Education Council, Business Education Council, Central Council for Education and Training in Social Work, National Nursery Examinations Board, the Royal Society of Arts, the 'Union of Educational Institutions', Institute of Management Services and Manpower Services Commission.

Figure 17   Network of curriculum decisions.

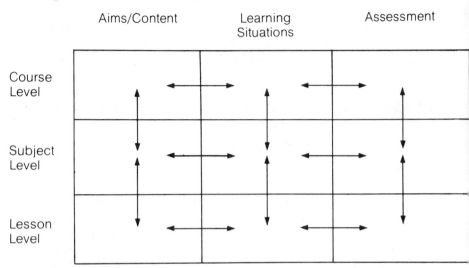

In effect it is the central body that decides the answers to these questions and thus what they do may be regarded not so much as determining the curriculum, but determining a decision-taking framework in which the curriculum comes about.

Part one of this research was a consideration and analysis of the varying approaches taken by the central bodies to their task of curriculum design. The details of the wide variations are given in part one. In the summary to part one a further consideration was given to the analysis of the key points of difference and the view was given that the three most important variations in curriculum design styles could be summed up as three types of relationships between central bodies and colleges as being:

a. *Examining body relationship*: where the central body exercises firm control over syllabus and examinations with little intervention in the curriculum decision areas of the learning situations at any levels or in content or testing at the 'lesson' level.

b. *Validating body relationship*: where all initiative in syllabus and examinations comes from the college with central body monitoring and control, and where there is little intervention in the curriculum decision areas of the learning situations at any levels or in content or testing at the 'lesson' level.

c. *Controlling body relationship*: where the central body maintains firm control over the syllabus either by setting it or strongly recommending it, monitors carefully local examinations and makes strong attempts to influence the other decision areas.

Each represents a different form of partnership between colleges and central bodies in solving the key problems of the curriculum and solving them in terms of analysing the students' needs, deriving goals for the students, defining the learning and selecting experiences to convey this content.

Within all these variations, however, there appear to be a number of common elements that must be taken into account in describing and evaluating the varying processes of curriculum design. These elements are by and large traditional, so there are in the central bodies varying degrees of awareness of these traditions. They are frequently the taken-for-granted assumptions upon which all else rests.

All central bodies use governing council structures that they use to take all key decisions. These councils are composed of people holding honorific office as representatives of what are usually described as users and providers of certificates. The central bodies nearly all use committees and sub-committees, also of users and providers, as central approving mechanisms for both their decisions concerning the curriculum process in general and any specific or draft curriculum outlines.

There is a very heavy reliance on these committees. It is a tradition that much work is done by them. Only very recently has there been much initiative taken by officers in the form of the production of papers. Often, perhaps usually at the level of decisions concerning individual curricula, both the initiative for and the approval of decisions lie with these committees. There is an assumption that their authority derives from their representative nature and the widespread information networks and flows to which they have access. The requirements of the users and providers in terms of curriculum design and development are fed through these committees where they are evaluated and compared. Of course, if this is to be effective, the role of the committee members has to be known and understood by those from whom they are to derive their information.

The committees of users and providers are also relied on very heavily in reviewing the progress of any particular scheme. The evaluation of specific curricula is done by the committees. Once more the initiative tends to lie with the committee rather than the officers, although in general routine-monitoring data are provided by the officers and many central bodies have a formal rule that some sort of review should take place every five years. More recently though, the bodies exercising a controlling relationship have, via their officers, initiated very much more thorough evaluation processes than previously, spending considerable sums of money on them. These have not yet come to fruition, but decisions will lie with the committees and councils.

In all parts of the curriculum world there seemed to be a widespread acceptance of the value that it is desirable to present the student with a set of learning experiences that are coherent or integrated within themselves and that integration is something which has to be manifest in the classroom. This is clearly regarded as the normal situation even where it recognized that for a minority of students a more modular programme might be desirable. What remains uncertain is the strategy for integration and the administrative techniques to try to enhance the possibility of integration in the classroom. The older of the two curriculum approaches to course integration is the single vocational purpose; and that is still the dominant tradition.

A second tradition for integration of a course is that of 'intellectual coherence'. In this situation a group of professionals, who are assumed to have a common identity, agree on the typical or essential boundaries for the course. In order to give a clear purpose to the course they agree to a minimum of learning patterned into a traditional configuration. They may, of course, allow for optional 'extras' which are consistent with, or at least not incompatible with, the dominant pattern. Modifications of this second traditional pattern are to be seen in 'interdisciplinary courses' where there is an attempt at, or at least the acknowledgement of, the possibility of the fruitful juxtaposition of traditionally separate subject areas. Even within this new trend the notion of a minimum-knowledge-set to achieve some reasonable coherence usually remains.

The final general comment which must be made is that concerning the growth of a general ideology of a 'professional curriculum commitment'. There seems to be a general tendency for there to be a steady shift from the concept of an officer of the central body as having a role in the system as 'servant-of-the-committee' towards one as a 'professional-in-the-system' with a deep understanding of the process of curriculum design and development. Nevertheless even within this new tradition there remains the role of the officer as 'servant' but a useful, prompting, catalytic servant of the committee. In origin this seems to have been derived from an increasing concern to assure more accurately that the centralized testing systems validly and reliably measure stated learning intentions. This attitude developed, at least in part, within the examining body relationship tradition, but when moved to the validating or controlling body relationship becomes transformed into a professionalism which emphasizes the close intermeshing of all curriculum decision-taking areas. This latter attitude, or consciousness, has spread back into the examining body relationship. There now seems to be a growing assumption that many of the more general aims proper to a curriculum are best guaranteed by a care and attention to the close relationship of the various stages of curriculum process and not simply to examination process and technique. Further, validation and control of the curriculum must pay great attention to what goes on in the college. There are ambivalences generated by this move which have implications for changing the college/examining body relationship from one of a traditional detachment to one of closer involvement.

Thus, there seems to be developing among the officers of the central bodies a definite, even if difficult to define, concept of professionalism. This professionalism extends in many cases beyond an exams professionalism to a 'curriculum professionalism'. There is also by implication a desire that this professionalism shall be spread into the colleges. There is no implication that these professional attitudes have their origin outside the colleges, but since in some sense or other the central bodies validate what is done in the colleges, the central body officers increasingly look for this development. This of course begins a slow change in three key aspects of the relationship of central bodies to colleges, namely:

a. the place and function of the user-provider committees in these processes;

b. the use of field officers or moderators by the central body;

c. the character of the attempts to look at college decision-taking processes (as well as outcomes).

In each of these three areas we find that the three main types of body (examining, validating, controlling) have developed their own characteristic relationships.

The oldest tradition is that the bulk of the curriculum design and definition is done by the user-provider committees of the central body. In this examining body relationship the committee, or subgroups of it, decides on the outlines of the syllabus, its definition, techniques of examination and so on. Frequently they go on to supplement these decisions with advice on reading lists, teaching strategies and so on and to monitor the examination instruments and processes. The validating body has assumed that this should all go on in the colleges, although the user-provider committees validate, by a variety of processes, *what* goes on. What distinguishes this from the newer controlling body relationship is that the validating body gives only the sketchiest of guidance to the college. The controlling bodies may use their committees for both designing some courses and validating others. Inevitably in designing some courses the central body gives a good deal of implicit guidance to college-designed courses. In general controlling bodies have little shortage of materials, general guidance and advice for colleges.

In guaranteeing the curriculum the central body may consider the part that officers of the central body can play 'in the field', interacting with the colleges. The older tradition of the examining bodies makes little use of field officers. Officers from the central body may visit colleges by invitation (although somewhat infrequently) but their role is to explain or publicize, not to monitor. Where college-based skills testing is included in the examination the central bodies usually make use of part-time assessors or moderators to visit the colleges. A similar pattern of activity for the officer exists for the validating bodies but these organizations require colleges to appoint local external examiners, subject to the control of the central body. In controlling bodies a very different pattern exists. The officers are available to the colleges but there is a much more closely controlled system of moderators who visit the colleges frequently, may receive specific training and have to report to the central body in great detail. These controlling systems closely monitor the college activity and by implication exercise a great deal of control over it.

Similarly we find great variation of central body concern with not merely the outcome of college decision-taking but also with the process. Examining bodies take very little cognizance of college organization or decision process, while validating bodies pay a great deal of attention to it at key points in their validation processes but do not monitor it in between. Controlling bodies monitor some aspects of this at regular intervals. Their college moderators are asked to report frequently on such things as team attitude or meeting of management boards for courses.

Thus a great deal of variation in procedures for relating to the colleges can be closely connected to the three main types of relationship between central body and colleges. Beyond that there is an immense wealth of variation in the detailed administrative procedures. These are of course in constant flux and the central bodies continuously adjust them for a variety of reasons that do not directly affect the main characteristics of the procedures, or relationships, for the design of the curriculum.

We have noted the variations in officer role which derive from the changes and developments in the concept of professionalism amongst the officers of the central bodies [. . .]. The older tradition of 'servant-of-the-committee' still exists because of the continuing use of user-provider committees to validate all that is done. It would appear though that officers have some role ambiguity about their functions as initiators, instigators, catalysts, prompters, diligent informers, or servants. We have described shifts in relationships between central bodies and colleges. These will all have to be put into operation by officers who are thus changing their roles. Their own degree of clarity will depend on the degree of clarity about the character of the process held in the committees that they serve.

One outstanding feature observed in the development of the three main types of relationship of central body to the colleges in the process of curriculum design was that all three types exist at all of the main 'levels' of curriculum (i.e. remedial, craft, technician, technologist, degree, professional) and across the vocational and subject areas. It cannot be consistently held that one system is appropriate to one level or area since the variations that exist are great. The three main methods seem to have evolved over time or in other words to be developmental. Further investigations may be needed to see why these took place. Certainly the development of validation as an attitude fitted its historical context. It was consistent with currently developing attitudes to college government and management and was consistent with ideas held in the whole society about participation and self-management. Moreover, research into curriculum innovations organized by the Schools Council and others (and in particular Kannetti-Barry's research on the implementation of the C&GLI craft – then – 500 series) meant that anyone aware of this research would have to be suspicious of the effectiveness of curriculum changes initiated in an examining board relationship. To explain the shift from validating relationship to controlling relationship is more difficult. Clearly it involves a greater attempt to guarantee (or control) the curriculum and has been seen this way. In part it stems from the increasing sophistication of curriculum professionalism at the centre and a desire to spread that knowledge.

What is most clear is that the controlling body relationships have been developed recently, exist in *all* areas of current major change and development, and are a lot more expensive even if the major costs are dispersed to the colleges and not identified. Technician education, business education, social work education, UVP schemes, new courses for the unemployed, and possibly wider-spread foundation courses, or 'A Basis for Choice' schemes all use a controlling body relationship. It is not certain that revision in craft schemes would use this relationship but it is not clear what reforms will take place. However, current trends do raise a number of consequential issues that ought to be considered not only by the central bodies themselves but also by the DES. This report has tried to identify the trends and consequent issues and problems. It is not an attempt to evaluate the processes, but to clarify the issues.

The most general issues seem to be as follows:

a. Teachers in colleges seem to be expected to spend increasing amounts of time in curriculum development activity, in internal validation and committee work, and in preparing the work for presentation to central bodies. How much time is involved for each individual is not clear, nor are there proven or agreed ways of measuring this involvement. This new development demand is not easily identified in the present system of allocating teacher workload while the standard system of defining, measuring and controlling the workload of individual teachers is the class-contact hour. The assumption that the ratio of class-contact to other associated work is a fixed ratio for each individual member of staff at each grade is just not true when development work is unevenly distributed. National systems for giving a class-contact relief equivalent may be clumsy. It could well be that the best way to control staff utilization in the newer curriculum systems is to allow greater college control and flexibility within an agreed overall staff–student ratio, thus allowing individual curriculum development and class-contact loadings to vary.

b. In a similar way, local education authorities and regional advisory councils have sought to control the provision of courses not only through basic systems of approval-to-run but also by minimum class size. Inasmuch as the curriculum systems now being designed are more modular, more flexible and incorporate more independent learning situations, class size (minimum or maximum) becomes a less appropriate formula within the system of administrative control. This should be reviewed.

c. The curriculum research design and development carried out by the central bodies is expensive. The more detailed the work, and the more research based, the more expensive it becomes. In addition any tendency to provide examples of teaching materials or to closely monitor or control the implementation in the colleges of centrally devised ideas adds to the cost.

The central bodies and their consultative systems are all moving in the direction of these relatively expensive techniques for reasons which this report must accept. The rising costs do raise the issues of funding to a considerable degree. To what extent can we routinely expect the central bodies to develop schemes thought to be appropriate on the income derived from student fees for certification?

d. The current distinction between education and training exists primarily as a device for costing and paying purposes. As education designs move progressively towards a vocational orientation and cognizance, and are focused on work skills, the distinction becomes weaker. Industry is increasingly asked to make significant contributions to the design of educational experience, the provision of work experience and even to supporting, reporting on and testing students. Can this always be supported by the individual enterprise? A very large percentage of the labour force remains 'out of scope' of the ITBs and while these may contribute to the development of a research-based curriculum there are limits. The establishment of a centrally funded research unit for curriculum development work could assist in these difficulties.

e. As curriculum design moves towards a closer partnership between the central bodies and the colleges there comes into existence a need for conference or workshop activity in which college staff may receive messages from the central bodies, but in a way and on grounds in which they may challenge the central bodies and express disagreements and tensions which arise from the structure of the power relationships between the central bodies and colleges. This is an important part of the information flow from the college system back to the central body and the need for it is greater, though more difficult to manage, when the curriculum system moves towards controlling relationships. The necessary provision becomes a problem. In a sense the colleges of education (technical) provide some of this, but neither they nor the central bodies are specifically funded for this work. The kind of situation in which it takes place usually also carries a staff-development function which creates yet a further demand. There is within all these needs an ill-defined place and responsibility for Her Majesty's Inspectorate, and for the LEA Inspectorate. Presumably it is part of their role to detect these needs and respond to them, but they may not have the expertise or resources so to do.

f. The extension of curriculum professionality into the colleges in a form which specifically demands an increase in the traditional amount of team work may create organizational tension. While we have argued that the emphasis on team work in part derives from a wider social and ideological emphasis on participation, many colleges have only experienced minimal changes in their organizational character. Not all colleges have introduced college academic boards that have a policy-making character, and there is always a tension between participatory management and the older forms of hierarchical management. Put simply, the tensions have not been adequately researched, particularly as they affect the structure of the decision-taking processes which lead to the curriculum. We do not know enough about what are the best organizational forms and climates for the kind of curriculum development required.

g. The monitoring of the success of any particular scheme or the need for a new scheme, has by and large been the responsibility of either the central body or its joint user-provider committee for the scheme. This remains the case, but even with more active officer work, and greater use of part-time moderators, this becomes more difficult because the standards that seem to be required for close meshing of course experience and learning and the world of work seem to be going up. Quite simply this requires more work to be done. Clearly within the generally raised standards of public accountability as well as the raised standards of curriculum requirement the effectiveness of such monitoring standards within an uncertain situation must be questioned.

h. Finally, the effectiveness of the central body itself, and the curriculum system it adopts, becomes open to question. Clearly public bodies of the sort under discussion are rational and responsible and take seriously the notion of accountability. Yet there is also some sort of monitoring of the central bodies by the DES. Much of this is known to the central bodies, and in particular their officers, but to few others in the curriculum system (despite its widespread college and industrial contact). The question arises, should this be more public?

Reference

Barry, S.M. Kannetti, *Engineering Craft Studies: Monitoring a New Syllabus.* Slough, NFER.

CHAPTER 5.5

CURRICULUM CHANGE: AN FEU EVALUATION OF TEC PROGRAMME DEVELOPMENT IN COLLEGES*
Preface to the report
JACK MANSELL

1   The [FEU report, *Curriculum Change*] represents a unique attempt to evaluate the curriculum process introduced by the Technician Education Council (TEC). The report is not insubstantial, it has taken almost three years and yet it samples only a modest fraction of the total output of TEC. This not only helps to describe the magnitude of the problem that has confronted the FHE system since 1976 but also indicates the way in which we appear to consistently underestimate the need to evaluate curriculum development.

2   Throughout the report and its conclusions, is the persistent criticism that because of pressure of existing work, of time and lack of support, local curriculum development had to be rushed: there were no opportunities for curriculum trials, Standard units were uncritically accepted, programme guidelines were rarely challenged and to many teachers the validation process became identified as an elaborate and sometimes desperate paper-game, rather than an opportunity for genuine curriculum reflection.

3   As such, with hindsight, many valuable opportunities were lost, and too many mistakes may well have been made. The general acceptance of the 15-unit certificate (and 25-unit diploma), coupled with demanding assessment schedules, undoubtedly overloaded teaching schedules and significantly reduced opportunities for practical work. The use of a particular simplified version of Bloom's Taxonomy of Educational Objectives, whilst no doubt an invaluable aid to analysis and discussion, has in many ways

*Curriculum Change: An Evaluation of TEC Programme Development in Colleges. London, Further Education Curriculum Review and Development Unit, December 1981, pp. vii–viii, pp. 113–118. Jack Mansell is Director of the Further Education Curriculum Review and Development Unit, and an ex-president of NATFHE.

been interpreted as the ultimate in curriculum and assessment design, to the detriment of more creative curriculum innovation. The autonomous and sometimes idiosyncratic demands of the individual programme committees often produced confusion, duplication and ambivalence in the development and validation process.

4   The strategy of this study involved 78 colleges and the methodology of data collection included questionnaires, interviews, case studies and an analysis of documentation. This study has largely concentrated on 'internal' curriculum issues. A complementary study by the National Foundation for Educational Research, due to be completed in 1982–1983, will be concentrating on more 'external' factors such as the perceptions, progress and attitudes of students and the views of employers in relation to involvement and standards, etc. Inevitably, for the sake of completeness, some duplication may exist but this, hopefully, has been kept to a minimum.

5   Many of the issues identified in the study are not unique to TEC or indeed to further education. Problems arising out of inadequate teacher training, dated industrial experience, inflexible teaching modes and poor curriculum dissemination, were not created but aggravated by the demands of TEC. These problems have been around for some time. On the other hand, TEC appears to have created its own spectrum of problems. Its neglect of the regional examining bodies and RACs, in some cases heavily involved in existing technician courses, removed, initially at least, a source of local curriculum support for many teachers. The rapid production of the first generation of Standard units resulted, as the report says, in the 'widespread adoption of units of uncertain quality'. The continuing lack of well-validated, externally available tests, the 'apparent haste' in the development of the innovative TEC policies and the sometimes 'unnecessary' changes have, according to the study, undoubtedly contributed to uncertainties about standards by employers and teachers alike.

6   The suggestions in the report with respect to teaching and learning methods may not be entirely welcome to all readers. Generally the evaluation concludes that in spite of a major aim of TEC being concerned with this area, 'there have not been substantial changes in teaching methods'. It indeed goes further; and states that the way in which TEC has used and validated objectives and assessment plans, has put too much accent on *what* the students learn rather than *how* they learn. This neglect of the 'dynamic interrelationship' between ends and means is identified as a deficiency by the report, which goes on to suggest that colleges and TEC should consider the desirability of describing teaching and learning strategies in their

development and review of units and programmes.

7   The report describes examples of apparent underestimations by TEC of the demands it would place on the system: consultations with employers (a perennial problem in a diversified industrial society); a complex and demanding administrative burden (now being simplified); the assumptions made with respect to resources (for staff and curriculum development); the phasing out of existing courses (hostility still remains) . . . It is tempting to conclude that if the expertise was not there to foresee what now appear to be obvious problems, then at least some form of evaluated pilot studies could have been set up. This concept, until recently, was strange to FE and perhaps therefore, if blame must be apportioned, it belongs to all those in education who acquiesce to untried curricular experiments.

8   Nevertheless, notwithstanding the above, what this study essentially describes is how a massive curriculum project in a complex technical area was generally accepted by the colleges, in spite of its many problems, as an improvement in the way we provide technician curricula. The publication of this report will coincide with many reviews and revalidations of TEC programmes, and it is hoped that it will facilitate those processes.

9   On a more global basis, this report also illustrates, not for the first time, the way in which we under-resource curriculum development in FE. Sooner or later it must be realized that attempting massive curriculum change on the cheap is false economy. The price is eventually paid in terms of failure, expensive modification and non-productive hostility. In this context the generalized lessons that emerge are briefly:

i. no major curriculum innovation can succeed solely on the basis of issuing unilateral policy statements to the centres of implementation;

ii. large-scale innovation processes should not concentrate only on curriculum elements but should also take into account the organizational and resource implications of the changes they propose;

iii. new proposals should be trial tested and supportively evaluated, where appropriate by an independent project, and staff development needs should be an essential element of this process.

In the case of TEC, who are proving to be responsive to college demands and currently reviewing their policies, this study is, in many respects, eight years too late. Nevertheless it is to be hoped that the report will not only be of assistance to those engaged in TEC work, but will contribute to the fundamental change of attitude that appears necessary to bring about a revaluation of curricular change.

Summary of the report
CHRISTOPHER PARKIN*

Introduction

The focus

This report describes and evaluates the introduction of new programmes in colleges in the further education sector, leading to awards of the Technician Education Council, in mechanical engineering (A5), building studies (B2) and science (C1). Evidence for the evaluation was collected during 1978–1980.

Curriculum and curriculum development

A simple model of curriculum development identifies the interactive stages of analysis of the context, design, implementation and evaluation. Decision-making in curriculum design and in realizing the curriculum in action requires exploration of the interrelationships between the curriculum elements, objectives, subject matter, teaching and learning methods and assessment in the achievement of aims.

Research strategy

The report seeks to reflect typical practice and experience drawing on a random selection of 78 colleges in various components of the study. The principal sources of evidence include data from questionnaires and check-

---

* Christopher Parkin was FEU Development Officer and is now Head of Science at Bedford College of Higher Education.

lists about teachers' work activities and experience, interviews with teachers of selected TEC units, case studies of programme development, relevant documentation of developments.

The teachers of TEC programmes

Qualifications and experience

The teachers of the technical units are older and possess a little above average teaching experience compared with FE lecturers as a whole. Teachers of general and communication studies are younger and have less FE teaching experience than their technical colleagues. The teachers of technical units in general mechanical engineering and building studies have substantial industrial experience although for about half of them this dates from 15 years ago. The industrial experience of teachers of science programmes is much less and a substantial number have none. For many teachers less than half of their work is assigned to TEC programmes.

General attitude of teachers

Teachers generally accept many of the educational approaches of TEC but not the accompanying administrative consequences and changes within existing resource limits. The more senior staff are generally more favourably disposed than those with day-to-day teaching responsibilities. The most favourably disposed group of teachers, in this sample, by discipline area appears to be that of general and communication studies, the least favourably disposed being technical teachers of the A5 programmes. Many teachers did not feel that a major change in the nature of course specification and assessment was necessary. Teachers' anxieties arose due to uncertainties about the standards, the additional effort and the apparent haste in development of the innovative TEC policies.

The students of TEC programmes

Student achievement before entry

A high proportion of students (67 percent) in the opportunity sample possessed qualifications which would have normally allowed them entry to the previous National Certificate/Diploma courses. The sample is skewed relative to a figure of 43 percent in a larger NFER sample.

Curriculum issues

Learning objectives

The use of behavioural or near behavioural objectives is of value in specifying intended outcomes of technician curricula but their limitations should be more fully understood. Care must be exercised to ensure the modified Bloom taxonomy does not dominate and limit rather than assist effective curriculum design and implementation. For example, teachers do not find the skill category 'invention' easy to use. The units analysed, at levels I, II and III, showed a high proportion of skills in the information and comprehension categories which may in part be due to the simplified version of the Bloom taxonomy. Unit designers should improve the specification and analysis of objectives. This may require, in the long term, a modification of the taxonomy at present used. Objectives written in the format generally adopted in TEC Standard units often contain ambiguities, and a high degree of precision in matching assessment to these objectives should not be expected. Teachers generally find objectives to be acceptable in principle, expressions of dissatisfaction relating to instances of their vagueness and imprecision. About one-third of the teachers feel constrained to follow the sequence of objectives in devising teaching and learning, the remainder making a more liberal interpretation but usually within the specified topic areas of the unit. Teachers' early experiences were that Standard units were too demanding on the student in relation to their design length of 60 hours' 'class-study'. The present listing of objectives with a corresponding assessment plan can provide a more balanced and controlled assessment of a range of knowledge and skills than less systematic approaches but it is unlikely to lead to a precisely uniform provision by different teachers in different colleges.

Teaching and learning methods

The TEC Standard unit format with objectives and an assessment plan has caused teachers to think about their general approach. In general there have not been substantial changes in teaching methods. A reduction in laboratory or practical activities by the student is the most marked change. In some colleges new materials for overhead projector transparencies and handouts for students have been developed. Students, in the sample questioned, generally held favourable views about the teaching methods they experience although some report that they find the expected rate of learning to be too rapid. Over half seemed sceptical about the value of general and communication studies in helping them to communicate technical information to others. Student learning experiences continued to be centred around a formal input and study rate determined by the teacher and the college. In general, colleges find it difficult to organize tutorial or less formalized approaches to learning for the day-release student. TEC's policy aspirations in this direction are generally not yet being achieved.

Subject matter

The building studies B2 certificate programmes generally have greater uniformity than the mechanical engineering A5 or science C1 programmes, reflecting the fewer Standard units available. The unit structure provided opportunity for programmes to be designed to meet the more specialist needs of particular technicians and industries, although the content of programmes appears to be strongly influenced by TEC programme committees and requirements of professional bodies. TEC policy has generally enhanced the status of general studies and communication studies. The relationship between general and communication studies and O-Level English language, and the assessment of affective objectives requires further study and development work.

Assessment of learning

The requirement by TEC for colleges to provide detailed assessment specifications implied a precision to the assessment process which in practical terms has proved unattainable and untenable. A wide diversity of plans have been drawn up typically based on intelligent guesswork and limited previous experience. However, such plans offer a more balanced and controlled assessment of knowledge and skills than less systematic approaches providing teachers receive appropriate guidance in their use. The further TEC Guidance Note No. 8 eases the demands upon colleges but de-emphasizes the role of formative assessment in the learning process compared with earlier intentions. In the case of the units analysed, the overall numbers of students gaining merit and pass grades were similar. About 16 percent of the students, overall, failed to meet the pass requirement. A large variation in the distribution of grades at different colleges underlines the importance of moderation. TEC should monitor and publish data which analyse the patterns of student achievement and in relation to student and college characteristics (e.g. student achievement patterns before entry).

Teachers generally believe that their involvement in assessment and examination is likely to lead to more successful educational provision, endorsing TEC policy. Many believe that 'the assessment processes are effective in measuring whether students achieve the programme objectives'. Teachers of mechanical engineering A5 programmes indicated that they would prefer external examination of level III units to college-based assessment. This probably reflects their concern for the concept of an external national standard as much or more than the work demands made upon them by the internal college provision. TEC's policy on assessment provides opportunity for a 'mastery' approach to learning, and 'criterion-referenced' testing. However, it also acknowledges testing to discriminate levels of achievement, and a conflict between a mastery and 'norm-referenced' approach. This is not always apparent to the teacher. In practice colleges have found the organizational and resource demands too great to successfully change from an essentially group-paced learning approach to a new provision which potentially caters for individual learning and achievement rates.

Curriculum statements

TEC policies and validation practice emphasize the definition of aims, learning objectives and an associated assessment specification. In so doing TEC has caused teachers to focus on the *ends* to be achieved rather than the *means*, the learning experiences, through which they may be achieved. There is a strong case for including valued teaching and learning activities in the curriculum specification. Not to recognize the dynamic interrelationship between these ends and means in decision-making when specifying the curriculum can result in a curriculum out-of-balance on implementation. In the development and review of units and programmes, colleges and TEC should consider the desirability of describing teaching and learning strategies for the guidance of teachers.

The process of curriculum development

Development at national level – the origin and nature of the change

The Haslegrave Report recommended the machinery at national and regional level for administering a new broad pattern of technician courses. However it did not consider organizational change at the college level and TEC began one of the most wide-ranging curriculum validation exercises ever attempted without guidance in this respect. The policies formulated by

TEC on the basis of the report required radical curriculum change from the previous provision in terms of curriculum administration, structure and specification, of teaching approach and assessment procedures and of teacher participation in development and assessment. With insufficient resources to undertake research and development work before wide-scale implementation, the consequential organizational problems experienced by colleges in the early years of implementation are not surprising. The magnitude of the changes emanating from TEC's implementation of the Haslegrave Report do not appear to have been anticipated.

Some assumptions apparent in TEC policy

The authoritative TEC Policy Statement of June 1974 emphasizes organizational and administrative rather than pedagogical matters. It assumed there was little need to provide rationale for many of the decisions. In further development the reasons for particular policies or changes in policy should be explained as part of the process of engendering an acceptance of the need for change. Programmes of teacher development were not initially perceived as a systematic part of the process of curriculum development. TEC appears to have assumed, following the Haslegrave Report, that teachers and colleges were likely to be receptive to the new proposals, to cooperate within and with other colleges, and to have time to undertake curriculum development. Whilst teachers have found sufficient enthusiasm and willingness to sustain the development, collaboration is constrained by commitment to existing courses and students, and by the time and resources available.

Programme development

The guidelines for Standard programmes and the Standard units have much influenced programme development in colleges. The almost universal adoption of 15-unit certificate programmes illustrates colleges' rapid acceptance of the norms they perceived acceptable. The early years were characterized by hasty development without trials, inevitable with few full-time TEC officers but many committee members undertaking a heavy validation load. The rapidly produced Standard units enabled colleges to make, and TEC to validate, a large number of submissions in accordance with the scheduled timetable. The lack of trial resulted in wide-scale adoption of units of uncertain quality and uncertain demand upon teachers and students. The autonomy of programme committees was in accordance with the policy of flexibility. A more phased introduction might have allowed sector committees to achieve more commonality of practice across committees. The Council, contrary to the recommendations of the Haslegrave Report, established its independence of the regional bodies for the purposes of validation and assessment. Whilst minimizing the influence of the old on the new provision in establishing a national system of awards, an opportunity to profit from existing mechanisms was lost. The regional advisory councils generally have facilitated curriculum development meetings of college staff in so far as their own resources have allowed.

Development in the colleges

Analysis of needs before curriculum design

TEC's validation requirements have encouraged colleges to identify the needs of employers. The accent has been on what students learn rather than how they should learn. TEC's policy that decisions regarding the teaching of the programme are not the subject of validation risks the implementation of the real 'curriculum in action' being unnecessarily divorced from the curriculum design.

Consultation with industry

The extent, depth and effectiveness of consultation has varied from college to college, involving in particular employer participation in development committee meetings. Difficulties of consultation have been most acute for colleges with many small employers in their neighbourhood. Colleges reported that many employers were often unaware of the proposed change in course provision and did not understand the need for a major change in structure. They were concerned that the standards which they associated with existing courses should be maintained. Colleges often found difficult the task of identifying specific technician functions. The need for student technicians to develop communication skills was widely recognized. Satisfaction with an existing provision is a barrier to innovation. In maintaining and making new contacts with employers, colleges should supply local firms with succinct reports of relevant TEC programmes and invite opinion on draft curricula through personal contact and visits wherever possible.

Completing TEC programme validation forms

Validation forms completed by colleges and submitted to TEC exercise a strong influence and control upon the deliberations of colleges and teachers at the programme design stage. When little or no resources are specifically allocated for curriculum development, then attention is only likely to be given to those aspects for which information is directly requested. Political expediency prevails. The validation process is a postal exercise, with unavoidable limitations, involving analysis of the 'internal coherence' of the curriculum proposals on paper. The extent of commitment or involvement of the teachers individually or as a team is left to the college. Where colleges adopt guidelines of the Council or programme committees (e.g. lists of aims, or Guidance Note No. 8 on assessment) without accompanying rationale or discussion, the validating committee has little evidence as to the extent which these have been discussed or have influenced teachers. TEC's encouragement that colleges should select their own unit assessment plans has led to a diversity of proposals. In the absence of trials TEC officers were unable to advise on good practice, hence many experimental plans were developed.

Teacher participation in programme development

Heads of department have generally been the members of staff most involved in programme development both in decision-making and in development work. Many principals, seniors and lecturer IIs took part in writing objectives and particularly assessment analyses. Few lecturer Is were involved in these tasks and in decisions made. They had the greatest time allocation to teaching the existing courses alongside which curriculum change takes place. Principals and vice-principals appear to have substantial involvement only when their own academic discipline or professional experience coincides with the areas under development. In accordance with their major commitment, heads of department were seen by their colleagues to be the people most influential in determining the time-scale of programme development. Departmental boundaries often provide barriers to easy development and negotiation across them can be difficult.

Inter-college joint programme submissions

Depending on programme area, 30–55 percent of the colleges have been involved in developing programmes jointly with other colleges. Such collaboration enabled the workload of early development to be shared and the teachers involved to gain mutual support necessary in undertaking innovative development work. Advantages perceived included the opportunity for sharing ideas and experience and for common standards and assessment. Collaboration must overcome problems of rivalry between colleges, of scarcity of time for travel and attendance at meetings, and organizational complexities of institutions working together. Compromises have to be made which may be on political rather than educational grounds, and which give doubts that the needs of local employers are being met. Colleges participating in joint schemes have experienced the administrative complexity of making changes in agreed programme specifications and in maintaining continuity of joint development, for example in establishing assessment item banks. Collaboration seems particularly appropriate and advantageous in the case of smaller departments. In the case of large departments and heavily subscribed programmes the disadvantages may outweigh the advantages. Joint developments risk reducing the numbers of staff involved and committed to development. Disparate college sizes and resources for development and allegiance to different local education authorities may inhibit collaboration.

Programme implementation

Effects on the day-to-day work activities of teachers

New procedures mean more work at least until they become familiar. Teachers in the 1979–1980 session were spending a greater proportion of their time on tasks associated with the assessment of learning, compared with previous technician courses. The effect on their teaching activities appears to be much less, although apparently there is more collaboration between teachers, and more preparation of handouts for students. The three categories in which teachers spend most of their time are 'assessment', 'preparation for teaching' and 'teaching', the former two categories having increased relative to work on non-TEC courses. When teachers say the introduction of TEC programmes has caused more administration and paperwork, they are generally referring to the work they associate with the assessment procedures. A provision which gives the teachers a predominant share of the responsibility for the assessment of their students with external monitoring through validation and moderation will almost inevitably require more documentation of intentions, practice and performance. Colleges have found it necessary to introduce new procedures to record details of student entry qualifications, achievement and progress, as a consequence of the unit structure. However, the keeping of records is an essential part of the teachers' role and can assist effective counselling. Much of the implementation of the newly validated programmes appears to be characterized by colleges responding to problems as they arise rather than prior anticipation of needs or difficulties. Continuing change is a characteristic of curriculum development but had evidence been available from trials unprofitable experimentation might have been avoided.

Adoption of Standard units

The majority of colleges adopted many Standard units making few amendments, in spite of the criticisms of the quality of expression of some of the objectives. This reflects the limited expertise at writing objectives in many colleges, the lack of time and resources for this development work and the belief that their adoption would facilitate the validation of the programme.

The unit-based programme structure

TEC wisely constrained the choice of units available in a programme by requiring each combination of units to be validated in an attempt to ensure coherent courses. The availability of approved combinations can be severely restricted by factors such as viability of student numbers, employer and teacher influence, teacher availability and expertise, pattern of study release given by employers, availability of classrooms. Colleges often found they were unable to offer all the alternatives which they had envisaged. Alternative combinations may be more or less academically or practically orientated, and cannot be directly comparable in terms of the intellectual demands made on the student. Whilst the grouping of students of different programmes (e.g. electrical, mechanical, motor-vehicle, medical, laboratory science technicians) to study common units is advantageous from a timetabling and resource point of view, teachers often believe that students learn best if working together in a group who share common vocational intent. For the advantages of the unit structure to be maximized employers need to be flexible in their approach to the pattern of release for the part-time student and colleges need to consider how the variable study rates of individual students can be catered for. The unit structure has increased the demands on the teacher in his role as counsellor.

Assessment and reassessment

In the absence of information from trials, colleges designed assessment plans too elaborate to operate in terms of available resources and expertise. The self-contained nature of each unit and its own assessment plan has generally resulted in each unit being assessed as a separate entity. Teachers have found difficulty in interpreting assessment plans to take account of the categories of knowledge and skills. The requirement that students should obtain a minimum mark in each assessment component has caused problems in organizing 'retests' for part-time students. A variety of solutions has been attempted. There is a danger that requiring students to pass all phase-tests before proceeding may unduly limit their time to assimilate new material. Whether units are assessed by phase-tests or end-tests may be the consequence of rather arbitrary decisions. Teachers have found it necessary to ensure that students do not abuse procedures which provide opportunity for resitting phase-tests. Clear distinction should be made wherever possible between testing which is primarily to aid the process of learning (e.g. by providing feedback and help to the student and teacher) and testing which is to measure the achievement of competency. In the former case assessment may be less formal and retesting may not always be necessary.

Factors helping and hindering change

Factors helping the development process

Teachers have found much benefit from external contacts, meetings and working groups which have enabled them to overcome uncertainty and gain confidence. Collaboration can stimulate creativity. The innovation process is facilitated by external agents who can mediate between TEC, at the centre and the colleges. In this respect TEC advisory officers played a key role in so far as their time allowed. Teachers found personal contact with them more rewarding and beneficial than correspondence. Care must be taken to ensure that the advisory function does not lead to central solutions inappropriate to local problems. Innovation is facilitated in those colleges where there is efficient information flow, where teachers have a clear understanding of the rationale for change and opportunity for developing new skills. Fortunately many teachers are motivated to do their best for their students. The provision of Standard units enabled some colleges to gain validation of a programme at an earlier date than would otherwise have been possible.

Factors hindering development

Innovation implies change in values and value conflicts are a significant barrier to change. People prefer the familiar to the unfamiliar. Many teachers believed in the adequacy and standards of the pre-TEC courses, and the new TEC proposals engendered a climate of uncertainty. Teachers reported a lack of information and a slow response from TEC in the early stages of development, due to its limited resources. In some colleges communication problems were internal. Many teachers were unfamiliar with the 'jargon' used by TEC and needed more consultancy/workshop support than was available. The geographical separation of staff workrooms in some colleges gave rise to relationship and communication difficulties which are barriers to innovation. Developments were carried out in too much of a rush and TEC was criticized for not setting up and monitoring some pilot schemes. Lack of clarity of purpose can be major causes of innovation failure. Colleges generally did not have sufficient resources and experience to do other than develop programmes for different technician fields independently of each other reflecting the TEC programme committee structure and working within their own departmental boundaries. Lack of formal allocation of time for development work caused staff to give priority to looking after the needs of students on existing courses. Many staff did not have the training and guidance necessary to undertake the tasks of writing objectives and in particular, designing assessment plans.

Evaluation

Moderation

The first handbook for part-time moderators was issued in autumn 1979, although moderators were first appointed for the 1976–1977 session. More systematic training of moderators in the early years would have enhanced the credibility of the provision. Colleges have welcomed the moderator as an external agent linking the college to a national TEC system. Teachers tend to respect a moderator's competence as a subject specialist, but doubt whether he can make valid commentary on the programme as a whole, or assess the standard of the programme in relation to national provision. This in part is due to their previous understanding of the role of an external examiner as a 'subject' assessor. The demands on a moderator of programmes with large numbers of students are severe. Moderation should be regarded as no more than a sampling procedure. Training and guidance for moderators are needed to develop a more uniform interpretation of TEC policy and practice. Moderators, in the autumn of 1979, were concerned about the problems of communication between themselves and TEC, about their role and duties, and about the marks and grades to be awarded when students resit phase-tests.

Aspects overlooked in programme design and changes which have been or should be made

The amount and administrative burden of assessment were not anticipated nor were the logistics of the reassessment of students. Inadequate attention was given in the design of units to the possibility of overlap and fragmentation and the time needed for students to absorb the level and amount of learning required. The amount of time needed for basic curriculum development work in introducing a new system and the lack of resources and costs required for effective implementation were underestimated. Much of the most time-demanding work of curriculum development occurs at the implementation stage since this is close to the curriculum in action. TEC has responded to the pressure to reduce the demands of the assessment process by issuing revised Guidance Notes. Many colleges have made changes to assessment plans and reduced the content of some units. Teachers vary in the extent to which they believe change is legitimate without seeking formal approval of the moderator or revalidation. Where changes have not been made teachers believed there should be a reduction in the amount and time spent on testing, a reduction in unit content and in administrative and paperwork. They identified the need to plan and review programmes as a whole reviewing the links between units.

Other review and formative evaluation

Although TEC did not formally build formative evaluation into its early curriculum planning, the Council and its officers have been responsive to many of the changes required by colleges following initial experience of programme operation. Review meetings by agencies external to colleges and TEC highlighted the diversity of practice and uncertainties experienced by teachers in their initial response in individual college contexts to new national policies.

Staff development

Effective curriculum development will not occur without concomitant staff development. In the absence of a national phased system of planned staff training to accompany the introduction of TEC policy, the support which teachers received varied enormously from college to college and teacher to teacher. Responsibility for ensuring that all those involved in curriculum development have adequate guidance lies with the DES, LEAs, TEC and the colleges themselves. When there is inadequate opportunity for teachers to learn of the purpose and rationale of proposed curriculum change, then the consequences are likely to be a climate of uncertainty and individual interpretations of what should be done. Planned involvement of teachers in curriculum development can improve the quality of teaching and learning and be an effective form of teacher development. The introduction of TEC programmes has been curriculum development by trial and error. One of the most urgent needs is to provide opportunities for staff to update their technical knowledge skills and experience. Training in assessment procedures and in the effective use of less formal teaching and learning approaches is needed. Lack of required skills can be a cause of curriculum innovation failure.

Resource provision

TEC officers and college teachers have undertaken major change with a minimal allocation of resources for the necessary development process, for example, of research and dissemination. Recent budget proposals for an Open Tech illustrate the relatively low national commitment made to the development costs of establishing TEC, yet the requirements were similar; finance for learning materials, an information service, teacher development. TEC has caused an increase in demand by colleges for material resources. The efficient organization of learning requires increased reprographic facilities.

Other outcomes

The reported increased communication and cooperation between teachers are likely to mean a more favourable climate for further development.

SECTION 6

STAFF MANAGEMENT AND DEVELOPMENT

CHAPTER 6.1

INDUSTRIAL RELATIONS: ATTITUDES AND APPROACHES*
MICHAEL P. JACKSON

Frames of reference

Sociologists have made a variety of contributions to the study of industrial relations (see Hill and Thurley, 1974). One of the most widely discussed of recent years has been made by Fox (1966), initially in his research paper for the Donovan Commission. In this paper Fox did not attempt to provide an all-embracing theory, nor even to provide a particular methodology; rather he attempted to demystify industrial relations. He argued that 'sociology as a discipline confers its greatest strength when it helps us, at least to some limited degree, to reduce our dependence on the blinkers of our own social reconditioning and thereby to escape from the self-fulfilling prophecies of what is, must be' (Hill and Thurley, 1974, p. 149).

Initially his attempt at demystification was based on the discussion of two frames of reference. In defining what is meant by a frame of reference he referred to the work of Thelen and Whitehall:

> Each person 'perceives and interprets events by means of a conceptual structure of generalisations or contexts [which consists of] postulates about what is essential, assumptions as to what is valuable, attitudes about what is possible, and ideas about what will work effectively. This conceptual structure constitutes the frame of reference of that person'. (Fox, 1966, p. 2)

Thus the frame of reference embodies 'the main selective influences at work as the perceiver supplements, omits and structures what he notices' (p. 2).

---

* *Industrial Relations*. London, Croom Helm, 1982, pp. 28–37. Michael P. Jackson is a Senior Lecturer in the Department of Sociology, University of Stirling.

The two frames of reference outlined in his initial research paper were the unitary and the pluralistic. The unitary frame of reference, he argued, stressed the importance of a common goal for the enterprise; there is no room, given this frame of reference, for divisions within the enterprise, for all participants have the same basic aim (the efficient functioning of the enterprise) and all will share in the rewards which will accrue from the attainment of this aim. According to people accepting a unitary frame of reference, the closest analogy to the industrial enterprise is that of the team.

> What pattern of behaviour do we expect from the members of a successful and healthily functioning team? We expect them to strive jointly toward a common objective, each pulling his weight to the best of his ability. Each accepts his place and his function gladly, following the leadership of the one so appointed. There are no oppositionary groups or factions, and therefore no rival leaders within the team. Nor are there any outside it; the team stands alone, its members giving allegiance to their own leaders but to no others. (Fox, 1966, p. 3)

Those who subscribe to the unitary ideology will, therefore, tend to define transgressors as aberrants. The manager who firmly believes in the unitary ideology will find it difficult, because of his conviction of the rightness of management rule, not only to acknowledge the legitimacy of challenges to it, but also to grasp 'that such challenges may at least be grounded in legitimacy for those who mount them' (Fox, 1973, p. 189). To him the transgressors must know in their own hearts that they are doing wrong and hurting others needlessly. Explanations for their actions will stress the failure of the men concerned to understand the true position, poor communications and the work of agitators.

The unitary ideology has a great deal of support in industry and in governments. Many managers accept the unitary ideology (it is, as Fox points out, a useful instrument of persuasion and can serve to confer legitimacy on their actions) and go to some lengths to promote its acceptance; it is also implicit in many government statements which discuss issues in terms of 'the national interest'. Many government inquiries and reports have shown an acceptance of the unitary ideology in aspects of their work; for example, the Devlin Report on labour relations in the port transport industry argued that one of the causes of industrial conflict was the work of unofficial shop stewards committees. It recognized that many of the unofficial leaders were genuine in their desire to improve conditions on the docks and operated with the best of intentions. However, it argued that others

. . . find industrial agitation a satisfactory way of life, bringing personal influence and prestige, and whose concern it is to make sure that there is always something to agitate about. Such men put forward extravagant programmes so that they can be sure of being well ahead of any settlement that is made and at the same time be able to represent the settlement as a move towards what they have always advocated. All such men, whatever their motives, are wreckers. (Ministry of Labour, 1965)

Fox argues that the unitary ideology played an important part in the provisions of the Industrial Relations Act. One of the central aims of the Act was to reduce the incidence of what was termed 'disruptive' and 'disorderly' behaviour by the use of external legal controls.

The unitary ideology also has considerable support in the academic sphere. A great deal of the work of the human relations school[1] falls into this category. The human relations school emphasizes the importance of social relations in industry. It argues that a great deal of conflict is the result of poor social (or human) relations. In order to avoid or overcome conflict they suggest methods of improving human relations; for example, better communications (see Miller and Form, 1964). However, they largely ignore differences in interest as a source of conflict; a common interest is merely assumed.

The pluralistic frame of reference, on the other hand, Fox argues, adopts a different approach. The pluralistic ideology accepts that an enterprise contains people with a variety of different interests, aims and aspirations; it is, therefore, a coalition of different interests rather than the embodiment of one common goal. Ross (1958), for example, argues that we should view an organization as a 'plural society, containing many related but separate interests and objectives which must be maintained in some kind of equilibrium'. This clearly has implications for the government of an industrial enterprise.

The problem of government of a plural society is not to unify, integrate or liquidate sectional groups and their special interests in the name of some over-riding corporate existence, but to control and balance the activities of constituent groups so as to provide for the maximum degree of freedom of association and action for sectional and group purposes consistent with the general interest of the society as conceived, with the support of public opinion, by those responsible for government. (Ross, 1958)

Given such views conflict is not abnormal, but is to be expected. Management and governments should not expect blind obedience, nor try to suppress any ideas or aims which conflict with their own; their aim rather should be to try to reconcile conflicting opinions and keep the conflict within accepted bounds so that it does not destroy the enterprise altogether. The pluralist ideology, like the unitary ideology, has a large number of adherents; it, too, has found considerable support in the academic sphere. It has links with the work of Schumpeter, Durkheim, Kornhauser and Kerr, and its use in industrial relations recently has been defended by Clegg (1975). Its influence can also be seen in a number of Government reports; the most striking example is that of the report of the Donovan Commission. In one of its early passages the Donovan Commission described the nature of the business enterprise:

> The running of large businesses is in the hands of professional managers . . . while in the long term shareholders, employers and customers all stand to benefit if a concern flourishes, the immediate interests of these groups often conflict. Directors and managers have to balance these conflicting interests, and in practice they generally seek to strike whatever balance will best promote the welfare of the enterprise as such. (Fox, 1973, p. 203)

The pluralist ideology also has found support in certain management circles. For example, Kelly, in an article entitled 'Make conflict work for you', argues that the old human relations theories which assume that conflict is harmful should be avoided because they do not square with the facts. He says that if it is handled properly conflict 'can lead to more effective and appropriate arrangements . . . The way conflict is managed – rather than suppressed, ignored or avoided – contributes significantly to a company's effectiveness' (Fox, 1973, p. 215).

However, the pluralist ideology itself has been attacked consistently not only from the unitary but also from a more radical perspective. One of the major sources of criticism has been that the pluralist ideology, while it recognizes the inevitability of conflict, also implies a degree of equality between the conflicting parties. Many have argued that such an equality does not exist. Eldridge (1973), for example, quotes the following passage from Milliband:

> What is wrong with pluralist-democratic theory is not its insistence on the factor of competition but its claim (very often its implicit assumption) that the major organized 'interests' in these societies, and notably capital and labour, compete on more or less equal terms, and that none of them is therefore able to achieve a decisive and permanent advantage in the process of competition. This is where ideology enters and turns observation into myth. (p. 146)

Eldridge (1973) argues that pluralism must accept that there are important inequalities in society and that what might be defined as 'disorderly and undesirable industrial conflict from one pluralistic perspective might from another pluralist perspective be regarded as promoting a new and more desirable form of integration' (p. 162). Similar criticisms of the pluralist perspective can be seen in the work of a number of other writers including Gouldner (1971), Rex (1961) and Wright Mills (1959).

From such a perspective pluralism can be just as important a method of mystification as the unitary ideology. The implication that there is some kind of balance of power between the different parties in the organization, combined with the insistence on the importance of compromise, creates a climate in which it will be suggested that each side in the conflict should be allowed to express and maintain 'its own point of view'. Such a climate is an ideal mechanism for resisting fundamental change and, according to the radical criticism, for ensuring the maintenance of existing inequalities.

Such criticisms have now been accepted by Fox. In a number of pieces of work he seems to have moved away from his early adherence to the pluralist stance. In an essay published in 1973 he concluded that 'pluralism may operate as an ignoble myth by offering a misleading picture of the realities of social power, thereby serving those who, by the test of "cui bono", have an interest in the propagation of a comforting and reassuring message' (p. 231). In that particular essay Fox did not dismiss pluralism completely: he argued that although it may not have intellectual validity it might be valuable as a way of achieving a more acceptable society within the status quo (more civilized ways of conducting business, and a reduction in social inequalities). However, in a later publication, Fox (1974) appeared to go further and challenge pluralism even on the pragmatic level. He suggested that if managers tried to operate on the basis of the pluralist ideology they would find it very difficult to meet shopfloor leaders and workplace groups who did not accept the validity of the pluralist image, and saw their interests as being very different to those of management.

Whether Fox has really moved away from pluralism and accepted a more radical perspective, though, has been the source of debate; Wood and Elliott (1977) argue that, even in his later work, Fox has not abandoned pluralism: rather his recent work 'is best viewed as an attempt to develop and modify pluralism in response to changing conditions'. They claim that Fox's approach, based on more rank-and-file participation in management and the development of a shared purpose of social justice, implies that Fox still accepts evolutionary social change rather than a revolutionary socialist perspective.

Clegg has also questioned whether Fox has moved away from pluralism by arguing that the definition of pluralism used by Fox in his recent works has been wrong. According to Clegg, pluralism does not imply (as he says Fox seems to suggest) that there is a balance of power and that compromise will be the inevitable result of industrial conflict. There is, Clegg (1975) argues, reason to believe that normally conflict will be resolved by compromise because there are 'few associations – or governments – which do not prefer to make a further concession rather than take the chance of destroying the social order' (p. 311). Nevertheless, pluralism, he says, accepts the possibility that because of the strength of other moral values, a compromise need not necessarily be reached. He points to two examples to back up his statement – the dispute between the mine owners and mine workers in 1926 and the dispute between the Government and the miners in 1974. There were, he says, 'many skilled and patient hands at work on both occasions but none of their products served to forestall the starvation of the miners into submission in 1926, or the electoral defeat of the Conservative government in 1974. It seems reasonable to conclude that no acceptable compromise was available' (p. 312). Clegg suggests, then, that the criticisms made by Fox of the pluralist position are misdirected, and the points he makes could be accepted by the pluralist. Not everyone accepts this view: Hyman (1978), in a review of the origins of pluralism (in which he shows the different assumptions of the American and British pluralist tradition), questions Clegg's interpretation of the pluralist position.

Whatever the precise nature of the stance adopted by Fox it is clear that the criticisms of the pluralist perspective, that he and others outlined, could be linked to an alternative more radical approach. Such an approach is presented most clearly through the Marxist thesis. This emphasizes the central importance of the division between those who own the means of production and those who merely have their labour to sell.

> Capitalists and wage-workers stand at each side of the labour market as buyers and sellers respectively of the commodity 'labour'. Wage-workers, as the owners of this commodity, present themselves on the labour market in order to sell their labour in exchange for the financial means to sustain their existence. This labour is completely valueless to them until it is combined with the means of production. However, since these are owned by the capitalists, wage-workers can capitalise on their labour only by selling it. Capitalists, for their part, present themselves on the labour market in order to purchase the labour required for the profitable deployment of their means of production. (Schienstock, 1981)

From this point of view, then, the interests of capitalists and workers directly conflict. The advance of one set of interests must be at the expense of the other. 'An unceasing "power struggle" is therefore a central feature of industrial relations' (Hyman, 1975, p. 26).

However, unlike some pluralists, Marxists do not assume a rough equality of power between these different interests. To the contrary, they explicitly assume an imbalance of power, with the owners of the means of production using their superior power to influence events. This is not to suggest that workers can do nothing to combat the power of the capitalist. The development of trade unions is an important advance, strengthening individual workers by reducing the competition between them. Nevertheless, although trade unions may provide some protection and some advancement, the owners of the means of production remain the strongest side. 'Marx believed, moreover, that industrial development would increase the imbalance; mechanization would create a growing pool of unemployment, undermining trade union strength' (Hyman, 1975, p. 28).

In the long term the Marxist theory is not pessimistic for it predicts the overthrow of the capitalist system. Nevertheless, until that happens, industrial relations are crucially affected by the conflict between capital and labour, and by the superior power of capital. This superiority does not simply affect the price to be paid for labour but also affects working arrangements and conditions. 'Because capitalist enterprise is concerned only with the pursuit of profit and labour is bought and sold as a commodity, and treated impersonally as a factor of production, the economic and human interests of employees are sacrificed under the coercive power of the capitalist. It is this inherent exploitation that builds conflict into the social relations in production' (Walker, 1977).

Although there are numerous different interpretations of the Marxist thesis, and many of these interpretations differ over more than simply detail, the inevitable conflict between the interests of the worker and the interests of the capitalist, and the exploitation of the worker by the capitalist are common themes, and represent a radical alternative to pluralism.

Summary

The aim of this chapter has been to introduce a number of different approaches to the study of industrial relations. The approaches selected have been influential [. . .].

One of the main difficulties with presenting approaches, or categories, is that it may give the impression that such approaches have tight boundaries and are exclusive, when, in practice, this is not the case. For example, pluralism is very difficult to define, there are many variants, and the boundary with a more radical approach is far from easy to determine. Further, while the unitary, pluralistic and radical frames of reference are all addressing a similar question, they are addressing a different question to systems theory and the social action approach. As a result, the acceptance of one of the three frames of reference does not necessarily imply the acceptance or rejection of systems theory or the social action approach, even though commonly it may be associated with a particular stance.

Note

1   See, for example, the work of Elton Mayo.

References

Clegg, H.A. (1975) Pluralism in industrial relations. *British Journal of Industrial Relations*, vol. XIII, no. 3, pp. 309–316.

Eldridge, J.E.T. (1973) In: Child, J. (ed.) *Man and Organisation*. London, Allen & Unwin.

Fox, A. (1966) *Industrial Sociology and Industrial Relations*. Research paper 3. London, HMSO.

Fox, A. (1973) Industrial relations: A social critique of pluralist ideology. In: Child, J. (ed.) *Man and Organisation*. London, Allen & Unwin, p. 189.

Fox, A. (1974) *Beyond Contract*. London, Faber.

Gouldner, A.W. (1971) *The Coming Crisis of Western Sociology*. London, Heinemann.

Hill, S. and Thurley, K. (1974) Sociology and industrial relations. *British Journal of Industrial Relations*, vol. XII, no. 2, pp. 147–170.

Hyman, R. (1975) *Industrial Relations: A Marxist Introduction*. London, Macmillan.

Hyman, R. (1978) Pluralism, procedural consensus and collective bargaining. *British Journal of Industrial Relations*, vol. XVI, no. 1, pp. 16–40.

Miller, D.C. and Form, W.H. (1964) *Industrial Sociology*. New York, Harper & Row, p. 245.

Ministry of Labour (1965) *Final Report of the Committee of Inquiry under Rt. Hon. Lord Devlin into Certain Matters Concerning the Port Transport Industry*. Cmnd 2734. London, HMSO, pp. 42–43.

Rex, J. (1961) *Key Problems in Sociological Theory*. London, Routledge & Kegan Paul.

Ross, H.S. (1958) In: Hugh-Jones, E.M. (ed.) *Human Relations and Modern Management*, quoted by Fox (1966).

Schienstock, G. (1981) Towards a theory of industrial relations. *British Journal of Industrial Relations*, vol. XIX, no. 2, pp. 180–181.

Walker, K. (1977) Towards useful theorising about industrial relations. *British Journal of Industrial Relations*, vol. XV, no. 3, p. 311.

Wood, S. and Elliott, R. (1977) A critical evaluation of Fox's radicalisation of industrial relations theory. *Sociology*, vol. 11, no. 1, p. 109.

Wright Mills, C. (1959) *The Power Elite*. New York, Oxford University Press.

CHAPTER 6.2

RELATIONS WITH TRADE UNIONS*
JOHN C.N. BAILLIE

1   It is not the purpose of this sub-section to attempt guidance on how to proceed in a dispute at college level between management and trade union(s). In such a situation, recourse will be advisable to the advice of one's trade union and/or the local authority. This sub-section concerns itself with the establishment of a regular procedural framework designed to avoid disputes before they arise.

2   Relations between management and trade unions at college level should be viewed in the context of industrial relations at national and local education authority level. Their purpose and nature have been defined by LACSAB (1978) as follows: 'Industrial relations are about the relationships between employers and the people they employ – their aspirations, expectations, achievements, successes and failures. The satisfaction of the employee in doing a good job contributes to the successful implementation of the policies of the employer and the effectiveness of his undertaking. Conversely, the anxieties, frustrations and failures of employees in their working environment can diminish the effectiveness of the organization. Employers and employees therefore have a mutual interest in maintaining and developing good industrial relations.'

3   Industrial relations are thus essentially the transactions occurring between employer and employee. Employer responsibilities for maintained establishments of further, higher and adult education attach to individual

* *College Administration: A Handbook*, edited by I. Waitt. National Association of Teachers in Further and Higher Education, 1980, section 4, pp. 150–154. Reference should be made to other sections of *College Administration* in order to fully understand the issues raised in this chapter.

local education authorities, and the essential nexus is therefore between the local education authority and the trade union's organizational unit responsible for the LEA area – for teachers, the NATFHE Liaison Committee, and for other occupations, the union branch and Joint Works Committee. In the case of certain establishments of higher education maintained jointly by two or more LEAs, employer responsibilities attach to a joint education committee drawing its membership from the constituent authorities. Voluntary or grant-aided establishments are usually constituted as employers in their own right; it is often, and appropriately, a condition of grant that employee's terms and conditions of employment are comparable with those in maintained establishments.

4 Conventional wisdom, however, continues to describe education as 'a national service locally administered'. The local authority associations and the trade unions concerned have found it helpful to establish national negotiating and consultative machinery, in order to conclude agreements binding at least in honour upon all local education authorities and upon the trade unions concerned at all levels of organization [. . .]. In respect of teachers, such agreements may leave scope for determination of certain matters at local authority level; both national and local authority level agreements may leave scope for discussion as to implementation at college level. In respect of non-teaching staff, variations will also occur at Provincial Council and local authority level. What is crucial for all concerned in such discussions is a realization that both the college management (however constituted: for example, principal and chief administrative officer) and the college union membership are constrained by agreements made elsewhere. For the college management, there is also the overriding constraint that the level of financial resources (whether for accommodation, staffing, or equipment and materials) is determined outside the college, so that while discussions at college level may influence the deployment of resources already allocated, such discussion cannot increase the resource allocation without reference to the authority.

5 An intermediate stage of discussion may involve the college governing body, whose powers are determined by the articles (and instrument) of government for the college concerned. If the local education authority has expressly delegated some of its powers and responsibilities as an employer to the governing body, any local discussions must have regard to the fact: on the whole, however, industrial relations are better handled through other channels. Similarly, the academic board is not normally a satisfactory vehicle for the ventilation of industrial relations issues as such.

6   In the previous paragraphs, the term 'discussion' has been used to describe exchanges of view at college level. A great deal of heat has been expended on the question of whether such discussions constitute 'consultation' or 'negotiation', and it may be helpful to attempt working definitions of the two. Consultation concerns matters which are regarded by the management as responsibilities which it cannot or will not share, but on which it is prepared to inform the trade union(s) concerned of actions intended or envisaged, and to receive representations thereon before acting. The intended actions are sometimes modified or abandoned in the light of representations made, and sometimes not: the decision is with the management. Occasionally consultation may be statutorily prescribed, for example where there are impending redundancies. Negotiation concerns matters which are mutually accepted by employer and union(s) as suitable for collective bargaining, the outcome of which is expected to be a collective agreement freely entered into by the parties concerned, which then becomes binding at least in honour upon them. Both consultation and negotiation can take place at college level, so long as a negotiated agreement restricts itself to matters where the college management has power to decide: if not such an agreement would need confirmation or repudiation at local authority level. In the event of a continuing difference of opinion over intended action which has been the subject of consultation, or over a matter which has been the subject of unsuccessful negotiation, the situation may become serious enough to describe as a dispute[. There is a] negotiated procedure for dealing with disputes involving teachers' unions which may arise at college level [. . .]. Grievance and disputes procedures governing non-teaching staff are covered by the national agreements. The college principal may be called upon by staff in the college and by the local authority to act as the agent of the employer in initial discussions on any matter; such discussions will often resolve the problem without the need to refer beyond the college.

7   Examples of issues for discussion at college level include the following:

i.   *Manning levels*
   a.   current establishments of full-time and part-time staff, their deployment within the college and between departments;
   b.   future estimates of manning requirements for submission to the local education authority; and
   c.   departmental and other staffing patterns (it is helpful for any

changes to have been discussed before they are implemented).

ii.   *Staff selection and development*
    a.   procedures within the college for the appointment of staff;

    b.   procedures within the college for the promotion of staff; and

    c.   staff development procedures within the college.

Note: Any such college procedures will naturally have to satisfy the requirements of procedures at authority level, but these usually incorporate scope for variation.

iii.   *Timetabling*

The teachers' conditions of service agreement [. . .] requires access to timetables on request for representatives of the recognized trade unions.

iv.   *Working conditions*
    a.   variations to daily starting times for classes;

    b.   (for technicians) the timetabling of laboratory use to permit access for preparatory work; and

    c.   provision of working space outside teaching areas.

Note: There may well be 'welfare' issues more suitably considered by a college Safety Committee established within the purview of the Health and Safety at Work etc. Act 1974 [. . .].

8   It would be possible to multiply the examples in the previous paragraph almost indefinitely: a college union branch or group of members could well carry a resolution on almost any matter of concern within the college for presentation to the college management. A major concern, however, is almost certain to be the position of individual union members in multifarious contexts – the situation familiarly described by the teaching unions as 'casework'. Much of this casework arises from misunderstanding at some level; by the union member or representative on the one hand or by a senior member of staff on the other. A recent NFER survey (Bradley and Silverleaf, 1979) has found that most teachers regard the head of department as their 'boss', a view shared by some heads of department! It is important that any delegation by the principal or chief administrative officer of managerial responsibility for industrial relations should be clearly defined. In particular, the power to 'hire and fire' part-time staff should be explicitly assigned, if assigned at all (at least one large LEA forbids the termination of part-time teachers' contracts by staff other than the principal). Teachers and principals should avoid coming into conflict. Where

conflict seems likely to arise, either party should seek advice from the LEA or its relevant officers, or from their professional association or its full-time officials.

9   Consideration should be given at college level to the procedure for management–trade union discussions. Casework is often urgent, and may require access to a designated member of the college management team by a union representative without undue formality. Other matters merit prearranged meetings with defined agenda and a proper record of proceedings available to the representatives of both parties. A reliance on meetings arranged ad hoc is seldom satisfactory, and a regular calendar of meetings (which can always be cancelled in the absence of business to consider) is both mutually beneficial in itself and facilitates adjustments to the timetables of the teachers concerned to avoid adverse consequences to students.

10   The three main negotiating groups of trade unions recognized nationally are as follows:

Teachers – NATFHE (including AACE), NSAE, APC, AAES.
APT&C – NALGO, GMWU, NUPE, TGWU, COHSE. (Administrative, Professional, Technical and Clerical grades.)
Manual – GMWU, NUPE, TGWU. (School meals staff, caretakers and cleaners, residential employees.)

At college level, the three groups may have formed a Joint Union Committee (JUC) to coordinate policies and action on matters of common concern, and it may be appropriate on occasion for JUC representatives to meet college management. This may be particularly suitable in the context of health and safety matters. For most issues, however, separate meetings will probably be more helpful. All the unions mentioned above favour local consultation and negotiation (except of course in respect of matters which can only be determined elsewhere in the bargaining structure) and believe that problems should be resolved at local level wherever possible. The manual workers' unions' particularly encourage the development of shop steward or workplace representative systems and most unions provide some access to industrial relations training for their workplace representatives. The NATFHE Rules give specific authority for a college Branch or Coordinating Committee to discuss with the college principal and governing body all matters domestic to the institution. The involvement in discussions of a full-time official from the union concerned may be arranged; the union(s) will more usually be represented by elected lay members, on most occasions drawn from the college staff.

11   Good industrial relations at college level can thus be seen not just as a one-way process involving a management decision followed by its willing and successful implementation; to paraphrase LACSAB (1978), good industrial relations involve give and take, with the staff, through their unions, influencing the decisions that have to be taken and their subsequent implementation. With good industrial relations, this influence is of benefit to the college, and thus to the authority. With indifferent or bad industrial relations, important decisions may be deferred or, if taken, may be impossible adequately to implement.

References

Bradley, J. and Silverleaf, J. (1979) *Making the Grade*. Slough, NFER.

Local Authorities' Conditions of Service Advisory Board and Local Government Training Board (1978) *Employee Relations: Reference Guide for Chief Officers and Managers in Local Authorities*.

THEORIES AND MODELS OF STAFF DEVELOPMENT IN UNIVERSITY TEACHING*
DESMOND RUTHERFORD

Introduction

Institutional attempts to develop teaching and learning in British universities – often referred to as academic staff training and development programmes – have expanded considerably during the 1970s: some successes and some notable failures have been recorded. However we suspect that academic staff in general have tolerated but remained largely uninvolved and sceptical of the value of these initiatives. To make matters worse, there is widespread disagreement among those who have a more direct responsibility for organizing such programmes – often referred to, without enthusiasm, as 'staff developers' – as to the scope of their responsibilities. For example, Matheson (1980) has argued that since the work of academic staff encompasses teaching, research and administration:

> concentration solely on improving university teaching is the siren of staff development which in the end will devalue the activity to a worthless level. (p. 10)

This disagreement is compounded by the lack of consensus among staff developers as to how even programmes designed to develop teaching should be carried out. On one hand there are those (Brown, 1977) who believe that improvements in teaching arise out of practical activities, whereas others (Sayer, 1977) emphasize the growth of self-awareness through discussion resulting in changes in attitudes to be followed later by changes in teaching behaviour. Of course, such a divergence of approach is to be expected and

* *Higher Education*, 1982, vol. 1, no. 2, pp. 177–191. © 1982 Elsevier Scientific Publishing Company. Dr D.J. Rutherford is Organizing Tutor for the Advisory Service on Teaching Methods at the University of Birmingham.

even welcomed in a new and speculative area: much depends on the personal philosophies and skills of those involved and the institutional context in which they work. However, the resultant climate of uncertainty heightens the danger that even the present modest level of activity will not survive.

The purpose of this article is neither to offer another definition of the scope of staff development nor prescriptions of how to achieve specific aims. Rather we will explore the possibility of developing a strategy to facilitate the improvement of university teaching that will engage the interest and commitment of those academic staff and staff developers to whom the institution has given this responsibility. Hewton (1979) has already discussed the value of an organizational perspective on staff development and it is this that we wish to develop. First of all we will examine the relevance of theories of innovation processes and then review possible roles for staff developers.

Theories of innovation and staff development

Chin and Benne (1976) have offered a very useful classification of general strategies to effect planned change. Three quite distinct approaches were identified: power/coercive; empirical/rational; normative/re-educative.

Power/coercive strategies

Power/coercive strategies are characterized by the application of superior power (i.e. the use or the threat of the use of political, economic or moral sanctions) from those in authority in order to secure the compliance of those in subordinate positions. Such a strategy runs a great risk – perhaps an inevitable risk – of exciting conflict and covert resistance to proposed innovations. Nevertheless, power/coercive strategies have been successfully employed from time to time by both students and governments to implement change in universities.

With respect to staff development, Hewton (1979) has suggested that:

> The power/coercive approach is of interest in so far as it is regarded as important in the implementation of a development programme. It represents the political side of the coin and involves: the gaining of support, the overcoming of resistance, the steering of proposals through committees, obtaining and increasing budgets and the general manipulation of the system. This is a part of the job which fascinates some but is reluctantly regarded by others as a necessity which takes time away from what they see as their real work. (p. 4)

Empirical/rational strategies

Empirical/rational strategies lay great stress on the value of research and development producing ideas and proposals for change that can be rationally justified and shown to benefit the potential audience – a relatively passive audience – to which they are directed. Such a strategy has a strong appeal to the academic mind – dispassionate, disinterested and essentially logical – especially since the standard response to a problem is more research. However, any success appears to depend on the readiness of the audience to accept the suggested innovations and the strength of the links between them and the researchers. Lack of success has sometimes been attributed to an inadequate understanding of the factors which affect the diffusion and implementation of innovations rather than to the failure of the strategy itself.

Again Hewton (1979) has given some examples of this strategy as it operates in practice.

> The empirical/rational approach involves a special interest in research, testing, quantitative analysis, carefully prepared statements and materials, high standards of accuracy and well worked out theoretical positions.

> The rationale behind such an approach, when applied to staff development, follows the logic that this is the way academics work and this therefore is the way to win their respect. The absence of careful research and clear evidence will reduce credibility – but if these are present, the academic mind will be guided by reasoned argument. The problem becomes one of communication, of how best to make the message clear and readily available. Books, learned papers, audio-visual material and displays, newsletters, information services and consultancy are offered. Occasionally learning packages on particular themes or topics in connection with teaching and learning are prepared and distributed. (p. 4)

Normative/re-educative strategies

Normative/re-educative strategies emphasize that change cannot be imposed externally but can only be brought about by the persons involved as they themselves recognize, clarify and seek to solve their own problems. Experience-based learning is regarded as the essential vehicle for promoting innovation with the reorientation of personal and group attitudes and values as important as intellectual development. Hewton (1979) has described this strategy as follows:

> The normative/re-educative approach involves working with academic staff much more than in the rational/empirical mode. The developer assumes a

collaborative, participative stance. An awareness of research and theory may underpin the approach but the starting point is located in the ideas and problems of the client; these are paramount and must be explored. Workshops normally figure large and there are examples of the formation of experiential learning groups and of counselling opportunities of various kinds. (p. 4)

Chin and Benne argued that normative/re-educative strategies are likely to be the most effective in implementing change. Nevertheless, two rather different approaches can be discerned which emphasize either the improvement of the problem-solving and task-orientated capabilities of individuals and groups concerned or the personal development of those individuals. In some respects these two approaches may reflect the different philosophies of Brown and Sayer which were described earlier. However, it does appear that in British universities at the present time strategies which are directly aimed at personal development (i.e. forms of human relations training) are less successful than might at first be anticipated (see Elton, 1981; Hatch, 1980). In this article we will focus on the alternative strategy – the improvement of problem-solving and task-orientated capabilities.

Problem-solving strategies and the social and organizational context

A recurring theme in analysis of strategies to promote innovation in higher education is the importance of gaining institutional support for such activities. Some years ago Eraut (1975) suggested that the 'teaching climate' of an institution was the key issue. He identified some of the particular constraints affecting innovation in higher education (e.g. no priority to teaching and learning, no dissatisfaction with present solutions, few resources for innovation, ignorance of possible innovations and lack of guidance as to how to develop profitable innovations). Eraut argued that insufficient attention was paid to the identification and clarification of problems as they actually confronted academic staff; this led to the all too common situation of specific innovations chasing teaching problems (e.g. How can I use television? What about writing a Keller-Plan course?) rather than specific problems leading to planned change. In order to overcome this he proposed that problems should be investigated by a multidisciplinary task force consisting of academic staff, students and educational consultants working through a five-stage process – problem awareness, problem diagnosis, problem study, problem attack, problem evaluation. Such a strategy lies well within the normative/re-educative tradition, since the main responsibility and a substantial part of the work involved rest squarely with the consumers of any proposed solution – the academic staff themselves. This approach appears to hold great potential when there is an awareness of a particular problem and a willingness to devote resources – particularly the time and energy of the academic staff directly affected – to its solution.

The challenge of devising a theoretical model which would help academic staff to solve teaching and learning problems has attracted other authors as well as Eraut. For example, Havelock (1973) has proposed a very similar six-stage model – building relationships, diagnosing the problem, acquiring resources, choosing the solution, gaining acceptance, stabilizing the innovation. However, innovations do not occur in vacuo according to an idealized 'process of planned change': success depends on a clear understanding of the social and organizational context in which an innovation takes place as well as on its intrinsic merits. What then are the relevant characteristics of our institutions of higher education?

Hogan (1980) has claimed that institutions in general – particularly large institutions – are no longer capable of reaching a consensus over common goals, that is, they cannot be regarded as 'purposive systems'.

> Thus it is believed to be positively dysfunctional to treat the organisation as a purposive system. It should rather be seen as an area of negotiation, exchange and conflict between diverse and conflicting interests, out of which – hopefully but transiently – shared purposes may arise. (p. 129)

In such circumstances it is extremely difficult to introduce planned change, especially when there is competition for decreasing resources.

> Many of our larger organisations now look remarkably like feudal systems with great departmental barons competing for ever larger shares of the spoils to support sectional interests. (p. 130)

It can readily be appreciated that such institutions are highly resistant to external demands for change. Typically, solutions to problems are sought through the establishment of an interdisciplinary working party which bypasses existing structures and allegiances or the creation of a new appointment. Neither approach, of course, guarantees a solution. Hogan's analysis – although somewhat uncomfortable – is particularly relevant to developing an understanding of how universities function and the strategies and tactics that are necessary to facilitate innovation.

Berg and Ostergren (1977, 1979) have argued that it is essential to examine an innovation in terms of the social and organizational context in which it takes place and indeed that change itself is a form of political process. They have developed an apparently simple yet powerful theory to explain why some innovations are successful and why others are not. The theory was derived from a thorough investigation of seven innovations in course development and teaching methods in Swedish universities. Each represented a fairly radical departure from previous practice rather than a change of a more conventional and less controversial nature, namely a system-divergent rather than a system-convergent change. They also suggested that the theory would be widely applicable since the basic properties of higher education as a social system (i.e. membership, ideology, technology, organization and relationship with the environment) are largely the same in all countries.

The scope of their investigation was described as follows:

> The functional study in its entirety can be characterised as a clinical examination of governance, planning systems, and innovativeness in higher education. The purpose is to chart dysfunctions in the system as related to planning for change. (Berg and Ostergren, 1977, p. 12)

Each innovation was analysed in the total context in which it took place and this led the authors to conclude:

> an innovation process is first and foremost determined by the interaction between social systems. The interests and positions of the systems essentially determine the needs, positions and actions of individual participants. (p. 20)

In other words, the actions of individuals are largely determined and can be best understood by reference to the various groups – social and organizational – to which they belong and the success or otherwise of an innovation is largely determined by the interplay among these groups. For each of the seven innovations, the various groups that formed the social system were first of all identified and then their interactions were analysed according to the following four decisive factors:

1 *Gain/Loss*

This concept proved to be of primary importance and reflected the extent to which the various groups and to a lesser extent the various individuals in the system gained or lost through the innovation. Particular examples of gains would be increases in the areas of security/stability and personal satisfaction/self-realization.

2 *Ownership*

This concept reflected the degree to which the various groups and individuals felt that the innovation belonged to them, that is, the extent to which they had created and introduced the innovation and hence their commitment to its success. Direct ownership, either total or partial, could be claimed by those who had actually created and introduced all or part of the innovation respectively while indirect ownership could be claimed by those who gave it their support.

3 *Leadership*

This concept was seen as a system-related concept in that the individual was also the leader of a group. Innovation leaders were defined as those who had created and introduced the innovation (i.e. having direct, total ownership), secondary leaders were those who had been involved in part of the innovation (i.e. having direct, partial ownership) and formal leaders were generally those in positions of authority who supported the innovation (i.e. having indirect ownership). Opposition leaders were also identified.

4 *Power*

The exercise of power or the threat of the exercise of power was found to be essential in order to implement, sustain and, in particular, to institutionalize an innovation. The degree of power that was available depended on the position of a group or individual in the constellation of forces that constituted the social system.

The concept of power was of crucial importance as Berg and Ostergren emphasized that institutions are essentially conservative and seek to defend themselves against intrusions. Although the application of power forms a necessary part of a power/coercive strategy, it may also be consequent on the usual processes of consultation and deliberation that contribute to decision-making in universities and so can also form part of a normative/re-educative strategy.

To summarize, the theory would predict that an innovation was likely to be successful if there were clear *gains* and few *losses* to be made, a strong sense of *ownership*, effective *leadership* and, most importantly, a sensitive and timely exercise of institutional *power* that could be mobilized to secure the innovation. However it must also be appreciated that innovation processes are dynamic rather than static, so gains and losses, ownership, leadership and power may all change with the passage of time.

The preceding analysis of theories of innovation processes leads us to suggest that the basis of a strategy to facilitate the development of university teaching lies in a problem-solving approach such as that described by Eraut coupled with an appreciation of the social and organizational context as provided by Berg and Ostergren's theory. But what, in this strategy, is the role of those academic staff who are employed on a full- or part-time basis to support such developments – the staff developers?

Possible roles for the staff developer

Davies (1975), Havelock (1973) and Schein (1976) have all described various ways in which a staff developer can establish a professional relationship with a member or group of academic staff. Four quite distinct philosophies can be identified: product-orientated; prescription-orientated; process-orientated; problem-orientated.

Product-orientated model

In this model academic staff identify a specific need for information or a particular service and call upon the expertise of the staff developer to satisfy that need. In turn, the staff developer may suggest an immediate solution or provide a range of alternatives from which staff can then choose. The difficulties with this approach are that the staff developer must respond to a problem that is already well defined – which may not be the 'real' problem – and provide a ready-made solution or solutions which staff then are supposed to implement. Feedback on whether or not a solution was indeed implemented and how effective it proved to be may well not be forthcoming.

For example, what possible response could a staff developer give to a member of academic staff who sought advice on how to improve the reading speeds of his students. Some suggestions could be made but perhaps the real problem was that the students were not being given adequate advice on what reading they should be doing and the purposes of that reading. And so both staff developer and staff run the risk of attending to superficial problems, 'fire-fighting', rather than undertaking a detailed analysis of the problem and identifying the actual difficulties and the possibilities.

The product-orientated model is perhaps best thought of as being most closely related to the empirical/rational theory of change which was described earlier.

Prescription-orientated model

In this model academic staff are unable to identify a specific problem but rather experience a feeling that there is 'something wrong' and the staff developer is brought in both to diagnose the problem and to suggest an appropriate remedy. The relationship between staff developer and staff is somewhat akin to that between doctor and patient: some staff developers find such a role attractive as it appeals to their own sense of professionalism. The difficulties with this approach are that very few staff developers are likely to have the knowledge, skills and personal qualities required and that academic staff are unaccustomed and generally extremely hostile to any notion of being investigated by 'outsiders'.

For example, how could a staff developer respond to a head of department who, without consulting his colleagues, invited him to 'look over' the department and 'check out' that all was well? If such an invitation was accepted without a very great deal of preparatory work, the staff developer would surely find that the 'patients' (i.e. academic staff) were very unwilling to reveal any disparaging information about themselves and possibly even less likely to accept any analysis of problems and solutions.

This particular example would be classified as a power/coercive strategy on the part of the head of department but if the invitation had come from the department as a whole then the rational/empirical model would have been more applicable.

Process-orientated model

In this model the staff developer works with academic staff as a 'process consultant' in the diagnosis and solution of problems. His particular contribution is to facilitate the problem-solving process and, in so doing, to provide training in problem-solving skills for those with whom he is working. However, he does not offer information, ideas or advice on the intellectual content of a problem. Schein (1978) has defined process consultation as follows:

> . . . the ultimate function of the process consultant (is) to help the client perceive, understand and act upon the process and content events that occur in his or her environment in order to improve the functioning of that client. (p. 342)

The process consultant does not then assume responsibility for a problem or offer prescriptions as to its solution: his priority, at all times, is that academic staff should develop their own skills and solve their own problems. Difficulties in personal relationships are only raised – and even then with great caution – when the academic staff themselves indicate their readiness to confront such issues and when they seriously inhibit the problem-solving process. As previously mentioned, attempts to involve academic staff in British universities in human relations training of one kind or another have been made but on the whole the response has not been encouraging. Misunderstandings may obviously arise if the role of the process consultant is not fully understood and accepted by the academic staff.

This strategy clearly lies in the normative/re-educative tradition where the emphasis is placed on developing the personal and professional qualities of individuals.

Problem-oriented model

In this model academic staff and staff developer work together in a joint enterprise to diagnose and solve problems. The staff developer may have in mind a well-defined model of the problem-solving process. He will also be conscious of the need to manage his personal relationships with those with whom he is working as the project develops and the institutional context into which any proposed solution must fit. The staff developer will be particularly concerned to ensure that a wide range of possible alternative solutions are explored but that any decision-making is clearly left to those directly involved – the academic staff themselves.

This strategy also lies within the normative/re-educative tradition where the emphasis is primarily on a mutual process of problem-solving. It is also arguably the most effective strategy for staff developers to employ in present circumstances. The working party approach is a common one in a university environment and in this all participants – academic staff and staff developer – have a contribution to make in the solution of problems and the execution of joint responsibilities.

Although the process-orientated and the problem-orientated models are not mutually exclusive, the former emphasizes the personal and professional development of individuals whereas the latter focuses on the resolution of the task in hand. This difference in emphasis reflects a very real difference in underlying philosophy which we encountered earlier in our discussion of normative/re-educative strategies.

[. . .]

Conclusion

Obviously any single strategy that an institution adopts to facilitate innovation in such a complex and diverse area as university teaching will prove inadequate. The many differences among institutions – differences in personnel, context, history, available resources and so forth – necessitate different strategies which inevitably change as circumstances change.

It is important to recognize, nurture and seek to understand the often unique ways in which universities have responded to the many challenges of developing teaching, learning and assessment methods and the competencies of their academic staff. The theoretical perspectives outlined in this chapter may help towards that understanding.

References

Berg, B. and Ostergren, B. (1977) *Innovations and Innovations Processes in Higher Education*. Stockholm, National Board of Universities and Colleges.

Berg, B. and Ostergren, B. (1979) Innovation processes in higher education. *Studies in Higher Education*, no. 4, pp. 261–268.

Brown, G. (1977) Some myths of staff training and development. *Impetus*, no. 6, pp. 2–8.

Chin, R. and Benne, K.D. (1976) General strategies for effecting changes in human systems. In: Bennis, W.G., Benne, K.D., Chin, R. and Corey, K.E. (eds) *The Planning of Change*, 3rd ed. New York, Holt, Rinehart and Winston, pp. 22–45.

Davies, I.K. (1975) Some aspects of a theory of advice: the management of an instructional developer–client, evaluator–client relationship. *Instructional Science* no. 3, pp. 351–373. Reprinted in Hartley, J. and Davies, I.K. (eds) (1978) *Contributions to an Educational Technology, Vol. 2*. London, Kogan Page.

Elton, L. (1981) Can universities change? *Studies in Higher Education*, no. 6, pp. 23–24.

Eraut, M. (1975) Promoting innovation in teaching and learning: problems, processes and institutional mechanisms. *Higher Education*, no. 4, pp. 13–26.

Hatch, J. (1980) Research and creative teaching: reflections on a workshop. *Teaching News*, no. 11, p. 18.

Havelock, R.G. (1973) *The Change Agent's Guide to Innovation in Education*. Englewood Cliffs, N.J., Educational Technology Publications.

Hewton, E. (1979) Towards a definition of staff development. *Impetus*, no. 11, pp. 1–8.

Hogan, D. (1980) New directions in the study of innovation. *Royal Air Force Education Bulletin*, no. 18, pp. 127–134.

Matheson, C.C. (1980) The boundaries of concern of staff development. In: *Improving University Teaching: Proceedings of the Sixth International Conference*. Maryland, University of Maryland, pp. 1–10.

Sayer, S. (1977) Development and discourse. *Impetus*, no. 7, pp. 34–36.

Schein, E. (1976) Process consultation. In: Bennis, W.G., Benne, K.D., Chin, R.

and Corey, K.E. (eds) *The Planning of Change*, 3rd ed. New York, Holt, Rinehart and Winston, pp. 327–330.

Schein, E.H. (1978) The role of the consultant: content expert or process facilitator. *Personnel and Guidance Journal*, no. 56, pp. 339–343.

CHAPTER 6.4

THE INTERVIEW IN EDUCATION: SOME RESEARCH EVIDENCE AND ITS IMPLICATIONS FOR PRACTITIONERS*
COLIN R. RICHES

Interviewing is a common activity in education. An interview can be defined as a conversation, in gesture as well as words, aimed at a definite purpose (which will always include the obtaining of information of quality) with the interviewer(s) in control. There are numerous situations when interviewing takes place between personnel in schools and colleges – staff, students, parents, employers, local authority administrators and so on – ranging from casual encounters to the highly formal setting. There are various ways in which one can classify interviews in education and other circles, but a simple and workable differentiation can be made between interviewing for (1) selection, (2) staff appraisal and (3) counselling.

In the *selection* interview (on which this chapter concentrates) the end is clear, at least in outline, that is, to pick the potentially most effective (however ill-defined) person for a post in an organization. In an *appraisal* interview the purpose is to make an organization more effective by helping people to be more effective and may include a number of purposes such as evaluation, discovering training needs, motivating staff, developing individuals, checking on their effectiveness and giving performance feedback (Randell, 1975). *Counselling* interviews are focused more on the individual than the organization and involve the counsellor assisting an individual to adjust more effectively to himself, and his world. While all three types of interview involve assessment of one sort or another, selection and counselling are usually at opposite ends of a continuum because in the selection situation the interviewee will certainly attempt to demonstrate his or her

---

* The Open University (unpublished). Colin Riches is Lecturer in Educational Administration, at the Open University.

more attractive traits, whereas in a counselling situation the individual is looking for or needing help. Clearly the varying degrees of frankness represented along the continuum will influence the reliability and validity of an interview.

In practice the processes and ends of interviewing in general are often ill-defined and inadequate and the effectiveness of the interview can be called into question. Unfortunately the research evidence on the interview in education is severely limited and the findings give inadequate guidance on sound practice. This chapter draws attention to the research data on staff selection in education, and examines more general research on the employment interview in the belief that this can lead to a greater appreciation of some of the problems involved in interviewing as applied to education. Interviewing continues to flourish in its various forms without any convincing evidence to justify the confidence invested in it. Interviews are popular because they are considered easy to give, personnel resources only are required, apparently no specific training is needed and many people feel they are very competent in giving interviews. While the evidence tends to suggest that the interview is the least effective way of assessing people, out of a variety of assessment procedures, it is the most popular. For this reason it is important to attempt to evaluate the evidence with a view to improving existing techniques of interviewing, while at the same time recognizing that other instruments such as references and psychological, written and group tests could be used more often in the selection and other types of interview.

Evidence from education

Major studies of staff in schools (Hilsum and Start, 1974) and colleges (Bradley and Silverleaf, 1979) make critical but only passing reference to the interview. The former research revealed widespread dissatisfaction with interview procedures: there was even reference to one instance where a candidate, after an interview for a post, immediately bought the local evening paper and to his horror read details of who had been appointed! But Hilsum and Start recorded participants' reactions to interview procedures and did not investigate the predictive power of the interview for the selection and promotion of staff. Similar limitations are to be found in Bradley and Silverleaf's study of staff in further education, which highlighted a variety of procedures for conducting selection interviews. There were divided views for teachers and managers in further education about the advantages of various procedures, but dissatisfaction was widespread. College principals were uncertain about the merits of different patterns of interview, for example the panel or one-to-one interviewing. Teachers who had been interviewed and appointed to college posts complained about there being too many people on the interviewing panels who lacked detailed knowledge of the post they were selecting for (41.7 percent of the sample) and too many irrelevant 'superficial and highly subjective' questions asked (42.3 percent) (see also Nicholson, 1968, pp. 246–247). Principals, however, were more assured about the efficiency of a formal final interview when 'a larger exchange of views with college staff' also took place, although 59.6 percent felt that the formal interview was not conducted on the lines of giving information as well as receiving it (Nicholson, 1968, pp. 53–54). A similar pattern of ambiguity and the absence of a rationale has been lately observed at school level in a study of the selection of secondary heads (Morgan and Hall, 1982). From this evidence on selection interviewing it is clear that a reappraisal of procedures is necessary.

Such limited research – as distinct from advice on the use of the interview in staff selection for colleges and schools (e.g. Field, 1971; Stoddart, 1978; Morris, 1982; Ferguson, 1979) – is all that is available. Some teachers' professional associations have laid down 'model' procedures; for example, in 1977 NATFHE produced a draft policy of appointments and interview procedure.

Interviewing

Over the years many different methods of interviewing have developed. All of them have advantages and disadvantages and the Association does not wish to advocate one method in preference to the others. The Association's prime concern is that whatever method is chosen it is applied fairly between the candidates. In some cases, candidates have claimed that their interviews were biased and included questioning on matters which, in fairness, ought not to have concerned the interviewing panel. (This matter is dealt with below where the general theme of discrimination in appointments is considered.)

Concern has been expressed about the role of lay members serving on interviewing panels. The Association recognizes that this is a delicate area since lay members cannot be expected to be versed in interviewing techniques or always distinguish thoroughly the appropriate from the inappropriate question. It may help to avoid these problems if the interviewing panel decides in advance the nature of the questions which are to be put to the candidates.

The Association believes that it is important to keep the size of the interviewing panel to a reasonable size. The size of of the panel should allow for the proper representation of interested parties but overlarge panels should be avoided. (Waitt, 1980, pp. 682–683)

Such advice is based on so-called 'good practice' but does not pretend to have been developed from basic research in the area. For guidance one is obliged to examine evidence outside the sphere of education. We look first at the major issue of the validity and reliability of the interview as an evaluative instrument.

Validity and reliability in the interview

The measure of the effectiveness of any test is that it should be both valid and reliable. *Validity* is the extent to which a test predicts a criterion, the criterion being a measure of some degree of success in performance. In the case of the interview it is important to know the extent to which the information gained there will predict success in the post in question. The interview is often used either without any knowledge or with conflicting evidence about how a particular interview will accurately predict job performance. This begs the question of what is an appropriate criterion, for example immediate success or long-term success at higher levels of responsibility. In other words, do we know what we are looking for in the interview and will the process enable us to successfully ascertain whether the interviewee can achieve the desired end?

Reliability is the extent to which test results are consistent with one another. An indication of reliability is whether a repetition of the test will produce the same result. It follows from the above discussion that if a test is unreliable its validity is bound to be low. Of course, if reliability is high it does not follow that validity will be high; for example, if two interviewers thought that candidates who had beards were desirable for a post this would give high reliability but per se a low validity. The problem of validity and reliability is compounded in the interview (as distinct from a written test) because of the difficulty of precise measurement of situational and personality factors. The wide use of the interview (together with some other measures) suggests that there is widespread optimism about its predictive power, but these expectations are not fully justified if one examines the research literature.

Problems of research

A great difficulty in research in this area arises from the number and complexity of the variables involved. These have been conceptualized by Schmitt (1976) as:

1   Applicant variables such as age, race, sex, physical appearance, educational and employment background, psychological characteristics, expectations and verbal and non-verbal behaviour which may influence the perceptions of the interviewer and influence the result decision.

2   Situational variables, e.g. the political, legal and economic forces operating at the time, the role of the interview in the total selection system and the setting and structure of the interview.

3   Interviewer variables (as for (1) above).

These variables interact in a number of ways to influence subsequent decisions made on selection. Some variables are referred to *en passant* by Stoddart (1978) when he offers a critique of present procedures of selection in further and higher education.

> Little thought appears to be given to what qualities are to be assessed, the conditions under which the assessment is to be made, and the experience and qualifications required by those who are to make the assessment. In addition, little preparatory work is done before the interview; publications are often counted rather than read; references are often taken up at short notice and may not be available at interview; little checking on candidates' experience is done. On the interview day itself, although total man hours spent on the process may be adequate, they are not necessarily effectively deployed. (pp. 6–7)

When researching into the interview the 'qualities' looked for in the interviewee, the 'conditions' for making the assessment and the competence of the interviewing body are too difficult to control, even in test conditions, to enable dependent and independent variables to be established. In spite of the difficulties, most of these variables have been investigated over the years.

A selective review of research

The long history of interview research cannot be examined in detail here, so we have decided to highlight the findings which have relevance to those aspects of the interview that can be improved without insuperable difficulties. The most frequently quoted early study on the employment interview is that by Hollingworth (1922), in which 12 sales managers in the USA who interviewed 57 applicants for a sales job, failed to come anywhere near to agreement on their interview ratings of the salesmen. However, this and other findings do not prove that the interview need be necessarily unreliable because, in this case, experienced sales managers were not necessarily experienced interviewers, there was no clear job specification, little planning for the interview and no system for recording information on which an assessment could be made. Subsequent research has suggested that when such defects are remedied then the degree of unreliability will be reduced, although this does not solve the problem of validity.

Major reviews of the research literature on employment interviewing have been carried out by Wagner (1949), Mayfield (1964), Ulrich and Trumbo (1965), Wright (1969), Schmitt (1976) and Arvey and Campion (1982). Wagner found a dearth of empirical work but concludes that, on the evidence then available, information-gathering at the interview should be seen as part of a quantitative measure; in addition, he found value in candidates performing a number of tasks as part of a package of selection instruments. Mayfield (1964) stressed the importance of a micro-analytical approach, namely a close study of one or two variables which might influence interviewer judgements. In summing up the evidence over the previous 15 years, he gave a number of pointers towards more effective practice: while interview *validity* was low interrater *reliability* could be improved by a more structured approach, because in the unstructured type interviewers tended to talk too much and to make decisions about selection too early. He concluded that interviewers are more influenced by unfavourable, negative information than by favourable, positive information and the way questions were formed influenced the type of answer obtained. Ulrich and Trumbo's (1965) survey came to similar conclusions about the existing evidence on validity and reliability and argued that the interview should be limited to a well-defined purpose, particularly in the area of the assessment of personal relations and career motivation.

Schmitt (1976) has reviewed a number of specific variables and findings affecting interview outcomes. He concludes from the research evidence in the intervening years that:

1 interviewers come to a decision about the candidate probably within the first four minutes of the interview;

2 the impressions formed early in the interview are more important than actual information in influencing judgements;

3 candidates tend to be judged by idealized stereotypes;

4 they attach more importance to negative than to positive information;

5 if interviewers have clear details about the job to be filled interrater reliability is increased;

6 different people give different weight to certain categories of information;

7 non-verbal clues have considerable influence on decision-making;

8 factors such as interviewer attitudes and sexual and racial differences affect candidate assessment;

9 there is a so-called contrast effect whereby individuals are judged by the quality of the previous candidates;

10 experienced interviewers are not more reliable than inexperienced ones, so systematic training is needed with feedback mechanisms built into the selection procedures to enable interviewers to learn from their experience (i.e. to improve reliability).

The most recent review (Arvey and Campion, 1982) draws attention to the contrived experimental designs found in much of the research on the interview, for example the transcripts of interviews and the excessive use of graduates and undergraduates as subjects. They argue for more research on the way the variables of race, age and handicap affect interview outcomes, and for a closer analysis of the perceptual processes which operate during the interview. However, they are encouraged by the increasing evidence that when the interview is confined to 'specific predictions of job behaviour, less distortion is found' (p. 297).

These brief summaries give some indication of the state of the research evidence. Arvey and Campion (1982) conclude their survey by stating that we should now move towards:

> converting the findings and results stemming from research into applied guidelines for interviewers and interviewees. There is a dearth of guidelines and suggestions concerning the improvement of interview effectiveness based on research findings. Instead, many guidelines, suggestions, 'how to interview' workshops, and techniques are founded on intuition, beliefs, and what seems more comfortable, rather than on research results. There need to be greater efforts made to merge research with application in this domain. (p. 137)

In the rest of this chapter I intend to concentrate, in more detail, on a few aspects of the research which point the way forward along the above lines through practicable changes in interview practice, preceded by adequate training programmes in staff selection, appraisal and counselling.

The panel or board interview: its reliability and validity

Research on the interview tends to reinforce scepticism about its validity and reliability although there is some evidence that board interviews may improve the situation. Landy's (1976) extended study of nearly 400 applicants for the police, who were interviewed by a board, suggested that prediction of performance was higher than might have been the case with one-to-one interviews. Anstey (1977), in investigating the working of the Civil Service Selection Board (CSSB) over a period of 30 years, concluded that board interviews had predictive validity in terms of the ultimate ranks reached by the people selected 'particularly at the higher end of the scale' p. 155). However, Anstey goes on to argue that a selection procedure is improved by including a personal interview preparatory to the board interview because it 'makes on average better predictions of personal qualities. A progressive sequence of tests, personal interview, Board interview, makes a pretty efficient selection procedure; not as good, of course, as a fully extended interview procedure like CSSB but considerably better than an unassisted Board interview' (p. 156). Thus the evidence suggests that the use of board interviews is a way of improving the validity and reliability of the interview, probably because the sharing of different perceptions between different interviewers leads to greater awareness of irrelevant data for the post in question.

Observers of selection procedures in further education have argued for the use of board panel interviews. Nicholson (1968, p. 247) supports this procedure but argues that if the panels are poorly selected and untrained the outcomes will be unsatisfactory. Field (1971, p. 76) similarly favours a panel but believes that the interviews should be planned, well conducted and properly assessed; this requires considerable training. What emerges from the research evidence and general experience is that the judgements of several people are preferable to individual judgement in selection. But this does not rule out a number of separate one-to-one or one-to-two interviews, provided that proper comparison can be made between them and that time is given for bringing all the data together. However, the number and combination of people used will have little impact if they have inadequate skills for conducting the interview.

Types of interview

Here we are thinking of the structured, semistructured, unstructured and stress interviews. In the structured type of employment interview a list of questions is prepared in advance, the interviewer(s) seldom deviates from them and there may even be a prearranged sequence of questions. This approach is very restricted because it does not adapt to the individual applicant who may well be inhibited by the experience. In a semistructured interview only basic questions are prepared in advance and there is greater flexibility with the interviewer being left free to probe in areas which seem to need further investigation. The unstructured interview may well involve little preparation apart from drawing up a list of some possible topics to be covered, but while this may allow more freedom for adaptation to the characteristics of different applicants, so-called spontaneity may lead an interviewer into digression, discontinuity and eventual frustration. At the counselling end of the interview continuum, when used by skilled interviewers, an unstructured format may lead to important insights. Research on the employment interview demonstrates a link between structure and reliability and this is not surprising because structure facilitates comparability between candidates (e.g. Carlson et al., 1970).

Another type of interview, on which there is very little research evidence, is the stress interview. Here the format adopted is meant to evaluate an applicant's ability to cope with stress, on the grounds that the candidate will experience stress in his post and ought therefore to be tested before he is appointed. Pressure is purposely applied to the applicant in order to test his responses, for example the rapid firing of questions by a 'hostile' interviewer. But the stress created in an artificial situation is rarely similar to that found in day-to-day work. There is no proof of the validity of this type of interview which, incidentally, can place almost as much stress on the interviewer(s) as on the candidate. Not only are the structure of the interview and the composition of interviewers important, but so are the judgements made during the interview, and it is this aspect which is considered now.

Standards of comparison and the contrast effect

Wexley et al. (1973) have found that the influence of contrast effects is surprisingly tenacious: warnings of the dangers involved and the provision of absolute standards as anchors failed to eliminate the contrast errors in their experiment, and the only successful strategy was the use of intensive workshop experience. In addition to the contrast effect it has been shown that when interviewers evaluated more than one candidate at a time, they did not have an absolute standard; those average candidates whom they considered 'good' had been compared with mediocre ones (Carlson, 1968). The inference from these findings is that the evaluation system should be well standardized with a careful consideration of job and person specifications and a system established for recording data, with appropriate training sessions. These sessions would include practice interviews when well-defined person-specification criteria for selection are agreed upon and the trial candidates are questioned to see the extent to which they meet established criteria *before* making comparisons.

Recall of interview information

A study by Carlson et al. (1971)

> tried to determine how accurately managers can recall what an applicant says during an interview. Prior to the interview the managers were given the interview guide, pencils, and paper, and were told to perform as if *they* were conducting the interview. A 20-minute video tape of a selection interview was played for a group of 40 managers. Following the video tape presentation, the managers were given a 20-question test. All questions were straightforward and factual. Some managers missed none, while some missed as many as 15 out of 20 items. The average number was 10 wrong. In a short 20-minute interview, half the managers could not report accurately on the information produced during the interview! On the other hand, those managers who had been following the interview guide and taking notes were quite accurate on the test; note-taking in conjunction with a guide appears to be essential. (p. 271)

The more important question is of course the extent to which inadequate recall affects interviewer judgement. Carlson et al. found that interviewers with less satisfactory recall rated interviewees more highly and with less variability between them, while the more accurate interviewers rated the interviewees average or below average and with greater variability. The less accurate interviewers appeared to use a 'halo strategy', when one feature possessed by the interviewee becomes a prevailing influence that governs the interviewer's total perception of the interviewee, as when the notion that someone who is attractive and articulate is extended to the assumption that he/she is also intelligent.

It reasonably follows from the evidence that selection decisions based on the interview (and other measures) ought to be made on the basis of good record-keeping during the interview itself – and on weighing up all the evidence, not just the last piece from the interview; but that is a consideration outside this brief.

Non-verbal exchange in interviews

This has been an area of considerable research interest in the USA and Britain. The impression an interviewer forms of a candidate will be related to both verbal and non-verbal exchange at the interview. Keenan (1976) found that the interviewer's style of communication (as seen in head nods, smiling and eye contact) affected the perception of the interviewer and the performance of the candidate. An interviewer's non-verbal style may significantly influence the behaviour of the candidate he is trying to evaluate.

But as Forbes and Jackson (1980) point out, in this and other related studies findings were based on video recordings and judgements made by observers. However, their research into non-verbal behaviour (NVB) used real-life interviews of school-leavers being interviewed by a four-member panel for places on an engineering apprentice training scheme. They discovered that if the interviewer looked a school-leaver in the eye quite often during this job selection interview there was a good chance that the candidate would be selected, and if the interviewer smiled and moved his head around frequently the job was almost guaranteed. They also pointed out that where candidates seem closely matched in intelligence and aptitude (as these subjects were), the role of NVB assumes greater importance. There is some suggestion of 'behavioural echo' in the process; in other words, interviewers make up their minds about a candidate's suitability soon after the start of an interview and then, through their behaviour, transmit either negative or positive reinforcement of their decision. Such findings seem to call for *more uniform* and consistent responses to candidates' answers, both *verbally* and *non-verbally*, otherwise wrong impressions will be given and reacted to by the candidate, which may well influence the decision-making process. Interviewers themselves should be non-judgemental in both their verbal and non-verbal responses.

The character of the interview

The research evidence analysed above has, as we have seen, clear implications for practice, as well as sounding a very cautionary note about over-reliance on interview data. Because of the ambiguity of the evidence, at the very least considerable thought ought to be given to other measures for obtaining information on which to make judgements and to *the use of all that evidence* at the assessment stage. In this way the interview, which invariably comes at the *end* of the selection procedure, does not assume the importance which contiguity to evaluation so often gives it.

Research suggests the value of a closely defined structure and a well-thought-out process when conducting an interview. The aspect of the process which has not really been discussed is the role of *questioning*, because research evidence on questioning in the interview is scant. But there is ample general evidence from research on verbal exchange which shows that the degree and quality of information obtained in communication are dependent on the way questions are phrased and developed. They should be straightforward, unambiguous, open, probing and uncomplicated. Space does not permit an exploration of this most vital aspect of the interview.

Another important inference from the evidence is the desirability of establishing rapport by means of a favourable setting, without distractions or barriers to communication, and a friendly, listening and relaxed interviewer style. But, as we saw in our definition of the interview, it is a conversation directed to some purpose and therefore the interview ought to have clear aims and a structure to achieve these aims. Yates (1975) has identified four phases of the interview: (1) ice-breaking, (2) exploration, (3) detailed development and (4) termination. For phases 2 and 3 a clear strategy needs to be worked out to avoid repetition of questions on the same subject and to ensure that gaps in information are filled. In general candidates should be given every opportunity to display fully their competencies.

Such skills have to be worked upon; but this is a small requirement compared with the magnitude of decisions made in selection, particularly at a time of much decreased staff mobility. Jones and Bracegirdle (1979), in a critical statement on interviewing, bemoan the fact that often too little time and care are taken in selecting people for junior posts in further education.

> It should be emphasised that in many cases an appointment of an L1 is an appointment of someone new to the profession. Once accepted, he may be in the profession for another forty years. This, at today's prices, is a capital investment of approximately £150,000. Would any Authority buy a piece of equipment or undertake a new building, of a similar cost in the same casual way that many appoint an L1 to his or her first post? (p. 197)

I am not suggesting that such a casual approach is commonplace in our colleges, polytechnics and universities, but although evidence of practice has not been fully evaluated there seems a good *prima facie* case for a closer analysis of institutional selection procedures and the role of the interview within them. Field (1971) has done this exercise in relation to his own college and has evolved a series of selection steps which he commends to others:

1   Prepare an adequate job specification.

2   Prepare a person specification setting out the optimum qualifications, experience and other qualities looked for.

3   Attract applicants through the most suitable advertising media.

4   Prepare a shortlist of suitable candidates by the use of a weighting form for grading the information on the application form and letter of application.

5   Pre-interview arrangements consisting of a call to the candidate to attend for interview and an offer to him to meet the head of department (HoD) (in the case of a junior teaching post) before the formal interview; the taking-up of references which ask for *specific* information, a request for notes for a lesson on a part of the syllabus or 'on aspects of course planning, depending on the grade of the post'; the preparation of abstract sheets giving vital information on each candidate and an interview record form for the interviewing panel.

6   Interviewing procedures that start first with a meeting with the HoD while other senior staff assess the notes and make a written assessment. 'The formal interviews are normally held in two parts: the first part is mainly concerned with the candidate's career to date and is usually fairly short. At the end of this part the candidate is given a topic concerned with teaching or administration on which he is expected to talk (for five minutes) when he returns for the second part . . . This is followed by questions on all aspects of the candidate's suitability for the post . . . and the panel is prepared to discuss any relevant questions raised by the candidates' (pp. 53–54).

7   Guidelines for questioning are laid down: questions seeking a 'yes' or 'no' answer should be avoided – the candidate should be allowed to complete his answers to questions; the same basic questions should be asked of each candidate; candidates should not be penalized for failing to give information which has not been asked for; on questions of opinion interviewers must be prepared to accept as valid, answers based on sound arguments although they might be in conflict with their own views.

8   The final assessment.

This example has been outlined at length because it is an attempt to think through the role of the interview(s) in a carefully planned set of procedures (evolved over time through feedback and experiment) and to conduct the interview taking into account *some* of the evidence discussed above. It is not necessarily the most effective or efficient way of proceeding but it demonstrates the outcome of careful planning. Moreover, staff are trained in the techniques involved in the selection of staff and particularly in successful interviewing. Besides exercises constructing a job and person specifications, the preparation and completion of weighting forms, the assessment of letters and forms of application, they carry out mock interviews designed at 'rationalizing interview techniques' (Field, 1971, p. 51). The case presented in this chapter is that it is, to say the least, unsatisfactory for managers in education to ignore the existing empirical evidence on selection interviewing when they seek to appoint staff, and the application of this evidence to appraisal and counselling interviews. In practice, interviewing in educational management sometimes lacks professionalism, but this *can* be improved by a careful examination of the evidence, analysis of each particular interviewing procedure and continued attempts at improvement.[1]

Notes

I should like to thank the editors for their constructive criticism in the course of preparing this paper.

1 For further analysis of the techniques of interviewing see Riches, C.R. (forthcoming) *Developing Interviewing Skills in Education*. London, Croom Helm.

References

Anstey, E. (1977) A 30-year follow up of the CSSB procedures with lessons for the future. *Journal of Occupational Psychology*, vol. 50, pp. 149–159.

Arvey, R.D. and Campion, J.E. (1982) The employment interview: a summary and review of recent research. *Personal Psychology*, vol. 35, pp. 281–322.

Bradley, J. and Silverleaf, J. (1979) *Making the Grade; Careers in FE Teaching*. Windsor, NFER.

Carlson, R.E. (1968) Selection interview decisions: the effect of mode of applicant presentation in some outcome measures. *Personnel Psychology*, vol. 21, pp. 193–207.

Carlson, R.E., Schwab, D.P. and Henneman, H.G. (1970) Agreement among selection interview styles. *Journal of Industrial Psychology*, vol. 5, no. 1, pp. 8–17.

Carlson, R.E., Thayer, P.W., Mayfield, F.C. and Peterson, D.E. (1971) Improvement in the selection interview. *Personnel Journal*, vol. 60, pp. 268–275, 317.

Ferguson, S. (1979) The outmoded ritual we call teacher selection. *Education*, 25 May 1979.

Field, B.R. (1971) *The Development of Selection Procedures for Full-time Teaching Staff Within a Technical College*. Thesis for the Fellowship of the College of Preceptors (unpublished).

Forbes, R.J. and Jackson, P.R. (1980) Non-verbal behaviour and the outcome of selection interviews. *Journal of Occupational Psychology*, vol. 53, pp. 65–72.

Hilsum, S. and Start, K.B. (1974) *Promotion and Careers in Teaching*. Windsor, NFER.

Hollingworth, H.L. (1922) *Judging Human Character*. New York, Appleton-Century-Crofts.

Jones, P. and Bracegirdle, B. (1979) Appointing lecturers. *Education*, 24 August 1979.

Keenan, A. (1976) Effects of the non-verbal behaviour of interviewers on candidates' performance. *Journal of Occupational Psychology*, vol. 49, pp. 171–176.

Landy, F.J. (1976) Validity of the interview in police officer selection. *Journal of Applied Psychology*, vol. 61, pp. 193–198.

Mayfield, E.C. (1964) The selection interview: a revaluation of published research. *Personnel Psychology*, vol. 17, pp. 239–260.

Morgan, C. and Hall, V. (1982) The POST Project: What is the job of the secondary school head? *Education*, 18 June 1982.

Morris, G. (1982) Week by week. *Education*, 8 January 1982, p. 19.

Nicholson, S. (1968) *The Application of Management Principles to the Internal Administration of Technical Colleges*. MSc thesis, University of Salford (unpublished).

Randell, G.A. (1975) Staff appraisal and development through interviewing. *Training Officer*, June, pp. 166–169.

Schmitt, N. (1976) Social and situational determinants of interview decisions: Implications for the employment interview. *Personnel Psychology*, vol. 29, pp. 79–101.

Stoddart, J. (1978) *The Recruitment and Selection of Teaching Staff*. London, NATFHE.

Ulrich, L. and Trumbo, D. (1965) The selection interview since 1949. *Psychological Bulletin*, vol. 63, pp. 100–116.

Wagner, R. (1949) The employment interview: a critical summary. *Personnel Psychology*, vol. 2, pp. 17–46.

Waitt, I. (ed.) (1980) *College Administration*. London, NATFHE.

Wexley, K.N., Sanders, R.E. and Yukl, G.A. (1973) Training interviews to eliminate contrast effects in employment interviews. *Journal of Applied Psychology*, vol. 57, no. 3, pp. 193–207.

Wright, O.R. Jr (1969) Summary of research on the selection interview since 1964.

Personnel Psychology, vol. 35, pp. 281–322.

Yates, T. (1975) Interviewing . . . foundation of fact finding. *Systems Management*, October, pp. 14–16.

CHAPTER 6.5

PROBLEMS OF INSTITUTIONAL MANAGEMENT IN A PERIOD OF CONTRACTION*
TOM BONE

The management of educational institutions in a time of contraction, along with the tensions which accompany this, is a subject which has attracted a good deal of attention in recent years (e.g. Morris, 1980) and may expect to be of continuing interest throughout much of the 1980s because of the falling rolls which will be affecting first schools and then colleges and universities throughout that period. This chapter is written from the perspective of the head of an institution of higher education in the United Kingdom, and is based partly on personal experience within that institution, and partly on more general experience derived from membership of the Education Committee of the Council for National Academic Awards, which has given the author the opportunity to become acquainted with institutional problems in many other parts of Britain. An attempt has been made to relate that experience to some of the writing on the subject.

In a number of instances throughout the United Kingdom, although not in the author's own, the basic problem for management in the past year or two has been that of the survival of the institution as falling student numbers have brought its viability into question. Such a situation creates exceptional pressures both on an institution and within it and there are some effects which may be beneficial, like the sense of corporate unity which is engendered, but the position is so unusual and normally so brief in its duration that it has little to offer others not similarly placed. [. . .]

A much more common position however, indeed one that is becoming almost the norm, is that in which an institution is able to survive but finds

* The Management of Educational Institutions. Theory, Research and Consultancy, edited by H.L. Gray. Falmer Press, 1982, pp. 263–283. Dr T.R. Bone is Principal of Jordanhill College of Education, Glasgow.

that its resources are contracting because of a decline in student numbers and income. Sometimes there is direct pressure for the reduction of staff. What happens then is that there has to be consideration given to the reduction in the number of academic and non-academic staff employed, and it is the group of problems associated with that reduction which is the first to be given some detailed treatment in this chapter.

Before any reduction in staffing actually takes place there is usually a period in which attempts are made to avoid this and, while there may typically be some people in the organization who simply hope that the problem will go away, there are possibilities for constructive planning at this stage which may be beneficial to the institution and to the community it serves, as well as to the individuals whose jobs may be saved. In the author's experience there are three steps that may well be taken, two of which will probably be ineffective and one which may in fact be useful. The first step, which is perfectly natural but which will probably fail, is that both the management of the institution and the leaders of the staff unions will argue for some change in the basis for the calculation for staff entitlement so that the funding body will allow more staff to be employed for any given number of students. Often good arguments will be put forward for this, but the case should have been pressed at a time of more generous treatment, and it is likely that in times of financial stringency governments will not accept it. They are seeking to make cuts in public expenditure, and a reduction in student numbers seems to offer them a legitimate means of doing so (Bone, 1980).

The other technique, which will be even more certain of failure, is to avoid reducing staff by cutting expenditure in other ways – for example by making savings on equipment, the maintenance of buildings, departmental expenses, etc. This fails simply because it does not save enough, and because any savings that are made are likely to be totally offset by consequent necessary expenditure in future.

The one constructive step that may be taken at this stage, before staff are actually lost, is that attempts can be made to diversify the service provided, or to make use of staff in ways that have always been justified but which have not been happening in more comfortable times. In England and Wales the colleges of education were encouraged by the James Report (DES, 1972a) and by the DES (1972b, 1973) to develop DipHE courses of a general kind, and did so in the mid-1970s with varying success (Lynch, 1979). The Scottish colleges of education were able between 1977 and 1980 to preserve the posts of 214 academic staff across the system by a major movement into school-focused in-service training of teachers, and in the author's own college further posts were saved by a significant expansion of externally funded research, as well as by the attraction of students from overseas countries whose governments were prepared to pay for special courses. All of these things required members of the staff to move into new forms of work, and made demands upon them which might not have been so readily accepted in another climate, but in the situation which existed at that time there was an energetic and enthusiastic response. A significant number of staff, for example, were willing to go away from their own homes for periods of as long as a year to acquire new qualifications and expertise.

Yet there are limits to the possibilities of diversification, and it is unlikely to do more than ease the problem. Any institution worthy to have been there in the first place will not have totally neglected all its opportunities for interesting work and, when it begins to widen its field of activity, it is likely quite quickly to encounter the sphere of influence of some other institution. In the United Kingdom the colleges of education, which have thus far suffered more than any others in respect of declining rolls, have often found that their attempts to diversify have brought them into conflict with the colleges of further education and the polytechnics, which in the 1960s and 1970s had expanded their work to cover most of the areas in question. Indeed for the principals of many of the English colleges, caught between the conflicting demands of the Department of Education and Science and neighbouring universities or the CNAA, and with the psychological stresses arising from the attempt to keep as many options open as possible, the process of diversification proved a particularly exhausting one (Shaw, 1978).

Quite quickly there will come an acceptance of the need to reduce the numbers of staff, and there are three normal ways of doing this. The first is to make use of natural wastage by not filling the posts which become vacant as people die, retire and move away to other fields. This will be accepted by the staff in general, as doing least harm to any individual within the institution, but by itself it is inadequate and unsatisfactory as a method for dealing with the problem. It is inadequate because it is slow and because there are not enough people who leave at such a time (partly because promotion opportunities are becoming less available elsewhere), and it will only work in places where the decline in numbers is occurring very gradually, like some secondary schools. It is unsatisfactory because it is so unpredictable, and because it produces imbalances within the general pattern of staffing. Deaths and retirements tend to occur in a random way which may spread themselves evenly across an institution over a lengthy period, but which certainly do not do so in the short term, and promotions to posts elsewhere are more likely to be available to some kinds of staff than to others. For example, those involved in such fields as physics and mathematics, if they are good, will continue to be mobile, but those who teach in such areas as art, music, drama, physical education, etc. are likely to be less so, while in recent years those who have taught history, geography, economics, etc. have had very few prospects at all. The result is that reliance upon natural wastage is likely to lead to too many staff in certain areas, and too few in others, and it is in the areas with most staff that there will probably be the greatest decline in student numbers. That certainly has been the case in teacher training. If this is allowed to continue without any check, it will be very damaging to morale among the staff in general.

There is, therefore, almost always a move to supplement natural wastage by a process of early retirement or voluntary redundancy, with both assisted by financial treatment more generous than the usual. Contrary to what might have been our expectation some years ago, this is not always inadequate, but experience suggests that it is still unsatisfactory. It is not always inadequate because a surprising number of members of staff are likely to opt for redundancy if the financial settlement is sufficiently generous, especially if the process is not rushed and there is time for those who are more cautious to wait to see how things turn out for their colleagues. It is not simply those who are approaching retirement who will choose to go, for experience shows that there are many, especially married women in their late forties and early fifties, who have been working partly for satisfaction but also partly for money and who will find the financial settlement more attractive than the prospect of continuing to work until they are sufficiently old to secure the normal pension. In the Scottish colleges of education nearly 400 staff, out of a total of around 1400, chose voluntary redundancy between 1978 and 1980 (under the Grant Aided Colleges (Compensation) (Scotland) Regulations of 1977).

Yet even if the voluntary process proves numerically adequate, it will be attended by serious disadvantages, especially for the management of the institution. Like natural wastage it will not affect all departments similarly and, if all volunteers were accepted, there would be both general imbalance and a loss of staff in fields where they could not readily be spared. The management will have to refuse some volunteers, and great care will have to be taken if this is not to antagonize the unions and staff in a damaging way. That point will be taken up in a later paragraph. Even if that problem is avoided, there is another aspect which will be just as serious. Inevitably the voluntary redundancy terms will attract some of the senior staff, including heads of department and key personnel, and it will be difficult for the management to replace these persons from within the institution without loss. Normally it will be possible, where good relationships exist, for the staff unions to be persuaded that a lecturer in mathematics cannot be released because his department is not overstaffed but, if it is clear that the department of history is overstaffed and the head of that department seeks redundancy, it is too much to hope that the staff unions will accept that no one else within that department is fit to assume his position. Yet that could be the case. The result is that voluntary redundancy will produce too many internal promotions and the institution will suffer from this, as is indicated more fully later.

In this position there is another alternative, that of forced redundancy, and this is likely to be considered both by the funding body or government and by the management of the institution. It is frequently employed in industry and commerce, and there is no obvious reason why education should be exempt from it. If it is used it may have the merit of being quick, and it can be effective in tackling specific problems – for example, cuts can be made where they are felt to be most necessary instead of being left to the random working of natural wastage or voluntary redundancy, and it may be possible for the institution to shed those persons who are regarded by management as being least effective, so that the staff is reduced to the desired level with the minimum damage to the college's work. The power of unions is so strong today, however, that it may be over-optimistic to count on this happening, and even when compulsory redundancy is employed it is possible that some formula may have to be agreed which will result in the candidates for redundancy being selected on criteria other than the effectiveness of their contribution. 'Last in, first out' may not always be insisted on, but it is a phrase which represents a typical union attitude, and it is simply not to be expected that unions will readily agree to any system which distinguishes among workers on the basis of such factors as energy, intelligence or application to duties. Thus even compulsory redundancy may not result in the best solution from the point of view of management.

The main objection to compulsory redundancy, however, is concerned with its side-effects, which cannot all be predicted and which usually are harmful to the institution. Redundancy of a forced kind is always accompanied by fear, suspicion and tension, and is very damaging to the morale of the staff. Perhaps if one quick cut was all that was necessary the fear and suspicion would not be long-lasting, and the tension would gradually evaporate, but even in industry staff reductions are rarely effected on a necessary scale at one blow and, in education, where student numbers tend to fall annually for a period, it is almost impossible that this could happen. Any prolonged period of fear and suspicion will be thoroughly damaging, and will result in the working behaviour of staff regressing to a kind which is entirely motivated by a need for security rather than by professional thinking. To take only one example, it will become very difficult to secure agreement to any changes in courses, regardless of how desirable these may be, since any member of staff who agrees to a lower teaching commitment will automatically have increased the likelihood of being selected for redundancy.

There is, therefore, no way of reducing staff which will not produce problems for management, and in education what will happen in most cases is that there will be a dependence on a combination of natural wastage and voluntary redundancy, with an attempt being made to minimize the worst effects of the latter. If forced redundancy is employed, it will probably only be in specific and very limited areas. In the author's experience, however, based upon what he has seen in a number of colleges of education in the United Kingdom, the same basic methods of tackling the problem can produce very different results, depending upon the ways in which they are implemented. In his view there are certain management tools which are essential if the damage to the institution is not to be so great that it ceases to carry out its basic functions effectively.

The first of these tools is the employment of a regular and effective system of communication with the staff in general (Fielden and Lockwood, 1973). What individual members of that staff find hardest to bear is uncertainty, and it is vital that they should be kept informed as accurately and as fully as possible of what is happening. It is the task of management to do this, and it is unwise to delegate something so important to any other group such as a union, which may view the matter from a different point of view. As is well known, over-communicators are ineffective communicators in that people cease to listen to what they are saying, but there are few who are uninterested in matters affecting themselves, and in a redundancy situation, it is a more serious mistake to communicate too little than too much. Naturally, it is best if a variety of methods can be employed, and if the people doing it are personally good at it. Those in senior positions in education ought to be. What certainly must be avoided is the encouragement of any small clique of people who know what is going to happen before others do and who take pleasure in dropping hints of their knowledge.

If the management communicates regularly with the whole staff, it must also, however, have an effective system of consultation with the unions, and in a time of redundancy this will probably have to be quite formal. In the United Kingdom the law (Employment Protection Consolidation Act 1978) actually requires consultation with the unions on this matter, but in countries where that is not the case it is nevertheless desirable. The author found it helpful that, in his own college some years before student rolls ever began to fall, he had taken the initiative in establishing a joint management/union committee, based upon a procedural agreement whereby all decisions affecting the conditions of service of staff collectively had to be the subject of consultation before they could be implemented. Over a period of several years this system had come to work fairly well, and a relationship of some trust had been built up, which was to be of great value in the period of most severe contraction.

[. . .]

A process of steady retraction in any institution is inevitably accompanied by a decrease in the recruitment of new blood, and over a period of some years this becomes increasingly serious. In higher education it is essential that there is a steady flow into universities and colleges of people who have recently been working at the frontiers of their subjects (Blau, 1974). In a university department of mathematics or physics, for example, it is common to find that people do their best work when they are relatively young, while in a teacher training institution it is vital that there is a regular supply of people who have themselves recently been facing the problems of teachers in ordinary classrooms and in ordinary schools. When the supply of such people begins to dry up it may be hardly noticed at first, especially if the institution is then preoccupied by what appear more serious difficulties, but the effects will show fairly soon and they may last for a long time (Hirsch and Morgan, 1978). At the very worst (and the author has not yet seen this happen, since contraction is still a relatively fresh phenomenon in the UK) an institution could lose its natural authority, in that it might cease to have a sufficient number of people with personal experience of what they are teaching others about.

The problem is seen most clearly when too many internal promotions take place. As already explained, the combination of natural wastage and voluntary redundancy will almost certainly take a greater toll among the senior staff than among the junior, and there will be a higher than usual incidence of heads of department posts becoming vacant. Although everyone will recognize that these should be advertised nationally, this will probably not happen – partly because the institution is overstaffed and the funding body cannot agree to the rejection of any opportunity to reduce that problem, and partly because staff in the institution (and the union) will oppose any external recruitment which might increase the danger of existing staff being made redundant in a compulsory way. So with regrets the management will advertise such posts within the institution alone, and will have to take the best person that can be found there. Often this will be a good person, one who in many ways is suitable for the post, or who would be suitable for appointment to a similar post in another institution. But if he has worked in the department for a number of years, the changes which he will wish to make will tend to be relatively small and, although of course there are exceptions to this, it is unlikely that he will adopt any radical policies which will be unsettling to all his colleagues. If several such appointments have to be made at one time, the disadvantages will hardly be noticed, indeed it will appear that everything is going very smoothly, but a price is being paid in terms of the institution's development which may well be serious, and the current managers could be taking steps which their successors will regret in the future.

Staff development is important in any institution at any time, but in a period of contraction it becomes even more so. The lack of fresh blood and the probable spate of internal promotions make it essential that there be a deliberate and systematic plan designed to strengthen the experience and qualifications of those who are going to remain in the institution for some time to come. This is widely recognized and any external body looking at the quality of an institution, not only in its current work but in its plans for the years ahead, will certainly wish to examine its staff development programme. In the United Kingdom the Council for National Academic Awards has placed considerable emphasis on this (CNAA, 1974, Section 9) in its institutional reviews and has looked for a strong programme of this kind in the polytechnics and colleges which teach for its degrees. It has not merely been a matter of seeing that some individual lecturers have gained the qualifications and experience necessary to undertake new tasks, but rather the emphasis has been placed on the existence of an environment in which the continuing education of staff is seen as important. Institutions which in recent years have proclaimed and supported the call for recurrent, lifelong education for others, should certainly be able to show that they believe in this to the extent of putting it into practice themselves.

There is an extensive literature devoted to staff development (e.g. Piper and Glatter, 1977; Greenway and Harding, 1978; Teather, 1979), and attention is being paid here only to the ways in which it may be encouraged in a time of contraction. It is assumed that the idea of staff development is in no way new to the institution, and that it has always been common for some staff to be engaged in study designed to raise their qualifications through masters' or doctors' degrees etc., that there have always been some staff who are engaged in research, that many have contributed to and attended conferences, that some have gone back for periods of development work in the field with which their teaching is concerned, and that some have served on national committees, working parties, etc. The first danger in a time of contraction is that arguments may be presented for the curtailment of these activities on two grounds, one being that if reductions in expenditure have to be made, they can most simply be made by reducing attendance at conferences etc., and the other being that the institution must devote all its resources to activities which earn staff. And thus, for example, it could be argued that in a teacher training college the provision of in-service courses for others, which counts towards the staff entitlement, should be supported by staff even to the exclusion of the raising of their own qualifications or membership of national committees. Both these arguments are fallacious. There can justifiably be a reduction in the support for some of the peripheral conferences which grow up in times of expansion, and whose benefits are almost entirely social (although there is some value to institutions in that too), but even if the total budget has been cut and financial restraints are necessary, in a time of contraction it is still important to encourage staff to raise their personal qualifications and widen their experience. Fees for attendance at courses elsewhere should still be paid, and other forms of financial support should also be considered. The suggestion that the institution should concentrate all its activities on teaching others so that it earns the maximum number of staff must be firmly repudiated, since it has no right to set out to teach others unless it continues to be a learning environment itself.

Most people would accept that statement, but since contraction is accompanied by fears, suspicions and tensions, it is too much to hope that there will not be some lecturers who will not resent having to carry the burden of teaching work while they see their colleagues going off to courses and conferences, especially if it is suspected that this will enhance the likelihood of their colleagues being promoted at a later stage. For this reason it is important that the matter be discussed openly within the institution, and that decisions as to which individuals should receive the financial support for courses etc., should be taken by a group which includes representatives of staff interests. In times of expansion it will probably have been left to a member of the management team, without anyone caring very much about it because any reputable cause has always been supported, and management could well wish to hold on to this power when contraction comes, in that it helps to control an element of expenditure at a difficult time, but this is a mistake. The element of patronage which has always existed in such matters will now be perceived and resented, and although the management will be suffering from a loss of power in a number of ways, as will be discussed more fully later, it should be prepared to give up some of this, retaining only that share which is the legitimate interest of the financial guardians.

[. . .] Sabbatical leave may pose particular problems. The institution will probably have had a policy of granting such leave in the past, with conditions relating to length of service and worthiness of intention, and probably in the past it will have been open to any member of staff who could meet these conditions. When contraction occurs a stage will arise in which some departments will have lost so many staff that they are genuinely unable to allow anyone to be away for a lengthy period, while other departments will have a surplus which would make this comparatively easy. The other problem is that the fear of compulsory redundancy will probably remain in the background for some time, and individuals may be afraid to ask for leave in case this shows that they can readily be done without, and therefore may be making themselves prime targets for that redundancy. What the author has found himself, and has indeed observed elsewhere, is that applications for sabbatical leave tended to dry up, and this has been in some ways convenient for the institution's management, but if it were to continue too long it would represent a serious diminution in staff development, taking away the longest periods available for uninterrupted refreshment of experience.

[. . .]

The most important need for staff development, however, may not be at the grade of ordinary lecturers, but rather at that of head of department, for two reasons. The first is that conditions both inside and outside the college will be changing very rapidly; the second is that, as has already been explained, there is likely to be an unduly high incidence of internal promotion to head of department posts. If the departments have a fairly high degree of autonomy in the institution, as is very common in higher education, then a head of department who is not responsive to changing conditions, or who wishes simply to keep matters ticking over in a routine way, can impose a very serious brake on progress. It is essential that all heads of department should continue to have opportunities to develop themselves and to be placed in situations which will encourage creative and constructive thinking.

Such opportunities can sometimes be provided by experience away from the person's own institution, and an attempt should be made to ensure that as many as possible gain from this. All too often there are a few heads of department in an institution who have a national reputation and who are invited to participate in all sorts of external bodies and committees, while the remainder receive little experience of this kind. The management of the institution does not have the power to issue these invitations, but should do what it can to see that the opportunities go round as far as possible. It is especially important that those newly appointed to the head of department posts should be found the chance to widen their vision and understanding.

Probably the best single experience of this kind available throughout the United Kingdom in recent years has been that of serving the Council for National Academic Awards through membership of one of its committees, panels or boards. These take their members to visit other institutions for consideration of the validation of new course proposals or for the review of the working of whole institutions, and both of these situations, while very demanding on the membership of the visiting parties if they are doing their job well, provide almost unrivalled opportunities for gaining fresh experience, understanding and insights. The members are taken away from the restraints of their own institutions and placed in a situation which is not simulated but real, in which they can learn a great deal from both the senior members of the visiting party and from the institution being visited. They have to test their skills and their ideas against those of their peers, and few members would deny that their early experiences in serving such visiting parties have been of considerable benefit to them personally. The institutions being visited do not suffer, since the Council's officers and the senior members of the party will ensure that undue weight is not given to the views of those who are still in the process of being bloodied, and this form of association with the CNAA is something that is highly valued. Institutions receive opportunities to nominate members of the committees, panels and boards every four years, and of course the number who go from any college is fairly limited, but across the country the CNAA involves more than 1000 people in its work, and this has been of great benefit to the higher education system (CNAA, 1979).

[. . .]

Outside the institution there are many other useful, if less prestigious, forms of staff development available. Whatever the financial difficulties of the time, it is worth while to see that heads of department, especially new heads of department, attend important conferences, are placed on local working parties and committees, and find themselves where it is likely that they will have to discuss their ideas with others engaged in similar and related work. It is particularly important that they are kept conscious of the views of the professions for which they are training future members.

The best forms of staff development take place within the institution itself, and they tend to be associated with the practice of participative management. They are therefore side-effects of something which is introduced for its own and even more important purposes – purposes with which this chapter now goes on to deal – but side-effects are very helpful too.

Education as a whole has been slower to adopt the participative style of management than has industry, probably because failure to achieve objectives in education generally has less calamitous results for the managers, and a relatively old-fashioned style of authoritarian leadership remains not unknown in many schools. In higher education, however, there has been a quite distinct and widespread movement towards the location of control in the hands of academic boards and committees, partly because of external pressure (as through the Weaver Report (DES, 1966) and the work of the CNAA in England and Wales) and partly through internal pressure from academic unions and from the institution's own social scientists. There also has been considerable influence exerted, especially in the United States and in Canada, through the courses in educational administration which are commonly taken by those who aspire to promoted posts, and gradually this is having its effect on the schools sector too.

The basic concept of participative management is that an organization will be more effective, in the sense of achieving its goals, when the work groups most affected by the consequences of any decisions which are required are actively involved in making those decisions. The approach is a direct application of the motivation theories and social systems theory of the 1950s, 1960s and 1970s, especially as these were expressed in the writings of Kurt Lewin (1947), Abraham Maslow (1954), Douglas McGregor (1960) and Frederick Herzberg (1966). Although later writers have found weaknesses in Herzberg's two-factor theory of motivation, and there has been a movement towards the more sophisticated expectancy theory as formulated by Vroom (1964) and others, so that it is now recognized as necessary to individualize the incentive system to satisfy the varying needs of employees, it is still generally accepted that the organization will be more effective if workers can be given the opportunity to participate in making the decisions on what they themselves will have to do. And while McGregor's theory X/theory Y is an oversimplification which has been shown even by some of its supporters (e.g. Maslow, 1965) to have limitations in application, it has nevertheless been the most powerful single contribution to the movement away from paternalistic control and towards the sharing of power.

The most obvious feature of participative management is that decisions are generally taken in boards and committees, and there is nothing particularly new in this even in education, where universities have had their senates for a very long time. Nevertheless the role of the president or principal has perceptibly changed in the past 20 years or so and, in smaller institutions of higher education where the influence of one individual tended in the past to be greater, the position and stature of academic committees have certainly grown. Although the legal position varies, and there are places where academic boards are still in theory advisory, in practice all major academic decisions, along with the responsibility for academic standards in the institution, lie with the academic board, which normally has a system of subcommittees which give an opportunity for a large number of academic staff to play a part in the process. Strong support for this position is provided by the Council for National Academic Awards, which validates degree courses in most polytechnics and colleges in the United Kingdom, since this is one of the 'minimum requirements' for the award of degrees:

> The Council believes that advanced work can only flourish in an institution which has made considerable progress towards becoming an academic community within the sphere of advanced further and higher education. Normally this can only be achieved if there are opportunities for the staff and student body to participate in the formation of academic policy, in the determination of priorities as between the various activities in the institution, and in the other major issues, which are likely to arise. (CNAA, 1974)

The arguments for such devolution of power within an institution are strong, and provided that it has not been carried to excessive lengths (as is rumoured to have happened in some institutions in North America) those who have experience of a change in this direction would not readily return to the previous position. This is true of the managers as well as of the teaching staff, for there are positive advantages for them too. When problems are being tackled, more minds are brought to bear on them and it is helpful to have the views of those who are nearer to the situation and have more immediate experience of it. There is more likelihood of fresh ideas, and communication throughout the whole of the staff is enhanced as more have first-hand knowledge of what is happening. Since authority lies in a body on which everyone has either membership or representation, it is less remote and less likely to be misunderstood. If members of the teaching staff are involved in looking at the whole of a problem rather than only at their own little piece of it, they are more likely to share in contributing to the common good, and interdepartmental cooperation becomes more probable. Most important of all, when a much larger proportion of the academic community is involved in making a decision, there come to be far more people committed to making that decision work.

[. . .]

References

Blau, P.M. (1974) *The Organization of Academic Work*. New York, Wiley, ch. 4.

Bone, T.R. (1980) Current trends in initial training. In: Hoyle, E. and Megarry, J. (1980).

Council for National Academic Awards (CNAA) (1974) *Regulations and Conditions for the Award of the Council's First Degrees*. London, CNAA.

Council for National Academic Awards (1979) *The Council: Its Place in British Higher Education*. London, CNAA.

Department of Education and Science (DES) (1966) *The Government of Colleges of Education* (the Weaver Report). London, HMSO.

Department of Education and Science (DES) (1972a) *Teacher Education and Training* (the James Report). London, HMSO.

Department of Education and Science (DES) (1972b) *White Paper, A Framework for Growth*. London, HMSO.

Department of Education and Science (DES) (1973) *Development of Higher Education on the Non-University Sector*. Circular 7/73. London, HMSO.

Fielden, J. and Lockwood, G. (1973) *Planning and Management in Universities*. London, Chatto and Windus, ch. 7.

Greenway, H. and Harding, A.G. (1978) *The Growth of Policies for Staff Development*. Research into Higher Education, Monograph No. 34, University of Surrey.

Herzberg, F. (1966) *Work and The Nature of Man*. Cleveland, World Publishing Company.

Hirsch, W. and Morgan, R. (1978) Career prospects in British universities. *Higher Education*, vol. 7.

Hoyle, E. and Megarry, J. (1980) *The Professional Development of Teachers*. The World Yearbook of Education. London, Kogan Page.

Lewin, K. (1947) Frontiers in group dynamics. *Human Relations*, vol. 1, no. 5.

Lynch, J. (1979) *The Reform of Teacher Education in the United Kingdom*. Guildford, Society for Research into Higher Education.

Maslow, A.H. (1954) *Motivation and Personality*. New York, Harper & Row.

Maslow, A.H. (1965) *Eupsychian Management*. Homewood, Ill., Irwin.

McGregor, D. (1960) *The Human Side of Enterprise*. New York, McGraw-Hill.

Morris, J. (1980) *Management, Stress and Contraction*. Sheffield, Association of Colleges for Further and Higher Education.

Piper, D.W. and Glatter, R. (1977) *The Changing University*. Slough, National Foundation for Educational Research.

Shaw, K.E. (1978) Contraction and mergers of United Kingdom colleges of education: Some logistic comments. *The Journal of Educational Administration*, vol. 16, no. 2. Armidale, NSW, Australia.

Teather, D.C.B. (1979) *Staff Development in Higher Education, an International Review*. New York, Kogan Page.

Vroom, V. (1964) *Work and Motivation*. New York, Wiley.

CHAPTER 6.6

PROFESSIONALS AND REDUNDANCY*
DEREK PORTWOOD

Of the many implications of the recent reorganization of the colleges of
education (see, for example, Hencke, 1978), one of the most significant is
that the college lecturers have set a precedent in the occupational sphere.
This is because they are the first professional group to have experienced (as
a group) the kind of reorganization which involves not only redeployment
but also large-scale redundancy. From a peak of 10,800 in 1974, their
numbers have been cut by at least one-third. One consequence has been
their change of status from a separate profession to a segment of a larger
professional grouping.[1] Another consequence, and this is where the interest
of this article lies, is that they could be proto-typical and in some respects
ideal-typical for professionals in the future, especially in respect of what is
happening to professional careers.[2]

Clearly this is a broad subject, and this article will focus only on what
happened to the careers of individual lecturers from their point of view.
Indeed, it is even more restricted, because their experience depended
heavily on what happened to their own colleges and this took a variety of
forms. The most extreme of these was closure,[3] but even this was of diverse
kinds, depending largely on the extent of 'outside' help offered to redundant staff. Thus, in order to obtain as comprehensive and extreme form of
professional redundancy as possible, a college was chosen for study which
was not only closed against its wishes but received neither support for its
survival[4] nor any offers of, or any assistance in finding, alternative employment for its staff. In every sense, these lecturers were on their own.

The question, then, was what happened to their careers in this situation?

* *Journal of Further and Higher Education*, 1980, vol. 4, no. 3, pp. 3–19. Derek Portwood is a
Senior Lecturer in Sociology at Wolverhampton Polytechnic.

From their side, this involved the perceptions they formed, the policies they adopted and the actions they took. More generally, it was a question of control. Plainly they were experiencing involuntary change, but were there different forms and extents of involuntariness? The theme of this article will be that redundancy for these professionals was differentially viewed and handled by them largely on the basis of career contingencies and professional commitment, which themselves were strongly affected by the lecturers' career histories.

The study itself was in the first instance part of a PhD research project on involuntary change in professional careers, which spanned 1973–1979. Most of the data for these lecturers, however, were gathered from (late) 1975 to (late) 1978 during numerous and lengthy visits to the college and to the lecturers' 'new' places of work. Research techniques included document analysis,[5] observation,[6] but primarily interviewing of a loosely structured kind and on a sequential basis. Forty-seven of the 54 staff[7] were interviewed in this way (for an analysis of the college staff, excluding the principal and vice-principal, see *Table* 13). To organize and analyse the data, I adopted a case history approach and found Glaser and Strauss's (1971) concept of status passage particularly helpful.

Clearly this article, therefore, can give only a limited view and appraisal of what happens when professionals face redundancy. This must be so, even for the college of education lecturers themselves. Nonetheless, its contribution to the subject is on the grounds of its intensive study of a *physical unit* of a profession (for professionals, this is frequently their meaningful grouping) as well as its humanistic emphasis. Thus, it seeks to describe and analyse what professionals actually thought and did (general statistical analyses omit this crucial aspect of experience). As such, it can at least contribute towards the construction of a model of the structure of control of change in professional careers as well as provide information and suggestions for other professionals who face redundancy.

In order to explore these matters I will approach the subject, first, by giving background information on the college's development and struggle for survival and I will draw out the implications which this held for the lecturers' view of their work situation and careers; secondly, I will describe and analyse their decisions and actions following the announcement of the closure of the college, mainly in order to classify their career destinations and to chart the consequences of their career policies, but also to examine the utility and validity of other analyses of how workers face redundancy; finally, I will note and comment on the practical application of this research.

Table 13 Analysis of staff, August 1975

Age grouping	Education department												Academic subject department												Total	No. interviewed
	Graduate						Non-graduate						Graduate						Non-graduate							
	Men			Women			Men			Women			Men			Women			Men			Women				
	L2	SL	PL	L2	SL	PL	L2	SL	PL	L2	SL	PL	L2	SL	PL	L2	SL	PL	L2	SL	PL	L2	SL	PL		
Under 40	2	1		2	1	1							4	8	1	3	1		1			1			22	21
40–49				2	1	1				1			7	2	1	1	1		4						20	18
50–54							1			1			2			1			1						6	5
55 and over													3						1						4	1
TOTAL	2	1	2	1	1	1	1			1	1		4	15	8	4	3		1	6		1			52	
No. interviewed	2	1	2	1			1			1	1		4	15	5	4	2		1	4		1				45

The history of the college and the lecturers' careers

The college was one of the first to be founded in England in the mid-nineteenth century. It was situated in the suburbs of a large city, where it became hemmed in with industrial development and high-density, low-grade housing. Styled on Oxbridge colleges with enclosed trees and lawns, the college boasted the only open space for miles. The site encouraged isolationist attitudes, even as its voluntary status gave it legal autonomy. Such dispositions, combined with physical and financial constraints, held back its growth (it did not exceed 250 students until the mid-1960s). On the other hand, its local independence fostered aspirations to be regarded as a national college. The combination of these factors resulted in the college letting several (locally generated) opportunities for expansion slip by. It was not until the late 1960s, when various policy changes took place (e.g. the admission of women students) and a new principal arrived, that a rapid development in the size of the college occurred. Ingenious means were then found to squeeze new buildings on the site and, within five years, student numbers nearly trebled and staff numbers doubled.

All this was a belated response to the implications of the Robbins Report (1963) and its speed tended to make the college even more preoccupied with itself. Nonetheless, it did not reach a size which could safeguard its future. In any case, old attitudes remained entrenched and bred caution during various negotiations with other local bodies (university, polytechnic, other colleges and the local authority), following the James Report (1972) and White Paper (1972). Possible lines of survival were either not created (e.g. with the polytechnic) or were not seized (e.g. with the university). With no powerful 'friends', the college's fate was sealed in 1975 when the Department of Education and Science refused to support new intakes of students, and it closed in 1978.

In general terms, the college was a 'powerless pawn' (Newton et al., 1975, p. 1) in the hands of the DES, which had ultimate control of the 'guaranteed clientele' of all the colleges. However, the question was why this college and not another? Among a range of answers, a crucial one was not simply that of the college's structure of relations but, more especially, its perception of that structure. To a considerable extent, its self-dependency had been self-defeating. In Nias's (1976) terms, it was not merely that it had not resolved its 'crucial dependency' on the state (at national and local levels), but rather that it had not even recognized it.

Such attitudes and developments had many implications, of course, for the lecturers' careers. For a start, the 'negotiations' had brought into the open a division between what were known as the 'old guard' and the 'young brigade' (i.e. 'pre- and post-expansion' staff). The latter set up its own working party to formulate and present an alternative plan to that of the hierarchy for the college's future. The point is, however, that the division itself had not been discernible prior to the struggle for survival, because expansion had meant easy and rapid promotion for all and the club-like lifestyle of the college had promoted easy relationships. Indeed, collegiate principles had led many of the staff to regard their work not so much as a career but more as a way of life. Accordingly, career security and advance had become taken for granted. In fact, while the growth in size of the college had led to some bureaucratization of its organization, the college could be regarded as a 'bureaucracy of low constraint' (Newton et al., 1975, p. 11) and, for the staff, much of their job satisfaction had been derived from the style of their relations among themselves and with their students. The only distinguishing mark between the two staff factions had been the pronounced academic orientation of the younger staff.

The college's traditions and situation and its version of the collegiate principle had the further implications, on the one hand, of promoting a moral basis to the relationships (especially noticeable in the principal's approach to his staff) and, on the other, of inhibiting political awareness and skills (seen in the little regard given to the professional associations – both ATCDE and NATFHE). In consequence, the lecturers viewed their careers as professional commitment of a moral kind and a legalistic approach emerged only when their careers came under threat. Even then, many staff were slow to investigate and, in some cases, to take advantage of the provisions for redundancy contained in the Crombie Code.[8]

To summarize: the lecturers' (collective) control of their careers had been within their localized sphere of work. Here, the state connection at both national and local levels had been decisive, because of the state's control of the rate and scale of change in the size (expansion and contraction) of the guaranteed clientele. Another major influence, however, had been the bureaucratic-collegiate principles of the college, because, although these principles produced a highly satisfactory style of career, the preferences of the principal and his senior colleagues had held sway. Thus, the acquiescence of the lecturers had been secured in times of expansion because there were 'prizes for all', and in times of contraction because initially they adopted a united front in order to save their college.

The question then arises, what happened when events left behind the 'save us' stage and individual lecturers were confronted with a 'save me' situation? In short, what did they individually make of the announcement in 1975 of the impending closure of their college and their own inevitable redundancy? Thus, the cardinal issue was the personal control of their careers, which meant in effect the ways and extent they individually could control not only their career destinations but also the path to it. Accordingly, I will now turn to a description and analysis of these individual reactions.

The lecturers' response to redundancy

One view of the staff's response to the announcement of the closure of the college can be gained by tabulating the date of their departure on the basis of their age groupings,[9] as in *Table* 14. Thus, the falling numbers of the college were related to a series of waves of staff departures. An interesting feature of those waves is that the early ones comprised the lecturers who were most successful in continuing their careers. Even more interesting is that, in the early waves, younger staff were conspicuous, as indicated by *Table* 15. Thus, age was clearly a primary career contingency. However, a fuller analysis of career outcomes (*Table* 16) indicates that other factors relating to career history were also significant. Among these were academic qualifications, job status and length of service.

Table 14   Departure of staff from college, 1976–78, by age groupings

Age grouping	Total*	Left 1976		Left 1977		Left 1978		
		For jobs	On secondment	For jobs	On secondment	For jobs	On secondment	Retired/ unemployment
Under 40	22	5	2	3	3	1	8	
40–49	20			4	2	2	7	5
50–54	6				1		2	3
55 and over	4							4

*Excludes principal and vice-principal.

With 16 of the 52 staff on secondment and another 5 unemployed but seeking work, it was still (in early 1979) far from clear what the final pattern

Table 15   Career destination of staff by age groupings, August 1978

Career destination	Under 40	40–49	50–54	55 and over	Total
Career advancement (universities)	5	1			6
Career maintenance (polytechnic, schools, advisory)	8	6			14
Career extension (on secondment)	7	7	2		16
Career undecided (unemployment)	2	2	1		5
Career terminated		4	3	4	11
Total	22	20	6	4	52

of career outcomes would be, but even at that stage it was possible to trace the lines, strategies and tactics of the lecturers' reactions to the termination of their existing career paths. Particularly, it was possible to mark the stages of the various lines of reaction through using the notion of status passage. This is because it raises the issue of the management of the phasing and timing of the constituent actions of the passage.

Indeed, the reference to status passage is more widely applicable to this analysis, because not only does it lead one to consider how individuals handle and cope with such change but it poses other key questions, such as the composition of the grouping of status passages (aggregate, collective, solo), how long the passage takes, and how far can it go.

On the composition of the passagees' grouping, it was noted earlier that the announcement of the closure of the college switched the career interest from an aggregate to a solo concern. Yet this was not readily apparent in all the immediate reactions to the announcement. It is necessary, therefore, to identify when and for whom such an awareness arose and to trace its influence on the eventual career outcomes.

As for the question of the duration of the passage, this was especially important in this case, because it could have lasted as long as four years (September 1975 to August 1979), which not only gave a protracted period for the formulation and pursuit of private plans[10] but also gave scope and opportunity for psychological and social adjustment. Here was a major (structural) contribution to the minimization of the consequences of involuntary change.

Finally, the extent of the status passage raised the questions, first, of its limits which, according to this analysis of career outcomes, could stretch

Table 16 Careers outcomes of college staff at August, 1978

Career outcomes	Career placement	No. of staff	Characteristics of staff
Advancement	Universities	6	Men, very high academic qualifications; 5 under 40; 4 obtained posts after secondment and, in 2 cases, after temporary part-time university work following secondment; 5 were married and 4 of their wives were teachers (occupation of other lecturer's wife not known) and 2 of these were university teachers; service at college was from 3–5 years
Maintenance	(1) Polytechnic	1	Man; retained former status and work on account of transfer of (shortage subject) course for which he was organizer
	(2) Schools (heads of department or equivalent)*	6	2 women, 4 men; high academic qualifications; all under 40; all left in 1976 or 1977; all academic subject teachers; all married and 5 of spouses were teachers
	(3) Advisory or administrative	7	Men; mixed range of qualifications but all posts linked with professional qualifications and experience; 2 advisory posts in shortage subjects (both these lecturers late 40s, otherwise under 40); all served over 5 years in college; all married and 5 of their wives were teachers
Replacement	'Self-employed'	2	Men; late 40s; long service at college

Career outcomes	Career placement	No. of staff	Characteristics of staff
Extension (temporary)	Secondment	16	Completely mixed as to sex, age, status, qualifications and length of service
Loss	(1) Unemployed	5	4 women, 1 man; 4 following secondment in 1977; 4 L2s
	(2) Retirement	9	1 woman, 8 men; older age grouping (2 in late 40s, otherwise over 50); all (except woman) long-serving at college

* In addition to these, the woman vice-principal (middle-age) secured the principalship of a girls' (private) secondary school. Although highly qualified, she had no success in applications for a wide range of jobs in higher education.

from advancement to loss, and second, of the degree of these gains and losses. For instance, even in the case of career loss, the provisions of the Crombie Code were at least ameliorative at the financial level. In any case, self-respect in that situation could be partly salvaged by reference to the compulsory and involuntary nature of the career loss itself.

Clearly such questions are of vital concern to the whole subject of involuntary change in professional careers, and to the question of redundancy in particular. Thus, features of the involuntary process such as its prolongation and limitation make some of the existing analyses of reactions to redundancy somewhat inappropriate to this case. For instance, such features throw into question the accuracy or adequacy of the listing of reactions both by Johns (1973, p. 44: i.e. shock, fight or flight, gradual acceptance and adjustment) and by Sofer (1970, pp. 280–287: he adds to Johns' list removal from stressful situation, tolerating emotions and construction of defensive ideologies). The response of the lecturers at this college appeared to be far more complicated.

For a start, the announcement of the closure was received not so much in a state of shock as in a condition of confusion. The lack of shock may have been due to the length and tenor of the college negotiations, which had at least 'half-prepared' many of them for this possibility. More subtly, it may have been because their approach to career security and progression had gone beyond that of assumption to presumption, and this state of mind was not fundamentally undermined by the bald announcement of the college's future. For them, there was an underlying conviction that 'there would always be jobs for teachers'.[11]

Thus, they were thrown into a condition of confusion which meant to most of them that, for once in a long time (indeed, for some, if ever at all), the private plans aspect of the career dialogue became a prime concern. Their response in this connection largely determined their own part in the final career outcomes.

The career policies of the lecturers

Broadly, there were three responses to the prospect of redundancy. The first was to attempt to define and exercise control of the situation. The second was to accept it as providing a possible solution to other career difficulties or uncertainties. The third was to let the confusion continue. In brief, three career policies emerged, those of control, acceptance and drift.

The control policy centred on deliberate action to achieve at least career continuity, but this was approached in two ways: one was to go all out to make an immediate change, while the other was to take things a little more slowly. Thus, the difference between the two approaches lay in how far the lecturers viewed their career situation in emergency terms. In turn, this view primarily arose from their perception of what was happening in the colleges and higher education generally, and also of what would happen in their college in particular. Those who were the most pessimistic on the one score and most intolerant on the other acted quickly. Hence the young academics whose policies for saving the college had not been adopted, moved first. Their radical plans for the college had attuned them to make urgent and radical plans for themselves. Moreover, a further (major) contributory factor in their case was the realization of their professional commitment on a household as well as on a personal basis – clearly, the actual careers of spouses heavily influenced their views and judgements.[12] Thus, while their attempt at political action within the college had clarified for them the context and direction of their careers, their empathy with their spouses on the subject spurred and sustained their determination to obtain at least career continuity and at most career advance.[13]

The other grouping which adopted the control policy was itself divided into two sections. The distinction here lay in how long they were prepared to wait for what they considered to be an acceptable career outcome. The difference was between short delay and 'as long as possible' delay. Their problem, of course, rested on their definition of what was acceptable and the difference between the sections was, therefore, partly to do with the clarification of their professional commitment and career expectations. This was achieved mainly through the response they received to their job applications and their interpretation of its implications for them. Thus, while all in this grouping wanted to delay a career decision until they found what was right for them, some hastened the process through altering their career expectations and taking what appeared to be available and accessible to them.

Naturally, some were more fortunate than others in this regard, because their particular qualifications, experience and skills were in short supply, but all of those who, despite 'needing time' to sort themselves out, were prepared to move at the earliest opportunity (even if in some cases this meant 'lowering their sights') were characterized by intense career activity. Their spur was both their reading of career contingencies and family obligations. Thus, the grouping which consisted mainly of middle-aged men became acutely aware of the disadvantages attached to their age and length of service, while at the same time they urgently realized that, for standard of living purposes, they required the safeguarded salary provisions of the Crombie Code rather than its redundancy compensation.

But, while most of those who used a 'delaying' strategy on a short-term basis succeeded in obtaining career parallels (10 out of 14), some did not. For them, career anxiety flared into career crisis. Acceptable jobs were either not available or they could not obtain what were. For them, this was a situation of 'career crunch'[14] and resulted in every case in reduced career activity. All looked far more carefully at the compensation provisions and two sought professional advice regarding them. Furthermore, all began to develop 'defensive ideologies' concerning their impending career loss and, thereby, their change of professional and social status and identity. Two decided to prolong the process as long as possible (hoping in the meantime that 'something might turn up'), while the other two settled for retirement at that stage (with the possibility of 'self-employment' afterwards).

The second section of those who adopted a policy of control on a delayed basis wanted to take as long as possible over their choice of career outcome. This was because, while all of them wanted career continuity, the younger ones (three out of the eight) felt this would take considerable time and could involve improving their qualifications, while the middle-aged (none was over 50) wanted to ensure by this means the maximum compensation benefits if they could not get another post. Hence, this grouping was marked, first, by fewer and a slower flow of applications for jobs than the others and, second, with one exception,[15] by opting for secondment. By August 1978, three of this section had secured posts (two in universities and the other as an adviser), four were on secondment and the other 'temporarily unemployed'.

The grouping which adopted an acceptance policy did so because they felt that they had little choice over the termination of their careers. In their view, their age in particular was decisive (all six were over 50, and four were over 55). Moreover, in the main, they welcomed this development,[16] considering that they had had 'a good run for their money' (even in the case of the only woman among them, who had been recently appointed – she had been aware that her job would be 'short-lived'). In any case, two of them were on the brink of retirement and this simply foreshortened the process, and another two were glad of the opportunity to retire on health grounds. Thus, this grouping simply waited for the college to close.

In this respect, they differed from another small grouping (three men) who similarly saw early retirement (without previous secondment) as a desirable end. Yet, in so far as they could not justify it in age terms only (they ranged from 45 to 52), they were rather in the position of the 'long-term' section of the 'control' grouping, in that they needed to secure it on as favourable terms as possible. Thus, their actions were highly calculative and they accordingly applied for the minimum number of posts which they thought would 'satisfy the regulations'. For them, financial considerations predominated, but all of them had 'other irons in the fire'. However, in their view, they were simply making the most of a situation which was not of their choice or creation. Thus, they could be regarded as a hybrid control-acceptance grouping.

The last grouping adopted a drift policy or perhaps, more accurately, they simply drifted. Most of them had been recently appointed to the college (only three of the 12 had exceeded four years' service) and, consequently, they were only at the beginning of a new stage of their career when the closure of the college was announced. Hence, they were completely uninformed about it and unprepared for it. None of them knew what to make of it, because none of them had more than a faint knowledge of why and how it had happened. Moreover, in that they had only just made the transition from school to college on the grounds of career promotion, they could not adjust themselves to return there immediately. Thus, they 'just 'sat tight' and adopted an attitude of 'wait and see', although taking the precaution in every case 'of prolonging the day' by obtaining secondment. The nearest that any of them came to career plans was to contemplate emigration or setting up their own businesses.

The grouping itself was predominantly young (eight of the 12 were under 40) and female (seven women, of whom four were under 40). On the women's side, two of them 'took the opportunity to have a family', while another older woman gained (unmarketable) graduate status. Indeed, all three of the older women entertained few hopes of employment in education, whereas the younger ones thought that 'something might turn up'. But, whether women or men, there was very little or no career activity. Certainly there was a degree of career anxiety among them, but it was insufficient to make them take positive steps to overcome their career uncertainty. Unquestionably, this state of career inertia was fostered by the possibility of temporarily extending their careers through secondment, but, even at that stage, career activity was still lethargic (the reason advanced was 'nothing available' – this may well have been the case, because all four who had completed secondment in August 1978 were unemployed). Yet, among the younger men in particular, there was an air of optimism about finding work, although just what that would be was decidedly vague.[17] What was conspicuous for this grouping was, first, its lack of developed personal professional commitment[18] and, second, that it was the nearest of all of the groupings to a somewhat carefree attitude towards career contingencies.[19] In fact, the younger ones had adopted an attitude of calculative hedonism, openly declaring that they had stayed 'until the end' on the basis of 'making hay while the sun shone'.[20]

Looking over the college as a whole, then, we can summarize in diagrammatic form (*Fig.* 18) the reactions of the lecturers to the prospect of redundancy.

Practical application of lecturers' experience

The general application of this study is to those professional groupings whose status and practice are heavily dependent on a guaranteed clientele and, thereby, are vulnerable to imposed change in their careers during shifts in government policy on the provision and distribution of that clientele. In the field of education at present, the most obvious example is that of the schools, where the decreasing number of pupils and changes in government policy on public spending have already affected primary school

Figure 18 Chart of the directions and consequences of career policies of college lecturers, August 1978.

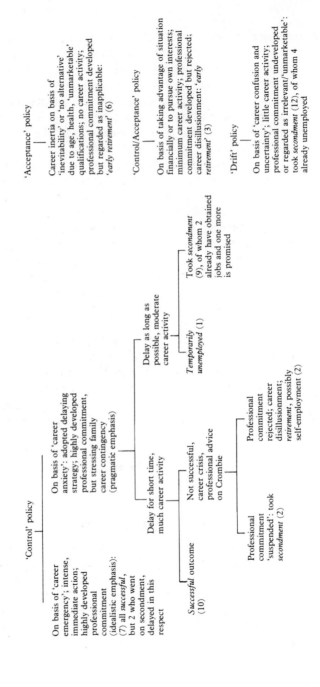

'Control' policy

On basis of 'career emergency'; intense, immediate action; highly developed professional commitment (idealistic emphasis): (7) all *successful*, but 2 who went on secondment, delayed in this respect

On basis of 'career anxiety'; adopted delaying strategy; highly developed professional commitment, but stressing family career contingency (pragmatic emphasis)

Successful outcome (10)

Delay for short time, much career activity

Not successful, career crisis, professional advice on Crombie

Professional commitment 'suspended': took *secondment* (2)

Professional commitment rejected; career disillusionment; *retirement*, possibly self-employment (2)

Delay as long as possible, moderate career activity

Temporarily unemployed (1)

Took *secondment* (9), of whom 2 already have obtained jobs and one more is promised

'Acceptance' policy

Career inertia on basis of 'inevitability' or 'no alternative' due to age, health, 'unmarketable' qualifications; no career activity; professional commitment developed but regarded as inapplicable: *'early retirement'* (6)

'Control/Acceptance' policy

On basis of taking advantage of situation financially or to pursue own interests; minimum career activity; professional commitment developed but rejected; career disillusionment: *'early retirement'* (3)

'Drift' policy

On basis of 'career confusion and uncertainty'; little career activity; professional commitment undeveloped or regarded as irrelevant/'unmarketable': took *secondment* (12), of whom 4 already unemployed teachers and are beginning to affect teachers in secondary schools. More broadly, it can be applied to other state-sponsored professions, especially where they are organized on a local basis (e.g. in large hospitals). However, the most direct application is to teachers in professional training schools, especially those outside the universities. In all such cases, the study provides data for planners of change, that is, both those who initiate and those who implement it. The data, of course, relate to the human factors and costs involved in professional redundancy.

The crucial information, however, is for individuals who are confronted with the prospect of redundancy. Here, the study stresses two factors. One is the immediate physical and political context of their careers and the other is the nature and extent of their personal commitment to their careers.

On the matter of the local unit of their profession, this is important not only because it provides a clientele and thereby a career structure, but also because the traditions and policies of that particular unit shape and direct their conceptions of their careers. Thus, the local unit can breed false security and unrealistic aspirations based on presumptuous attitudes.

In the light of this study, a significant question would appear to be the status of the professional grouping in the local area. Here, the key issue is the grouping's view of its autonomy, which is reflected in the extent of its physical, social and political separation from the local community. Clearly, this should not be taken to the point where the group contributes minimally to the local economy and civic pride and exerts no political influence. The slogan 'united we stand' is pointless, if the group stands alone. Instead, the aim of the group should be to establish a community *within* a community. However, the study indicates that this realization is unlikely without a political as well as a social basis to the relations of the professional group itself. Indeed, without this, it seems that the group will have neither an appreciation of the political dimensions of its situation nor much competence in political negotiations. An important issue, therefore, is the group's attitude towards the role of its professional association in its own situation.[21] The political naïvety of these college lecturers, for instance, was clearly related to their casual attitude to and lack of involvement in their professional association. Hence, the professional who is facing the prospect of redundancy needs in the first instance to analyse and assess his career history and commitment in the context of the traditions and policies of his immediate professional group. This plainly affects the formation of his own career policies.

Then there is the matter of the more personal sources of the professional's commitment. Here, features of the professional's career history such as length of service, qualifications and job status are important, but equally so is the household dimension of the professional's career. This is the case not only in terms of family obligations arising from the stage of the professional's family life-cycle, but also in respect of the occupation of his/her spouse. This can give rise to a family or household professional commitment which may provide the moral and practical support necessary not only to cope with redundancy itself, but also to generate and justify career aspirations and lines of action which would not be considered wise or legitimate under 'normal circumstances'.

Thus, the study provides guidelines for an understanding of the sources and dimensions of professional commitment and the career policies which these produce. In so doing, it questions common-sense policies such as 'keep your options open' and 'delay as long as you can'. It indicates that redundancy is a process which has a variety of outcomes and that the more desirable of these may be the result of early and sustained action.

In these ways, the study shows that redundancy throws long-held assumptions about professional careers into the melting-pot. Plainly, they are not sacrosanct. Moreover, norms which formerly were regarded as necessary for career advance (mature age, high status, high qualifications, long service) can readily become hindrances (too old, too high a status, too well or too narrowly qualified, too long in the job). Nonetheless, it indicates that, even in such an extreme instance as that of this college, there are structural factors serving to minimize the adverse consequences of redundancy for professionals. In this case, they ranged from institutional provisions (e.g. Crombie Code and secondment policies) to the availability of career 'switching points' and 'replacements', and to the professional's own (idealized or pragmatic) commitment. Hence, the women lecturers who apparently fared worse than the men[22] considered that, where their career investment matched that of the men, they could generally achieve similar outcomes.[23]

In all these respects, therefore, the analysis of the experience of these lecturers should assist policy-making and decision-taking, both for organizations and individuals when they contemplate or are confronted with career redundancy.

Notes

1   For a discussion of the college lecturers as a profession, see Warwick (1976). The change

in professional status was marked by the merger of the Association of Teachers in Colleges and Departments of Education (ATCDE) with the Association of Teachers in Technical Institutions (ATTI) to form the National Association of Teachers in Further and Higher Education (NATFHE) in January 1976.

2 Wilensky (1960) noted that this is a crucial sociological concern.

3 Of 163 colleges in 1974, only 19 remain in their previous form. Over 40 were closed and the remainder were involved in a variety of mergers (with each other, with polytechnics, with universities and with colleges of further education). Teacher training now takes place in 75 separate institutions.

4 The college had voluntary (Church of England) status. The Church of England Board of Education sided with central and local government over its closure.

5 Most of the records of the college were placed at my disposal for unhurried scrutiny. A history of the college written by a former vice-principal was made available to me in draft form.

6 Apart from private interviews, I spent many hours talking with staff in small groups, especially in the senior common room where I gleaned not only new information but was able to check what had been told to me privately.

7 One lecturer declined to be interviewed, four others declined 'private' interviews but freely conversed in the senior common room, and the other two were 'too ill' (and thereby absent from college) for interviewing.

8 This was the popular name for the Colleges of Education (Compensation) Regulations (1975). There were two main provisions. One was the safeguarding of salary in the event of transfer to jobs covered by the Burnham scales, and the other was a system of compensation for loss of employment. The provisions had previously been used for the local government reorganization of 1974.

9 The significance of this lies not only in the often mentioned observation that age is a primary feature of careers (e.g. Sofer, 1970, p. 53) but more particularly because the provisions of the Crombie Code operated largely on this basis.

10 Pahl and Pahl (1971, p. 18) defined career as 'the dialogue between private plans and public expectations'.

11 Compare the experience of the workers at Casterton Mill, where a sudden and unexpected announcement of redundancies came as 'a complete shock'. Was this simply because they had been assured by management earlier that the merger would not necessitate redundancies, or because they did not hold presumptions about job security and continuity which inured them to realizing the direct implications of the announcement? (Martin and Fryer, 1973, p. 119).

12 This was the case for the woman lecturer in this group as well as for the men. However, perhaps the factor weighed most heavily with the two men in the first wave of departures who went on secondment. Both their wives were university lecturers and they were intent on securing similar positions themselves. This involved not only improving their academic qualifications but becoming unemployed afterwards. They adopted the strategy of cultivating personal contacts and taking on 'bits and pieces' in higher education. Although both of them spoke of 'a lot of pain' in this policy, it did eventually achieve their aim – both of them have now secured university work.

13 In their analysis of dual-career families, the Rapoports say nothing on this question of household professional commitment, despite presenting the cases of several husbands and wives who work in the same profession as each other. Perhaps this was because such commitment is articulated only when one of their professional careers is threatened. However, the Rapoports seemed to be interested mainly in the husbands' 'motivations'

towards their wives' careers and paid little attention to the reverse 'motivations' or to combined 'motivations' (Rapoport and Rapoport, 1971, p. 27).

14 Pavalko (1971, p. 156) defined this as where the expectations that individuals hold concerning their present and future occupational activities are inconsistent with the expectations that the reality of the situation presents.

15 The exception was the only woman in this grouping (she was middle-aged, single and a non-graduate). She preferred 'temporary employment' and possibly work outside education.

16 The one exception was a 53-year-old non-graduate. He accepted the ending of his career not only because his career chances were slim but also because he simply did not want any other post in any other place. In our terms, his identity was *physically* located. Rather, he began to explore what 'voluntary' work he could undertake in education. The other older lecturers held a similar view. One of them said, 'This place gets into your gut'.

17 Although several remarked in passing that, just to 'hedge bets', they might contact schools.

18 Often there was a vague household professional commitment, as several of their spouses were teachers, but, even where personal commitment existed (e.g. among the older women), it did not bestir career activity, because they considered their career position to be 'hopeless'.

19 Three of this grouping were single and had no family obligations, but the main reason for their attitude appeared to be the confidence that many of them had that their various skills (professional and otherwise) would stand them in good stead. Nonetheless, there was a fair amount of disquiet about their financial position, despite a few of them reckoning that their spouse's earnings kept them from a 'make or break' situation.

20 This was palpably the case, but I noted as well that there was also an element of affected bravado which provided a defence against feelings of career insecurity.

21 The study of change in six other colleges of education (Newton et al., 1975) is illustrative of this theme, i.e., that the kinds and degrees of political action by professional groups are related to differing attitudes and levels of participation in their professional association.

22 Three of the 13 women, including the vice-principal, had obtained new jobs compared with 17 of the 40 men.

23 Thus, those women lecturers who spoke of being 'phased out' in both the younger and older age categories had held their college appointments for only a relatively short time. Moreover, the married lecturers whose husbands were teachers were emphatic that their careers were of equal importance.

References

Glaser, B.G. and Strauss, A.L. (1971) *Status Passage*. London, Routledge and Kegan Paul.

Hencke, D. (1978) *Colleges in Crisis*. Harmondsworth, Penguin.

James Report (1972) *Teacher Education and Training*. London, HMSO.

Johns, E.A. (1973) *The Sociology of Organizational Change*. Oxford, Pergamon Press.

Martin, R. and Fryer, R.H. (1973) *Redundancy and Paternalist Capitalism: A Study in the Sociology of Work*. London, Allen & Unwin.

Newton, D., Shaw, K.E. and Wormald, E. (1975) *Change in the Colleges of Educa-*

tion. Occasional Papers in Sociology and Education, No. 2, ATCDE Sociology Section.

Nias, J. (1976) Colleges of education: external pressures and negotiation of internal power. In: Page, C.F. and Yates, M. (eds) *Power and Authority in Higher Education*. Guildford, Society for Research into Higher Education.

Pahl, J.M. and Pahl, R.E. (1971) *Managers and Their Wives*. Harmondsworth, Penguin.

Pavalko, R.M. (1971) *Sociology of Occupations and Professions*. Itasia, Ill., Peacock.

Robbins Report (1963) *Higher Education: A Report of the Committee Appointed by the Prime Minister, 1961–63*. London, HMSO.

Rapoport, R. and Rapoport, R.N. (1971) *Dual-Career Families*. Harmondsworth, Penguin.

Sofer, C. (1970) *Men in Mid-Career*. Cambridge University Press.

Warwick, D. (1976) *Professional Properties: The Case of the College Teachers*. Occasional Papers, No. 3, Sociology, University of Leeds.

White Paper (1972) *Education: A Framework for Expansion*, Cmnd 5174. London, HMSO.

Wilensky, H.L. (1960) Work, careers and social integration. *International Social Science Journal*, vol. 12, pp. 543–560.

CHAPTER 6.7

TENURE*
GRAEME C. MOODIE

In the autumn of 1981 British universities seemed to be in a 'catch-22' situation created for them by the impact of government policy upon the conditions of academic employment. The government cuts in university income demanded economies that were unattainable without a reduction on the bill for wages and salaries (which together make up some two-thirds of total expenditure). In the time available this reduction could not be achieved merely by 'freezing' vacant posts; many, possibly including 3000 or more academics, would need to be dismissed, the alternative of lower salaries being unacceptable to the AUT and many staff. Only an uncertain number of universities had the legal right to dismiss for purely financial reasons. Elsewhere, and possibly everywhere, immense sums would be due by way of damage or compensation for dismissal. If these came from the government the universities would survive, if only at reduced levels of performance and at the cost of the initial purpose of the exercise (a significant reduction in public expenditure). If, as seemed possible then, the government did not pay, several universities would be bankrupted, all their staff would presumably end up with neither employment nor compensation, the AUT's policy would have helped destroy what it had set out to protect, and the government would be left with yet another sector of national life sacrificed on the altar of a controversial economic doctrine – and all this in part because academics seemed to have a secure property right in their jobs.

From the full force of this folly the government and higher education seem (at the time of writing) to have been rescued by agreement on a level of

---

* *Higher Education Review*, Summer 1982, pp. 49–55.

compensation which is neither penal nor contemptible. Even so, it offers no guarantee against litigation by a threatened academic and it is therefore still possible that the dilemma will be resurrected by judicial decision confirming the legal immunity of academic employment to economic forces.

By the time this appears the legal issues may have been settled, and/or redundant academics quietly be accepting their farewell cheques. Whether or not that is so, one hare at least will still be running, and that is the debate about security of academic employment. Is there any place, it is being asked, for a contract which in effect offers a virtual lifetime of employment provided only that a teacher is neither incapacitated nor grossly (and frequently) immoral? Many say 'no' and urge the adoption of new forms of academic contract, while those universities with posts to fill are prudently offering limited-period appointments in as many cases as possible. It is clearly time (or past time) to examine the principle of tenure more closely and publicly than it has been usual to do in this country.

Some three-quarters of university teachers have tenure, in the sense that 'they cannot be dismissed except for infringements of contractual obligations of a fairly specific nature' (Williams et al., 1974), and many of the rest are likely to obtain tenure at the end of a probationary period that rarely exceeds three years. One remarkable feature about this prevalent condition is how little has been written about it. It is not even mentioned in the report of the Robbins Committee (1963). It is mentioned, however, in Halsey and Trow's (1971) classic study of British academics; a footnote on p. 147 promises a discussion in their Chapter 9, but that is the only mention, for the promised discussion is omitted. Tenure is safeguarded by the provision of some university charters, but not of all nor for all academic staff, and elsewhere depends on the precise nature of unstandardized local contracts of service (France, 1971), hence some of the uncertainty about its legal status. On the other hand, academics generally 'have tended to operate with the assumption that in practice they enjoy security of tenure until the normal retirement age', and have done so with some justification in that 'the relatively few dismissals appear always to have followed instances of "gross misconduct" ' (Startup, 1979).

One consequence is the lack of recent defences, or even explanations, of the principle. It may be assumed, however, that the standard line of defence would resemble (if in less incisive language) that put forward by Jacques Barzun (1969) with reference to the USA: 'The practice of giving tenure to university professors is justified on the same grounds as the tenure of judges . . . to make them independent of thought control . . . What generates the truly scholarly atmosphere is the property right in the post itself, voided only by mental incapacity or moral turpitude. Therefore uncensored speech and tenure. On these unusual and inseparable supports academic man walks in freedom.' In essence, it must be emphasized, tenure is a necessary condition of academic freedom, and that freedom is in turn a necessary condition for the highest level of scholarship, teaching and research. In other words, tenure is not a mere privilege of rank, it is a *functional necessity*.

Historically, however, tenure in British universities is rooted at least as much in privilege as in instrumental rationality, and in concepts of community membership as of working efficiency. In the ancient universities (those founded before the nineteenth century) both the Oxbridge college fellows and the Scottish professors had virtual life tenure. Many of the former were not involved in teaching whereas the latter carried the main burden of teaching in their respective institutions, but they had in common the facts of autonomy and of citizenship in largely self-governing communities. The newer English and Welsh universities originally had neither, and even professors were liable to be dismissed by their lay employers 'without giving any specific reason' as in Nottingham (Coats, 1969) or on some 'principle of expediency' as in London (Ashby, 1970). However, the influence of the older traditions, ideas about academic freedom imported from Germany, and an increasing recognition of the benefits tenure brought to the universities ensured that it was generally accorded to professors by 1919 and, under the additional influences of the newly established AUT and UGC, to most other staff by 1939 (Perkins, 1969). But none of these reasons for the extension of security necessarily is eternally convincing, and the principle must therefore be inspected from time to time in the light of changing circumstances and of other, possibly competing, functional necessities.

Today even those who grant the importance of academic freedom in the realms of teaching, research and publication subscribe to the need to 'review the university teacher's contract of service' or 'academic's freehold' as it was moderately put in a *Times* leading article (1981). Envy and spite apart, there are four main lines of argument that demand much more serious consideration by academics than has yet been manifested:

1   Tenure is not unconditional even now; it is normally given only to those who have satisfactorily served a probationary period of up to four years and is subject to at least a minimum level of continuing competence thereafter. But, so it is said, the conditions are so loosely

defined and laxly applied that universities carry too many people who abuse the system by (to quote from *The Times* again) 'retiring on the job'.

2 Tenure, it has been argued by the *Times Higher Education Supplement* (1981), is either unnecessary today as a protection of people with unpopular views or it is a 'feeble' defence if the views are 'sufficiently unpopular to established authority, particularly at a time of political stress'.

3 Security of employment may well operate against the flexibility and innovation needed for the successful pursuit of excellence, and especially so if the whole tertiary system is to be expanded and tailored more to the needs of anything approaching comprehensive higher education. Alternatively, tenure ought to be extended to the colleges and polytechnics instead of being 'arbitrarily' confined to the universities. (Both arguments are put forward by the *THES*.)

4 Tenure can lead to the present situation in which saving money is either too expensive or unselective or both, however great the need for economy. Tenure has been perverted, according to the *THES*, into 'a defence of the jobs of university teachers faced with the sack'.

Let us look at each of these in turn. It is undeniable that incompetents manage to survive despite the conditions on which tenure is granted. Only in the newest universities, for example, are there no stories about students still using their fathers' notes on some venerable academic's lectures. It may even be true that it is as difficult to sack a university teacher for inefficiency as it is a shop-steward in times of full employment in an industrial closed shop or the owner's son in some family businesses. But the same can be said of many sections of Britain's economic life (to judge by results and the experience of consumers), not to mention those areas in which legal or customary security obtains (the judiciary and civil service for example). The appropriate remedy, however, seems to lie in a tightening of the definitions of competence and/or a fuller statement of the normal duties of an academic rather than a removal of all protection from dismissal. Moreover, incompetence must be distinguished from normal ageing, and 'dead wood' from that state of partial decline resulting from having been 'squeezed dry' by overwork in youth: staff complacency must not be replaced by institutional ingratitude. Accepting that the highest level of intellectual work requires freedom in which to operate, it must not be forgotten that the rule of law is a necessary element in freedom. Similarly, since rules cannot totally replace the exercise of judgement, the application of new rules of competence must continue to be applied according to the traditional procedural safeguards (essentially: the right of defence against known charges in front of personally qualified but uninvolved arbiters). At the same time, it remains desirable to provide adequate compensation for those rendered incompetent by misfortune (illness or accident) or old age.

It is sometimes suggested that universities should go beyond a mere sharpening of the criteria for tenure and should also limit it in substance, for example by extending the initial probation period or by appointing people only for fixed, if renewable, periods. Alternatively, tenure might be made only relatively secure, for example by instituting a system of rolling three-year appointments terminable only for appropriate reasons and subject to appeal instead of the present system which might be described as 'absolute within limits' (i.e. indefinite tenure except for very specific good cause). In principle these are plausible, or even attractive, propositions, or would be but for certain practical objections: they are liable to induce excessive anxiety of a kind that would interfere with rather than stimulate scholarship; they may well lead to that pressure to publish which is the enemy not only of dedicated teaching but of civilized reading; and they would provide all too many oppportunities for that 'subtle peril' denounced by one of the founders of the American Association of University Professors, 'attacks on . . . academic freedom . . . officially disguised as something else' (Caston, 1981). The danger is that an increase in the number of 'hurdles' or 'reviews' would lessen the chance of remaining vigilant against abuse.

To worry about abuse of probationary or other tests is, of course, implicitly to reject the second argument against tenure. There is, to begin with, a logical problem concealed in the suggestion that tenure is no longer necessary to protect unpopular beliefs. The lack of cases of clearly 'political' dismissals might be evidence either that no defence is necessary or, with equal superficial persuasiveness, that no one dare stick a neck out for fear of the consequences; it might also be a testament to the efficient filtering power of the initial selection processes. History, memories of the McCarthy witch-hunts of the 1950s in America, and general experience all argue against the first of these hypotheses, so that no prudent man would wish to experiment with the abolition of tenure.

None of the points just made weaken the other, linked, argument that tenure may be ineffective, either because of screening before appointments are made or because of other reasons, relating (it may be) to extracurricular or non-intellectual behaviour. The *THES* (1981) offered no evidence for its judgement that in 'really hard cases . . . tenure is either irrelevant or brushed aside', but the point is taken that vigilance is the price of liberty here as elsewhere. Here, too, is perhaps the greyest area – and that not only because of the difficulties of obtaining and interpreting the evidence. The perils may be real as well as subtle, but not all academic 'dissidents' deserve to obtain or retain a teaching post, though any who are dismissed will certainly claim that it was because of their 'dissidence' and not, for example, their incompetence, idleness or total lack of integrity (personal or intellectual). It is arguable, in any case, that there are certain academic principles, of the kind that Lord Ashby (1969) has suggested should be incorporated in a scholars' 'Hippocratic Oath', from which dissent ought to be a possible ground for dismissal. Undeniably, unorthodoxy must not be censored or punished per se, but it is not always easy to tell the creative unorthodoxy from perverse error or from anti-intellectual claims to personal revelation or certainty that are more appropriate (if they are appropriate anywhere) in a church, politics or a proselitizing campaign than in the classroom. Such considerations argue for caution both in appointing and dismissing academics and in denouncing particular instances of either function; but, as the biography of many a judge bears out, it remains the case that security of tenure *after* appointment is the crucial safeguard of freedom and is one whose justification is unaffected by the difficulties of extending the principle of tenure beyond its immediate sphere of application.

Perhaps conscious of the vulnerability of these arguments the *THES* leader-writer goes on to his (her) main objection: that tenure hampers new thinking and hinders innovation because 'there is simply no way in which new needs, which are inevitably tentative and unconventional, can be satisfied if this must be done within the iron framework of a tenured teaching staff. There is considerable and immediately recognizable force to this argument. Inflexibility and stagnation are ills to which universities have proved themselves to have no immunity, and from which various forms of external intervention have had to rescue them at various times in the past. At a time of constant or declining resources, moreover, tenure does limit what a university can do or what it can do with its existing ageing staff. Tenure may thus conflict with the pursuit of excellence (as well as with innovation) despite also being a condition for it.

But academic vitality does not depend solely on either recruits or redundancy. Neither the survival of a critical tradition which dissolves congealed orthodoxy nor the free flow of communication which breaches the walls of any ivory tower depend solely, if at all, on the lack of tenure for academics. On the other hand, any institution is likely to be more venturesome if its liability for failure is, as in the commercial world, limited; universities might therefore innovate more radically if they could do so through expendable organizations and programmes. But it is not obvious that such 'disposable' undertakings are necessarily incompatible with offering some security of employment somewhere within the system, as other posts were found for security risks in the civil service (not to mention those senior officials who did not fulfil their early promise). Universities are rightly conscious that it may take time to distinguish clearly between the meritorious and the meretricious, or between the trendy and the true; others are rightly conscious that universities sometimes use this as an excuse for not even examining the claims of the new; but the proper control would seem to lie in public scrutiny and pressure rather than in abolishing a necessary safeguard against arbitrary dismissal by either outsiders or insiders.

Finally, we must return to our starting-point, money, and to the strongest of all the current arguments for modifying the existing system of tenure. That argument, in a nutshell, is that tenure may be the enemy of excellence and development simply because it is the enemy of economy and, in so far as it is taken to mean a guaranteed lifetime job at a given level of reward, because it may amount to petrifying the existing distribution of resources. That it would be preferable, for the universities, not to have to reduce expenditure goes without saying; but it is also irrelevant to the principle and, at some point in time, also unacceptable in practice. Why, therefore, should Britain not accept, as American academics have always done, that 'financial exigency' can constitute legitimate ground for terminating an academic post even if its current incumbent has tenure? To anyone with any sense of responsibility about the future of universities and the longer-term interests for their teaching staff there can only be one answer in principle, and that is to accept financial stringency as a legitimate reason for enforced redundancy, but not for a purely individual act of dismissal and only on certain conditions.

No academic, least of all one within even remote hailing-distance of retirement age, can welcome the thought of redundancy; but in the last resort it seems impossible honourably to argue that the salary claims of all existing tenured academics have an absolute priority over all competing claims on resources either within or outside the university system – and that seems to be the logical corollary of an insistence on absolute tenure. (The argument here, let it be stressed, is not about present government policy on the existing legal status of tenured staff, but about whether the terms of employment for the future ought to be modified.) Having conceded this point of principle, it becomes the more important to state the conditions. If this new reason is to be added to the list of grounds that constitute 'good cause' for dismissal, it is crucial, first, that at least the traditional procedural safeguards be maintained. This is to say that, to minimize the risk of a new disguise for thought control, there must be established procedures for testing the assertion of financial exigency and for challenging the criteria by which particular posts or programmes are selected for abolition. There must, secondly, and as a built-in disincentive to hasty selection, be some guarantee that a post will not be re-established until after some minimum period (five or seven years, say) has elapsed, failing which the previous incumbent must either be reappointed or compensated for damages inflicted. Third, there would need to be some agreed system of compensation for loss of employment that is no less generous (at least) than those operating for judges, civil servants or members of Parliament. The *THES* leader was surely right to suggest that the AUT would be wise to start discussing the precise conditions to accompany the modification of tenure rather than continue its root-and-branch opposition to any change in academic conditions of service. Full and unqualified tenure is not the only functional necessity in higher education.

As a postscript, it may tie up at least one loose end if I say something about the relevance of these arguments to the rest of tertiary education. I do not believe that everything I have said necessarily applies to the non-university sector (about which I cannot claim any very detailed or intimate knowledge). Despite their overlapping concerns, however, I am inclined to believe that there are significant differences between the various sectors, both with respect to their relations with the market and to the kind of intellectual activity which distinguishes them. But I do not see that these differences entail or justify totally different terms of employment. It may well be that the precise definitions of 'competence', the list of duties, and the nature of the peers who should arbitrate in the case of dispute will differ – I would not presume to decide – but it is surely obvious that in all education teachers must be safeguarded from arbitrary dismissal however much their conditions of employment differ in other respects. It is not only in universities that some security of tenure is a functional necessity.

References

Ashby, Eric (1969) *The Academic Profession*. Oxford University Press.

Ashby, Eric (1970) *Masters and Scholars*. Oxford University Press, p. 23.

Barzun, Jacques (1969) *The American University*. Oxford University Press, pp. 59–60.

Caston, Geoffrey (1981) Who decides who chooses who goes. *Times Higher Education Supplement*, 23 October 1981.

Coats, A.W. (1969) Academic freedom in Nottingham during the 1880's. *Renaissance and Modern Studies*, vol. VII, p. 120.

France, P.R. (1971) Security of tenure. *Universities Quarterly*, vol. 25, no. 4, pp. 456–470.

Halsey, A.H. and Trow, Martin (1971) *The British Academics*. London, Faber & Faber.

Perkins, Harold (1969) *Key Profession*. London, Routledge & Kegan Paul, pp. 65–87.

Robbins Committee (1963) *Report of the Committee on Higher Education*, Cmnd 2154. London, HMSO.

Startup, Richard (1979) *The University Teacher and His World*. Farnborough, Saxon House.

The Times, 1 December 1981.

Times Higher Education Supplement, 23 October 1981.

Williams, Gareth et al. (1974) *The Academic Labour Market*. Amsterdam, Elsevier, p. 217.

CHAPTER 6.8

TERMS AND CONDITIONS OF SERVICE OF ACADEMIC STAFF*
PETER C. KNIGHT

Introduction

The prime question which has to be answered by an analysis of the terms and conditions of service for academic staff must be how can those terms and conditions be changed in the 1990s so that:

a.   the quality of education received by students is improved;

b.   the quantity of education at advanced level is changed appropriately';

c.   the efficiency in cost terms is improved;

d.   the acquisition of knowledge is enhanced.

A preliminary analysis indicates that the results will be depressing.

There may be difficulty in acknowledging that the terms and conditions of service of academic staff have a significant impact on the scale and scope of higher education. This is possibly because public debate, particularly about the level of salaries, does not usually concentrate on the educational consequences of the issues, but centres on the rather ritual posturing by the representatives of employers and employees, which is intended to influence the more private negotiations. Yet if several salary settlements reduced higher education salaries there would be an inexorable lowering of the quality of the service by reducing its ability to compete for able employees. Conversely, successive high settlements would increase the unit cost and might cause the government to take action that would reduce the quantity of

* Leverhulme Seminar on resources and their allocation, June 1982. This article is an abridged version. A complete version can be found in *Resources and Higher Education* edited by A. Morris and J. Sizer, Leverhulme Programme and Study into the Future of Higher Education no. 8, SHRE, Guildford. Dr Peter Knight is Deputy Director, Preston Polytechnic.

higher education that was available. Although such changes tend to be slow and subtle in their effect, [. . .]. Over a period of years the terms and conditions of academic staff could have far-reaching consequences for higher education.

Inertia

[. . .] In all questions of salary and conditions of service there is a massive inertia. Change is exceptionally difficult to achieve because the existing terms and conditions of service, even if totally inappropriate or irrational, are determined by historical circumstances. [. . .] A rate of pay is 95 percent history, 5 percent destiny. The opportunity for rationality or for logicality is restricted to a very small amount of adjustment at the margins.

Another factor which encourages and enhances this inertia of the system is the edifice of employment law that has been created over the past three decades. [. . .] Employment law governs the relationship between employers and employees and is as applicable in the most refined university college in the land as it is applicable in the smallest, most reactionary independent company. However inconvenient or misunderstood or inappropriate or counterproductive it may be, it is the law and applies to professors, vice-chancellors, lecturers and all other employees. The very fact that it is written as a general statement means that it will restrict and preclude actions which might otherwise have been in the interests of a developing system of higher education.

History

Universities

If it is accepted that the prime determinant of the existing system is the historical constraint that has acted upon it, then it is interesting to look at the different historical developments of the university sector as against the public sector. Such a study may indicate why these sectors have different characteristics in relation to pay and conditions.

The universities owe their origin to private enterprise, being created at various times by individual trusts and endowments. Consequently, in the early part of this century there was little, if any, uniformity in staff and salary structure between one university and another; salary levels reflected the size of endowments, the fees that could be charged and the number of potential students who could be enrolled.

The University Grants Committee (UGC) was appointed in 1919 at a time when it was decided to increase considerably the state aid given to university education, and from then until 1945 the UGC monitored the level of academic salaries. However, it never advocated that those salaries should be standardized between institutions, for to do so would have been regarded as an unacceptable attack on the individual autonomy of the universities. For example in 1930 it expressed the view that [. . .] 'Each university or college must be free to decide for itself what is best . . . it is not only natural but desirable, that the size, wealth and standing of different institutions should be reflected by difference in salaries' (National Board on Prices and Incomes, 1968). [. . .] This is plant bargaining, except that while the salary levels are fixed in each plant it is very unlikely that there will be any bargaining in terms of a collective discussion between employers and their employees.

After the Second World War, however, the less well-endowed universities found that they were unable to offer appropriate salaries without substantial government money. Following discussions between the UGC and the Treasury in 1946, the UGC specified a standing rate for the professorial salary. The Committee then announced a complete reversal of their previous policy for all staff, stating that there could be no justification for raising salaries 'beyond the level which the Treasury are prepared to subsidize' (UGC, 1964). [. . .] This policy was aimed at avoiding 'poaching', whereby the best endowed institutions might increasingly be able to bribe away from the less well-endowed institutions their most able staff by offering them higher salaries. [. . .] Consequently, the concept of a standardized rate of pay was inevitable.

In 1948 the Spens Committee reported on the pay of consultants and specialists working in the universities and introduced a standardized salary scale. In 1949 a new basic national salary framework was established for all other academic staff. [. . .] This was implemented with considerable speed and competence. Only the Universities of Oxford and Cambridge and the pay of clinical staff remained outside the system, which not only specified the pay, but also avoided poaching by specifying a maximum proportion of senior posts, namely senior lecturers, readers and professors, to lecturer posts. [. . .]

A secondary, but significant effect of the introduction of a national salary scale is that it avoided differential rates of pay among individual lecturers [. . .] such that a lecturer in a marketable subject, say physics, would have been paid more than a colleague in a less marketable discipline such as Ancient Greek. Individual colleges are obliged to pay the same amount of salary to lecturers irrespective of their discipline. This creates the concept of a rate of pay of a university lecturer, although the subjects upon which a lecturer is practising his profession will receive substantially different rates of pay in the outside community. This dilemma creates a tension within the pay structure that is probably more significant in the public sector than in the universities.

The university scales are interesting. First, they have always had equal pay for men and women, not because of egalitarianism [. . .] but probably because of the fact that there were, in complete contrast to the public sector, very few female academics. Secondly, the basic university lecturer scale is exceptionally long, extending over 16 years [. . .] with extensive use being made of an age tie-point, usually at 26. Such a scale is for time-servers; it is unimaginative, plodding and designed to discourage creativity and to eliminate incentives. [. . .] The only opportunities for rewarding merit remain in promotion to a more senior post. It is surprising that in a community that is meant to encourage initiative and reward creativity that the basic salary scale should be so lacking in incentives.

It is interesting to ask what the rationale is for the existing level of pay for university lecturers. It is notionally based on the concept of a 'fair comparison'. [. . .] In relation to university teachers the National Board on Prices and Incomes (1968) stated that:

> A principle which it thought was proper in looking at university salaries . . . (was) . . . the competition of several occupations for recruits from the same sort of supply . . . were obliged to look at the salaries offered by the others in order to judge what, in the context of the relevant circumstances of the whole field in which the competition operates, was required to restore the balance between several competitors.

The basic principle here is that in order to recruit able staff one needs to pay the same amount as one's competitors. [. . .]

There is an underlying attitude in all these debates. That is that one needs to pay university lecturers the sort of salary that will, largely, insulate them from the vulgarities of everyday life. While they will never be rich, they should not be poor, because if they are poor, they are unlikely to be able to discharge their duties. [. . .] This is an interesting attitude particularly as it does not extend down to research workers on limited-term contracts within the university system. It is the concept of a gentleman's salary for gentleman's work. [. . .]

This cynical analysis can be further supported by the fascinating contrast between the universities and the public sector. At no stage in the discussion on pay is there any debate about the duties which should be undertaken in order to justify that pay. Those duties are 'understood'. There are very few occupations in which such an understanding exists. The closest parallel is with members of Parliament, [. . .] where the concept of terms and conditions of service in determining their pay is clearly inappropriate.

Whether it remains inappropriate for 30,000 university academic staff is a radically different matter.

Although there is a standardized university superannuation scheme and statutory provision for sick pay, maternity leave and the like, all other matters, except for pay, are the responsibility of the individual university. [. . .] The basic principle is that conditions of service, if specified at all, are matters for plant bargaining in each individual university, in a situation where the universities usually decline to bargain.

Public sector

The public sector of higher education has developed from technical education and teacher training [. . .]. The origin of the existing salary structure is the salary structure that existed in primary and secondary schools as long ago as 1925, when the Burnham Committee was instituted to determine the pay of teachers. That Committee has, from time to time, undergone various changes in its statutory base and different committees have been set up to deal with particular types of teachers. [. . .] The existing situation is that the Burnham Primary and Secondary Committee determines the pay of school teachers and the Burnham Further Education Committee governs the pay of staff in further education colleges, agricultural colleges and all public-sector higher education institutions, including the pay of teachers, whether they happen to be teaching advanced work in a particular college or not.

In contrast with the university scales the scales that have applied in further education have been standardized as national scales from as long ago as 1925. It was in that year that the Rt. Hon. the Viscount Burnham, CH, wrote to the Secretary of State stating that:

I strongly recommend:

1 The Board of Education shall ensure that no local education authority shall gain financially by paying salaries on a basis lower than the appropriate standard scales.

2   No part of such sum shall be applied towards so increasing the salaries of classes of teachers as mentioned in the report that would be tantamount to altering the operation of the scales.

So for over 55 years there have been standard national scales operating in the public sector. [. . .] But it was not until 1961 that equal pay was finally introduced. The delay was because there was a high proportion of women teaching in primary education and the local authorities would not concede equal pay in further education because of the consequences on primary and secondary pay. This is clear evidence of the way in which a feature of the primary and secondary scales largely determines the characteristics of the further education scales, even when that particular feature is not relevant to further and higher education. [. . .]

[. . .] The single greatest determinant of the level as well as the structure of pay in the Further Education Burnham Committee is the offer that is made and accepted by the Primary and Secondary Committee. It is political reality that the management panel will not make an offer in the FE Committee that is greater than the offer they have made in the Primary and Secondary Committee. The Primary and Secondary Committee leads in determining the size of the global sum because the size of the salary bill in primary and secondary education is about £4.5 billion, compared with further education where it is slightly less than £1 billion. Further education can only tinker at the edges. Thus the salaries of lecturers doing advanced work in the public sector are primarily determined by the nature of the negotiations for the salaries of schoolteachers. That particular market force is overwhelming and cannot be ignored. A comparison of the settlements in primary and secondary education and further education reveals that over the years 1972–1981 the percentage increases have been nearly parallel.

Conditions of service in the public sector have both uncontentious and contentious elements. On the uncontentious side are questions of an appropriate scheme of sick pay, sensible pension arrangements, the amount of notice that is required on leaving a post – these are all matters that should be reasonably specified in the relations between an employer and an employee.

The contentious sensitive ground is the arrangements that exist in the public sector under the Conditions of Service Agreement which was negotiated in 1974 and 1975. This agreement specifies, as one of its most contentious provisions, the maximum class-contact hours that a lecturer can be required to teach in any one week. This idea would be completely alien to the university sector especially as the maximum lecturing hours that are required in the public sector are in excess of the lecturing hours that are usually expected within the universities, although the vacation periods (as distinct from study leave) are substantially longer than the arrangement for university staff. When this agreement was concluded there was a feeling that it was alien to the basic processes of higher education.

It is difficult now to separate legitimate objections to the arrangements from the political rhetoric that surrounded them at the time. The agreement had its origins in the way non-advanced further education operates. Its existence has, however, prevented class-contact hours for lecturers in both non-advanced and advanced further education from being unreasonably increased. For the basic grades of senior lecturer and lecturer grade II, the hours required are of the order of 15–20 per week. Those figures would represent the norm in many institutions. It can be argued forcibly that a lecturer who is required to teach those hours is not operating in a sensible or an efficient manner. A desirable characteristic of higher education, as it is offered by the university sector, is for students to be taught significantly less time in the week than their public-sector counterparts, and for the university staff to teach correspondingly less hours. Such a provision would enhance the quality of education offered in the public sector. Once maximum hours are specified there is pressure to ensure that staff are teaching those hours. A courageous college management which tries to prevent hours reaching the maximum is open to charges of inefficiency. [. . .] Yet it is quite clear that teaching styles can be adopted so that greater emphasis is placed on the preparation of lectures, seminars and tutorial work so that overall efficiency of the operation is not jeopardized. The day when the conditions of service agreement becomes an irrelevancy in advanced further education should be welcomed, but unfortunately that day is a long way off. A report of the District Audit Commission in the early 1980s paid particular emphasis to the question of maximum hours and seemed to suggest that there was something indecent in colleges not having their staff operating absolutely at the maximum, even though more sophisticated measures of efficiency, such as student–staff ratios, showed that the colleges concerned were operating in a perfectly satisfactory manner.

The main limitation of the conditions of service agreement is that it specifies only that which is measurable. The prime characteristic of an academic's job relates to the quality of the teaching, not necessarily the quantity, and it relates to the ability to carry out research and academic administration, all of which are not easily measurable. A lecturer who discharges his commitments under the conditions of service agreement, even if operating at the maximum class-contact hours, and does nothing else, is not contributing to the institution in the way that one would hope. While the conditions of service agreement is very valuable as a trade union bargaining tool, it is an inhibitor to the sensible development of teaching styles in public-sector colleges and prevents a professional and rewarding outlook on work for the academic staff concerned.

Flexibility

In both the universities and the public sector the salaries and conditions of service of the academic staff are frequently characterized as rigid and inflexible. It is often superficially thought that greater flexibility would lead to a more enriched and vibrant system. Envious glances are cast at the United States where there is often free bargaining on an individual basis between the academic and the university over the appropriate rate of salary; tenure largely does not exist for junior staff; academic appointments are not regarded as permanent; and there is a greater mobility between younger academics in the various institutions than there is in this country. [. . .] Before embracing flexibility with too much enthusiasm it is worth pausing for a moment to examine the so-called flexible employment opportunities of research workers [. . .] both in the universities and the public sector. The research worker, whether at doctoral or postdoctoral level, is in a situation where if he is not actually occupying a lectureship then he has no career structure. The rates of pay are depressed because the group concerned is in no position to bargain, and agreed terms and conditions of service are largely non-existent so that individuals can be exploited, [. . .] and will have little redress. [. . .]

The present arrangements for the employment of research workers have grown up with the institutions. It was previously regarded as a perfectly sensible way of ensuring that the most able undergraduates remained with their discipline for a further three years or more in order to obtain their doctoral degree. Then after a discreet interval of postdoctoral work the substantial number who had not dropped out moved into tenured academic posts. [. . .] The first signs that the system was beginning to fail occurred when more and more researchers were finding themselves in the position where they had to move from one post with a limited-term contract to another with a limited-term contract at postdoctoral level and their chances of obtaining secure employment were receding with each move. It became increasingly clear that this was not a career structure, but an employment trap into which one should not move. The chances of gaining permanent appointment through this route are vanishingly small. Hence we have moved to a situation where the students who are attracted into these appointments are only those who are not able to obtain outside employment, and the most able people are being filtered out, [. . .] whereas previously the flexibility of the system kept the most able in. [. . .] Given the structure of employment in the 1980s the continued use of limited-term contracts for people of ability is a very unsatisfactory way of providing employees for the research function. [. . .] Maybe the greater use of technicians or graduate assistants, particularly in the physical and engineering sciences, would be a better way of ensuring that the same volume of research was done, albeit by a smaller number of academics.

A study of the duties carried out by research students would lead a neutral observer to question whether such a student is in fact a student receiving instruction, or is employed to carry out certain prescribed duties. If the latter view is valid then they should not be paid a grant but should be paid a wage. [. . .] Interestingly the difficulty that the public sector has experienced in getting research students from the research councils has led most polytechnics to use the research assistant posts [. . .] in exactly the same way as a research student. [. . .] They are required to undertake a small amount of teaching and demonstrating duties in addition to their research, but the difference between this and the private sector is that the amount is often nominal. Consequently, in the public sector, the people who are being employed in research are employees, they are paid and at the conclusion of their limited-term contract they may well be eligible for and receive redundancy pay.

It would be wrong to give the impression that the public sector is in a more honourable position in its treatment of research workers than its university counterpart. The same general problem continues to occur in relation to the level of salaries. Prior to the study by the Clegg Commission of job comparability of lecturers, the rates of pay of research assistants were determined locally. Whenever pay of a group who are poorly organized is determined locally, the effect is that the level of pay is depressed. In many areas a research assistant, who presumably would have a good first degree, would receive less than his degree and qualifications would entitle him to in school teaching. The Clegg Commission was rightly appalled at these arrangements for local bargaining and as a result made a recommendation that a national scale should be introduced. Inevitably that national scale is substantially less rewarding in terms of salary that graduates would attract if appointed to the lecturer scale. Nevertheless that salary is still substantially greater than the amount of income that research students would receive as a result of their research council grant – a differential that can be acutely felt in departments where research students and research assistants are working side by side.

[. . .] There is no evidence that the quality of research is in any way enhanced by this type of flexibility, and a genuine concern must be that the line between flexibility and abuse of people's goodwill is a very narrow one [. . .]. The job of a research student is demonstratively that of an employee, not that of a student.

[. . .]

Myths of employment law

[. . .] The framework of employment law within this country, when coupled with the general attitude and expectations of people in white-collar employment, is not noted for its flexibility. This is not simply a matter of party political argument, although there are changes of degree with changes of government. There is a general attitude in this country that makes it difficult for a public employer to act in a cavalier or entrepreneurial manner to his employees. Hence it is exceptionally difficult for such an employer to operate a system of hiring and firing almost on a whim, which would be the characteristic of higher education in some other countries. [. . .] Even if tenure did not exist the universities would be exceptionally hard pressed to dismiss lecturing staff. Similarly the polytechnics do not find it easy to dismiss their academic staff other than for exceptional cause. The concept of hire and fire does not exist in this country for professional employees, and if it was introduced [. . .] the best would leave, the worst would try to stay.

If this is a depressing analysis there are isolated glimpses of hope. It has been argued that it is hard to sack academics. Putting questions of tenure to one side for the courts of law to resolve, it is not difficult to sack incompetent academics because of employment law, but because of the attitudes of employers and employees. There is a general principle of common law which provides that no one can be forced by law to work and no one can be forced by law to employ. If you dismiss an employee without good reason, no court in the land can require you to re-employ him, but it can reward the employee with compensation; for the employer it is a question of judgement as to how much he is prepared to pay in order to get rid of a particular inept or obstreperous individual. Hence if a polytechnic director was so minded, and received the backing of his governing body and local authority as appropriate, he could [. . .] summarily dismiss a person without cause if he was acting as an employer. There would then be a grubby and unpleasant battle through industrial tribunals and the net result would be that if the director failed to demonstrate good cause, he would be instructed to re-employ. He could refuse. [. . .] The industrial tribunal is then only able to award compensation for loss of employment to the member of staff concerned, and not to oblige the employer to take him back. As the compensation in such cases is not particularly large in relation to the salary that academics attract, it may well seem an attractive proposition for employers to pursue. Needless to say the circumstances described would be somewhat unusual in the placid world of higher education, and the union representatives of the individuals concerned may have something to say about it. However, it is worth emphasizing that the process of dismissal can occur and indeed has occurred in a number of cases. There have been dismissals for just cause and dismissals for unjust cause, but they have largely been dealt with quietly and without any attendant publicity. They are very much the exception, not the rule.

What can be done?

It has been a basic contention of the arguments presented in this paper that the terms and conditions of service of academic staff on both sides of the binary line are exceptionally difficult to change. Change is inhibited both by the inertia of the status quo and by the stultifying framework of employment law. The single example of flexibility, as it is applied to research workers, casts discredit on both the universities and the public sector as responsible employers. The question must now be asked as to whether or not there is any hope of a change in the system that would improve the provision of higher education in the 1990s.

An ideal system of employment could be defined as one where the individual employees had security yet were encouraged to change their jobs frequently; the rates of pay represented a just reward for the levels of skill and responsibility deployed and yet were economic; the system was lawful in that it was within the framework of employment law but that framework was recognized as a support for the system rather than an inhibitor.

It might be possible to introduce improvements that would achieve these objectives by changing the attitudes of mind of the staff and their employing colleges. For instance, on both sides of the binary line, emphasis, [. . .]

when considering questions of promotion, [. . .] could be removed from research and the key to promotion might be to have recently spent two or three years in industry, commerce or the professions. This would be a positive inducement to staff to seek contracts outside the institution. Security could be provided by the college seconding the member of staff concerned either on salary, or even on salary with an element of enhancement (say £1000 for the first year spent in industry, then £2000 for the second and third years) to recognize the contribution that that experience would make to the individual's ability to teach when he returned. [. . .]

Undoubtedly, a number of the people so employed would find the outside work sufficiently stimulating that they would prefer to continue their career there rather than to return to the academic life. While the loss of such a person would be the loss to the system, nobody is irreplaceable and a vacancy would be created for another appointment to be made. In making such an appointment emphasis could be placed on the desirability of bringing somebody into the institution in mid-career rather than continuing to recruit at the traditional level of postdoctoral experience. There would be nothing unlawful in such a process. All that would be required would be a change from the traditional attitude with its undue emphasis on research experience. There would be a number of technical details that would have to be tidied up. For instance, pension arrangements can often be an inhibition to such provisions. Once again if the will was there these problems could be overcome.

Clearly such arrangements for temporary transfer to outside employment are more relevant to some disciplines than others. [. . .] Also one suspects that such an option may not be particularly attractive to many academics. It should be recognized that for disciplines such as the arts and social sciences it is not so important that they maintain contact with outside professional interests. In these areas invigorating and broadening exchanges could be arranged between institutions and perhaps between countries. The problem once again is that the system offers no incentive for such activity. An incentive in salary would be an assistance. An incentive that recognized such a move as enhancing one's promotion prospects would be an encouragement and simple provision like assistance with the expenses associated with moving and rental of accommodation would be an added advantage. The net cost of all these provisions would, when compared with the individual's salary, be small but such arrangements would change the existing attitude of mind within the system as a whole. [. . .] One suspects that if the way to promotion for an Oxford don relied on him having to spend two years in a nearby polytechnic as a lecturer grade II, then the polytechnic would have to put up a barricade to keep out the applicants. Such exchanges would lead to a greater understanding of the values and attitudes within the sectors than exists at the moment.

The concept of job exchange or long-term secondment within the security of one's full-time employment is used all too rarely. Its introduction could significantly improve the quality of many academics and could provide at least one mechanism whereby there was a voluntary movement of people out of academic life into other forms of employment. An unfortunate feature of academic life on both sides of the binary line is the idea that it is a job for life. In this respect the concept of tenure in the universities is an anomaly which should be removed at the earliest opportunity. Security is one thing and academic freedom is necessary and should be defended, but the idea that those two objectives can only be achieved by a guarantee of a job for life is completely unacceptable in the current age.

[. . .] The single greatest change that needs to take place is a change in attitude towards the criteria for promotion. [. . .] The overemphasis on research ability as a primary criterion has a deadening effect on the encouragement of teaching ability. Unfortunately the public sector is making possibly the same mistake as the university sector in this respect. Research work is important in assisting the academic standard of the college, but to use it exclusively to determine the promotion prospects of staff is a very unsatisfactory employment practice.

Few changes need to or could be made in the salary structure that would have any significant effect on the nature of higher education. The general level of salaries is adequate when compared with the salaries of comparable professions. [. . .] There are minor irritants and differentials which are strongly felt. Nevertheless their removal is not likely to have a significant effect even though such problems should be resolved. In particular the levels of pay in the public sector should be made to mirror the levels that the universities attract, either by increasing the public-sector pay or decreasing that of the universities. There should be no differential between them. The existence of the differential, however small, is an irritant to sensible transfer between the sectors. This can only be guaranteed if the pay of lecturers in advanced further education is separated from the pay of their further education colleagues. Such an action will break the tie with the school scales which has been a deadening hand on the scales available for higher education. Strangely this very effect may come about, not because of pressure from the higher education sector, but because the development of tertiary education for the 16–19 age-group will require the pay of lecturers teaching non-advanced work to be more closely tied to the scales of primary and secondary teachers. Such a change will not be easy but the pressures that exist at the moment seem to be making it inescapable.

It is difficult to see any proposals for changes in employment law which would have a significant or constructive effect. As has been mentioned before, one cannot isolate academic life from the general framework of employment law. The consequences of so doing would simply be to make it less attractive to work in higher education and probably to drive the most able employees into other activities. [. . .]

Conclusion

Radical changes in pay and conditions will not provide a credible structure for higher education in the 1990s. If general agreement is reached on the nature of the provision in that decade it must then be accepted that the employees who will provide it will be on terms and conditions of service not drastically dissimilar from those that operate at present. Some improvements can be made but they are improvements more in the attitude of mind of the colleges and their employees rather than fundamental changes in the salary structures. The hope that should be expressed [. . .] is that over the next few years the universities and the public sector will grow closer together in the principles and attitudes that determine their terms and conditions of service. Such similarity can only enhance the interchange between the sectors. In no way need it be viewed as weakening the essential distinctiveness of either side of the binary line.

References

National Board on Prices and Incomes (1968) *Report 98. Standing Reference on the Pay of University Teachers*, Cmnd 3866. London, HMSO, pp. 4–6.

Spens Committee (1948) *Report of the Inter-Departmental Committee on the Remuneration of Consultants and Specialists*, Cmnd 7420. London, HMSO.

University Grants Committee (1964) *Report on University Development 1957–62*, Cmnd 2267. London, HMSO.

AUTHOR INDEX

SUBJECT INDEX